832
Goethe
I

Interpreting Goethe's
"Faust" today.

$40.00

DATE			

3/12-6x

θc 7/18-7x

BAKER & TAYLOR

Interpreting Goethe's Faust Today

Interpreting Goethe's
Faust Today

Edited by
Jane K. Brown, Meredith Lee,
and Thomas P. Saine

In collaboration with
Paul Hernadi and Cyrus Hamlin

CAMDEN HOUSE

Copyright © 1994 by
CAMDEN HOUSE, INC.

Published by Camden House, Inc.
Drawer 2025
Columbia, SC 29202 USA

Printed on acid-free paper.
Binding materials are chosen for strength and durability.

Jacket: Ernst Barlach, "Faust und Mephistopheles" II, 1922.
Courtesy of Ernst und Hans Barlach GBR Lizenzverwaltung
Photographs from the 1990 UC Santa Barbara Faust production by Christopher Vore.
Printed in the United States of America
First Edition

Simultaneously published as:
Goethe Yearbook, Special Issue No. 1. Publications of the
Goethe Society of North America.

ISBN:1-879751-49-6

Library of Congress Cataloging-in-Publication Data

Interpreting Goethe's "Faust" today / edited by Jane K. Brown,
  Meredith Lee, and Thomas P. Saine ; in collaboration with Paul
Hernadi and Cyrus Hamlin.
      p.   cm. -- (Studies in German literature, linguistics, and
culture)
    "Simultaneously published as: Goethe yearbook, Special issue no.
1. Publications of the Goethe Society of North America."
    Includes bibliographical references and index.
    ISBN 1-879751-49-6 (acid-free paper)
    1. Goethe, Johann Wolfgang von, 1749-1832. Faust. I. Brown,
Jane K., 1943- . II. Lee, Meredith, 1945- . III. Saine, Thomas
P., 1941- . IV. Series: Studies in German literature, linguistics, and
culture (Unnumbered)
PT1925.I58
832'.6--dc20   93-32513
                                                                    CIP

Contents

RECEPTION

Preface and Acknowledgments

As FORMER DIRECTOR OF THE Interdisciplinary Humanities Center at the University of California, Santa Barbara, I am happy to preface the present volume with a few words about the book's origins in two events hosted by the Center: the 1990 institute on "Goethe's *Faust* and the Humanities Curriculum," from which the idea for a conference emerged, and the 1992 international conference on "Interpreting Goethe's *Faust* Today," at which early versions of the contributions to this volume were presented. But I hasten to point out that the Santa Barbara campus of the University of California has long been a notable site of *Germanistik* due in large part to the presence of Stuart Atkins, the widely acknowledged dean of American Goethe studies and a guiding spirit of both the institute and the conference. In honor of Stuart's eightieth birthday on 8 March 1994, the editorial committee wishes to acknowledge his manifold contributions as teacher, scholar, and translator to the interpretation of Goethe's *Faust* over a period of almost six decades.

The six-week summer institute of 1990, funded by the National Endowment for the Humanities, brought together more than thirty university and college teachers from twenty states and ten different disciplines. Cyrus Hamlin of Yale University and Jane Brown of the University of Washington joined me in planning and conducting an intensive scholarly program of almost daily lectures and workshops. These were open only to institute participants, but some two thousand members of the Santa Barbara community enjoyed the accompanying book exhibit, film series, a costumed performance of scenes from Faust operas, and the ambitious stage production, discussed in the present volume, of an abridged English version of both parts of Goethe's *Faust*. As we searched for an opportunity to continue the fruitful discussions of the institute, it seemed especially timely to explore how the international community of scholars approaches Germany's foremost cultural icon in the wake of German unification. Our call for a large-scale gathering led in August 1992 to a five-day bilingual conference of over forty active participants from Europe, North America, and Australia, as well as many additional registrants (including twelve junior scholars with modest travel stipends) from all over the United States.

Organizers and participants alike felt that a selection from the wide array of conference papers could and should yield a book with a coherent design. We therefore welcomed the suggestion of publishing the revised conference proceedings as a special issue of the *Goethe Yearbook* published by the Goethe Society of

Paul Hernadi

North America. During the conference, the three organizers invited Thomas P. Saine and Meredith Lee (both of the University of California, Irvine, where the GSNA is headquartered) to join them on an editorial committee with a view to making a cross section of the proceedings available to the general public. To be sure, some papers had already been committed for publication elsewhere and several others (particularly those tracing Goethe's influence on subsequent appropriations of the Faust theme) could not be accommodated within the limited space and design of the present volume. It is safe to predict, however, that most presentations at the Santa Barbara conference will find their way into print.

Needless to say, our collection of carefully revised papers is intended to do more than transpose the élan of a successful conference into the medium of print. The book will, I trust, leave its mark on the ongoing international dialogue about one of the most German, as well as most cosmopolitan, works of literature. The broad participation of Goethe scholars and of prominent humanists working in related fields could not have been secured without financial assistance from a number of institutions and funding agencies. The timely publication of the present bilingual volume has also required subsidy. Thus it is my pleasant task to express sincere gratitude for generous contributions by the following sponsors: the Goethe Institutes of Los Angeles, Boston, and New York, Fritz Thyssen Stiftung, Deutscher Akademischer Austauschdienst, University of California Humanities Research Institute, Max Kade Foundation, University of California Center for German and European Studies, Deutsche Forschungsgemeinschaft, Akademie der Geistes- und Sozialwissenschaften (Switzerland), Goethe Society of North America, Monash University (Australia), University of Washington, Yale University, and, last but not least, the University of California, Santa Barbara. Further thanks are due to the staff of the UCSB Interdisciplinary Humanities Center (Dr. Barbara Harthorn, Randi Glick, Linda James) and two graduate student assistants (Perry Bennett and Lorna Clymer) who saw to it that the conference was well prepared and ran very smoothly. Laura Jackson, of the University of Washington at Seattle, assisted in preparing the manuscript for publication and in proofreading. Readers of the present volume may also be interested to know that my successor as director of the UCSB Interdisciplinary Humanities Center is Simon Williams, a theater historian whose paper here sums up his experience of playing the role of Mephistopheles in the 1990 Santa Barbara production of Goethe's *Faust*. I have no doubt that Simon finds his current assignment equally congenial because the Center's director, to cite the Lord's words from the Prologue in Heaven, "*muß als Teufel schaffen.*"

Paul Hernadi

Introduction

THOUGH *Faust* HAS LONG SERVED as a carrier of Germany's national identity, it continues to resist conclusive interpretation. Thus, the title of our volume, "Interpreting Goethe's *Faust* Today," does not signal an attempt to assess the relevance of the text for "today" or to showcase selected newer modes of inquiry that, in a prescriptive mode, are designed to replace older readings of the text. Rather the title announces an interest in sampling current readings in all their diversity. The collection is deliberately open to modes of inquiry *still* in use today as well as to those new or currently relevant. Like *Faust* itself, the volume offers neither closed structure nor final conclusions, but is rather a ragout (line 100) or, as Gerhard Kurz reminds us, "eine große Schwammfamilie." Some of the essays present us with a dramatically new *Faust*, while others present a *Faust* being read in some continuity with readings familiar from, say, twenty years ago. But in none of the essays does *Faust* look quite the same as it once did. In this spirit the essays have been arranged according to traditional topics of *Faust* scholarship: The Faustian, The Demonic, The Eternal Feminine, Representation (what used to be called Art), and Reception. Nothing, perhaps, could show more clearly the drift away from traditional readings, even in scholarship that is not aggressively iconoclastic, than the ways the essays converge with and diverge from these traditional categories.

The Faustian, and particularly the relentless striving of the eponymous hero which once enjoyed such privileged affirmation in the political reception of *Faust*, is revisited in a series of essays concerned with issues of politics, gender, technology, and history. In Virgil Nemoianu's general typology of political forms in the play, Faust's ceaseless activity and his adaptive capacity in the political realm is understood as a (not unproblematic) display of liberal energies checked and challenged within the play by Goethe's preoccupation with historical memory and his deep ambivalence toward the irreversible forces of modernization. Under revision in Nemoianu's essay, the whole concept of Faustian striving and our moral and political evaluation of it blows up when Robert Tobin considers how it is gendered—the traditional ambivalent opposition between Faust and Mephistopheles emerges here as the fluid complementarity of male and female in the play. With this incorporation of passivity into striving the concept of "Streben" once associated with violent progress at all costs seems ineluctably on its way to a merger with the Eternal Feminine. In contrast to these surprisingly

affirmative readings, Jeffrey Barnouw attacks the Spenglerian equation of the
Faustian with the modern ethos of technology in order to rescue technology
from the play's condemnations of Faustian excess. He decouples the two while
rethinking the relationship of magic and technology in Act V. Finally, Hans
Vaget responds to the long German tradition of affirmative readings of Faust's
role by undermining GDR readings of a socialist Faust and showing the negative political and moral significance of Faust's involvement in the war in Act IV.
Both sides of the traditional love/hate relationship of the scholarship toward
Faust are thus represented, as "The Faustian" turns out to be anything but the
familiar striving.

Similarly, the concept of the Demonic, most often embodied in Mephistopheles, becomes in the papers presented here ever less metaphysical and absolute:
only one of the essays even begins to concern itself with the problem of evil.
Harald Weinrich offers us a Mephistopheles who embodies, less for Goethe
perhaps than for his readers into the twentieth century, the French Other with
which German culture has struggled so ambivalently. Only with this context
established does he readmit the problem of evil into the discussion and now in
new terms—he probes the complexities of a metaphysical principle whose theatrical embodiment is all surface and social form. In a similar spirit of revision, evil
yields to an anti-gothic counterplot when Marshall and Jane Brown read *Faust*
in the context of the romantic gothic and conclude that Goethe's playful exploitation and parody of the gothic ultimately triumphs over it, especially in the
premature burial of the final scene. In her reading of the "Walpurgisnacht"
Meredith Lee connects the demonic to the real (within the play's real-ideal
dichotomy) rather than to a principle of evil as she disputes Albrecht Schöne's
restoration of Goethe's rejected paralipomena and demonism to the scene. And,
finally, based on his own experience playing the role, Simon Williams interprets
Mephistopheles not as the agent of metaphysical evil, but rather as the player
par excellence, all role and mask—no inner identity, no consistent moral principle of anything. All play and no work makes Goethe's devil much more interesting.

The Eternal Feminine, a deliberately vague term to begin with, suffers
perhaps the greatest encroachments. Hannelore Schlaffer sets the tone as she
explores a general tendency to irony, parody and self-parody in the endings of
Goethe's late works. In the process she in effect assimilates the term "eternal
feminine" into the definition of formal closure. Gail K. Hart offers a different
context—Sacher-Masoch's exploitation of *Faust* in the articulation of his theories
of masochism—to reread the issues of feminine leadership and seduction so
complexly intertwined throughout the play. Choosing yet another nineteenth-
century context, Herbert Lindenberger analyzes musical settings of the end of
Part II to relate it to the nineteenth century's unwillingness to bring things to
ends. It is still possible to address eloquently the ethical aspects of Gretchen's
seduction, as Christoph Schweitzer shows, but in this context he stands alone.
In Cyrus Hamlin's reading "das Ewig-Weibliche" becomes the paradigm of the

epiphanic fulfilled moments in the play to be connected with other equivalent moments elsewhere, such as the epiphany of Galatea at the end of Act II. In all these readings, the feminine virtually disappears as it is assimilated to Faustian striving or transformed into a principle of structure.

If the Eternal Feminine disappears through a process of abstraction, the same process runs rampant with regard to explicit questions of form. Representation covers no longer the thematics of art in *Faust*, so firmly established as a topic by scholars as different as Wilhelm Emrich and Katharina Mommsen; instead all of these essays address, from very different perspectives, the way the text represents and the ways that it thematizes its own status as representation. Starting from a careful reading of the "Vorspiel auf dem Theater," Ulrich Gaier argues that *Faust* stages the dialectic of interrelated but incommensurable modes of thinking–distinct, comprehensive, yet incompatible. Focusing more on the structures of discontinuity rather than on dialectics, Gerhard Kurz demonstrates the pluralistic structure of the play with the example of the poetological metaphor of eating and drinking and roots its pluralism in the process of composition. Clark Muenzer seems to operate within fundamental dualities in the play's representation of the world when he asserts the gothicism of Goethe's classicism, but in his reading a complex historicizing effacement of boundaries replaces the play of polarities. Christoph Jamme once more raises questions of discontinuity and irony in his discussion of mythological *bricolage* in *Faust*. All these concerns are effectively summarized in Martin Esslin's paper on the post-modern affinities of *Faust*. Yet underlying these different foci on discontinuity is a strong concern for Goethe's sophisticated historical sensibility and the ways in which it nevertheless–through irony and parody–re-weaves these discontinuous forms into interpretable structures.

The standing of *Faust* today is addressed, finally, most directly in a group of essays on reception, which range from surveys to individual responses, from translation to theatrical performance. Stuart Atkins's remarkable survey of some fifty *Faust* translations of the last twenty years in dozens of languages testifies perhaps most compellingly to the uncanny vitality of this most bizarre of texts. The specifically German reception is analyzed by Karl Robert Mandelkow as he reviews the history of reading *Faust* from the second empire to the recent opposition between the affirmative readings of the GDR and radical deconstructive readings in the West. The final two essays deal with *Faust* in the theater, from opposing perspectives. Peter Lackner's account of his 1990 staging of an English version in Santa Barbara reveals on the one hand the difficulties in staging *Faust* outside the German context, and, on the other, the opportunities afforded by the freedom from the German tradition of reception. The recent European productions surveyed by Bernd Sucher, and described by him in good part as "interesting failures," mostly attack the play and its monumental status: the contrast between his and Lackner's accounts demonstrates the continuing power of the traditional *Faust* reception in Europe.

The volume leaves us, then, with a very open text. Yet this is not the open-ness of indifference or despair, nor yet the openness of radical post-structuralism. These readings share some core of agreement on the issues the text addresses, and on its significance. What is astonishing is that so many people of such disparate backgrounds and persuasions find it worth their while to spend time together discussing *Faust*. How remarkable this phenomenon is was dramatized for me by the NEH Institute from which this volume ultimately grew. On arrival the attitudes of the Institute participants were extraordinarily disparate; they ranged from naive enthusiasm to ambivalence and even down-right hostility. Charges of authoritarianism, sexual bias (in all directions), naive materialism, intolerance all surfaced as our discourse replicated the standing controversies of the contemporary academy. In the end we came together—partly through the intense reaction evoked even among such seasoned intellectu-al sophisticates by the "Gretchentragödie," and even more through reading Part II, which reminded us that every conceivable intellectual tool we can bring to bear on *Faust* is useful, necessary, and still insufficient. The challenge, we discovered, is not the play's resistance to interpretation, but rather its incorrigi-ble responsiveness to any question posed to it. Reading *Faust* today may be fraught with more than its fair share of the pitfalls attendant on all reading; nevertheless it is still possible and still exhilarating.

Jane K. Brown

Bibliographical Note

Verse passages of *Faust* are cited throughout by line number. Goethe letters and conversations are referenced for the most part by date only. Other passages in Goethe's works are usually cited according to the following editions, by volume and page number:

WA = *Goethes Werke*. Herausgegeben im Auftrage der Großherzogin Sophie von Sachsen (Weimar: Hermann Böhlau, 1887–1919).
HA = *Goethes Werke*. Hamburger Ausgabe in 14 Bänden. Herausgegeben von Erich Trunz (originally Hamburg: Christian Wegner Verlag, 1948ff.).

Several scholarly works cited in more than one of the contributions to the volume are abbreviated in the notes as follows:

Bennett = Benjamin K. Bennett, *Goethe's Theory of Poetry: "Faust" and the Regeneration of Language* (Ithaca: Cornell University Press, 1986).
Brown = Jane K. Brown, *Goethe's "Faust": The German Tragedy* (Ithaca and London: Cornell University Press, 1986).
Emrich = Wilhelm Emrich, *Die Symbolik von Faust II: Sinn und Vorformen* (Berlin: Juncker und Dünnhaupt Verlag, 1943).
Gräf = Hans Gerhard Gräf, *Goethe über seine Dichtungen: Versuch einer Sammlung aller Äußerungen des Dichters über seine poetischen Werke*, 9 vols. (Frankfurt/Main: Literarische Anstalt, 1901–1914).
Mandelkow I = Karl Robert Mandelkow, ed., *Goethe im Urteil seiner Kritiker: Dokumente zur Wirkungsgeschichte Goethes in Deutschland*, 4 vols. (München: Verlag C.H. Beck, 1975–1984).
Mandelkow II = Karl Robert Mandelkow, *Goethe in Deutschland: Rezeptionsgeschichte eines Klassikers*, 2 vols. (München: Verlag C.H. Beck, 1980, 1989).
Schöne = Albrecht Schöne, *Götterzeichen, Liebeszauber, Satanskult: Neue Einblicke in alte Goethetexte* (München: Beck, 1982).
Schwerte = Hans Schwerte, *Faust und das Faustische: Ein Kapitel deutscher Ideologie* (Stuttgart: Klett, 1962).
Staiger = Emil Staiger, *Goethe*, 3 vols. (Zürich: Atlantis, 1957–59).

THE FAUSTIAN

VIRGIL NEMOIANU

Absorbing Modernization: The Dilemmas of Progress
in the Novels of Walter Scott and in *Faust II*

I

ANY ATTEMPT TO DECODE THE POLITICAL-HISTORICAL implications of Goethe's
Faust must begin with the reminder that Goethe's positions on contemporary
politics, and on historical development in general, have been a subject of puzzle-
ment for almost two centuries now. Goethe's stands have been read as ambivalent, timid, opportunistic, slyly toadying, even downright backsliding. Indeed his
work (and *Faust* in particular) has been seen as open to reactionary and exclu-
sionary exploitation. A comparable number of readings has highlighted progress,
tolerance and Enlightenment broadmindedness in the writings of Goethe and
tried to define *these* as the center of gravity in his work.[1]

Such debates reflect Goethe's continuing socio-cultural influence; they also
embody the questionable enterprise of translating accurately and completely
literary-aesthetic discourse into ideological-political formulations. In fact, confronting these two modes of discourse can be truly helpful only if their relation
is envisaged not as the passive *mimesis* of one sphere by the other but rather as
a genuine intermeshing in which the literary-aesthetic rhetoric and utterance is
a senior participant that can explain the historical text at least as much as it is
explained by the latter.[2]

Each of the opposing positions on Goethe's socio-historical role is marred by
the unfortunate and deep-rooted prejudice that Goethe's Olympian stature
somehow precludes indeterminacies ("Goethe knew"). It is closer to fact to say
that Goethe was struggling honestly with a phenomenon of enormous historical
proportions, trying to enact it dramatically before articulating answers, which
in any case often proved unsatisfactory. Goethe was indeed trying to shape a
synthesis by formulating a centrist answer, but he was simultaneously trying to
make sense of an unfolding historical process: for better or for worse, such
wrestling for the truth was considered at the time an essential part of being fully
human, and Goethe certainly shared this view.

The debate on Goethe's role also founders on the fantastic-utopian categories of Hegelian-Marxist pedigree that obfuscate, sometimes hopelessly, historical readings.[3] The writers and thinkers who (like Goethe) were busy at the Enlightenment/Romanticism intersection read history not in Hegelian or Marxist terms, but, as it turns out, in terms much closer to those of Max Weber, Ralf Dahrendorf, Ernst Gellner or W.W. Rostow—what is called nowadays "modernization theory."[4] In these terms the problem confronting the age can be summarized as a series of accelerated displacements from traditional, organic-biological modes of governance and social behavior to rationalist and transactional social structures, from rural to urban and industrialized existence and production; from tribal to individualist consciousness, from communitarian constraint to contractual and alienated modes of association; from stability and harmony to speed, homogeneity and creativity; from eccentricity and tentativeness to streamlining and discipline. These broad tendencies had been gathering momentum since the Renaissance, but the industrial revolution in northwest Europe and the political upheavals in France, North America and elsewhere rendered them painfully visible and forced conscious deliberation upon both intellectuals and society at large.

Goethe's political opinions *per se* are not especially acute or profound, perhaps just symptomatically interesting, as the views of one intelligent individual at the time.[5] By contrast, in the enactments of his literary works Goethe puts forward sophisticated and nuanced responses to the historical situation of his time—to my mind, some of the most complex and satisfying ever put forward. The encodings and decodings of historical dilemmas and aporias, the enactments of tradition and progress, of transactional versus organic, of liberal versus conservative that are incorporated in *Faust* are all better described by taking a comparative approach (something done rather seldom) in order to place Goethe more firmly inside his age, rather than the age "inside" Goethe.

II

Scott is the closest literary counterpart of Edmund Burke. Scott lacked Burke's rhetorical energy, subtlety and precision, but he made a rather similar case with the additional efficiency that the ambiguities of dramatized situations can provide. Reflection on the accelerated movement of history was forced upon him by the local example that he knew in great detail, for Scotland represents one of the first cases of violent colonial imposition of technological and economic advance, with the concomitant political "loosening" of biologically rooted social forms. The tragic undecidabilities of historical progress were painfully immediate for Scott as he observed the century-long struggle between the Hanoverian regime and the archaic clan organization of the Scottish Highlands. In novel after novel such as *Waverley, Old Mortality, Rob Roy, Redgauntlet*, Scott tried to assess the advantages and the drawbacks of the one civilizational model as opposed to the other, and tried to delineate their value systems and their human costs. The answers become clear enough after perusing several of his novels: Scott wants us to accept the inevitability of the historical movement away from the organic bindings of blood and soil[6] towards the society of unattached individuals whose rationally negotiated contracts shape their personal destinies. At the same time, worried about the loss of values invested in the historical past, Scott declares the novelist's primary task to be salvaging these values by providing images of balance that would be fully human, rounded and integrated. This can be done, he suggests, by detaching the values of an archaic, natural and organic society from their previous material (physical and social) environment, and *transferring* them into a new medium by finding new vehicles for them. (It goes without saying that even the mere *contemplation* of such an abstract exercise already places Scott into the imaginative world outlined by Adam Smith and Adam Ferguson.) These older values, once implanted in the minds and souls of younger people, could survive and perhaps even revive, albeit in new bodies and with entirely new meanings and languages.

Scott returned with amazing doggedness to this his favorite topic, looking at it from different angles and in different historical circumstances. Harking back to the etymological roots of "revolution"[7] he often tried out on his readers combinations in which the "reactionary" and the truly "revolutionary" were allegories of each other or overlapped in different ways (*Old Mortality*). The enormous international impact of Scott's novels proves, in my opinion, that his political philosophy responded to an acutely felt need. Major figures such as Manzoni, Victor Hugo, Pushkin (*Kapitanskaya Dochka*), and others in Eastern and Southern Europe immediately came up with their own versions of Scott's scenario. I also believe that Balzac was more deeply marked by the example of Scott (i.e. well beyond his early and rather unsuccessful *Les Chouans*) than usually assumed. Perhaps Scott's most faithful and thoughtful follower was James Fenimore Cooper, who masterfully translated the opposition between the archaic Highlands clan-based civilization and the modernizing individual and contractual civilization into the opposition of Native Americans versus settlers, with their opposing systems of values and alternative versions of paradise, in the "Leatherstocking" series and elsewhere. Similarly the broadest acceptance of Scott's views of history may have been in the Old South of the new United States, although with its own local distortions.[8]

Comparable attempts at an uneasy balance can be found in the work of Chateaubriand, who once (trying to place himself inside the constitutional crisis of 1830) claimed that "Républicain par nature, monarchiste par raison et bourbonnien par honneur, je me serais beaucoup mieux arrangé d'une démocratie si je n'avais pu conserver la monarchie légitime, que de la monarchie bâtarde octroyée par je ne sais qui."[9] In a more disorderly and dispersed way, Chateaubriand engaged in the same kinds of enactments as Scott; he elaborates the possibilities inherent in Scott's narrative model and assays them in unexpected ways. Throughout the *Mémoires d'Outre-Tombe* for instance we find the continuous suggestion that the writer is at the crossroads, witnessing the end of a world and negotiating with the dawning age of modernity. The final essay in the *Mémoires*, on the future of the twentieth century, pessimistic though it is, summarizes, not much differently from Tocqueville, what Chateaubriand saw as the challenges of a natural humanity with its rich interiority abruptly confronted with artificial and manipulated social environments.

This tone of moderate (or liberal) conservatism, of reformist progress, of change and preservation, of orderly advancement, of continuity in transition soon became diffused throughout Europe.[10] It can be illustrated sufficiently by examples from opposite ends of the continent. In Spain, the school of the "costumbristas" tried in its short essays to outline the dialectic of change and continuity, rather in the spirit of Jovellanos (the "Spanish Burke" and Goya's good friend), while the "liberal Romantics" of Hungary, as they have been called (István Szécheny, Jozsef Eötvös and others) took surprisingly analogous positions.[11]

Let me return to Sir Walter and the peculiar inter-connections between him and his Weimar contemporary. Scott was an enthusiast of German literature and knew it well, though in somewhat disorderly fashion. Goethe was one of his early favorites, and Scott's first book-length publication was a translation of *Goetz of Berlichingen* (1798; with the active support of "Monk Lewis"). Despite numerous and hilarious linguistic howlers (he admitted this himself in letters written in his old age; his German improved steadily over the years), the work was considered worthy of inclusion in the prestigious Bohn's Library (with due corrections) because of Scott's capacity to catch the flavor of Goethe's style (see also his translation of "Erlkönig," admirable, despite Scott's belief that the action was placed in the "Black Forest of Thuringia"). *Götz* exerted a clear influence on Scott's *Lay of the Last Minstrel* and on *Marmion*. (The title hero of the latter work was patterned after Weislingen, the main female character of the former after Elisabeth.) Further Goethean influences have been detected in *Ivanhoe* (by as early a commentator as Lockhart) and in the play *The House of Aspen* (1799), a "remake" of an obscure play by G. Wachter, and in other works. Fenella, for example, in *Peveril of the Peak*, is modeled on Mignon in the *Lehrjahre*, while the portrait of Louis XI in *Quentin Durward* seems to be indebted to the figure of Mephistopheles. Smaller borrowings have been noted in *The Antiquary* and the Leicester/Amy Robsart relationship in *Kenilworth* (after Egmont and Clara.)

Scott kept abreast of Goethe's main publications. His son-in-law Lockhart visited Goethe in Weimar and eventually the two exchanged long and highly complimentary letters (12 January 1827 from Weimar and 9 July 1827 from Edinburgh); both correspondents were pleased and flattered by the other's letter; in 1832, just two weeks before his death, Goethe (responding to a letter from an already seriously ill Scott, from Italy) invited the novelist to come to Weimar. In 1831, at Carlyle's initiative, fifteen distinguished Englishmen offered Goethe as an anniversary gift a golden seal inscribed with "Ohne Hast aber ohne Rast"; Scott was one of them.

Meanwhile Goethe had started reading massive amounts of Scott (his introduction was *Kenilworth* in 1821): not only novels (*Waverley, Ivanhoe, Rob Roy, The Black Dwarf, The Fair Maid of Perth*–about which he was highly complimentary–but also other works such as *The Life of Napoleon* and *Letters on Demonology and Witchcraft*. Goethe also read and sometimes summarized articles from the *Edinburgh Review* and other Scottish and English journals. The reception of Helena by Faust (Act III, "Innerer Burghof") is indebted, it has been convincingly argued, to the reception of Elizabeth I by the Earl of Leicester as described in Scott's *Kenilworth*. It is also generally accepted that some of the material in Act IV of *Faust II* is indebted to Scott's *Letters on Demonology and Witchcraft* (which, in turn, contains precisely the materials on Nicolai that had excited Goethe's lampoon in the "Walpurgisnacht").[12]

There can be no doubt that we are faced with a close and intimate connection. The reflections of Scott and Goethe on the movement of history were remarkably similar, primarily, I believe, because of parallels in their fundamental philosophical orientations. However, I do not exclude certain kinds of ideological reinforcement through direct influence. Goethe must have been heartened by the kinship he sensed in Scott's novels in the years when he was writing *Faust II*. For Scott, in turn, the ambiguous and tragic loneliness of Götz in the turbulence of historical progress, and Goethe's own vacillations with regard to progress in that play may well have motivated his later (novelistic) treatments of the dilemmas of progress.

III

In any case, where do Goethe and his *Faust* fit inside this wider European scene? Above all Goethe is bound to these contemporaries by the shared view that imagination, beauty, and subjectivity, all symbolic and emotional resources can and should be used as legitimate tools for cognition, human action, and historical *praxis*. This view was increasingly abandoned after 1850, but until then (in romantic historiography, in travel literature, and indeed, everywhere) one can observe many kinds of entwining of the fictional with the mimetic and reproductive. Practically this was a vindication of the past (in which sentimental and aesthetic factors were supposed to have been prevalent) by demonstrating its continued utility for the present and future. If a passing civilization could be boiled down to its interiority–rather than to its externals which, as was almost unanimously admitted, could and must be discarded–then the issue would be to find an effective function for the faculties and values put in doubt by the advent of modernity. It is here that *Faust*'s relevance to the progress/conservation debate must be sought.

For cultural history *Faust* is most "usefully" read as a kind of document in which the dialectics and possibilities of transition are outlined and worked out in systematic fashion. I will review a few aspects briefly and dwell upon others in more detail.

Faust has been often described as a *summa* of the past, a repository of genres and meters, stylistic possibilities, etc. In the same sense it can also be seen as a survey of modes of government, of socio-political frameworks, in the manner of both Montesquieu's *Esprit des Lois* (typologically) and of Fénelon's narrative unpacking of possibilities in his *Aventures de Télémaque*. Fairly detailed presentations of the mechanisms of a medieval city-state are presented in *Faust I*, the functioning of baroque and/or enlightened absolutism (with its bureaucracies, financial dealings, internal power struggles, emphasis on spectacle and splendor, etc.) is seen in the first act of *Faust II*. Slightly more complicated (but also more stimulating) are the last two structures of governance presented in the play. The Faust/Helena monarchic experiment looks back to archaic clan organization; at the same time it depicts a modern alternative, in the guise of the Biedermeier *Kleinstaat*, to the imperialist macroeconomic frameworks that were emerging at the time. The same ambiguity obtains in the case of Faust's final governmental experiment. This is in some ways an egalitarian, democratic, state-socialist construct; but in other ways it is firmly *dirigiste*, directed by bureaucracies, *Realpolitik*, and collectivist volition. Needless to say, this survey is also historical in its progress from the Middle Ages through the centuries to the near and predictable future.

The fact that *Faust* is a repository of the past can be considered a conservative side of the drama; nevertheless the very fact that this array of shapes (aesthetic as well as historical-cultural) is now in need of preservation marks a radical turning point, as the inception of a new and progressive age that is thus acknowledged and accepted.[13]

IV

Like the contemporaries whose examples I briefly adduced at the beginning, Goethe is most anxious to identify elements of the past that can resist the socio-historical rush of an accelerated and inevitable future, to identify what can resist time. The answer is certainly not clear, not for Faust, nor for Goethe, nor for *Faust*. (We do not have, if I am not mistaken, a Bakhtinian reading of *Faust*, but it is not usually disputed that *Faust* is a work of plural voices and of thick layers of deliberate indeterminacy.)

The answer is least clear for Faust himself, who is not very strong on memorizing. He has to be reminded of his social efficiency by the country people during his early bouts of dejection (981–1063). He relies thereafter increasingly on Mephistopheles as a repository of memory. Faust does not quite recognize Gretchen during the "Walpurgisnacht" orgy (4183–88), nor does he seem to recognize her, or understand her as an agent of his salvation, in the final scene of *Faust II*. At least as typical are the repeated incidents of swooning and fainting, devices by which episodes are brought to an end, but which also illustrate Faust's general passivity and dream-like state. The first of these episodes occurs even before the pact, when Mephistopheles easily escapes his power by inducing

Faust's cataleptic sleep (1425–1525). Others occur at the conclusion of *Faust I* and the beginning of *Faust II*: the most significant of these discontinuities is the result of the grab for Helena ("Explosion. Faust liegt am Boden") commented on by Mephistopheles' exasperated-condescending

> Hier lieg, Unseliger, verführt
> Zu schwergelöstem Liebesbande!
> Wen Helena paralysiert,
> Der kommt so leicht nicht zu Verstande. (6566–69)

This explosion leads to a longer paralysis, but not to loss of memory, although it could be argued that the wanderings along the upper and lower Peneios show a rudderless and easily distracted individual. Finally, Act V of *Faust II* gives no indications of continuity with previous experiences.[14] Faust is unable to re-establish contact with his former students and colleagues and one may wonder whether any kind of actual growth process can be imagined as going on inside Faust. One could almost argue that the Lord is seriously mistaken in providing grace, salvation, and forgiveness to Faust on the basis of some putative "Streben" and "Bemühen" of which there is precious little evidence! In a curious way, it is not Mephistopheles who represents a side of Faust, but rather Faust who could be seen as a variant of Mephistopheles; Faust's much-vaunted creativity is merely a "Verneinung" of a historical environment made available to him through no merit or effort of his own.

V

Although Faust is thus a master of oblivion and of liberal discontinuity, *Faust* can be seen as a monument of the struggle with and for memory, and thus as a conservative work.[15]

The evolutionary continuity in *Faust* as a whole, and in *Faust II* in particular, must therefore be placed not at the level of the character's subjective consciousness, but at that of Goethe's objective understanding of historical movement. Precisely because Faust has a weak and unreliable historical memory he is more fully engaged in each given historical situation and responds with a relative lack of inhibition to the given circumstances. Faust the character pays little attention to his own past, he integrates readily into the power configurations inside which he is placed and does what is required of him. "Faust-in-the-context" is what should be subjected to examination.

In Act I ("Kaiserliche Pfalz") power relations and governance are based on the overwhelming nominal privileges of the ruler. Mephistopheles describes these in unctuous superlatives in the passage beginning

> Das bist du, Herr! weil jedes Element
> Die Majestät als unbedingt erkennt.

> Gehorsam Feuer hast du nun erprobt;
> Wirf dich ins Meer. (6003–6)

and ending with "Und, höchster Herr, die Erde hast du schon!" (6030; cf. also the flattery of the herald in 5072–76). In reality, however, the powers of the emperor seem limited not only by economic constraints, but also by the assertive intervention of advisors ("Saal des Thrones"), all jealous of their privileges and speaking for powerful constituencies, not least the astrologer (4955–70; 5047–56), the equivalent of the modern-day social scientist and think-tank guru.[16] The people are heard from often, they have their own identity and opinions (often cynical or skeptical, 4885–89 or 4951–54) and are implicitly taken into account in the decision-making process (4757–60, 5484–93, 5715–26, 5748–56). Indeed, there are complaints about the growth of individualism and "greedy self-interest" at the expense of common causes and of the central budget:

> Wohin man kommt, da hält ein Neuer Haus,
> Und unabhängig will er leben;
> Zusehen muß man, wie er's treibt.
> Wir haben so viel Rechte hingegeben,
> Daß uns auf nichts ein Recht mehr übrigbleibt.
> . . .
> Ein jeder kratzt und scharrt und sammelt,
> Und unsre Kassen bleiben leer. (4836–51).

In neat contrast to Act V, cabinet-minister Mephistopheles advises the Emperor: "Nimm Hack' und Spaten, grabe selber! Die Bauernarbeit macht dich groß" (5039–40), and the latter complies (5047) with meek fussiness ("Nur gleich, nur gleich! Wie lange soll es währen?") in a gesture that would be quite out of character with the imperial/socio-bureaucratic Faust of the final scenes.[17] At any rate, in Act I Faust, whether as Plutus or as himself, is merely a minister and advisor, with no sovereign powers.

By contrast, in Act III, Faust enjoys sovereign autonomy over his small fief north of Sparta. His image (and self-image) is that of a benevolent, paternal ruler. The Vossian/Homeric meters, the constant reminders, in adages of pompous piety, of a power based upon age and legitimacy (often with reference to Biblical-patriarchal modes of governance as much as or more than to ancient Greek ones), the mild and benign behavior of both Helena and Faust all point to this image. In particular the long tirade by Faust (9514–61) represents a veritable governmental program, since it comes close to the beginning of this reign.

Against this progress stand at least two elements. The first is the heart of darkness inside this benignity. The mode of governance is based upon ritual sacrifice, human destruction, slavery and a notably more ruthless treatment of subjects than in Act I. Faust's and Helena's tolerance is just that: toleration, when in fact there is no constraint against the most ruthless behavior (8920–30). The second is the artificial nature of this governmental concoction. There are repeated references to the artificiality of Faust's little state. Faust himself asks: "Was bin ich nun?. . . / . . . meine Mauern / unsicher" (9264–66) and the anguished feminine chorus wonders:

> Alles deckte sich schon
> Rings mit Nebel umher.
> Sehen wir doch einander nicht!
> Was geschieht? gehen wir?
> Schweben wir nur
> Trippelnden Schrittes am Boden hin?
> . . .
> Ja auf einmal wird es düster. . .
> . . . Ist's ein Hof? ist's tiefe Grube?
> Schauerlich in jedem Falle! (9110–25)

The artificial and uncertain nature of this "nation" is analogous to the hybrid and historically contrived nature of much of Biedermeier and nineteenth-century statehood, with its veneer of chivalric-feudal externalities and its modernizing deep-structures.[18] In a word, the society outlined in Act III is in its aims, and even in its *praxis*, more liberal than the empire of Act I; nevertheless, we notice that the power of the ruler (and/or of Faust personally) has been growing considerably, while the voice of the people or the participatory nature of the governance has been losing ground.

A comparison with the third socio-political experience, in Act V, confirms this pattern. The ideals of this last society portrayed in *Faust* ("the end of history" as it were) come much closer to a modern socio-liberal agenda, with its concerns for job-creation ("Arbeiter schaffe Meng' auf Menge, / Ermuntere durch Genuß und Strenge, / Bezahle, locke, presse bei!," 11552–54), ecology ("die Erde mit sich selbst versöhnet," 11541), civil rights and communitarian options ("viele Millionen," "paradiesisch Land," "Völkerschaft," "Gewimmel," 11563–79)—to the point that, as I said earlier, a number of readers were convinced that Goethe was projecting, wittingly or unwittingly, a socialist future. If not Goethe, then at least Faust thought along these lines. The transfer into practice of these high ideals looks different, and of course we see here the other, conservative side of the coin, or to be more precise, the kind of *corrective* that conservative skepticism and realism ought to bring, in Goethe's scenario, to the utopian pressures for progress exerted by the collectivist project. On the one hand, Faust, immersed in the dynamics of his activist improvement activities, forgets all about his own mortality and about how one can lose touch with reality; as Mephistopheles comments with a malice bordering upon pity: "Den letzten, schlechten, leeren Augenblick, / Der Arme wünscht ihn festzuhalten" (11589–90), when all along the construction activity consisted only of funeral preparations: "Man spricht, wie man mir Nachricht gab, / Von keinem Graben, doch vom Grab" (11557–58). On the other hand, Goethe pointedly identifies the human cost of a radical progress that all too easily succumbs to (imperialist and administrative) coercion as the best means to hasten the achievement of the social good and to implement lofty ideals. Three of the seven scenes of Act V are devoted to Philemon and Baucis and their destruction. For Faust, the "Jeffersonian in a hurry," the possibility of imperfection or of an exception to collective goals is intolerable: "Daß sich das größte Werk vollende, / Genügt *ein* Geist für tausend Hände" (11509–10). Individual traditions, even the least threatening, become unacceptable from the vantage point of the socially desirable: "Das Glöckchen läutet, und ich wüte!" (11258). Procedural short-cuts, streamlined judicial procedure are impatiently resorted to: "Daß man, zu tiefer, grimmiger Pein, / Ermüden muß, gerecht zu sein" (11271–72). Faust's subsequent regret, whether sincere or hypocritical, at the liquidation of conservative minorities is quickly dispelled by the renewed opportunity for creative work, much in the vein of a (blind) totalitarian ruler.

It would be wrong to read immediately into the Philemon und Baucis episode a full-scale condemnation of the liberal-globalist project: if nothing else, Faust's redemption in the last scene of the dramatic poem indicates the contrary. The most plausible and convincing reading is one that highlights the dilemma posed by the episode and the centrality of a dialectics of peril in it. In any case a pattern can be recognized as we advance in the reading of *Faust II*: the ideal of a liberalized civilization gains ground, indeed seems to advance triumphant, while at the same time the possibilities for manipulation, control and social engineering grow and are, indeed, implemented by Faust.

VI

Another pattern of contradiction and uncertainty, while not identical with the one just described in the section above, nevertheless tends to reinforce it, and occasionally overlaps with it. I refer to the growth of abstraction, rationality and artificiality, as the "socio-political experiences" of *Faust II* unfold. There is, unquestionably, manipulation at work in the "Kaiserliche Pfalz": adornment, pretense, *Realpolitik*, outright lying. Nevertheless we also observe a certain ingenuousness and directness in the conversations between Emperor and advisors, and in any case, the very resort to allegory (the "Mummenschanz" in "Weitläufiger Saal") reaffirms belief in a one-to-one relationship between illusion and reality. At bottom, only the introduction of paper currency indicates a decisive orientation toward the artificial, abstract and transactional. Of course this money literally "undermines" the foundation on which the empire rests.

Not so north of Sparta. Crisp, apposite, to the point as usual, Phorkyas/Mephistopheles explains what the Northern invaders are bringing new and different into Hellenic lands:

Und seine Burg! Die solltet ihr mit Augen sehn!
Das ist was anderes gegen plumpes Mauerwerk,
Das eure Väter, mir nichts dir nichts, aufgewälzt,
Zyklopisch wie Zyklopen, rohen Stein sogleich
Auf rohe Steine stürzend; dort hingegen, dort
Ist alles senk- und waagerecht und regelhaft.
Von außen schaut sie! himmelan sie strebt empor,
So starr, so wohl in Fugen, spiegelglatt wie Stahl.
Zu klettern hier—ja selbst der Gedanke gleitet ab.
Und innen großer Höfe Raumgelasse, rings
Mit Baulichkeit umgeben, aller Art und Zweck. (9017–27)

The spirit of geometry takes over here as order, abstraction, logical linearity, abstract shapes replace the natural agglutinations of the past. Similarly the companions of Faust, the ". . . kühn Geschlecht / . . . dringend aus cimmerischer Nacht," (8999–9000) seem artificially bred in their "geregelter Zug" (9155) and are unattractive sexually to the otherwise bold and lusty female followers of Helena:

Gern biss' ich hinein, doch ich schaudre davor;
Denn in ähnlichem Fall, da erfüllte der Mund
Sich, gräßlich zu sagen, mit Asche. (9162–64)

The abstract and artificial atmosphere is further heightened precisely by the uncertainty of present reality: "Vielleicht auch irrt sie zweifelhaft im Labyrinth / Der wundersam aus vielen einsgewordnen Burg" (9145–46), in which everybody suspects the reality of everybody else and thick mists obliterate the surroundings.

Once Faust is no longer a feudal leader, but a modern one, he and Mephistopheles can shed all inhibitions; naturally derived modes are abandoned in favor of rational abstractions.[19] Mephistopheles's engineering helpers are mechanical and robot-like; their masterpiece is a "großer, gradgeführter Kanal" ("Palast," stage direction between 11142 and 11143). Faust avows that "der Tüchtige" should abandon the search for ultimate truths and turn to pragmatic pursuits: "Was er erkennt, läßt sich ergreifen" (11448). The family—Faust himself had been notoriously luckless in raising one, whether in the test-tube or otherwise—must give way to manipulated organizations. The clouds and mists of the Lacedemonian hills now are replaced by full blindness, the precondition of sterile rationality and arbitrary abstraction, ironically at the very moment that Faust clamors obsessively for visual control. Does not Lynkeus resemble a supervising guard on top of the wooden tower at the corner of a penal colony or prison camp? Does not Faust console himself for the misfortune of Philemon und Baucis by saying:

> Doch sei der Lindenwuchs vernichtet
> Zu halbverkohlter Stämme Graun,
> Ein Luginsland ist bald errichtet,
> Um ins Unendliche zu schaun (11342–45)?

On the whole, Act V reminds us of the theories of Goux on the growth of abstraction as the foundation of modern societies.[20]

The increase in abstraction and replaceability, as well as the decline of the sensorial and the concrete, signal for Goethe mankind's relentless modernization; he is deeply ambivalent about them. This is not to say that he is hostile: armies of readers (even in our own time a good majority, I would guess) have looked upon the progress outlined by Goethe in *Faust II* with approval: the capitalist growth ("Nur mit zwei Schiffen ging es fort, / Mit zwanzig sind wir nun im Port" 11173–74), the ensuing social sharing, the ceaseless advance ("Im Weiterschreiten find' er Qual und Glück," 11451). Surely this means that there is enough semantic gesturing to offset any outright opposition by the author to radical progress and to demote opposition to mere doubt. Thus the pattern described here resembles the one described in section V, the modernization of structures of governance, even though the two are not identical.[21]

Despite the pattern of progress from Act I to Act V, I am not too inclined to emphasize the historicity or chronology of these dramatic events, as many critics have done. Their arrangement is more a matter of communication and convenient rhetoric. In fact, it is more rewarding to think of these episodes as contemporaneous, as a series of existential and historical options offered to the reader, or offered by the author to himself as part of his reflection on what was happening to the world and where human society was heading. We may also wonder whether the tragedy of Gretchen could not be interpreted, in a political vein, as a "historical necessity"–the break of history with a small, secure and secluded environment, the break with the "micro-harmony" of modest personal happiness. In that case, the tragedy would be precisely the inevitability of individual sacrifice.

VII

Does *Faust II* offer any conclusions in the light of these considerations? Is Goethe pessimistic or optimistic about the direction in which the world is moving? I believe that the parallels with Tocqueville's considerations about American democracy are rather obvious.[22] The tone is amiable resignation, marked lack of enthusiasm, but therefore neither hostile opposition, nor, certainly, despair of human resilience and ingenuity to cope with radically modified historical environments or to preserve the features of humanity, as Goethe understood them.

Two qualifiers or accents ought to be added here. First, the evolution of environments in social history as imagined by Goethe and some of his more lucid contemporaries (not least Scott and Chateaubriand) oddly resembles the vision widely accepted at the end of the twentieth century and derived from Durckheim and Max Weber, or Ernst Gellner and Karl Polanyi. (If further names are needed to flesh out what I have in mind they could be those of the neo-classical figures of Friedrich Hayek, Karl Popper, Louis Dumont, or even Dahrendorf and Andrew János).

Second, quite central to the whole project of *Faust*, I am convinced, and probably also dear to Goethe's heart, was the argument that there are only systemic problems, no systemic solutions. Solutions can only be provided in and through individual *praxis*. Faust is the individual who must learn the virtues of the individual; *Faust* is the ultimate anti-*Candide*. Each episode that concludes with Faust's "unhappiness" or alienation indicates that the main hero is unable or unwilling to adapt. It also indicates that a system or framework as such is unable to respond fully to real individual human needs. The semantic value of the religious element at the very end is precisely this: it is extra-systemic. This is not to say that we should overlook the super-added irony of a religious framework that is itself placed inside the mode of contractual negotiation and arbitrary sign-attribution it is supposed to supersede, but only: Goethe indicates that imperfection and tragic tension are too integral to "being-human" to be eradicated except by transcendence of the human, irrespective of the nature (or probability) of such a transcendence.

Once we accept these two qualifications it is easy to see how Goethe's attempt to use history as a universalizing idiom has much relevance for today. Goethe thinks that history cannot be "made" in a real sense by the human person; but this does not involve him in either anti-historical negation, or the passive sufferance of a "whirlwind." He suggests in *Faust II* and elsewhere that history is or can be acceptable if it is responded to by moderating discourses of deflection and digression. This is Goethe's equivalence to romantic fragmentariness in the Schlegel-Nietzsche tradition. *Faust II* (or *Faust* as a whole) is itself such a deflective discourse, but it also contains inside itself instances of deflection, avoidance and moderation, like many smaller laboratories inside a medical building. Even if we do not accept this conception, we can still admire, or at least understand the strenuous honesty of its effort.[23]

The possibilities for the transfer of Faustian situations onto a global, late-millenium scale are considerable. The transitional pressures experienced by German/northwest European areas first around 1800 (and not entirely mastered even now) have been generalized to the entire globe by the end of the twentieth century. Showing how these pressures were processed in *Faust* and other contemporary works clearly vindicates the continuing relevance of some humanistic/canonical areas. I am sure I do not make an exaggerated claim in saying that works like *Faust* are a kind of "cushioning" area that allow everybody to work out the asperities of transitions in a more compassionate way than pure political-economic decisions, no matter how well-intentioned or democratically well-crafted they may otherwise be.[24]

NOTES

1. For a short discussion of Börne, Gregorovius and others see Walter Dietze, "Elemente evolutionären und revolutionären Denkens in der Humanismus-Konzeption Goethes und Herders," in Paolo Chiarini and Walter Dietze, ed., *Deutsche Klassik und Revolution* (Rome: Edizioni dell'Ateneo, 1981) 102–3. Cf. also Dieter Borchmeyer, *Höfische Gesellschaft und französische Revolution bei Goethe* (Kronberg/Ts.: Athenäum, 1977) 303.

2. Jens Kruse, *Der Tanz der Zeichen: Poetische Struktur und Geschichte in Goethes "Faust II"* (Königstein/Ts.: Anton Hain, 1985) 81–82 misses precisely this point in objecting to Heinz Schlaffer's interpretation of Goethe's readings on economics. Cf. also Ruth I. Cape, *Das französische Ungewitter: Goethes Bildersprache zur französischen Revolution* (Heidelberg: Carl Winter, 1991) 131, 141.

3. Thus my only main objection to Heinz Schlaffer's excellent *Faust Zweiter Teil: Die Allegorie des 19. Jahrhunderts* (Stuttgart: Metzler, 1981) is that it weakens its own argument by resorting to Marxist categories rather than e.g. to Karl Polanyi's tripartite sequence of reciprocity, redistribution, and market. Cf. Polanyi, *The Great Transformation* (originally 1944; Boston: Beacon Press, 1985)

4. According to John Tomlinson, *Cultural Imperialism: A Critical Introduction* (Baltimore: Johns Hopkins University Press, 1991) 142, Marx should also be included (along with Simmel, Durckheim and Tönnies) in this group of classical sociologists. Tomlinson also argues against understanding "capitalism" as "the single principle behind cultural modernity," although it "*inflects* modernity in a particular way" (141).

5. Perhaps of all Goethe's statements on his political philosophy, the most famous and the most significant are those noting the acceleration of the means of communication and the commercial speed of paper money, as well as the Eckermann passage in which he placed himself half-way between revolution and "arbitrary rule." See the comments on these in Wilhelm Mommsen, *Die politischen Anschauungen Goethes* (Stuttgart: Deutsche Verlags-Anstalt, 1948) 276–77, 284 and Arnold Bergstraesser, *Goethe's Image of Man and Society* (originally 1949; Freiburg: Herder, 1962) 90, 199–203.

6. Octavio Paz uses the term "condemned to modernity," cf. Tomlinson 136, 141. Numerous commentators noticed the attitude expressed by this phrase in Goethe's case. Cf. besides the above-cited Mommsen and Bergstraesser also Borchmeyer 307–8, or Gerhard Wild, *Versöhnungsbilder: Eine geschichtsphilosophische Untersuchung zu Goethes späten Werken* (Stuttgart: Metzler, 1991) 89, 95.

7. This was in fact still true about German usage at the time. See e.g. Thomas P. Saine, *Black Bread–White Bread: German Intellectuals and the French Revolution* (Columbia, S.C.: Camden House, 1988) 328.

8. For Goethe's knowledge of Scott and of Scotland see among others John Hennig, *Goethes Europakunde* (Amsterdam: Rodopi, 1987) 70–88; also Staiger 3:414.

9. Cf. Jean-Paul Clément, ed., *Chateaubriand politique* (Paris: Hachette Pluriel, 1987) 141. The phrase appears in an essay published in 1831 as a political pamphlet, "De la nouvelle proposition relative au bannissement de Charles X et de sa famille."

10. It is very difficult to dig out on the theoretical level a "conservative" position in the full and strong sense of the word during the "Goethezeit" and even before 1789. Thus none other than Prince Metternich thought of himself as just a pre-revolutionary liberal. Cf. Heinrich von Srbik, *Metternich*, 2 vols. (originally 1925; Munich: Bruckmann, 1957) 1:60–66, 227–28. Jacques Godechot in his fundamental work *La Contre-revolution: Doctrine et action, 1789–1804* (Paris: Presses universitaires de France, 1961) has difficulty finding pure ultra-conservative doctrines, before as well as during the revolution. The closest would be the handbook used for teaching politics to the future Louis XVI and his younger brothers, i.e. the original short (and specifically commissioned!) form of Jacques Nicolas Moreau's later enormously expanded *Principes de morale, de politique et du droit publique puisés dans l'histoire de nôtre monarchie* (cf. Godechot 18–20). I also tend to agree with more recent historical work that thinks of the revolutionary terror of the 1790s as a persecutory and paranoic ploy meant to cover up the despair of the victors at the absence of genuine opposition.

11. Gaspar Melchior de Jovellanos (1744–1811), unlike his English counterpart, and although he was also twice in government, was deemed a dangerous liberal; he was banished from Madrid (1790–1797) and imprisoned in Majorca (1801–1808). See, among others, Ricardo de la Cierva, *La Derecha sin remedio* (Barcelona: Plaza y Janes, 1987). For the Hungarians see Mihály Szegedy-Maszák, "Romanticism in Hungary," in Roy Porter and Mikulás Teich, ed., *Romanticism in National Context* (Cambridge: Cambridge University Press, 1988) 217–39 and J. Christopher Nyíri, "Tradition et liberté: le conservatisme autrichien d'Eötvös à Musil," in Miklos Molnár and André Reszler, ed., *Le Génie de l'Autriche-Hongrie* (Paris: Presses universitaires de France, 1989) 131–42.

12. For some full treatments see J.M. Bulloch, *Scott and Goethe: German Influence on the Writings of Sir Walter Scott* (originally 1925; Port Washington: Kennikat Press, 1970) and particularly George H. Needler, *Goethe and Scott* (Oxford: Oxford University Press, 1950).

13. I explored the separate issue of the ambivalent nature of creative originality in *Faust* in *Micro-Harmony: The Growth and Uses of the Idyllic Model in Literature* (Bern: Peter Lang, 1977) 69–75.

14. These episodes are much in keeping with the depiction of Scott's main heroes in some of his "Waverley" novels (Edward in *Waverley*, Frank Osbaldistone in *Rob Roy*, Darsey Latimer in *Redgauntlet* and others) who are similarly sleepwalking, manipulated individuals with only a sketchy grasp of what they are experiencing; dream-like passivity rather than action likewise characterizes many of Chateaubriand's figures, as well as Renzo in *I Promessi Sposi*.

15. Of course, ultimately *any* true literary writing is about memory, as Czeslaw Milosz once remarked. I would add: it is thus conservative at heart, hence the determined struggle of the *Zeitgeist* of each age, regarding itself as the embodiment of progressive values, against literature. See also Heinz Schlaffer, "Goethes Versuch, die Neuzeit zu hintergehen" in Paolo Chiarini, ed., *Bausteine zu einem neuen Goethe* (Frankfurt/Main: Athenäum, 1987) 19–28.

16. Schlaffer, *Faust Zweiter Teil* 124.

17. Other parallels, usually not noticed by critics, are to be found in the parade of Graces, Fates and Furies in "Weitläufiger Saal" (5300–5455) in opposition to "Mitter-

nacht," and Faust's much more intense and dangerous involvement with similar figures, e.g. the "Vier graue Weiber" or, indirectly, "die drei gewaltigen Gesellen."

18. Mark Girouard, *The Return to Camelot: Chivalry and the English Gentleman* (New Haven and London: Yale University Press, 1981). Arno J. Mayer, *The Persistence of the Old Regime: Europe to the Great War* (New York: Pantheon, 1981).

19. This has been very well depicted by Schlaffer 130–34, 143 and elsewhere. Cf. also Wild 120–28. Rudolf Eppelsheimer, *Goethes Faust. Das Drama im Doppelreich: Versuch einer Deutung im Geiste des Dichters* (Stuttgart: Verlag Freies Geistesleben, 1982) 386–417 argues more intemperately that the Faust of Act V is an anti-Faust, alien from the ecologist, anti-colonialist and spiritualized figure of the rest of the drama.

20. Jean Joseph Goux, *Les Iconoclastes* (Paris: Seuil, 1978).

21. As Schlaffer 54–55, 82–86, and others (e.g. Wild 8–9, 32–33, 40–41; Borchmeyer 171–73; Bergstraesser 301) have shown, Goethe's interest in and awareness of socio-economic developments and trends was extensive, covering the whole range of options, from Adam Smith and his followers (Georg Sartorius in Germany) to Saint-Simon and utopian communism.

22. Bergstraesser 310–11; Mommsen 106–15, 198; Borchmeyer 255–87; Cape 14, 139; Wild 1–6; the influence of Möser was processed by Goethe in the same direction, cf. Mommsen 29–33, also Ekkehart Krippendorff, *"Wie die Großen mit den Menschen spielen": Versuch über Goethes Politik* (Frankfurt/Main: Suhrkamp, 1988) 27; Borchmeyer *loc. cit.* Goethe in fact intuited Max Weber's basic insight as to the connection between Luther-an Reformation and modernity, Cape 138.

23. I am not saying that the quintessentially dialectical and anti-systemic nature of both Goethe and *Faust* (and their insistence on the concept of imperfection) have gone unobserved. See Ortega y Gasset's essay of 1932, also Borchmeyer 200–7; Heinz Hamm, *Goethes "Faust": Werkgeschichte und Textanalyse* (Berlin: Volk und Wissen, 1978) 20–21, 159; Mommsen 205–75; Krippendorff 116, 118 (on lack of enthusiasm for history; Schlaffer in Chiarini, *Bausteine*, 12; even Staiger 3:456.

24. I am grateful to Jane Brown, Harry Redner, and Jeffrey Barnouw for suggestions on terminology and substance.

Robert Tobin

Faust's Membership in Male Society:
Prometheus and Ganymede as Models

Two of the bits of Faustian flotsam and jetsam which wash up occasionally on literate shores for use in the general press, "the Faustian bargain" and "the eternal feminine," reflect the story's masculine origins and Goethe's addition of the feminine to that legacy. The entire Faust tradition, beginning long before Goethe, has always contained a bargain or deal, usually a male-male affair. The resonance of Goethe's addition of the feminine to the masculine Faustian world is audible in the common currency of the phrase "eternal feminine," along with the popularity of Margarete, whose tragedy within the drama has captured the sympathy of countless readers since its first publication. In adding the feminine to the Faustian tradition, Goethe does not, however, displace the male-male dynamics of the pact. Instead, he establishes a triangle of desire which confounds and upsets traditional gender dichotomies: Faust's masculine desire for the eternal feminine must be routed through the male Mephistopheles, in the process putting into question the nature of male and female.

Goethe's lifelong interest in questions of gender make clear why he would turn to the masculine Faust tradition and add to it the feminine. Although many examples from his oeuvre might serve as well, "Prometheus" and "Ganymed" provide a useful example of how Goethe consistently directs male desire for the feminine through other men. Throughout his life, Goethe linked "Prometheus" to other literary works he composed entirely or in part between 1773 and 1775, writings such as "Ganymed" and *Faust*.[1] While he intended these linkages to block radical political receptions of "Prometheus," they also underscore a series of seemingly fundamental dichotomies in Goethe's thinking. Ever since Goethe published "Ganymed" and "Prometheus" together in 1789, the two poems have embodied for critics opposing yet complementary postures toward the world, with "Ganymed" seen as dissolution of the self and "Prometheus" as an assertion of the self.[2] Often critics see "Ganymed" and "Prometheus" as exemplifying, respectively, the feminine and masculine as well,[3] but gender disrupts these elegant bifurcations, because both Ganymede and Prometheus are male. A gendered analysis, in fact, conflates the binary oppositions of the two poems into a single masculinity, striving, but unable to represent the feminine and construct a larger dichotomy.

On the pronominal level, "Prometheus" (HA 1:44–46) strongly asserts identity, from its elision of the "Du" in the opening lines to its resounding, self-confident line, "Wie ich" (line 58). The Promethean strength found in grammar carries over to other areas as well. In the first stanza, Prometheus alludes to the hut he has built and the fire he has created, pointing to his own technological prowess. In the fourth stanza, he refers to his victory over the Titans and his escape from death and slavery, claiming for himself freedom and autonomy. Not surprisingly for an eighteenth-century bourgeois fantasy, this assertive, technologically gifted, free self is also male. The speaker's masculinity emerges in references to his unfulfilled "Knabenmorgen / Blütenträume" (lines 50–51). While these boyhood dreams were in the past, the speaker makes clear that now it is Zeus who is boyish ("Und übe, Knaben gleich," line 3), as time and fate have initiated him into manhood:

> Hat nicht mich zum Manne geschmiedet
> Die allmächtige Zeit
> Und das ewige Schicksal? (lines 43–45)

This linkage of a powerfully asserted self and autonomous, technological strength with outspoken masculinity suggests why critics have frequently linked the Promethean with the masculine.

This masculinity, however, goes beyond Zeus's castratory ability to chop off the tops of oak trees and mountains, an ability which Prometheus belittles by comparing it to playing with thistles. The last stanza also shows that the poem's strongly asserted "I" is fertile enough to produce his own descendants, when it refers to Prometheus creating human beings after his own image. While this passage reflects eighteenth-century thinking about the metaphorical meaning of Prometheus as a poet who is a kind of god, a "second maker,"[4] it is also graphic enough to retain the strength of its literal image: a man creating life without procreating. Besides male parthenogenesis, the Promethean plentitude includes the ability to still pains and quiet tears—maternal, rather than paternal, charac-teristics. Indeed, even Prometheus's technical inventions, home and hearth, belong to the feminine sphere. The Promethean masculinity thus attempts to transcend the traditionally male to incorporate or appropriate the generative, nurturing, healing characteristics of the feminine.

In stark grammatical contrast to "Prometheus," "Ganymed" (HA 1:46–47) positions the "Du" prominently, from the emphatic "Du" of the poem's second line to its final lines, ending in the second person with an elided "ich." Whereas "Prometheus" had defiantly asserted the identity of its speaker, "Ganymed" is a poem of self-dissolution. Correspondingly, while "Prometheus" celebrates the autonomous individual, "Ganymed" speaks of a porous, vulnerable individual, into whose body the spring's warmth, the flowers and the grass all force their way ("sich drängen" is the verb). Recurrently, outside forces, such as the night-ingale's music which calls toward him ("drein") and the clouds, have an effect on Ganymede. Whereas Prometheus acts, Ganymede is a passive object of actions, penetrated by nature and spring. Ganymede's selflessness and porous-ness contribute to the "Verweiblichung" which some critics have noted in the hymn.[5] Specifically, this passivity has led to a critical understanding of Ganymede as the feminine object of masculine, divine love. The rape or rapture of Ganymede could then be seen neoplatonically as the story of the soul rising to God, or a fable with a moral having to do with a passive openness to pene-trating divine powers.[6] Goethe could have learned of such interpretations via his mystical studies of Pietism and alchemy, traditions which relied heavily on Neoplatonic thinking[7]; in his work, the "Ganymedic" can express the selfless-ness, vulnerability, and openness which humans need to experience divine and spiritual forces.

Just as interpretations of Prometheus's ability to create his own descendants as the poet's ability to create new worlds ignores the literal idea of male preg-nancy, the refashioning of the rape of Ganymede into the story of a feminized soul rising to God dismisses any discussion of male homosexuality from the scholarly discourse. Since Ganymede is a boy, however, the relationship be-tween Ganymede and Zeus is of course a male-male one. The subject matter gives the critics pause: "Doch merkwürdig," exclaims one, "der Frühling ist *der* Geliebte, nicht *die* Geliebte."[8] In the first sentence of his essay, another critic suggests avoiding the issue entirely: "Man sollte zunächst versuchen, sich diese Hymne zu vergegenwärtigen, ohne ihren Namen allzusehr in den Vordergrund zu stellen."[9] Although these essays are fairly old, they remain the ones to which the 1981 edition of the Hamburger Ausgabe refers its readers (HA 1:487). In any case, the limited amount of new scholarship on the subject is just as reticent: as recently as 1985, Pietzcker writes: "Doch viel mehr als ein Name ist Ganymed hier nicht."[10]

While Goethe was certainly familiar with Neoplatonic thinking, he did not feel the need to interpret the sexual out of his symbolic purview. Alongside the edifying, Neoplatonic, interpretation, another tradition, almost as old as the myth itself, has flourished, a tradition which adduced the Ganymede story as a defense of a non-critically understood homosexuality.[11] In the Renaissance and in the eighteenth century, Ganymede had become a symbol for male-male desire, in whatever form it manifested itself in those eras, without allusions to transcendent meaning.[12] Goethe's allusions to the Ganymede story throughout his life indicate his awareness of this non-Neoplatonic tradition. In *Götter, Helden und Wieland* (also composed in the early 1770s), Merkurius expresses his desire to see Wieland with the following command: "Und wenn er Ganymeds Hof-meister wäre, sollt er mir her" (HA 4:205). Given the slipperiness of the distinc-tion between pedagogy and pederasty in the Greek tradition, calling Wieland Ganymede's teacher fit neatly into a text designed to tweak the older author's dignity.[13] A Venetian Epigram of 1790 (#38) alludes to the sexual nature of Zeus's relationship with Ganymede:

> Kehre nicht, liebliches Kind, die Beinchen hinauf zu dem Himmel;
> Jupiter sieht dich, der Schalk, und Ganymed ist besorgt.
>
> (WA I, 1:317)

Goethe's subsequent translation of the passage in Benvenuto Cellini's autobiography in which the Italian artist defends sodomy with an allusion to Ganymede shows the translator's knowledge, at least by 1797, of the tradition equating Ganymede, quite non-neoplatonically, with sodomy.[14]

Time spent demonstrating the awareness of Goethe and his era that Ganymede was a signifier of male homosexuality is not idle provocation, but an important step in interpretation, because this knowledge makes clear that "Ganymed" is not about a feminine loss of individuality, but a male imitation of femininity in the form of passive male homosexuality. While Prometheus attempts to attain femininity through a phallic plenitude which allows for male mothering, Ganymede attempts to attain femininity through passive receptivity to male power. Thus, the apparent dichotomy between the Promethean and the Ganymedic pales in comparison to the unspoken dichotomy between masculine and feminine.

As suggested earlier, "Promethean" and "Ganymedic" are simply labels for attempts in Goethe's works at achieving the feminine through male-male relationships. Similar structures appear in Tasso's struggles with Antonio, which are a part of his love for Leonore von Este, in Werther's competition with Albert, which is a part of his love for Lotte, and perhaps most clearly in Wilhelm's bonding with Lothario and other members of the "Männerbund" of the Tower Society as he graduates to the love of Natalie. Precisely this structure also appears in *Faust*, where an analysis emphasizing gender shows the collapse of the distinction between Mephistopheles and Faust into an eternal masculinity incapable, but desirous, of reaching the feminine.

Dichotomies, between the Promethean and the Ganymedic as well as between the masculine and the feminine, obviously play a role in the philosophy outlined in *Faust*. Faust's famous speech to Wagner about the "zwei Seelen" in his breast (1112ff.) shows, within one person, a pattern of polar opposites. While a simple structure of dual desires is the main point here, a very tentative linkage could be made between the Promethean self-assertion of the one soul which "hält. . . sich an die Welt" and the Ganymedic desire for rapture or ascension to another world expressed by the other soul which "hebt gewaltsam sich. . . zu den Gefilden hoher Ahnen." This admixture of the Ganymedic and the Promethean can be seen in many of the early scenes of *Faust*. In "Nacht," for instance, Faust yearns in a Ganymedic way for a divine force that will penetrate him and fill his heart (434–81).[15] Once confronted by the spirits, however, he asserts his identity in a Promethean fashion (499–500).[16]

Faust claims in his speech about the two souls in his unhappy breast that they want a divorce: "Die eine will sich von der andern trennen" (1112). A close analysis of the play will show that, while Faust can never sort out these categories, he develops the Promethean at the cost of the Ganymedic. When making the pact with the devil, Faust's initially receptive posture–thrice asking Mephisto to enter (1530–32)–exemplifies his early Ganymedic tendencies.[17] The spirit world's program of teaching Faust a more Promethean approach toward the world begins with the "Geisterchor," which calls Faust "ein Halbgott" and "Mächtiger der Erdensöhne" (1612, 1617–18), titles appropriate for the Titan Prometheus. As ironic as these lines are, they point to Mephisto's plan to teach Faust a more phallically penetrating attitude toward women and men. He teaches Faust to penetrate "recht ins Innere" (3047) by seducing Margarete. Near the beginning of this process of seduction, he introduces Faust to the art of entering rooms by bringing the newly rejuvenated scholar into Margarete's chamber. In the room, Faust's masculine daydreams of a paternal throne ("Väterthron," 2697) reveal his incipient phallic desires. After Mephisto has taught Faust to seduce Margarete, he teaches him how to use phallic instruments for the less romantic penetration of men. He has Faust pull out his "Flederwisch" (3706) and fight Valentin. Valentin, who is concerned with Margarete's lost virginity, most painfully when he calls her a whore (3730), is certainly aware of the phallic nature of Faust's intrusions.

Throughout the play's second part, Faust gains more and more control over the phallic idiom. In *Faust II*, Act I,[18] he receives "das kleine Ding," for instance, the all-important key to the Mothers, which shares with the male member the property of growing when it is handled (6261).[19] Shortly after the herald strikes Mephistopheles, he lends his staff to Faust, who is dressed as Plutus:

> Wie's blitzt und platzt, in Funken sprüht!
> Der Stab, schon ist er angeglüht. (5743–44)

In Act IV, the Kaiser refuses to give Mephistopheles the general's staff, preferring to lend it to Faust:

> Den Stab kann ich dir nicht verleihen,
> Du scheinst mir nicht der rechte Mann. (10703–4)

Mephistopheles responds to this slight to his manhood with sour grapes: "Mag ihn der stumpfe Stab beschützen!" (10707). Notwithstanding the aspersions Mephistopheles casts on the size of Faust's masculinity, by this point the trend is clear that Faust is becoming more phallic and thus more Promethean. By Act V, Faust's "Bildung" to a phallic Promethean outlook on life has reached the point that, like Prometheus, he is creating new worlds, although sometimes with criminal means.

In contrast to Faust, Mephistopheles begins the play as a phallic presence. In the "Prolog im Himmel" he assertively introduces himself, attacking God just as Prometheus attacked Zeus. When he intrudes into the receptive Faustian study, he comes bedecked in phallic symbols, wearing a cock's plume in his hat and a long, sharp rapier at his side:

> Die Hahnenfeder auf dem Hut,
> Mit einem langen spitzen Degen. (1538–39)

Before Faust has sat on his paternal throne in Margarete's room, Mephistopheles sits on the throne in the witch's kitchen holding a phallic scepter:

> Hier sitz' ich wie der König auf dem Throne,
> Den Zepter halt' ich hier, es fehlt nur noch die Krone. (2448–49)

Here, in this feminine space, in which Faust becomes entranced with the image of femininity ("Das schönste Bild von einem Weibe," 2436), Mephistopheles insists on respect for the trappings of his masculinity:

> Hast du vorm roten Wams nicht mehr Respekt?
> Kannst du die Hahnenfeder nicht erkennen? (2485–86)

Mephistopheles tries to convince Faust to ride phallic broomsticks to the Walpurgisnacht party (3835), where the coarse old witch vulgarly praises the size of his endowment (4140–43). In "Trüber Tag," Mephistopheles echoes the Promethean scorn of the supposedly divine ability to throw lightning bolts and provoke storms:

> Greifst du nach dem Donner? Wohl, daß er euch elenden Sterblichen
> nicht gegeben ward! Den unschuldig Entgegnenden zu zerschmettern, das
> ist so Tyrannenart, sich in Verlegenheiten Luft zu machen. (HA 3:138)

While Mephistopheles is primarily mocking Faust's undirected and helpless rage, his argument contains a secondary critique—reminiscent of Prometheus—of the gods in general who use their strength to punish the innocent tyrannically. Finally, appearing in the "Mummenschanz" as "Geiz," Mephistopheles seems to emphasize his masculinity by undergoing a sex change from female avarice to male greed and declaring: "Bin männlichen Geschlechts, der Geiz!" (5665). In this scene, he parades his masculinity even more outrageously by molding gold into offensive figurines, presumably penises (5781–94).

But perhaps Mephistopheles protests too much: despite his offensive figurines and assertions of masculinity, he no longer controls the phallic symbols in Act I. Indeed, as early as "Nacht," in Margarete's room, where Faust learns of the "Väterthron," Mephistopheles, not his pupil, cries out, twice, "Herein" (2684).

When he appears in the "Mummenschanz" as Zoilo-Tersites, Mephistopheles receives a blow from the herald's phallic rod:

> So treffe dich, du Lumpenhund,
> Des frommen Stabes Meisterstreich! (5471–72)

Similarly, after his escapade with the gold figurines, the herald drives him away with his "Stab" (5796). Obscenely well-endowed in the first Walpurgisnacht, in the Classical Walpurgisnacht he, as Phorkyas, worries about the accusation of hermaphroditism: "Man schilt mich nun, o Schmach, Hermaphroditen" (8029). Throughout *Faust II*, Mephistopheles becomes increasingly emasculated and feminized. He continues his female impersonation in the play's final act, when Faust wants the property of Philemon and Baucis and Mephisto acquires it for his master with illicit means. Mephistopheles refers to the Biblical story of Naboth's vineyard to explain his role: according to the metaphor, Baucis and Philemon are Naboth, who loses his vineyard, Faust is King Ahab, and Mephistopheles takes on the role of Isabel, the king's beloved, who arranges the immoral takeover (11286–87).

Increasing evidence of Mephisto's homosexuality accompanies his loss of masculinity. Subtle traces of this homosexuality manifest themselves in Mephisto's overly warm descriptions to Helen of Faust's beauty. Asked about his appearance, Mephisto, as Phorkyas, replies:

> . . . mir gefällt er schon.
> Es ist ein munterer, kecker, wohlgebildeter,
> Wie unter Griechen wenig', ein verständ'ger Mann. (9010–12)

To Helen's attendants, Mephisto-Phorkyas describes Faust's entourage as a "goldgelockte, frische Bubenschar. / Die duften Jugend!" (9045–46). These fairly innocent indications of Mephisto's susceptibility to male beauty become much more obvious in the final scene, after the angels shower him with rose petals. He wants to kiss the angels: "Ihr seid so hübsch, fürwahr ich möcht' euch küssen" (11771). He tries to turn the reproach of homosexuality around by claiming that the heavenly forces are worse than the hellish ones because the angels seduce both men and women (11780–83). He thereby implies that the devils seduce only women, but his come-hither calls to one angel in particular belie his words: "Dich, langer Bursche, dich mag ich am liebsten leiden" (11794). Mephisto's interest in the "Glieder" of the angels also points to his appreciation of male beauty:

> . . . so senkt euch nieder,
> Ein bißchen weltlicher bewegt die holden Glieder. (11787–88)

By this point, the formerly phallic Mephistopheles has become as receptive and Ganymedic as the formerly receptive Faust has become phallic and Promethean.

The seesaw relationship between Faust and Mephistopheles reflects the Goethean structure—already seen in the poems "Ganymed" and "Prometheus"—of two forms of masculinity, each approaching the feminine from a different perspective and playing against the other in order to achieve a more complete femininity. While a discovery of the Ganymedic within the Promethean and vice versa unsettles the dichotomy between Mephisto and Faust, it strengthens the one between the masculine and the feminine. As Avital Ronell has Margarete say to Ernst Jünger in a discussion which also includes Marguerite Duras: "I was the excluded negativity that made it possible for you to displace virility."[20] The truly feminine figures—Margarete, Helen—are excluded by their effacement as the generalized "eternal feminine," so that the passive Ganymedic and the virile Promethean, like Faust and Mephistopheles, can intertwine.[21]

The way in which Faust's discourse, while attempting to undermine the distinctions between the Promethean and the Ganymedic, remains trapped in the masculine reveals itself in the angelic exclamation, "Gerettet ist das edle Glied" (11934), which elucidates Goethe's resolution of the polarity between the Promethean and the Ganymedic. By the play's conclusion, Faust's drive to become more Promethean has been so successful that his "Unsterbliches" is nothing but a "Glied." "Glied" can mean "limb," of course, and chaste ears may choose to hear that meaning in Mephisto's infatuation with the "Glieder" of the angels. But Goethe is bawdy enough that there could easily be an allusion to the meaning of the word as "male sexual organ" in both of these passages, especially when one recalls Mephisto's parodic line "Gerettet sind die edlen Teufelsteile" (11813), uttered just after Mephisto has withstood the homoerotic temptation of the angels.[22] As the "Glied" is at the same time "Faustens Unsterbliches," the word is also linked via the concept of soul to the Promethean goal of identity. In becoming a "Glied," Faust's Promethean, phallic striving reaches a climax.

Since for Goethe, however, the Promethean is only one of two necessary approaches to life, he chooses the word "Glied" to represent these Promethean qualities, for "Glied" in the sense of "Mitglied" or "member" points in a Ganymedic direction toward losing one's sense of phallic identity as a member of a larger group. The angelic refrain, "Gerettet ist das edle Glied der Geisterwelt," can also be seen as calling Faust a "link" in the great chain of being which is the spirit world. Thus Stuart Atkins's straightforward rendering catches almost all of the possible meanings of this difficult line: "This worthy member of the spirit world."[23] Faust has become a member both phallic and selfless, both Promethean and Ganymedic.

As Faust loses his sense of identity by becoming nothing but a "Glied"—both a "(male) member," that is, autonomous, assertive phallic symbol, and a "member, for instance, of society," that is, non-autonomous and submissive—he achieves the status which Mephistopheles had when Faust asks him: "Du nennst dich einen Teil, und stehst doch ganz vor mir?" (1345).[24] At the culmination of

Faust's journey, concepts like part and whole, rebellious autonomy and selfless submission—indeed, even characters like Mephistopheles and Faust—conflate as seen by Goethe's use of the word "Glied." Two seemingly diametrically opposed approaches to the feminine, the Ganymedic and the Promethean, the passive and the active, the Mephistophelian and the Faustian, collapse, incapable of being differentiated, and unable to escape membership in masculine society.

NOTES

1. For information on the dates of composition of "Prometheus," "Ganymed," and *Faust*, see Trunz's commentary, HA 1:483–85; HA 3:477–78. For the link to "Ganymed," see Trunz's commentary, HA 1:485. For the link to *Faust*, see the letter of 11 May 1820 to Carl Friedrich Zelter: "Ich enthalte mich aller Vergleichung; nur bemerke daß auch ein wichtiger Teil des Faust in diese Zeit fällt" (WA IV, 33:28).

2. As Rudolf Drux writes, "Prometheus" traditionally manifests the Goethean concepts of "Systole," "Konzentration," "Verselbstung," while "Ganymed" is said to promote "Diastole," "Expansion," Entselbstigung" ("Dichter und Titan. Der poetologische Bezug auf den Prometheus. Mythos in der Lyrik von Goethe bis Heine," *Heine-Jahrbuch* 25 [1986]: 24).

3. Erich Heller, "From Love to Love: Goethe's *Pandora* and Wedekind-Alban Berg's *Pandora-Lulu*," *Salamagundi* 84 (Fall 1989): 100; Clemens Lugowski, "Goethe: Ganymed," in *Gedicht und Gedanke: Auslegungen deutscher Gedichte*, ed. Heinz Otto Burger (Halle: Niemeyer, 1942) 115; Rolf Christian Zimmermann, *Das Weltbild des jungen Goethe: Studien zur hermetischen Tradition des deutschen 18. Jahrhunderts*, 2 vols. (Munich: Fink, 1969–1979) 2:158–61.

4. A notion which came to the German tradition via Herder from Shaftesbury. Goethe's knowledge of this tradition is indicated by his essay "Zum Shakespeares-Tag," written in the same years as "Prometheus," in which he compares Shakespeare to Prometheus as a maker of humans: "Er wetteiferte mit dem Prometheus, bildete ihm Zug vor Zug seine Menschen nach. . . ." (HA 12:227). See Drux 11–12 and also John Pizer, "Gadamer's Reading of Goethe," in *Philosophy and Literature* 15 (1991): 268–77.

5. Lugowski 115. See also Zimmermann 2:158–61.

6. Erwin Panofsky, *Studies in Iconography* (New York: Harper & Row, 1962) 212–18; Lorrayne Y. Baird-Lange, "Victim Criminalized: Iconographic Traditions and Peacham's Ganymede," in *Traditions and Innovations: Essays on British Literature of the Middle Ages and the Renaissance*, ed. D.G. Allen and R.A. White (Newark: University of Delaware Press, 1990) 238–40; James Saslow, *Ganymede in the Renaissance: Homosexuality in Art and Society* (New Haven and London: Yale University Press, 1986) 59–62, 187–90.

7. Zimmermann 1:185–219, esp. 205.

8. Karl Otto Conrady, "Ganymed," in *Die deutsche Lyrik. Form und Geschichte: Interpretationen vom Mittelalter zur Frühromantik*, ed. Benno von Wiese (Düsseldorf: August Bagel, 1964) 229.

9. Lugowski 103.

10. Carl Pietzcker, *Trauma, Wunsch und Abwehr: Psychoanalytische Studien zu Goethe, Jean Paul, Brecht, zur Atomliteratur und zur literarischen Form* (Würzburg: Königshaus & Neumann, 1985) 21.

11. In *Laws I*, 636d Plato writes: "And you know it is our universal accusation against the Cretans that they were the inventors of the tale of Ganymede; they were convinced, we say, that their legislation came from Zeus, so they went on to tell this story against him that they might, if you please, plead his example for their indulgence in this pleasure too" (*The Collected Dialogues of Plato*, ed. Edith Hamilton and Huntington Cairns [New York: Pantheon, 1961] 1237). For more examples of the use of the "chartering power" of the Ganymede myth see Leonard Barkan, *Transuming Passion: Ganymede and the Erotics of Humanism* (Stanford: Stanford University Press, 1991) 29.

12. In the Renaissance, Ganymede is a "part of homoerotic lexicography" and a phrase in the "vernacular of homoeroticism." (Gregory W. Bredbeck, "Milton's Ganymede: Negotiations of the Homoerotic Tradition in *Paradise Regained*," *PMLA* 106 (1991): 264, 267).

As for eighteenth-century Germany, a travel guide published anonymously in 1782 refers to the younger denizens of a male homosexual bordello in Berlin as "Ganymedes." (Cited by James Steakley, "Sodomy in Enlightenment Prussia: From Execution to Suicide,"in *The Pursuit of Sodomy: Male Homosexuality in Renaissance and Enlightenment Europe*, ed. Kent Gerard and Gert Hekma [New York: Harrington Park Press, 1989] 170. The travel guide, attributed to Johann Friedel, has been republished as *Briefe über die Galanterien von Berlin, auf einer Reise gesammelt von einem österreichischen Offizier. Neu ans Licht gebracht und mit einem angeblich aufgefundenen Dreyßigsten Briefe versehen*, ed. Sonja Schnitzler [Berlin/DDR: Eulenspiegel, 1987]).

13. Goethe's association of Wieland with pederasty was not entirely unmotivated. In Wieland's *Agathon*, after pirates capture Psyche, their sodomitical captain, thinking she is a boy, indicates his desire to have his way with her by calling her "Ganymedes" (Christoph Martin Wieland, *Werke*, 5 vols., ed. Fritz Martini and Hans Werner Seiffert [Munich: Hanser, 1964] 1:395).

Indeed, according to Gleim, the rumor circulated that Wieland, whose poem "Juno und Ganymed" overflows with passages revealing a knowledge of the actuality of pederastic desire, had introduced German youth to the idea of "Greek love," whereupon that seemingly easily corrupted generation began to keep "Ganymedes" itself: "Sollt ihm [Wieland] wegen seines Jupiter und Ganymedes nicht irgend ein unberufener richter des schönen den vorwurf gemacht haben, gegen den ich meinen Wieland zu Braunschweig einst verteidigte, diesen, dass aus seinem munde die deutsche jugend zuerst von griechischer liebe gehört und bald darauf sich Ganymede gehalten hätte" (Gleim to Wieland, 2 January 1774; cited by Paul Derks, *Die Schande der heiligen Päderastie: Homosexualität und Öffentlichkeit in der deutschen Literatur, 1750–1850* [Berlin: Verlag Rosa Winkel, 1990] 234).

Incidentally, despite this mildly abusive passage, Goethe was not only aware of the homosexuals around him but also in general supportive of them—or at least not as proscriptive as others—as shown by his lifelong regard for Winckelmann, culminating in a warm eulogy which indicated enough about the art historian's sexuality for those who wanted to know (Derks 174–231), and for Johannes Müller von Schaffhausen, the historian entangled in a scandalously public homosexual affair (Derks 295–369).

14. Called a sodomite, Cellini retorts, in Goethe's translation: "O du Thor, sagte ich, du überschreitest das Maß! aber wollte Gott, daß ich mich auf eine so edle Kunst verstünde; denn wir lesen, daß Jupiter sie mit Ganymeden verübte, und hier auf der Erde pflegten die größten Kaiser und Könige derselben; ich aber, als ein niedriges und geringes Menschlein, wüßte mich nicht in einen so wundersamen Gebrauch zu finden" (WA I, 44:196).

15. Faust's upward striving, although generally perceived as aggressive and thus fitting into the Promethean mode, overlaps in many ways with the Ganymedic desire for transcendence, as indicated in the use of "streben" in the ode as well as in the play. This demonstrates how closely entwined the concepts of Ganymedic and Promethean are. For more passages lining up Faust's desires with Ganymede's, see Nicholas Boyle, *Goethe: The Poet and the Age* (Oxford: Clarendon Press, 1991) 1:222–24.

16. The Promethean side of Faust has been apparent to critics from Erich Heller (100) to Jane K. Brown, "Faust," in *European Romanticism: Literary Cross-Currents, Modes and Models*, ed. Gerhart Hoffmeister (Detroit: Wayne State University Press, 1990) 185.

17. Later, in "Trüber Tag," Mephistopheles cleverly twists the question of who seduces and who is seduced, who penetrates and who is penetrated, when he asks: "Drangen wir uns dir auf, oder du dich uns?" (HA 3:138). It was Faust who passively received Mephisto's penetrating visits, implying that Mephisto is the aggressor, but it was also Faust who called for those visits, implying that he arranged his own seduction.

18. This act reveals considerable anxiety about the breakdown of distinctions between the masculine and the feminine, which manifests itself in the Chancellor's rejection of "Zweifel" as a hermaphroditic "Zwitterkind" (4902) and the discussion of gender in the "Mummenschanz," exemplified for instance by the flower girls' essentialist statement on the nature of women:

> Denn das Naturell der Frauen
> Ist so nah mit Kunst verwandt. (5105–6)

The herald, too, is concerned about gender when he tells Boy Charioteer that he looks like a girl: "Man könnte dich ein Mädchen schelten" (5548). Such concern turns out to be justified when Mephistopheles, disguised as "Geiz," changes from female to male (5665). This concern about gender may reflect Faust's development toward the Promethean and Mephisto's development toward the Ganymedic, both of which tendencies become increasingly evident in *Faust II.*

19. Bennett 83ff.

20. Avital Ronell, *Crack Wars: Literature, Addiction, Mania* (Lincoln and London: University of Nebraska Press, 1992) 157.

21. Jürgen Flimm, in his 1983 production of *Faust* in Cologne, seems to have captured the exclusion of the feminine from the male-male relationship between Mephistopheles and Faust. C. Bernd Sucher writes: "Das Gretchen interessiert diesen Kölner Faust weit weniger als der Mephisto" ("Faust, der Prahlheinz–Faust, der Zweifler," *Süddeutsche Zeitung,* 12 October 1992: 14).

22. Somewhat disapprovingly, because he sees the original meaning of the word as "joint," Adelung lists the male member as one of the meanings of "Glied": "Auf eine etwas uneigentlichere Art führet diesen Nahmen das männliche Glied, nach welchem

einige auf eine völlig unschickliche Art auch das weibliche Glied gebildet haben, welches eben so wenig ein Glied genannt werden kann, als solches von der Nase oder andern Theil des Leibes üblich ist" (Johann Christoph Adelung, *Grammatisch-kritisches Wörterbuch der Hochdeutschen Mundart* [Vienna: Pichler, 1807] 2:721).

The Grimms have fewer problems with the meaning of the word as penis, finding a long and complicated historical linguistic tradition: "verhüllend werden die geschlechtstheile durch gl[ied] bezeichnet. . . der gebrauch geht aus, entsprechend lat. membrum virile, von der bezeichnung des penis. . . auf die gesamten männlichen geschlechtstheile ausgedehnt" (*Deutsches Wörterbuch von Jacob und Wilhelm Grimm*, ed. by Ludwig Sütterlin [Leipzig: Hirzel, 1960]).

An observation by Hans Rudolf Vaget is useful here: "Zu der akuten Sprachnot, nicht nur Goethes, bei der poetischen Benennung des männlichen Gliedes, vgl. Goethes Epigram von 1790:

Gib mir statt "Der Schwanz" ein ander Wort, O Priapus,
Denn ich Deutscher ich bin übel als Dichter geplagt
. . .
Der Schwanz ist etwas von hinten,
Und von hinten war mir niemals ein froher Genuß."

(*Goethe–Der Mann von 60 Jahren: Mit einem Anhang über Thomas Mann* [Königstein/Ts.: Athenäum, 1982] 42; see also Dieter Borchmeyer, *Die Weimarer Klassik: Eine Einführung* [Königstein/Ts.: Athenäum, 1980] 138–39).

This little poem (*WA* I, 53:15-16) not only indicates that Goethe thought and wrote about the male anatomy, but also alludes to an awareness of sodomy, which is important for a discussion of the homosexual overtones of the relationship between Faust and Margarete. For more information on Goethe's writings and speculation about male genitalia, see Boyle 1:648.

23. Johann Wolfgang v. Goethe, *Faust I & II*, ed. and trans. Stuart Atkins (Boston: Suhrkamp/Insel Publishers, Inc., 1984).

24. See Michael Neumann, *Das Ewig-Weibliche in Goethes "Faust"* (Heidelberg: Carl Winter Universitätsverlag, 1985) 41: "als 'Glied der Geisterwelt' ist Faust ebenso Individuum wie Teil des Ganzen."

JEFFREY BARNOUW

Faust and the Ethos of Technology

ORIGINALLY THE FAUST STORY WAS A CAUTIONARY tale, an example of the *Magussage*, characterized by Robert Petsch as ending tragically, "indem der Zauberer an seiner eigenen Kunst zugrunde geht."[1] In the wake of the collapse of the German Reich at the end of World War II, a German critic explained the (implicitly associated) disfavor that the Faust figure had fallen into:

> Für die schrankenlose Herrschaft der konventionellen Faustauffassung muß bezahlt werden. Über ein Jahrhundert lang ist Faust mit dem Typ des rücksichtslosen Scientisten, des technischen Großorganisators. . . gleichgesetzt worden. Nicht verwunderlich darum, daß heute die Enttäuschung an diesen Idealen [!] zurückschlägt und vom "Dämon Faust," von "faustischer Blasphemie" usw. die Rede ist, wiederum am wirklichen Inhalt des Gedichtes vorbeiurteilend.[2]

It is customary for Germanists to point out how little connection there is between Goethe's text and "the Faustian" and in particular between Goethe's hero and "Faustian man," even granting the myriad forms the ideology or myth assumes. But given that Goethe was as deeply and lastingly committed to science, in his own understanding of it as a vocation and a social process, as he was to literature, it is a mistake to dissociate his *Faust* too readily from the vicissitudes of Faustian ideology as it relates to the social role and impact of modern science and technology. In this regard it may prove illuminating for us to see to what extent his text engages or bears upon Faustianism.

A German dictionary associates *faustisch* with "Wißbegierde, Wissensdurst, Forschungstrieb, Ahnungsdrang, Streben, strebsam, unersättlich."[3] This knowing and inquiring are not disinterested, purely intellectual; they have an eye to action and particularly the mastery of nature. Oswald Spengler, who gave the greatest currency to the characterization of Western culture as Faustian, saw the technological attitude as central to it. He writes, for example, "Das antike Lebensideal war die Interesselosigkeit (*apatheia*) am Lauf der Welt, gerade an dem, dessen Beherrschung dem faustischen Menschen der ganze Lebensinhalt ist."[4]

For Spengler the will to control nature informs Faustian science: "in dem Bewußtsein, daß keine Macht der Welt diese Berechnung [der Naturgesetze] erschüttern kann, liegt unser Wille zur Herrschaft über die Natur. Das ist faustisch."[5] This relation is expressed, for him, in the relation of the two parts of *Faust*:

> So ruft der Faust des ersten Teils der Tragödie, der leidenschaftliche Forscher in einsamen Mitternächten, folgerichtig den des zweiten Teils und des neuen Jahrhunderts hervor, den Typus einer rein praktischen, weitschauenden, nach außen gerichteten Tätigkeit. Hier hat Goethe psychologisch die ganze Zukunft Westeuropas vorweggenommen. Das ist die Zivilisation an Stelle von Kultur, der äußere Mechanismus statt des innern Organismus, der Intellekt als das seelische Petrefakt an Stelle der erloschenen Seele selbst.[6]

This litany of ideological dualities that have proved so fateful (not to say fatal) in German history is closely tied up with Faust, for Spengler, because he is reversing a positive or even enthusiastic identification of Faust and the cultural mission of modern science that was developed by the preceding generation. The modern age (from the sixteenth century on) was declared to be "Faustian"–and precisely for its "Forschertitanismus"–for the first time in 1882 by Erich Schmidt, following the lead of his teacher at Berlin, Wilhelm Scherer. Schmidt seems to have projected into Faust a sense of the social-political mandate of scientific research (taken in the broad German sense of *Wissenschaft*) that was epitomized at that time by the University of Berlin and perhaps above all by Hermann von Helmholtz. Already in 1862 Helmholtz could write:

> Wissen ist Macht. Keine Zeit kann diesen Grundsatz augenfälliger darlegen als die unsere. Die Naturkräfte der unorganischen Welt lehren wir den Bedürfnissen des menschlichen Lebens und den Zwecken des menschlichen Geistes zu dienen. . . . Daher ist denn auch jede Nation. . . nicht nur an der Ausbildung der Naturwissenschaften und ihrer techni-schen Anwendung interessiert, sondern ebensogut an der Ausbildung der politischen, juristischen und moralischen Wissenschaften [which he collectively calls "Geisteswissenschaften," just as Dilthey will].[7]

Helmholtz more than symbolically linked his own great philosophical as well as scientific achievement in the physiological optics to Goethe's Faust by the insistent use of quotations from *Faust* in his essays, "Die Tatsachen in der Wahrnehmung" (1878) and "Goethes Vorahnungen kommender naturwissen-schaftlicher Ideen" (1892).[8] This reflected a desire (shared with the Berlin Germanists) to enlist not only Goethe but his Faust in the representation of the national cultural and political value of "science."

Already by 1890, however, Julius Langbehn could write in his *Rembrandt als Erzieher*: "Faust, das Ideal der wissenschaftlichen Deutschen, hat seine Zeit gehabt." Spengler simply extended Schmidt's conception to an *Untergang* of Faustian civilization, "an der *logos* der *techne* zugrundegehend."[9]

Not all that different from Spengler, much twentieth-century German philosophy, from the left and the right in striking consonance, has made the criticism and condemnation (not to say demonization) of the "ethos of technology" one of its sustained and sustaining themes. From 1899 on Max Scheler repeatedly analyzed and attacked what he called *Arbeitswissen, Herrschaftswissen* or *Leistungswissen* (as distinguished from *Bildungswissen* and *Erlösungswissen*) in terms akin to those of Martin Heidegger's ruminations on the "essence of technology" and of the Frankfurt School critique of "instrumental reason," with the whole triadic scheme being revived in the set of *a priori Erkenntnisinteressen* laid down by Karl-Otto Apel and Jürgen Habermas. None of these any longer refer to Faust. This theme is increasingly associated in German thought not with Germany but with the United States as the homeland of Pragmatism, yet the Faust of legend and of Goethe is still caught up in the continuing conflict of values concerning the ethos of technology.

Erich Heller has not shied away from such connections. In "Faust's Damnation: The Morality of Knowledge," he writes,

> Dr. Faustus—is he damned or is he saved? Who would not suspect that the question has been emptied of meaning? [...] Where there is now talk of hell-fire, what comes to mind [is the Bomb]—yet, alas, not quite so readily that which has made it possible: the wings of the eagle that Dr. Faustus took upon himself in order to search out the uttermost parts of heaven and earth, and the innermost parts of life and matter, and to bring them within the reach of man's ever-blundering power. . . .[10]

With the eagle wings Heller is referring to the 1587 *Volksbuch*, the earliest known version of Faust, which already tells us that Faust had "fürgenommen, die Elementa zu spekulieren." Faust "wollte alle Grund am Himmel und Erden erforschen." But Heller's concern with the morality of knowledge is directed ultimately at Goethe's text and its striking ambiguity, or even ambivalence, as to the nature and outcome of Faust's culpability. He grants that Goethe grasped the danger inherent in technology, but adds,

> Yet the "modern man" in him would also have known that he could not live by [this] lesson. After all, he greeted with enthusiasm the plans for the Panama Canal and found no more fitting symbol for Faust's renunciation of magic than his assuming the position of a welfare engineer. The ambiguities of his *Faust* provide the measure of his lasting dilemma, a dilemma that is bound to stay with us.[11]

The resolution he would try to draw from *Faust* is ambiguous too, "If, as even Goethe's *Faust* might teach us, grace cannot be merited by man, he may yet try to earn his hope." And the final accent falls on the far less ambiguous "Sorcerer's Apprentice." Is cautionary "wisdom" about technology as "Faustian" part of the conclusion of Goethe's text? of the conclusion it forces on us?

In the typical *Magussage* the use of magic power was a form of hubris—ignoring human limitation—which brought the fall of the magus in its train. The pact with the devil is a second, distinct motif, which reinforces that of magic power. In some versions (followed by Lessing but not Goethe) it is possession of such power that leads to leverage over the devil and thus the power to use him, but always (until Lessing) at the eventual cost of damnation. Here it seems that the pact with the devil only reinforces a trap inherent in the use of magic, or one might say, conversely, that the very power to control forces of nature, as magic claims to, is of the devil and entails damnation and ruin.

There was very likely a humanist version of the Faust story in Latin which preceded the German *Volksbuch* version published in Frankfurt in 1587 and which possibly treated Faust's desire to know as nobly tragic, in that it expressed a high and essential human aspiration, epitomized at that time by Paracelsus. But the German folk version printed by Spies in 1587 told of "the Damnable Life and Deserved Death of Doctor John Faustus" (to quote the English translation that led Christopher Marlowe to write his *Tragicall History of D. Faustus*, probably within a year or two of the appearance of the German *Volksbuch*). In the German *Volksbuch* version there is nothing nobly tragic about Faust's quest or end. Curiosity itself is a sin, and tragedy applies only in the medieval sense of the high and mighty brought low, to cure others of vain aspirations. The analogy to the Titans and even to Lucifer might suggest some surreptitious grandeur, but only by reading against the grain.

> [Faust's] apostasy was nothing more nor less than his pride and arrogance, despair, audacity and insolence, like unto those giants of whom the poets sing. . . that they made war on God, yea, like unto that evil angel who opposed God, and was cast off by God on account of his arrogance and presumption.[12]

Heller points out that the English translation "replaced the original's very condemnatory statement, 'for his frowardness, lawlessness, and wantonness goaded him on,' by. . . 'for his Speculation was so wonderful'; [and] that the remorseful exclamation of the German Faustus, 'had I but had godly thoughts!' was changed in English to the far less contrite 'had not I desired to know so much.' "[13] The transformation which such changes hint at is carried through by Marlowe, who had had his earlier hero Tamburlaine justify political usurpation by the precedent of Jove, with the striking explanation:

> Nature that fram'd us of four elements,
> Warring within our breast for regiment,
> Doth teach us all to have aspiring minds.
> Our souls, whose faculties can comprehend
> The wondrous architecture of the world
> And measure every wand'ring planet's course,
> Still climbing after knowledge infinite,

And always moving as the restless spheres,
Wills us to wear ourselves and never rest
Until we reach the ripest fruit of all,
That perfect bliss and sole felicity,
The sweet fruition of an earthly crown.[14]

For Marlowe the pursuit of "knowledge infinite" is no purely intellectual curiosity, but a search for mastery or control that can plausibly end in and be satisfied
with political sovereignty. The idea that knowledge is power informs the quest
for knowledge, which proves itself in its application. Such ideas were abroad in
the late sixteenth century and the figure of Faust had to absorb them.

Marlowe's Faustus, when first tempted by the use of magic, imagines riches
and pleasures (including hearing "strange philosophy" and knowing the secrets
of kings), but then imagines technological marvels such as surrounding
Germany with a wall of brass, or making the Rhine circle Wittenberg. Even
after he has chased out the Prince of Parma so as to "reign sole king of all our
provinces," he will apply his magic to state-of-the-art weaponry. "Yea, stranger
engines for the brunt of war / Than was the fiery keel at Antwerp's bridge, / I'll
make my servile spirits to invent."[15]

Similarly, after making contact with Mephistophilis, he contemplates being
a great emperor and making a bridge to link Spain and Africa in order to rule
over them. Just as Paolo Rossi has seen links between the operational cast of
alchemy and the operationalist philosophy of experimental science in Francis
Bacon, whose ideas start up in the next decade, for at least some Elizabethans
the wonders of magic already stood for technology.

By the early eighteenth century, however, Germany's leading critic, Gottsched, could see the magic of Faust only as gross superstition of the sort that
was being dispelled forever by enlightenment, and the story of Faust as one that
could now only excite ridicule. It has been plausibly suggested that Gottsched's
condescending pronouncements may have provoked Lessing to take up the
Faust theme and to treat it in a very different way.[16] Lessing's friend, Moses
Mendelssohn, tried in a jocular way to dissuade him from taking the theme
seriously, but in his own jocular vein Lessing undertook to present Faust's
characteristic (and only) fault, "too great desire for knowledge [*Wißbegierde*]" or
passion for truth, not as leading to his downfall, as Lucifer was certain it would,
but as the basis of his redemption. As one report tells us, the play was to end
with an angel telling the devils they have not defeated humanity and science, as
they deludedly believe, "for divinity did not give man the most noble of drives
in order to make him unhappy."[17] But this was managed only by a divine ruse
which never put Faust at risk, and it is likely that Lessing did not finally take
Faust seriously as a vehicle for his favorite idea of the great value of the pursuit
(as opposed to the comfortable possession) of truth.[18]

The identification of the Faust figure with the endless striving characteristic
of modern science as a vocation, and equally with the sense of knowledge as
power (particularly the technological power to control and change nature) was

already established in various places, then, before Goethe took up the material and gave it its most distinctive, yet notoriously ambiguous, stamp. Goethe had certainly been aware of the drawn-out feud between Gottsched and Lessing that had Faust as one of its focal points. Moreover, *Faust I* was hailed by the Schlegels, Schelling and others in Jena, as an original myth epitomizing the modern age, in which Faust was an ideal representation of man,[19] so that the reception of Part I and Goethe's response to it is a factor in the genesis of Part II.[20] In the period when Goethe was struggling to get *Faust II* or at least part of it into print, he was all too aware that Faust was ideologically troublesome, a subject matter saturated with confused and contested values.

Hans Schwerte suggests that enthusiasm for "the Faustian" flourished in cultural and political discourse in ironic conjunction with a tendency in literary criticism to ignore the fault and guilt of the hero, such that his repeated error is transformed into a titanic Promethean achievement.[21] If we, on the contrary, focus on Faust's questionable actions toward Philemon and Baucis, which seem to reflect (if any part of *Faust* does) a technological will such as is associated with "the Faustian," we must ask how these actions are related to his (or the) tragedy.

Goethe's Faust introduces himself, in the *Urfaust* as in *Faust I*, as having moved beyond philosophy, medicine, law and theology, these being rejected as academic disciplines that do not lead to decisive action in the world, that is, to real knowledge. This has brought him close to despair,

> Und sehe, daß wir nichts wissen können!
> Das will mir schier das Herz verbrennen. (364–65)

He has turned to magic as another form of *Geistes Kraft*,

> Daß ich erkenne, was die Welt
> Im Innersten zusammenhält,
> Schau' alle Wirkenskraft und Samen
> Und tu' nicht mehr in Worten kramen. (382–85)

Contrary to normal expectations, magic is for Faust a form of inquiry that will take him out of the musty smoky Gothic study, surrounded by skeletons, beakers and books, and lead him back into living nature. All the Gottsched associations with magic have been displaced onto "scholastic" learning, leaving magic free to become the symbolic anticipation of a new, practically motivated science, directly engaged with nature. He feels the sign of the macrocosm fill his heart with joy "Und mit geheimnisvollem Trieb / Die Kräfte der Natur rings um mich her enthüllen." "Ich schau' in diesen reinen Zügen / Die wirkende Natur vor meiner Seele liegen" (437–41).

What a show! But, alas, only a show, a *Schauspiel*. The sign of the *Erdgeist* promises more, an enhancement of his powers, above all, courage to enter into the world and

Der Erde Weh, der Erde Glück zu tragen,
Mit Stürmen mich herumzuschlagen
Und in des Schiffbruchs Knirschen nicht zu zagen. (465–67)

It is unclear whether this means bearing and sharing the catastrophe of ship-wreck with others or simply experiencing it as the sublime power of nature, but the transition from a quest for knowledge to a hunger for experience is under-way. The Earth Spirit in fact rejects Faust as unequal to his grand pretensions, and he will have to turn to Mephisto, once the opportunity arises. The focus of Faust's character on a desire to know the workings of the natural world from within has been abandoned and will not return throughout Part I. While it may seem to refer back to the impasse of the old academic science, with its "Hebeln und. . . Schrauben" (675), which would be dramatically redundant, Faust's acknowledgement of the inaccessibility of nature actually shows a deflection of his desire, a change in what he would and will ask of the power of the devil.

Geheimnisvoll am lichten Tag
Läßt sich Natur des Schleiers nicht berauben,
Und was sie deinem Geist nicht offenbaren mag,
Das zwingst du ihr nicht ab. (672–75, cf. 1746–51, 1768)

Faust II unfolds within a new set of assumptions. In the second try at an announcement of *Helena* in 1826 Goethe looks back to Part I to build a bridge to the continuation and characterizes Faust as a man who "regards the posses-sion of the highest knowledge. . . as inadequate to satisfy his longing in the very least."[22] Now it seems Faust's frustration was not that true knowledge was not to be had, but that knowledge would not satisfy his *Sehnsucht*. Goethe treats this, I would argue, as a pathological symptom: "a mind which, turning in every direction, always returns to a more unhappy state." He goes on to link it with an implicit diagnosis of the times he lives in: "Such a disposition is so similar to the modern one that a number of clever heads have felt impelled to attempt to solve the problem." Goethe's own solution for a continuation is based on "the obvious thought," overlooked by all the others, "that in composing a second part one must necessarily transcend completely the melancholy sphere" of *Faust I*. This, of course, refers to the move to the classical world. But if in the process any remnant of the frustrated will to know is at first forgotten, perhaps as too *kummervoll* a theme for "worthier circumstances," that modern disposition in which Faust resembles those who thought of continuing his quest literarily is ultimately reflected in the world of *Faust II*.

The issue of Faust's will to master and mold nature emerges for the first time in Goethe's text, without being anticipated by any action preceding it, in the final act of *Faust II*. This is quite surprising in light of the importance of technological ambition among the thematic givens of the traditional Faust material. Part I construed Faust's interest in magic as seeking a knowledge of how nature works, but in an exception to the pervasive emphasis on activity this

is not characterized as being for the sake of application or any power other than
that of knowledge itself. Much of the magic surrounding him is conjuring, show
or illusion, and even though it may evoke the technologies of illusion of Goethe's time like the "Phantasmagoria," it does not "stand for" technology. Homunculus is significantly Wagner's project, not Faust's, and, for all its possibly
prophetic sense of genetic engineering, is presented as a perpetuation of the
pedantry of scholasticism in mechanical experimentation.

The plan to reclaim land from the sea is Faust's own and, more than anything else in *Faust II*, connects his urges or will and fate with the initial conditions of *Faust I*. The plan is first exposed in the first scene of Act IV, where,
having asked Mephistopheles to guess what great thing is attractive to him now,
Faust scorns the idea that it would be the appeal of luxurious living or an urge
to fly up to the moon:

> Mit nichten! dieser Erdenkreis
> Gewährt noch Raum zu großen Taten.
> Erstaunenswürdiges soll geraten,
> Ich fühle Kraft zu kühnem Fleiß. (10181–84)

Rejecting the imputation that his motive is fame, he exclaims,

> Herrschaft gewinn' ich, Eigentum!
> Die Tat ist alles, nichts der Ruhm.
> . . .
> Von allem ist dir nichts gewährt
> Was weißt du, was der Mensch begehrt? (10187–93)

This recalls Faust's words before closing the deal with Mephisto:

> Ward eines Menschen Geist, in seinem hohen Streben,
> Von deinesgleichen je gefaßt? (1676–77)

We seem to be back with the Faust of the original wager, yet now his interest
turns (like that of the traditional Faust) to new marvels of technology. He has
been studying the waves crashing in and rolling out, and has seen, "es ist nichts
geleistet." This vision of "Zwecklose Kraft unbändiger Elemente" threatens to
drive him to despair. It is this purposeless aspect of nature that he now wants
to combat and conquer, by pushing the waters back and reclaiming land, not yet
for any social purpose but simply to affirm his will against nature's lack of
purpose.

At the end of Act IV we learn that the land under the water has been
granted to Faust, and by the beginning of Act V he has completed the reclamation and built his palace. But we learn of this from the "lowly" perspective of the
old couple Philemon and Baucis, who hint that the project is not an unmixed
blessing. Building the dikes and digging the canal cost much human life, and

now the owner of it all wants to add the couple's small plot with its linden trees to his domain. He has offered them a fine estate in the new (drained) land, but they want to hold on to their high ground, their hut and grove. They are mistrustful, above all, because of Faust's high-handed masterful ways.

Faust, now 100 years old, is driven to distraction by their resistance, of which he is continually reminded by the tolling of their little bell. His *Hochbesitz* can give him no satisfaction as long as any part of the land is not his, and so he gives Mephisto the order to get the old couple out of the way. The fury of his will meeting resistance is mingled with the pride he takes (or wants to take) in his technological marvel, and thus the technological drive comes to seem contaminated by his absolutist egotism.

> Die Alten droben sollten weichen,
> Die Linden wünscht' ich mir zum Sitz;
> Die wenig Bäume, nicht mein eigen,
> Verderben mir den Weltbesitz.
> Dort wollt' ich, weit umherzuschauen,
> Von Ast zu Ast Gerüste bauen,
> Dem Blick eröffnen weite Bahn,
> Zu sehn, was alles ich getan,
> Zu überschaun mit einem Blick
> Des Menschengeistes Meisterstück,
> Betätigend mit klugem Sinn
> Der Völker breiten Wohngewinn. (11239-50)

A telling symbol, the linden trees he covets (while their smell tortures him with envy like the tinkling of the bell) will be made to support observation platforms from which his works can be surveyed and appreciated. For the first time we hear of the social aspect; it is a large-scale housing project, a colony, for the people. For Faust this may offer a supplementary justification for what he implicitly concedes is injustice toward Baucis and Philemon.

> Das Widerstehn, der Eigensinn
> Verkümmern herrlichsten Gewinn,
> Daß man, zu tiefer, grimmiger Pein,
> Ermüden muß, gerecht zu sein. (11269-72)

He still speaks as though Mephisto were simply going to transport them to their new home, but his command, "So geht und schafft sie mir zur Seite" (11275), makes him complicit in their destruction. And Mephisto's dry comment, "Auch hier geschieht, was längst geschah" (11286), recalls his observation on Gretchen's ruin, "Sie ist die Erste nicht" ("Trüber Tag. Feld," after 4398).

Even as he sees the old people's hut, linden trees and the rest going up in flames, Faust consoles himself that a watchtower can easily be built, "Um ins Unendliche zu schaun" (11345), and he looks across to the new home where he

imagines the couple settling in "im Gefühl großmütiger Schonung." Such innocence on the part of Faust, as in the tragedy of Gretchen, is itself culpable, an
exacerbation of his guilt. But whatever judgment one reaches on Faust's responsibility, we still need to ask what his fault says about the technological will he
seemed to embody. It is significant that, after he has learned of the death of
Philemon and Baucis and even before Care finds him, his first response is to
abjure magic:

> Noch hab' ich mich ins Freie nicht gekämpft.
> Könnt' ich Magie von meinem Pfad entfernen,
> Die Zaubersprüche ganz und gar verlernen,
> Stünd' ich, Natur, vor dir ein Mann allein,
> Da wär's der Mühe wert, ein Mensch zu sein. (11403–7)

Magic first promised to give him direct access to nature but now is seen as being
in the way, blocking Faust's immediate relation to nature, and by implication
keeping him from being fully and simply human. What is more, magic seemed
to stand symbolically or allegorically for modern technology, yet—as we soon
see—Faust is not swearing off his technological *magnum opus* at all. In a sense,
Goethe is rather simply sloughing off a significant piece of his allegory, saving
technology ("Ist gerettet!") from its now unfavorable association with magic.
The fault of Faust in destroying the world of Philemon and Baucis—which
represents the classical idyll as a cultural-historical phenomenon—is evidently not
the fault of a commitment to a technological mandate.

But what are we to make of Faust's fault itself? Blinded by Care, Faust finds
inner illumination which leads him to reaffirm his commitment to the coloniza-
tion and call upon his workers to bring to fruition what he has envisioned,
without the use of magic, but through labor directed by domination.

> Daß sich das größte Werk vollende,
> Genügt *ein* Geist für tausend Hände. (11509–10)

The grim irony of his mistaking the sound of shovels digging his grave for evidence that his civilizing work is being carried on suggests that the utopian
character of his project, announced only now, is itself largely still a mere intention, now illusory.

Yet Faust's delusion leads him to anticipate the moment when his plan
would be realized, and he might stand with a free people together on free
ground, as he says. In that moment he would utter (and does, in the subjunc-
tive) the words that concede the wager to Mephisto: "Zum Augenblicke dürft'
ich sagen: / Verweile doch, du bist so schön" (11581–82, cf. 1699–1706). In
anticipating it—and/or the fame that must follow from it (11583–84)—he says he
enjoys his greatest moment, and dies. The devil thinks he has won his bet at
last, but Faust's "soul" is spirited off by angels, who later offer a justification for
saving him which echoes the indulgent attitude of the Lord from the Prologue

in Heaven: "Es irrt der Mensch, solang' er strebt" (317). "Ein guter Mensch in seinem dunklen Drange / Ist sich des rechten Weges wohl bewußt" (328–29). As if reciting a divine anti-rule, they say,

> Wer immer strebend sich bemüht,
> Den können wir erlösen. (11936–37)

In a conversation with Eckermann on 6 June 1831 Goethe said, "In these lines is contained the key to Faust's salvation. In Faust himself there is an activity that becomes constantly higher and purer to the end, and from above there is eternal love coming to his aid."[23] Can we take this seriously? How did Goethe take Eckermann? The glimpse of Gretchen as Beatrice may be accepted as intertextual poetic license, but the idea that Faust's supposed striving should be the basis of his redemption makes a mockery of the fate of Philemon and Baucis, since burning their grounds was a direct consequence of Faust's incapacity to accept limits.

It is not clear that Faust himself has striven in the least. When Mephisto responds to his complaining about the old couple, "Mußt du nicht längst kolonisieren?" (11274), we may wonder how far his housing project has been realized. His statement of its utopian character is neither prepared nor supported by the context. It rather seems part of his delusion. By showing us the realization or objective reality of the project only through the perspective of its victims, Goethe may be trying to make Faust's subsequent redemption paradoxical or, as Jane Brown suggests, a deliberate affront to our sense of justice, because justice is in conflict with "the fundamentally rational order of the cosmos."[24]

Even if one were able to attribute such a notion to Goethe, it would be difficult to accept that the creation of the "utopia" entailed and justified the destruction of Philemon and Baucis: "To the extent that Faust's utopia exists in the real world, it is not perfect, it destroys the Arcadia of Baucis and Philemon; for if it is to exist really in the world it is of necessity imperfect and transient, 'tragic.' "[25] The destruction of the old couple (are they older than Faust's 100 years?) and their world cannot be seen as a tragic imperfection of the utopia, but rather as a sign that the utopia is tragically misconceived.

Brown explains "Baucis' naive mistrust of Faust's dikes" and puts it in a larger counter-balancing context:

> It seems profoundly improper to her that Faust should interfere with the natural boundary between land and sea and between human and supernatural spheres; but it is at least as improper to resist the more fundamental law of subjection to the temporal flux. There is no room either in the world or in human memory to preserve the past indefinitely; what resists the law of transformation into something new must pass, however tragic the consequences.[26]

But neither the words of Baucis which are cited here, "Denn es ging das ganze Wesen / Nicht mit rechten Dingen zu" (11113–14), nor any others suggest that she objects to Faust's interfering with the boundary between land and sea. The constant noise, the sacrifice of human blood, and Faust's overbearing manner as a neighbor are mentioned by her (11123–34), but her mistrust of the dikes ("Traue nicht dem Wasserboden, / Halt auf deiner Höhe stand!", 11137–38) seems based, quite reasonably, on mistrust of Faust.

Furthermore, if anyone is guilty (what would this mean?) of resisting the fundamental law of human subjection to the temporal flux, it is Faust. His penultimate words before dying are devoted to his self-assurance that he has left a mark from his earthly days that will last for ages. His refusal to accept limits to his desire, which led to the destruction of the world of Philemon and Baucis, is part of the characteristic "Faustian" denial of human finitude. Goethe may well have meant to show that *this* "striving" has its baleful consequences, its tragic side for others. Brown's caution, "Goethe's devil and his magic so consistently symbolize man's own creative power that we must hesitate to place the emphasis on any moral failure of Faust's,"[27] should rather attune us to the danger of any creative power that is taken to be beyond responsibility. In his expansive "striving" Faust embodies an indifference to our vulnerability and fallibility that is too often attributed misguidedly to a "Faustian" ethos of technology.

NOTES

1. Robert Petsch, "Magussage und Faustdichtung," in Petsch, *Faustsage und Faustdichtung* (Dortmund: Ruhfus, 1966) 6.

2. E.W. Eschmann, "Fausts Utopie," in: *Hamburger Akademische Rundschau* 3 (1948/49): 608ff., quoted in Schwerte 280, n. 9.

3. Anton Schlesinger, *Deutscher Wortschatz*, rev. ed. Hugo Wehrle (Stuttgart, [7]1940) 111, quoted in Schwerte 283, n. 42.

4. Oswald Spengler, *Der Untergang des Abendlandes* (Munich: Beck, 1923) 1:438. Cf. the contrast between Greek and Faustian modes of *Erfahrung*, i.e. *Beschaulichkeit* vs. experiment, 1:509–10.

5. Ibid. 1:507.

6. Ibid. 1:454–55. Cf. 1:550. Faust dies in *Faust II* because he has reached the end, a *Götterdämmerung* that epitomizes entropy.

7. "Über das Verhältnis der Naturwissenschaften zur Gesamtheit der Wissenschaften," in Hermann von Helmholtz, *Philosophische Vorträge und Aufsätze*, ed. Herbert Hörz and Siegfried Wollgast (Berlin: Akademie-Verlag, 1971) 79–108, 102–8. Wilhelm Dilthey strikes the same note throughout the first book of his *Einleitung in die Geisteswissenschaften* (1883, published in *Gesammelte Schriften*, I), and later connects this *Forschergeist* with the work not only of Helmholtz but of Scherer too (*Gesammelte Schriften* XI, 263 and 237–40).

8. *Philosophische Vorträge und Aufsätze* 247–82, 276–82, and 337–64, 358–63. Repeated contact with Goethe's ideas concerning the *Farbenlehre*, particularly the motives for his opposition to Newton, eventually led to a most significant development in Helmholtz's own sign-theory of perception and knowledge, on which see Jeffrey Barnouw, "Goethe and Helmholtz: Science and Sensation," in *Goethe and the Sciences: A Reappraisal*, ed. Frederick Amrine, Francis J. Zucker, and Harvey Wheeler (Dordrecht: Reidel, 1987) (*Boston Studies in the Philosophy of Science*, 97) 45–82.

9. Schwerte 176–78 and 329 n. 122. The last German phrase is my own, varying Petsch's at note 1. It should be noted that science is still a positive if subordinate factor in the Nazi appropriation of Faust prepared by Moeller van den Bruck, and that its worst aspect, the conviction that whoever is "auf ein tätiges Leben [verpflichtet], dem kann die Schuld nichts mehr anhaben," is anticipated from the beginning of the "Reichs-Optimist" appropriation, in Gustav von Loeper's 1871 edition and commentary which reverses Jean Paul's suggestion, "die Tragödie sei *gegen* die Titanfrechheit geschrieben," to claim the tragedy "schildere die *Berechtigung* titanischen Strebens." Loeper claimed that the Faustian idea demanded an "Erstürmen der Erde" for the sake of the *Gattung*, specified as *germanisch* and *arisch*. Schwerte 184–85, 155, 157.

10. Erich Heller, "Faust's Damnation: The Morality of Knowledge," in Heller, *The Artist's Journey into the Interior and Other Essays* (New York: Vintage, 1968) 16–17.

11. Ibid. 43.

12. Ibid. 4.

13. Ibid. 7.

14. *Tamburlaine the Great* II, vii, ll. 18–29, in *Elizabethan Plays*, ed. Hazelton Spencer (Boston: Heath, 1933) 17.

15. *The Tragicall History of D. Faustus*, I, i, ll. 94–96, in *Elizabethan Plays* 43.

16. Schwerte 30–31.

17. Lessing, *Werke* (Munich: Hanser, 1970–1979) 2:780.

18. The famous *Duplik*, in which pursuing the truth is preferred over possessing it, in *Werke* 8:32–33, referred essentially to religious truth, but Nietzsche's extension of it in *The Birth of Tragedy*, section 15 (*Werke*, ed. Karl Schlechta [Munich: Hanser, 1954] 1:84) to a paradoxical commitment to science as a social enterprise transcending its individual subjects is not without support in Lessing's other writings. Heller (note 8) 25 cites Lessing's comment on Maler Müller's Faust, "Anyone who today should attempt to represent such a subject in order to awaken serious belief in it. . . would be courting failure."

19. Friedrich Schlegel, *Philosophie der Kunst* (Darmstadt: Wissenschaftliche Buchgesell-schaft, 1966) 90, "so ist dieses Gedicht nichts anderes als die innerste, reinste Essenz unseres Zeitalters: Stoff und Form geschaffen aus dem, was die ganze Zeit in sich schloß, und selbst dem, womit sie schwanger war oder noch ist. Daher ist es ein wahr-haft mythologisches Gedicht. . . ."

20. Heinrich Luden told Goethe how confused he had been in 1799 at the "förmliche Diskussionen und Disputationen über den Faust" that Göttingen students had with others presenting the "Jenaische Weisheit," Schwerte 289–90.

21. Schwerte 11, 154–56.

22. Goethe, *Faust*, tr. Walter Arndt, ed. Cyrus Hamlin (New York: W.W. Norton, 1976) 399.

23. Ibid. 428.

24. Brown 253. "To complete the order of Faust's engineering projects—to complete God's order of the perfection of human striving—it is 'preferable' to murder the old couple." But this order is also a cultural and literary need. The death of Philemon and Baucis is unjust, Faust being "excused from the consequences of his part in their murder is also unjust. But it is equally without doubt that their deaths are demanded by the cosmic order portrayed in the play, whose historical aspect requires that Faust put antiquity behind him" (252).

25. Ibid. 239.

26. Ibid. 235.

27. Ibid. 233.

HANS RUDOLF VAGET

Goethe's *Faust* Today: A "Post-Wall" Reading

ACT IV OF GOETHE'S *Faust* CONSISTS OF only three scenes precariously poised between the conclusion of Faust's classical-romantic dream journey and the beginning of his rule over the land by the sea. These scenes–"Hochgebirg," "Auf dem Vorgebirg," "Des Gegenkaisers Zelt"–have proven remarkably resistant to the exegetical labors of generations of *Faust* scholars. Wilhelm Emrich characterized Act IV as "das große Schmerzenskind"[1] of *Faust* scholarship–an apt description, as even a cursory look at the relevant literature will confirm.[2] Jane Brown was hardly exaggerating when she observed in 1986 that Act IV has "traditionally been considered the least accessible part of a generally inaccessible work."[3]

A considerable part of the interpretive difficulty vis à vis Act IV has been self-induced, arising from the persistent and apparently irresistible temptation on the part of progressive-minded interpreters in the East and West to enlist Goethe in the service of a truly epochal project, whose purport has been, ultimately, to legitimize socialist utopian thought. Indeed, this was widely held to be the politically "correct" task of the historical moment. Now that that moment has passed and socialism has begun rapidly to disappear from the historical agenda, it may be the appropriate time to revisit Act IV and take a fresh look at its peculiar political implications for *Faust* as a whole.

Let us no longer concern ourselves here with Emil Staiger's famous dismissal of Act IV as poetically inferior.[4] Lamentably, many commentators have taken Staiger's verdict as a welcome license to dodge the overtly political and ideologically messy issues posed by Faust's participation in the war and his support of the emperor. Let us rather consider those commentators who have seriously reflected on Act IV precisely because it appears inaccessible: generally speaking, they have adopted two sharply differing interpretive strategies–strategies which, according to Karl Robert Mandelkow, have dominated the entire history of *Faust* exegesis since the time of Goethe's death.[5] One of these strategies is linked to the concept of nature; the other to the concept of history. It should be borne in mind, though, that for Goethe these were realms of a fundamentally different

order. The realm of nature was governed by certain evolutionary laws compre-
hensible to man. History, on the other hand, was governed by no such laws and
remained, in the last analysis, incomprehensible—a realm of "Tumult, Gewalt
und Unsinn" (10127) subject to demonic interventions. It should be obvious that
our readings of *Faust* will differ greatly depending on whether we lean upon
Goethe's concept of nature, or upon his concept of history. It seems to me that
the special challenge of Act IV lies in its remarkable, if reluctant openness to the
forces of history—incomprehensible and absurd though these forces may at first
have appeared to Goethe.

Adherents of the "nature camp," so to speak, employ Goethe's philosophy
of nature—with its key notions of "Entelechie," "Urphänomen," "Metamorphose," and "Polarität und Steigerung"—to construct a coherent, perhaps all-too
coherent, reading of *Faust*. The intention is almost always to demonstrate the
hidden unity of the text and to affirm the essential identity of Goethe's poetic
and scientific imagination.[6] This particular direction of *Faust* exegesis was greatly
strengthened by Wilhelm Emrich's book, *Die Symbolik von Faust II.* Emrich
postulated for Goethe's *Faust* in general an "Umschlag"—that is to say a translation—of historical phenomena into phenomena of nature.[7] Such a reduction of
"Realgeschichte" to "Urgeschichte"—the most seductive and persistent siren call
in Goethe scholarship—is still being practiced in many quarters. More than any
other trend in the literature on Goethe it has contributed to the mummification
of *Faust II.* As Mandelkow has reminded us, this type of interpretive practice
disengages Goethe's unusually charged text—charged with the energies of a
troubled but acute historical sensibility—from its immediate historical nexus.[8]

The other strategy has been to read *Faust* as a poetically encoded commentary, broadly speaking, on the history of the modern age. Two characteristic
recent titles in this regard would be Heinz Schlaffer's much discussed Benjaminian reading of the second part of *Faust* as an allegory of the nineteenth century,
and Marshall Berman's essay on Faust and modernity.[9] The great temptation
here is to make exaggerated claims for the prophetic and anticipatory powers
of Goethe's poem, without first embedding it as firmly as possible in the historical moment of its creation. Even more common has been the tendency to make
Goethe's text conform to certain preconceived notions about the course of
history and the causes of historical change.

No school has been more thoroughly committed to the task of historical
interpretation than the Marxists; and no one has had a higher stake in an ideologically coherent reading of *Faust* than *Faust* scholars of the former GDR. The
importance of articulating a politically "correct" interpretation of Goethe's text,
specifically of Faust's final statement, becomes immediately apparent if we recall
that the GDR defined its national identity with distinct reference to the progressive cultural heritage of German history; it prided itself on being not only the
guardian but also the executor ("Vollstrecker") of that heritage. In Deborah
Vietor-Engländer's recent comprehensive study of the GDR reception of *Faust*,
we have a most instructive analysis of that whole campaign for a progressive
political appropriation of the flagship of German literature,[10] a campaign initiat-

ed by the highest authorities of the state and the party. Alexander Abusch actually decreed in December, 1961 that the vision of the dying Faust anticipates the GDR's historical role of trying to drain the foul swamp of capitalism in Germany and to create the new land of the socialist state.[11] Walter Ulbricht went even further and declared in March of 1962 that Faust's vision of a free people on liberated land was being realized by the people of the GDR; that the third part of Goethe's *Faust* was being written by the German Socialist state; and that the completion of "Part Three" would be achieved through the unification of all Germans in a socialist state.[12]

Given such a broad historical agenda, it is understandable that the "correct" interpretation of *Faust* became a task of paramount importance–the secular equivalent of reading holy scripture in an ecclesiastical state. This required a more or less official reading–an orthodoxy; and it became the special assignment of a truly socialist *Faust* scholarship to produce it and to elaborate upon it. This task was begun by Gerhard Scholz in his popular and influential *Faust-Gespräche*,[13] intended primarily for the communist youth organisation (FDJ); it was continued in a series of GDR publications that never really swerved from the orthodoxy and that bore, more or less visibly, the official seal of approval.[14]

The linchpin of that orthodoxy–and this will take us back to Act IV–is the assertion that feudalism is overcome and destroyed by Faust. Other, more deviant voices in the Marxist camp were ignored or suppressed. Walter Benjamin's decidedly skeptical reading of *Faust*, for instance, was never quoted or discussed.[15] According to the official script, feudalism had to be overcome and succeeded by Faust's superior, forward-looking means of production as articulated in Act V. Without this crucial step, the fundamental assumption of all Marxist *Faust* interpretations would be untenable–the assumption of a historically inevitable progression from feudalism to capitalism and beyond to a vision of socialism. The outlines of such a view of Goethe's *Faust* were first sketched by Georg Lukács.[16] His progressive, and indeed "perfectionist" interpretation would have been unthinkable, however, without a long prior tradition of political appropriations of Goethe's *Faust*. As we know from Hans Schwerte[17] and Mandelkow,[18] there is indeed a long German tradition of reading ideas of progress and perfectibility into *Faust*, and of thereby adjusting Goethe's text, again and again, to the political agenda of the state–be it the Second or the Third Reich, or the "first socialist state on German soil."

The sudden disappearance from the historical scene of the state that claimed to be the heir and executor of Faust's utopian vision naturally casts a ghostly pall on the whole GDR project on behalf of Goethe's *Faust*. It is now, one would think, a closed chapter not only of German history but also of *Faust* exegesis. The once very vocal proponents of the Marxist reading of *Faust* in East and West are now faced with the sobering realization that they made an intellectual investment in a currency that was first depreciated and then withdrawn from circulation by the very power that was supposed to guarantee its value–history itself.

In what sense, then, can we speak of Act IV as the linchpin of the Marxist *Faust* orthodoxy? In essentially three regards, it seems to me. 1. Act IV, from the point of view of structure, provides the motivation for Faust's whole enterprise in Act V; it thereby reveals the moral and political underpinnings on which his rule is based. 2. Act IV—with its sequence of three scenes unfolding against the background of yet another crisis of the empire—decides the fate of feudalism. 3. Act IV, in a certain sense, represents Goethe's last word on *Faust.* It was written between January and July of 1831, that is to say, after Act V, with the exception of the Philemon and Baucis scenes, had been completed. Faust's death and salvation had long ago been settled. As soon as the final scenes were written, however, Goethe felt prompted to reconsider the question of how Faust acquired the land over which he rules. He decided to depart from his earlier plans for Act IV and to invent a set of three new scenes—"neue Erfindungen," as he confided to Eckermann.[19] His sketches of 1816 called for Faust to acquire his land through a war of conquest fought in medieval Greece against the "Mönche," i.e. a religious authority.[20] In 1831, Goethe decided to have Faust get involved in a civil war in the German empire and help the emperor win it.

What we need to understand, then, is this: what might have motivated Goethe, at the last moment, so to speak, to change his mind about such a crucial point as Faust's acquisition of land and power? There is evidence—compelling evidence, in my view—to suggest that this final revision of the Faust material was triggered by the July Revolution of 1830. It led Goethe once more to contemplate the issues of revolution and restoration; it further led him critically to reconsider the doctrine and religion of Henri Saint-Simon (1760–1825) with its revolutionary program of social engineering, and to rethink the issue of land ownership, which he was reading about just then, in Niebuhr's *Römische Geschichte.*

If Act IV has remained a problem child for *Faust* scholarship, therefore, this may be attributed in no small measure to the fact that matters relating to its genesis and ideological climate have been largely ignored. This appears odd when one considers that the relevance of the July Revolution and of Saint-Simonianism was ably demonstrated as long as 60 years ago by the German-American scholar Gottlieb Schuchard.[21] But Schuchard has been virtually ignored until recently, primarily, one suspects, because his findings did not square with the dominant currents of *Faust* interpretation. When in the early 1980s Nicholas Boyle and I, independently of each other, argued for a reconsideration of Schuchard's findings and questioned anew the Marxist orthodoxy on *Faust,*[22] the reaction ranged, predictably, from condescending rejection to benign neglect.[23]

It is now high time to attempt to bring our reading of Act IV into line with what we know about its genesis. As soon as we do that, a different set of questions needs to be raised—different from the favorite preoccupation of so many *Faust* scholars with their clouds, volcanos, and waves. These questions must focus on plot and motivation as the basis for all moral and political considerations. Questions that need to be asked: Why at this late stage would Goethe want to change his plans and again address the issues of revolution and civil war? What motivation does Goethe provide for Faust's participation in the war? Are there any compelling reasons for Faust to support the emperor, rather than his rival, the "Gegenkaiser?" What are the consequences of Faust's political involvement? And what light does Act IV throw on the question of Faust's salvation?

There is no denying that the introduction of war and revolution into this part of *Faust* is surprising. So, too, is the laconic, almost offhand manner in which this whole episode is executed, to say nothing of its grim, satirical mood and its overtly operatic design. Many commentators have thus felt entitled to treat Act IV in a cursory manner and to move from the opening monologue directly to Act V. But the fact of the matter is that Act IV provides badly needed evidence regarding Faust's road to power—evidence crucial to the understanding of the whole text, despite the highly laconic manner of the octogenarian poet at this stage of the work.

When news of yet another revolution in Paris reached Weimar in the summer of 1830, Goethe was haunted by the thought that the French Revolution, *the* political trauma of his life, was rearing its head again. He viewed the events of July, 1830 as the greatest intellectual challenge—"die größte Denkübung"—that he would have to encounter at the end of his life.[24] As we have seen, Goethe's plans for the remaining scenes of *Faust* did until then not call for revolution and civil war. We are therefore on safe ground in concluding that he was moved to address these matters as a result of the "größte Denkübung" concerning the events in Paris. That Goethe used such an expression—"größte Denkübung"—can only be because he related the events in Paris to his "Hauptgeschäft"—*Faust.*

The manner in which Goethe finally confronted the issue of revolution reflects two crucial decisions made at the conceptual stage. Thus, in the introductory exchanges of "Hochgebirg" it is Mephistopheles who argues for the volcanic theory of the earth's origin. Given the well-known associations in Goethe's mind of "Vulkanismus" with revolution and, conversely, of "Neptunismus" with "Darwinian" theory of evolution, we can see that the political dice were loaded from the outset. In another strategic move, Faust was returned to German soil, there to be confronted again with an empire in turmoil and on the brink of chaos. We are led to realize that Faust's and Mephistopheles' fraudulent rescue action in Act I merely postponed the present crisis. Having returned Faust to the political arena, Goethe makes him face the consequences of his actions in Act I. In similar fashion, Goethe has the consequences of Faust's actions in Act IV become apparent only in Act V. There is a very high probability that Goethe was prompted to draw Faust's political profile more distinctly as a result of his reflection on the events of July 1830.

The chief function of the scene "Hochgebirg," then, is to reveal the motivation for Faust's participation in the war. From much of the older literature, however, one would not be able to draw this conclusion. Indeed, it would be difficult to gather that Faust is engaged in any political action at all. Emrich, for instance, does not seem to believe that Faust should be considered an actor on the political stage. Like Kurt May, Emrich views Faust merely as a bored and passive spectator of the war; he considers the whole war action nothing but "Spuk und Magie"; it is said to have its purpose in itself ("Selbstzweck") and no political consequences or moral implications.[25]

The underlying pattern of the scene is familiar from Part I: Mephistopheles tempts Faust; Faust rejects what is offered and demands something else instead. For the reader, everything depends on the realization that Faust's rejection of a life of leisure and his desire for land and power are perfectly consistent and all of a piece. At this crucial stage, Faust's inner motivation is laid out with great economy and precision. He has no intention of governing the multitudes of a modern metropolis, for fear of having to deal with insurrection—"Und man erzieht sich nur Rebellen" (10159). Nor is he attracted to the pleasure-seeking life-style of the aristocracy; this option he rejects as "Schlecht und modern! Sardanapal!" (10176). The latter lacks the dimension of activity, the former that of complete, unchallenged domination.

Precisely these two conditions—meaningful activity and the exercise of power—are combined in what Faust now reveals to be his new goal. He has conceived the idea of claiming land from the sea and of controlling "zwecklose Kraft unbändiger Elemente" (10219). He desires nothing less than the domination of the sea and of nature. This project—in a certain sense representative of the ambition of Western man since the Renaissance—will offer him both creative activity and the delicious enjoyment of the exercise of power:

> Erlange dir das köstliche Genießen,
> Das herrische Meer vom Ufer auszuschließen. (10228)

Faust's high-minded desire to claim land from the sea has often been attributed to his encounter, in the previous act, with classical antiquity.[26] However, no such recourse to a mythical source of inspiration is needed here, for the desire to dominate is deeply rooted in Faust's nature and represents the ultimate, most radical articulation of his ceaseless striving. Goethe makes the point by placing Faust's culminating project in a highly political context, and by revealing, step by step, the motivation of his desire for power. It can be grasped in Faust's statement to Mephistopheles:

> Herrschaft gewinn' ich, Eigentum!
> Die Tat ist alles, nichts der Ruhm. (10187)

By "Eigentum"—this is crucial for the understanding of Acts IV and V in their entirety—Faust means "Landeigentum," landed property, specifically that stretch of land by the sea that had caught his attention on his return to Germany. He needs that land for carrying out his project; in addition, by owning it he acquires feudal rights and power over the people living there. The desire for power thus stands revealed as Faust's deepest motivation. Landed property will give him the opportunity to control the vast, aimless forces of the sea and to claim additional territory over which he intends to rule with no resistance from any "Rebellen." All this is designed to maximize his enjoyment of power. Whether the people living on Faust's land derive any benefit from this seems to be of secondary importance. So many optimistic voices to the contrary notwithstanding, there is really no evidence that Faust's motivation is in any way generous, idealistic, or specifically "philanthropic."[27]

And yet, at this juncture, there appears to be a certain contradiction in Faust's position, for his land reclamation project can be viewed as an audacious step; it points to the future and promises to improve the lives of the people. But this project cannot be realized without the acquisition of land. Eventually, Faust will obtain the land he desires, as Mephistopheles suggested, by rendering military service to the emperor and receiving from him a fief as a reward. In other words, Faust chooses the classical feudal road to power, a road that leads not to the future but to the past. If so, the argument advanced by Metscher, among others, that Faust's statement concerning "Herrschaft, Eigentum, Tat" signals the advent of "the new world of capitalist civilization—progress through the action of the individual self, the continuously revolutionary process of bourgeois development,"[28] is hardly tenable.

In light of Faust's previous activities at the imperial court, it may seem self-evident and perfectly logical to some that he would choose to ally himself again with the emperor. But is that decision—the most momentous political decision of his career—really self-evident? Goethe did see fit, though this is often overlooked, to present Faust with an alternative; he introduced a rival emperor and thereby indicated an alternative road to power. In Elizabethan drama, this is a familiar device. In *Doctor Faustus*, for instance, Marlowe introduces Bruno, a rival pope; Faustus sides with Bruno and thereby gains the favor of the emperor. And in *Richard II*, Shakespeare replaces the legitimate, but unfit king by Bolingbroke, the usurper, who, as Henry IV, will turn out to be an efficient and worthy ruler.[29] It seems to me that Faust scholarship has not wondered enough about Faust's political choice vis à vis the "Kaiser" and "Gegenkaiser." Why, precisely, does Faust side with the emperor and become the champion of restoration?

Faust clearly realizes that the emperor is chiefly responsible for the present political anarchy and unfit to rule. The only reason given for his alliance is a personal one, and it sounds strangely insufficient: Faust feels sympathy for the emperor in his present predicament—"Er jammert mich; er war so gut und offen" (10291). We already know, however, that Faust has a more compelling reason for acting the way he does: his power-driven desire to obtain land. Under normal circumstances, we would not question Faust's decision. He renders the emperor a vital service by bailing him out militarily in the expectation of a reward in the form of territory. Under the feudal system, this was the sole legitimate way to acquire land. But these are not normal circumstances. The empire's very existence is threatened by insurrection. A rival emperor has been elected; the two parties are preparing for war. Faust could just as well support the "Gegenkaiser," who, beholden to him for victory, would probably not hesitate to offer him an appropriate reward. From a purely practical point of view Faust could obtain his land from either the emperor or his rival. In fact, given the future-oriented, innovative aspects of his grand project, it would even make better sense to ally himself with the usurper, who at least promises reform.

Naturally, we would like to know more about the "Gegenkaiser" and his intentions. We do know that he is the chosen leader of a broadly based aristocratic opposition acting with the consent and blessing of certain clerics. No doubt is left as to the causes for their rebellion; the general state of anarchy has become intolerable:

> Doch war's zuletzt den Besten allzutoll.
> Die Tüchtigen, sie standen auf mit Kraft
> Und sagten: Herr ist, der uns Ruhe schafft.
> Der Kaiser kann's nicht, will's nicht—laßt uns wählen,
> Den neuen Kaiser neu das Reich beseelen,
> Indem er jeden sicher stellt,
> In einer frisch geschaffnen Welt
> Fried' und Gerechtigkeit vermählen. (10277–84)

Clerics, we hear, "waren mehr als andere beteiligt" (10287). Does this fact discredit the "Gegenkaiser's" cause, as orthodox Marxists would have us believe?[30] I think not, given the constitutional role played by the Church in the Holy Roman Empire regardless of the person of the emperor. Furthermore, the emperor's chancellor is also a cleric, an archbishop. After the restoration of the old empire he wields in effect even more power than the emperor, as was the case during most of the history of the Holy Roman Empire. There would seem to be no point, therefore, in arguing that the "Gegenkaiser" would bring about an even more church-dominated, i.e. reactionary, regime. Nor will it do to discredit the "Gegenkaiser's" cause by arguing that we cannot believe that he really stands for peace, order, and justice because we hear about it only from Mephistopheles.[31] This strikes me as a desperate and all too convenient argument. If we decided to discount everything Mephistopheles says, there would be no *Faust* at all.

Marxist commentators uniformly have discredited the rival emperor and his cause. They have been bound to do so by the premises of their historical master narrative; if they were to take the rival emperor for what he appears to be, they would be hard pressed to make sense of Faust's alliance with the emperor. Our positive assessment of the "Gegenkaiser's" position is further supported by one of Goethe's sketches for Act IV. Here the political conflict is defined as one between a foolish emperor ("thöriger Kaiser") and a wise prince ("Weiser Fürst").[32] I can find no compelling evidence in the final text of a change in this basic design. Let us further recall in this context that *Faust* commentators have again and again associated the "Gegenkaiser" with Napoleon. Goethe's unpatriotic admiration for the upstart emperor of the French is well known. Napoleon may indeed be viewed as the great contemporary rival to the legitimate emperor of the old Holy Roman Empire.[33]

An argument could be made that Faust sides with the emperor for reasons of legitimacy. Nominally, of course, legitimacy rests with the emperor. In reality, however, this emperor has undermined and squandered his own legitimacy by failing to maintain order and guarantee justice. The centrality of this point is stressed in Act I by none other than the chancellor:

> Die höchste Tugend, wie ein Heiligenschein,
> Umgibt des Kaisers Haupt; nur er allein
> Vermag sie gültig auszuüben:
> Gerechtigkeit!–Was alle Menschen lieben,
> Was alle fordern, wünschen, schwer entbehren,
> Es liegt an ihm, dem Volk es zu gewähren. (4772–77)

The emperor's failure in this crucial regard lends an aura of legitimacy to his rival. Under this emperor, the empire has sunk into a pre-revolutionary situation. As always with Goethe, the responsibility for anarchy and revolution is traced back to the rulers and laid squarely at their feet. As for Faust, if legitimacy were indeed a serious concern, he would presumably hesitate to ally himself with the emperor. But given his comportment in Act V, it can hardly be argued that he considers justice the "höchste Tugend." As soon as he himself exerts power, he, too, quickly tires of trying to be just (11272). In his disregard for justice, Faust proves to be of the same ilk as his playboy emperor.

It appears that the political configuration of Act IV is deliberately designed to contradict Faust's overtly non-political motivation and to plant questions in the reader's mind about the political and moral basis of his drive for power. Clearly, legitimacy and justice play no role here. If Goethe had wanted to display a Faust according to the GDR orthodoxy–a forward-looking man acting to overcome the injustices of feudalism–he would more likely have placed him on the side of the rival emperor. But Goethe seems to have had no interest in portraying Faust as the agent of progress and the grave-digger of the feudal system. The contrary is more likely the case: Faust enters into a pact with the emperor; he and Mephistopheles offer military aid that turns out to be the decisive factor in winning the day for the emperor and restoring the old, "legitimate" order. Goethe, it would appear, consciously departs from the Elizabethan model, and assigns Faust a place at the side of the old, legitimate, yet unworthy ruler. There is no indication that Faust acts reluctantly–as someone who sides with the emperor only for lack of a better, more progressive alternative, for example, as some Marxist-oriented commentators like to suggest.[34] Quite to the contrary, from his own point of view Faust's alliance with the emperor makes perfectly good sense. He desires to rule and to exercise power, and thus orients his political will accordingly to the emperor. And for good reason. There is a greater likelihood that Faust will be able to realize his will to power under a fully restored feudal system than under a reform-minded rival emperor. Faust will be able to carry out his plans for civil and social engineering more freely under the emperor rather than under the rival emperor. His actions in Act V clearly bear out this assumption.

Act IV comes to a surprising conclusion. We are led to expect the ceremony of Faust's "Belehnung," his investiture with his new fief. As reward for his service to the emperor, Faust would have had to be installed as the new lord over that coastal stretch of land that he requested. Goethe's notes call for such a scene.[35] He omitted it, however, and wrote instead a rather sarcastic scene, "Des Gegenkaisers Zelt," in which the emperor, in a satirical reenactment of the 1356 re-constitution of the German Empire, is forced to cede much of his power to the territorial princes. For the emperor, this turns out to be a Pyrrhic victory.

Do the omission of Faust's investiture and the curtailment of the emperor's powers signal the end of the feudal system? Can we therefore conclude with Marxist orthodoxy that the feudal system, at some unknown point between Act IV and Act V, was simply liquidated?[36] As we have seen, Faust needs this particular political system to acquire land and power for himself. By no stretch of the imagination, therefore, can he be dressed up as the enemy of feudalism. Even though we do not witness the award of his fief, we hear of it on several occasions as a legal fact. It has been announced to the population by an official imperial herald. Nor is there any indication in Act IV that the feudal system is no longer functioning. The emperor, ironically, may have suffered a loss of authority, but the feudal system endures, neither abolished nor weakened. What Act IV appears to evoke, then, is the transition, within feudalism, from an unchallenged central authority to a system of absolutism granting absolute power to the territorial princes, who recognize the emperor only nominally as their sovereign. Faust must be viewed as such a territorial ruler in the absolutist mold. As such, as Walter Benjamin has observed, Faust may fairly be judged as a regressive figure, historically and politically speaking. Benjamin, to be sure, spoke of a "utopian regression,"[37] but the utopian element is virtually crushed under the weight of the politically regressive practices in Faust's final stage. In the last analysis, as Benjamin recognized and the GDR Marxists did not, Goethe's *Faust* arrives at the restoration of feudalism—hardly a forward-looking perspective in 1830!

Thus the Faust of Act V—far from occupying a post-feudal space—appears to be operating in an advanced stage of absolutism—a system that he himself helped bring about. The way in which he takes possession of his land in order to subject it to his will bears all the marks of a man who experiences heavenly bliss—"Seligkeit" (10253)—when he commands and gives orders. Forced labor within the realm, and the inseparable triad of trade, war, and piracy (11187) in external relations, make this an evil empire by any civilized standards. What we are made to witness here is the inevitable outgrowth of a drive for power that appertains to Faust's striving from the beginning and that unmasks its pernicious propensity toward unchecked excess only now, in the last stage of Faust's career.

It is the function of the Philemon and Baucis episode—one of the very last additions to Goethe's 60-year-old Faust material—to demonstrate this point.

Faust has the old couple evicted from their inherited and tenaciously preserved land not for any justifiable reason, such as the common good, but simply because he cannot bear the thought of not owning and controlling everything. Without that plot of land, Faust finds himself unable to enjoy what he already possesses. And so he covets the old couple's small plot, deceiving himself into believing that this tiny addition to his property will be the last—the dot on the final "i." To a spirit like Faust's, however, there is always another undotted "i." He will discover new challenges and new frontiers until his dying moment. And indeed, in his last speech he envisages new ways to own and control more land. By that time, his crazed striving has gone completely out of control. Only a self-deluded *Faust* scholarship intoxicated by the heady dogma of the perfectibility and progress of the Faustian spirit could find anything admirable or elevating in Faust's dying vision.

To an unbiased mind, there is no way to morally justify the expropriation of their property and the death of Philemon and Baucis. On close inspection, however, such a justification of the unjustifiable turns out to be the *ultima ratio* of Gerhard Scholz's reading of Goethe's *Faust*. Scholz regards the enforced expropriation of the old couple as a sacrifice necessary for the good of the collective.[38] At this point, GDR orthodoxy fully reveals its moral insensitivity and political opportunism. Goethe's *Faust*, by means of some bizarre interpretive moves, is used to justify and make palatable the socialist policy of expropriation and collectivization.

Obviously, the striking prominence given to the question of landed property in the concluding parts of *Faust* cannot be tied to the socialist program of collectivization in our day. What weighed on Goethe's mind was a French forerunner of socialist collectivization, namely the "doctrine" of the Saint-Simonians. In the last years of his life, Goethe informed himself quite thoroughly about this latest ideology from France. His contemplation of its tenets formed part of that "größte Denkübung" of coping with the revolution of 1830. It was the Saint-Simonians who had called, among many other things, for a change in the laws governing land-ownership; they confidently declared this to be the last step to a new Golden Age.[39] Here we find a remarkable parallel to Faust's behavior in Act V. Before he announces his own vision of a Golden Age—a liberated people on liberated land—he orders, chillingly and incongruously, the expropriation of Philemon and Baucis!

The longer we contemplate Faust's political profile in light of Goethe's negative reaction to the events of 1830 in general and to the Saint-Simonian utopia in particular, the more we see him as the irresponsible and dangerous social engineer that Goethe had come to see in the French reformer and his many disciples. The resemblance appears especially striking in Faust's last speech. When Faust arrogantly claims to know what is good for the masses and takes the lead on the road toward that goal—"Daß sich das größte Werk vollende, / Genügt *ein* Geist für tausend Hände" (11509f.)—he essentially echoes the Saint-Simonians. Like the French reformers, Faust places the supposed concerns of the masses—variously referred to as "Menge," "Millionen," "Gewimmel," "Völkerschaft" and "Volk"–above the liberty and the dignity of the individual, whose existence is justified only to the extent that he/she contributes to the "improvement" of humanity. Very much in the spirit of the Saint-Simonians, Faust is bent on controlling land and on exploiting nature. The Saint-Simonian doctrine called for the abolition of hereditary title to land–a notion echoed in Faust's dying vision of a free people on a liberated land–liberated, above all, from the laws of inheritance. But Faust's inspired vision–the triumphant C-Major fanfare trumpeted by all Marxist readings of *Faust*–is about as trustworthy as the vow of sobriety of a derelict alcoholic. It is the vision of a blind man who is shown, most poignantly, to have deceived himself about such elementary matters as "Graben" and "Grab." Faust's last speech, all orthodox claims to the contrary, marks no conversion in a moral or political sense; it still bears the imprint of an authoritarian, power-hungry mind. Schuchard even went so far as to characterize this final instance of striving as Faust's greatest error.[40]

The implications of reading *Faust* in the historical context of 1830 can only be described as sobering. They contradict the deep-rooted and apparently ineradicable desire to attribute to Goethe's Faust some sort of self-improvement in order to justify his eventual redemption.[41] But there is absolutely no indication that Goethe, in the last years of his life, set much store in any program of social and political engineering. In his well-known last letter to Wilhelm von Humboldt–his final comment on *Faust*–Goethe refers to the misguided teachings and misguided actions of the day: "Verwirrende Lehre zu verwirrtem Handel waltet über die Welt."[42] It is time to recognize that Faust's last speech–the most politically exploited lines in all of German literature–is to be counted among those misguided teachings of the day.

In light of this we may begin to understand why in Marxist readings of *Faust* both the references to Saint-Simon and to the context of the 1830 revolution have been ignored, or played down. Heinz Hamm acknowledged as much only recently and reluctantly without, however, departing from the core of the orthodoxy.[43] Faust, despite his tactical alliance with the emperor, remains for Hamm the liquidator of feudalism and the bearer of a progressive, utopian vision. Hamm and with him virtually all "perfectionist" readers avert their eyes from the most disturbing feature of Faust's political physiognomy–his affinity with feudalism–and they dodge the implications of Goethe's profound pessimism, his disavowal–in the very spirit and manner of Faust–of all social and political engineering.

*   *   *

If Faust the ruler and visionary does not *merit* it, on what grounds are we to accept his so-called redemption? The poem itself offers an answer: striving *may* lead to redemption, but there is no certainty. What saves Faust is love in both its earthly and other-worldly, physical and spiritual, manifestations: once in his life, through Gretchen, Faust partook of love. Loving is also an activity, the complement of striving. Unlike the Faustian striving, however, with its potential

for destruction and inhumanity, love is essentially not the monomaniac, "unbedingte" sort of activity which, according to Goethe's well-known dictum, leads
to moral bankruptcy.[44] It is very much a "bedingte" activity, conditioned by
another person. Partaking of the experience of love is, as Faust dimly senses,
"the best" that life has had to offer. And it is the experience of love, as he also
senses in the pivotal monologue at the opening of Act IV, that is capable of
leading "hinan"–of performing that mystical "Steigerung" at which Goethe
decided to let matters rest. Faust is, of course, not privy to the mystical proceedings of the final scene. But he is granted a foretaste of that heavenly truth just
before he embarks on his high-minded but fatally flawed pursuit of power:

> Des tiefsten Herzens frühste Schätze quellen auf:
> Aurorens Liebe, leichten Schwung bezeichnet's mir,
> Den schnellempfundnen, ersten, kaum verstandnen Blick,
> Der, festgehalten, überglänzte jeden Schatz.
> Wie Seelenschönheit steigert sich die holde Form,
> Löst sich nicht auf, erhebt sich in den Äther hin
> und zieht das Beste meines Innern mit sich fort. (10060ff.)

NOTES

1. Emrich, 2. durchgesehene Auflage (Bonn: Athenäum-Verlag, 1957) 384.

2. For a condensed survey see Nicholas Boyle, " 'Du ahnungsloser Engel Du!': Some
Current Views of Goethe's 'Faust,' " in: *German Life and Letters*, NS XXXVI (1982/3):
116–47; John R. Williams, *Goethe's "Faust"* (London: Allen & Unwin, 1987) 47–62;
Hans Arens, *Kommentar zu Goethe's Faust II* (Heidelberg: Winter, 1989) 743–833.

3. Brown 217.

4. Emil Staiger 3:410: "Befremdliches zwar geschieht sehr viel, doch beinah nichts, was
zum Verweilen und ernstlichen Sinnen nötigen würde. Die Szenen des vierten Aktes
sind, von dem Eingangsmonolog abgesehen, die schwächsten der ganzen Faust-
Dichtung."

5. Karl Robert Mandelkow, "Natur und Geschichte bei Goethe im Spiegel seiner
Rezeption im 19. und 20. Jahrhundert," in *Geschichtlichkeit und Aktualität: Studien zur
deutschen Literatur seit der Romantik*. Festschrift für Hans-Joachim Mähl, ed. Klaus-Detlef
Müller et al. (Tübingen: Niemeyer, 1988) 69–96.

6. For a recent example of this line of reasoning see Dorothea Hölscher-Lohmeyer,
"Auf dem Hochgebirg. 'Faust II'–Die erste Szene des vierten Aktes," *Jahrbuch der
deutschen Schillergesellschaft* XXV (1981): 249–84.

7. Emrich (note 1) 347.

8. Mandelkow II, 2:114.

9. Heinz Schlaffer, *Faust Zweiter Teil: Die Allegorie des 19. Jahrhunderts* (Stuttgart: Metzler,
1981); Marshall Berman, "Goethe's 'Faust': The Tragedy of Development," in *All That*

Is Solid Melts Into Air: The Experience of Modernity (New York: Simon and Schuster, 1982) 37–86.

10. Deborah Vietor-Engländer, *Faust in der DDR* (Frankfurt/Main: Lang, 1987); cf. also Paul Michael Lützeler, "Goethe's 'Faust' und der Sozialismus. Zur Rezeption des klassischen Erbes in der DDR," in: *Basis: Jahrbuch für deutsche Gegenwartsliteratur*, ed. Reinhold Grimm and Jost Hermand, vol. 5 (1975): 31–57; Rüdiger Scholz, *Goethes Faust in der wissenschaftlichen Interpretation von Schelling und Hegel bis heute: Ein einführender Forschungsbericht* (Rheinfelden: Schäuble Verlag, 1983) 97–129.

11. See Alexander Abusch, *Goethes Erbe. Literatur und Wirklichkeit: Beiträge zu einer neuen deutschen Literaturgeschichte* (Berlin: Aufbau, 1953). Cf. Vietor-Engländer (note 10) 26f.; Scholz (note 10) 103ff.; Mandelkow II, 2:161ff.

12. See Walter Ulbricht, "An alle Bürger der DDR! an die ganze deutsche Nation," *Neues Deutschland,* 23 March 1962, 3–4. Cf. Vietor-Engländer (note 10) 27f.; Mandelkow II, 2:206f.

13. Gerhard Scholz, *Faust-Gespräche* (Berlin: Junge Welt, 1967; 2. Aufl. 1982); cf. Mandelkow II, 2:212–14.

14. See the items in note 16.

15. See Walter Benjamin's biographical essay, "Goethe," originally written for the *Great Russian Encyclopedia* (1929), in *Gesammelte Schriften,* ed. Rolf Tiedemann and Hermann Schweppenhäuser (Frankfurt/Main: Suhrkamp, 1977) 705–39.

16. See his "Faust-Studien," in Georg Lukács, *Werke,* vol. 6 (Neuwied und Berlin: Luchterhand, 1965) 525–621; for a brief excerpt see J.W. von Goethe, *Faust: A Tragedy,* ed. by Cyrus Hamlin (New York: W.W. Norton, 1976) 524–30. Cf. also Thomas Höhle/Heinz Hamm, "Faust. Der Tragödie zweiter Teil," in: *Weimarer Beiträge,* 20 (1974): 49–89, also in *Geschichte der deutschen Literatur: 1789–1830,* ed. H.-D. Dahnke, T. Höhle and G. Werner (Berlin: Akademie Verlag, 1978) 712–35; Thomas Metscher, "Faust und die Ökonomie. Ein literaturhistorischer Essay," in *Vom Faustus bis Karl Valentin: Der Bürger in Geschichte und Literatur* (Berlin: Argument Verlag, 1976) 28–155 (Argument Sonderband AS 3); Heinz Hamm, *Goethes "Faust": Werkgeschichte und Textanalyse* (Berlin: Volk und Wissen, 3. bearbeitete Auflage, 1984).

17. Hans Schwerte, see "Bibliographical Note."

18. Mandelkow II, vol. 1: *1773–1918.*

19. Johann Peter Eckermann, *Gespräche mit Goethe,* 13 and 17 February 1831.

20. See Paralipomenon Nr. 63, WA I, 15.2:177.

21. Gottlieb C.L. Schuchard, "Julirevolution, St. Simonismus und die Faustpartien von 1831," in: *Zeitschrift für deutsche Philologie* 60 (1935): 240–74, 362–84; neither Scholz (note 10) nor Mandelkow II mentions Schuchard.

22. Hans Rudolf Vaget, "Faust, Der Feudalismus und die Restauration," *Akten des VI. Internationalen Germanistenkongresses Basel 1980* (Bern: Lang, 1980) 345–51; Nicholas Boyle, "The Politics of 'Faust II': Another Look at the Stratum of 1831," in: *Publications of the English Goethe Society,* N.S. LII (1981/2): 4–43. Cf. also John R. Williams, "Die Rache der Kraniche. Goethe, 'Faust II,' und die Julirevolution," in: *Zeitschrift für deutsche Philologie* 103 (1984): 105–27.

23. Heinz Hamm, "Julirevolution, Saint-Simonismus und Goethes abschließende Arbeit am 'Faust,' " in: *Weimarer Beiträge*, XXVII, No. 11 (1982): 70–91; Thomas Metscher, "Faust's End: On the Present Significance of Goethe's Text," in *Our Faust: Roots and Ramifications of a Modern German Myth*, ed. by Reinhold Grimm and Jost Hermand (Madison, Wisconsin: U. of Wisconsin Press, 1987) 22–46.

24. *Goethes Gespräche*, 2. Teil, ed. Wolfgang Pfeifer-Belli (Zürich: Artemis, 1950) 718.

25. Emrich (note 1) 380; Kurt May, *Faust II. Teil: In der Sprachform gedeutet* (Berlin: Juncker u. Dünnhaupt, 1936) 200, 209, 215.

26. Cf. Deirdre Vincent, " 'Die Tat ist alles': A Reconsideration of the Significance of 'Faust II,' Act Four," in: *Seminar*, XVIII (1982): 125–41, 131.

27. It is widely assumed in the literature on *Faust* that the great land-reclamation project conceived in Act IV (10228) is inspired by idealistic and altruistic considerations. Such generous assessment begins to look suspect as soon as one realizes that in the feudal order the exercise of power is tied to land property, i.e. the fief. For a recent positive evaluation of Faust's project see Katharina Mommsen, " 'Faust II' als politisches Vermächtnis des Staatsmannes Goethe," *Jahrbuch des Freien Deutschen Hochstifts 1989* (Tübingen: Niemeyer, 1989) 1–36.

28. Metscher (note 23) 36.

29. Cf. Cyrus Hamlin (note 15) 265.

30. Hamm (note 23) 82; Metscher 46.

31. See Hamm 89f.

32. See Paralipomenon No. 179, WA I, 15.2:237.

33. For a recent example of this argument see John Gearey, *Goethe's Other 'Faust': The Drama, Part II* (Toronto: U. of Toronto Press, 1992) 149: "Yet the Anti-Emperor also surely represents Napoleon."

34. See Heinz Hamm (note 23); cf. also Manfred Birk, "Goethes Typologie der Epochenschwelle im vierten Akt des 'Faust II,' " in: *Jahrbuch der deutschen Schillergesellschaft* XXXII (1989): 261–80, who argues that Faust chooses "den zweckrationalen Weg über den Feudalismus" (277) in analogy to the historical upheavals at the beginning of the sixteenth and nineteenth centuries.

35. See Paralipomenon 182, WA I, 15.2:239.

36. Th. Höhle/H. Hamm (note 16) 79.

37. See Benjamin, "Goethe" (note 15) 737: "In einem geheimnisvollen, utopischen Ineinanderspiel agrarisch-technischen Wirkens und Schaffens mit dem politischen Apparat des Absolutismus hat Goethe die magische Formel gesehen, kraft deren die Realität der sozialen Kämpfe in Nichts sich verflüchtigen sollte. Lehnsherrschaft über bürgerlich bewirtschaftete Ländereien, das ist das zwiespältige Bild, in welchem Fausts höchstes Lebensglück seinen Ausdruck findet."

38. See Gerhard Scholz (note 13), who paints the cottage of the old couple as "Metapher für Zuständlichkeiten einer gesellschaftlichen Formation. . . , die in die Erdbebenzone historisch notwendigen Überfälligwerdens geraten war" (191), and who characterizes Philemon and Baucis as "Kleinsteigentümer" (190) and "nicht ganz unschuldig zu Tode gekommen" (200).

39. For a representative selection on Saint-Simon's program see Henri Saint-Simon, *Selected Writings on Science, Industry and Social Organization,* tr. with an introduction and notes by Keith Taylor (London: Croom Helm Ltd., 1975). For a useful survey of the Saint-Simonian influence in Germany, though without any apparent awareness of Goethe's interest in the matter, see Eliza M. Butler, *The Saint-Simonian Religion in Germany: A Study of the Young German Movement* (Cambridge: Cambridge University Press, 1926, reprinted New York: Fertig, 1968).

40. Schuchard (note 21) 384.

41. See Wilhelm Böhm, *Faust der Nichtfaustische* (Halle/Saale: Niemeyer, 1933) for an early example of resistance to the dominant "perfektibilistische" interpretations of *Faust.*

42. To Wilhelm von Humboldt, 17 March 1832; English version in Hamlin (note 16) 430–31.

43. See Hamm (note 23).

44. "Unrestrained activity, of whatever kind, leads at last to bankruptcy," Goethe, *Conversations of German Refugees, Wilhelm Meister's Journeyman Years or The Renunciants,* tr. by Jan von Henrik and Krishna Winston (New York: Suhrkamp Publishers, 1989) 296.

THE DEMONIC

HARALD WEINRICH

Der zivilisierte Teufel

The Civilized Devil

Madame de Staël, who judged Mephistopheles to be the hero of Faust I, also proclaimed him a figure demonstrably "civilisé." Indeed, Mephistopheles proves himself to be a man of the world, courteous, enlightened, adept in the art of conversation, and an acute observer of mores—all marks of the civilized individual in late eighteenth-century France. His accomplished cultivation renders him radically more evil than his eighteenth-century diabolical counterparts. Goethe has drawn on the example of Diderot's Rameau's Nephew to establish a new category of evil: "sublime" evil.

MEIN AUFSATZ BESTEHT AUS FÜNF TEILEN. Im ersten Teil beschäftige ich mich mit Madame de Staël, und zwar mit ihrem Werk über Deutschland, *De l'Allemagne*, aus dem Jahre 1813. Der zweite Teil heißt "Die Zivilität Mephistos." Es folgt ein dritter Abschnitt: "Kultur versus Zivilisation." Der vierte Abschnitt lautet: "Eine kleine Typologie des Bösen." Im fünften Teil gebe ich einen kurzen Ausblick auf Paul Valérys *Mon Faust.*

I

Madame de Staël kommt zu Recht am Anfang eines solchen Referats zu Wort, da sie sowohl das Werk als auch die Person Goethes gut gekannt hat. Sie hat Goethe sehr bewundert. In ihrem Buch über Deutschland steht ein kleines, sehr sympathisches Porträt Goethes, sie interpretiert ihn dort als Kompendium des deutschen Geistes. Alle bedeutenden Züge des deutschen Geistes, "le génie allemand," findet man nach ihrer Auffassung bei Goethe vereinigt, und zwar in eminentem Maße. Dann kommt sie im Kapitel I:23 ihres Buches auf den *Faust* zu sprechen. Und hier stehen zwei wichtige Sätze, die ich herausgreifen möchte. Der erste Satz lautet: "Der Teufel ist der Held dieses Stückes" ("Le diable est le héros de cette pièce"). Das bedeutet zunächst einmal—ich will den Satz nicht unterschreiben, aber ich referiere und erläutere ihn—, daß nach ihrer Auffassung zwei andere Kandidaten für die Hauptrolle dieses Stückes nicht in Frage kommen.

Zunächst Gretchen: Von Gretchen hält die Aristokratin Madame de Staël wenig. Sie ist eine Naive von niederem Stande und beschränkten Geistes, "d'un esprit borné." (Ich widerstehe hier schwer der Versuchung, "borné" mit "borniert" zu übersetzen.) Wir befinden uns also in der Nähe des Urteils von Carducci über "la stupida ragazza Goetheana." Auch Faust kommt nach Madame de Staëls Auffassung als eigentlicher Held dieses Stückes nicht in Frage. Zwar sagt sie nichts ausdrücklich Kritisches gegen Faust, aber auch wenig zu seinen Gunsten. Eine negative Anmerkung macht sie freilich. Sie nennt Faust nämlich einen unbeständigen Charakter, "un caractère inconstant." Das ist ein Urteil, das vor dem Hintergrund der aristotelischen Poetik beträchtliches Gewicht hat, da nach Aristoteles—und diese Lehrmeinung ist in der französischen Klassik dann noch verstärkt worden—die Charakterkonstanz zu den Grundbedingungen der Eignung eines Charakters für die Bühne, wenigstens als tragische Figur, gehört.

Der zweite Satz, den ich aus dem Buch von Madame de Staël herausgreifen möchte, lautet: "Mephistopheles ist der zivilisierte Teufel" ("Méphistophélès est le diable civilisé"). Ich weiß nicht einmal, ob ich hier "Le diable civilisé" mit "zivilisierter Teufel" richtig übersetzt habe, denn "civilisé" bedeutet in der französischen Sprache mehr als "zivilisiert." Ich hätte auch übersetzen können: "Der kultivierte Teufel." Die beiden zitierten Sätze werden später von Gérard de Nerval, dem maßgeblichen *Faust*-Übersetzer Frankreichs, der selber ein bedeutender romantischer Dichter war, herausgegriffen und bestätigt, und sie werden in Frankreich zur kanonischen Meinung über den *Faust*.

II

Aber stimmt es überhaupt, was Madame de Staël von Mephistopheles sagt? Ist er wirklich der zivilisierte Teufel, und wenn ja, worin liegt die Zivilität dieser dramatischen Gestalt? Ich bin der Ansicht, es gibt gute Gründe, so zu argumentieren und ich will das wieder in fünf Punkten tun.

Mephistopheles ist erstens in Goethes Drama ein Weltmann oder Weltmensch, wie ihn Thomas Mann in seinem Aufsatz über Goethes *Faust* interpretiert. Aus der Feder von Thomas Mann haben wir hier die schönste Beschreibung seiner weltmännischen Art. Thomas Mann spricht beispielsweise von der "achselzuckenden Überlegenheit des Weltmenschen." Sowohl Madame de Staël als auch später Valéry und viele andere lassen eigentlich keinen Zweifel daran, daß wir in Goethes Drama eine gewisse intellektuelle oder wenigstens intellektualistische Überlegenheit des Mephistopheles über Faust zu verzeichnen haben, mindestens aber einen Modernitätsvorsprung. Daß Goethe mit dem Begriff des Weltmännischen eine bestimmte, sehr deutliche Wertvorstellung verbunden hat, kann man auch daran sehen, daß er ausgerechnet für Madame de Staël einen eigenen deutschen Begriff neu geschaffen hat, nämlich den Begriff der "Weltfrau," um nämlich auszudrücken, daß sie eine "femme du monde" ist, und das mit deutlicher positiver Konnotation.

Zweitens ist Mephistopheles zweifellos die höflichste Gestalt des Dramas. Höflichkeit bedeutete den Franzosen sehr viel. Voltaire hat die Franzosen "das höflichste Volk" genannt, und Goethe hat selber an verschiedenen Stellen seines Werkes, beispielsweise in *Hermann und Dorothea*, deutlich gemacht, daß er die Höflichkeit für eine ganz besonders französische Tugend hält, der gegenüber auf der deutschen Seite eher Grobianismus zu verzeichnen ist. Die Schülerszene und die mit ihr korrespondierende Baccalaureus-Szene, die ja zum Urbestand des *Faust* gehören, bestätigen die Rolle, die Mephistopheles in diesem Stück einnimmt: er ist ein Lehrmeister der Höflichkeit, und natürlich ist er in diesen beiden Szenen gegenüber dem Schüler und dem späteren Baccalaureus aufgrund seiner Höflichkeit auch der Sympathieträger des Publikums. Man erinnert sich vielleicht an die berühmte Formulierung, die Mephistopheles hier gegenüber dem grobianistischen Verhalten des Schülers und Baccalaureus gebraucht: "Im Deutschen lügt man, wenn man höflich ist." Im Französischen natürlich nicht. Ich sollte hier noch erwähnen, daß auch Madame de Staël in ihrem Werk der Frage der Höflichkeit eine große Bedeutung beimißt. Sie hat ja sonst eine sehr hohe Meinung von den Deutschen, die ja alle Dichter und Denker, Philosophen und Musiker sind; nur mit der Höflichkeit haben sie's nicht so sehr, da fallen ihnen eigentlich keine anderen als nur zeremonielle Höflichkeitsfloskeln ein. Die richtige Höflichkeit beherrschen die Deutschen leider nicht.

Und so verhält es sich auch, drittens, mit der Konversationskunst. Bei allen guten Eigenschaften, die Madame de Staël sonst bei den Deutschen findet: die Kunst der Konversation liegt den Deutschen nicht. Nur einen einzigen Deutschen nimmt sie von dieser Regel aus: Goethe selber. Der beherrscht die Kunst der Konversation vollkommen, und wenn er in Paris wäre, würde man ihn, so schreibt sie, von einem Salon zum anderen zerren.

Wer beherrscht nun im *Faust* die Kunst der Konversation? Wer ist witzig? Wer ist frech? Wer kann in Sentenzen reden? Es steht ganz außer Frage, daß die einzige Person des Dramas, der die Konversationskunst stilistisch voll zur Verfügung steht, in dem Sinne des Wortes, den Madame de Staël dem Begriff gibt, Mephistopheles ist.

Viertens ist Mephistopheles die aufgeklärteste Person des Stückes. Man kann das an dem Losungswort der Aufklärung ablesen: Vorurteile. Mephistopheles ist in seinen Worten und Taten absolut vorurteilsfrei, sogar gegenüber seinen eigenen theologischen und dämonologischen Existenzbedingungen, gegenüber sich selbst also.

Und fünftens schließlich ist Mephistopheles der Moralist des Stückes. Bei dem Wort "Moralist" oder dem zugehörigen Abstraktum "Moralistik" ist nicht an Moral zu denken, sondern die Moralisten sind in der Geschichte der französischen Literatur—La Rochefoucauld, La Bruyère—, aber auch in der Geschichte der deutschen Literatur—Lichtenberg, Schopenhauer, Nietzsche usw.—die Beobachter der *mores*, diejenigen also, die sich in den Sitten der Menschen, so wie die Menschen mit ihren Schwächen nun einmal sind, genau auskennen und sie in vollendeter, geschliffener Form auszudrücken wissen. In diesem Sinne ist Mephistopheles Moralist.

III

Es ist nun sicherlich möglich, die fünf Punkte, die ich hier genannt habe, in dem Begriff der Zivilisation zusammenzufassen. Weltmännische Art, Höflichkeit, Konversationskunst, Aufgeklärtheit und schließlich Moralistik, das sind Kenn- und Kernworte der Zivilisation, so wie dieser Begriff in Frankreich in der zweiten Hälfte des 18. und der ersten Hälfte des 19. Jahrhunderts zu einem Leitbegriff des französischen Selbstverständnisses geworden ist.

Nun überspringe ich eine ganze Zeitspanne und komme zu Heinrich Heine, der ja in Paris gelernt hat, sich in diesem französischen Selbstverständnis auszukennen. Er hat im Jahre 1832, also gerade im Todesjahr Goethes, Frankreich ausdrücklich zum Mutterland der Zivilisation und Paris zur Hauptstadt der zivilisierten Welt gemacht. Gegenüber dieser französischen Selbstauffassung, hier auch von Heine bestätigt, ist dann auf der deutschen Seite zunehmende Zivilisationskritik zu verzeichnen. So zum Beispiel bei Herder, der sich kritisch gegenüber der "Letternkultur" äußert, dann deutlicher bei Pestalozzi und später bei Karl Marx.

Vor diesem Hintergrund, Zivilisationsbegeisterung auf der französischen, Zivilisationskritik auf der deutschen und deutschsprachigen Seite, entwickelt sich dann, und zwar schon im 18. Jahrhundert, eine deutliche Oppositionsstellung zwischen einer deutschen oder deutschsprachigen Kultur und einer französischen Zivilisation. Die ersten Äußerungen dazu finden sich schon bei Kant und Wilhelm von Humboldt. Hier zeigt sich bald, wenigstens bei Wilhelm von Humboldt, eine deutliche Tendenz, der deutschen Kultur–nach Abwägung alles Für und Wider–doch die besseren Zensuren zu geben. Die Kultur ist eben doch die tiefere und gründlichere Angelegenheit. Aber jedenfalls besteht zwischen Kultur und Zivilisation ein deutlicher Gegensatz. Nietzsche spricht später sogar von einem "abgründlichen Antagonismus" zwischen Kultur und Zivilisation.

Danach kommen wir zu Thomas Mann. Ich muß hier leider seinen wenig erfreulichen Aufsatz "Gedanken im Kriege" aus dem Jahre 1914 erwähnen. In diesem Aufsatz hat Thomas Mann den Antagonismus zwischen Kultur und Zivilisation zu einer (Erb-)Feindschaft zwischen deutscher Kultur und französischer Zivilisation weitergebildet. Er spricht in diesem Zusammenhang ausdrücklich–ich zitiere wörtlich–von einem "Krieg der Zivilisation gegen Deutschland" und als Ergebnis dieses Krieges, falls Deutschland ihn verlieren sollte, fürchtet er eine "Zwangszivilisierung Deutschlands."

Die Personen nun, an denen Thomas Mann auf der französischen Seite die Zivilisation und auf der deutschen Seite die Kultur prototypisch repräsentiert sieht, sind bezeichnend. Auf der französischen Seite ist es Voltaire, der "große Zivilist," wie er ihn nennt. Auf der deutschen Seite sind es einerseits Friedrich der Große, der große Soldat und Goethe als der faustische, der drängende, "der dämonischste Deutsche, den es je gegeben hat." Wir wissen heute, zumal wenn wir diese Gedanken weiter verfolgen bis in die *Betrachtungen eines Unpolitischen* hinein–daß sich hinter dem Antagonismus zwischen Deutschland und Frankreich, zwischen Kultur und Zivilisation der große Bruderstreit im Hause Mann versteckt. Auf der deutschen, der Kulturseite, steht Thomas Mann, auf der französischen, der Zivilisationsseite, steht der "Zivilisationsliterat" Heinrich Mann (der bezeichnenderweise auch über Voltaire geschrieben hat).

IV

Habe ich nun zu viel zum Lobe des Mephistopheles und der ihm verwandten Zivilisation gesagt und dabei vergessen, daß er ja auch der Teufel ist? Ich glaube, daß man eine kleine, sicher ganz unvollständige, Typologie des Bösen geben kann, die etwa so aussehen würde, jedoch natürlich präzisiert werden könnte: Es gibt in der historischen Typologie des Bösen zunächst einen Typus, den ich summarisch den gotischen Teufel nennen will. Er streckt seine Klauen nur ein wenig in den Faust hinein und ist poetisch nicht weiter bedeutsam. Den zweiten Typus des Bösen habe ich schon kurz besprochen. Es ist der zivilisierte Teufel. Ich will ihn jetzt nur noch kurz vor dem Hintergrund der aristotelischen Poetik beleuchten, wo es ja einen Passus über den Bösewicht gibt und wo Aristoteles deutlich sagt— und das werden die französischen Theoretiker des klassischen Dramas später noch stärker betonen—daß eine absolut böse Gestalt ohne jedes dramatische Interesse ist, da von ihr keine Katharsis ausgehen kann. Also: der Böse muß immer auch ein bißchen gut sein. In diesem Sinne können wir die fünf guten Eigenschaften, die ich oben bei Mephistopheles unter dem Begriff Zivilisation zusammengefaßt habe, als eine Milderung des Bösen ansehen, die diesen Typus Teufel überhaupt erst bühnenfähig macht und als dramaturgische Person legitimiert.

Die dritte Gestalt des Bösen will ich im Moment überschlagen und komme als nächstes auf die vierte Gestalt zu sprechen. Das ist eine Figur, wie sie im 19. Jahrhundert hauptsächlich von den Romantikern und ihren Nachfolgern entwickelt worden ist. Sie beruht auf einer Satanisierung der Ästhetik. Als Stichwort genügt es vielleicht, an Baudelaires *Fleurs du Mal* zu erinnern.

Der fünfte Typus, mit dem wir dann das 20. Jahrhundert betreten, ist jener Typus des Bösen, den Hannah Arendt entdeckt hat in ihrem bekannten Buch *Eichmann in Jerusalem*. Das Stichwort lautet: die "Banalität des Bösen." Ich will hier nur kurz darauf aufmerksam machen, daß dieser Typus des Bösen in der deutschen Literatur genial präfiguriert ist, und zwar in dem "Grauen" in Chamissos *Peter Schlemihl*.

Nun komme ich zurück auf den ausgesparten dritten Typus des Bösen, der über den Teufel im Sinne des aristotelischen Bösewichts ein Stück hinausgeht. Diesen Typus des Bösen will ich den Typus des "sublimen Bösen" nennen. Hiermit beziehe ich mich auf Goethes bekannte Übersetzung des Diderotschen Dialogs *Rameaus Neffe* aus dem Jahre 1804. Für *Rameaus Neffen* hat sich Goethe zweifellos vor allem deshalb interessiert, weil dieser amoralische Typus eine Form der Bosheit repräsentiert, die bisher in der Welt noch nicht da war oder die jedenfalls noch nicht genügend identifiziert worden war. Paul Valéry hat übrigens schon darauf aufmerksam gemacht, daß zwischen Mephistopheles und Rameaus Neffen eine deutliche Verwandtschaft besteht. Einen Satz will ich aus Goethes

Übersetzung herausgreifen. Dort sagt Diderot, mit Goethes deutschen Worten: "Wenn es irgend etwas Bedeutendes gibt, wo man sublim sein muß, dann ist es das Böse." Goethe schreibt hier "bedeutend" und es ist bekannt, welche Bedeutung das Wort "bedeutend" für Goethe hat. Der "sublime Böse," so wie er in gewissen Grenzen durch Rameaus Neffen repräsentiert wird, ist ein Typus, bei dem die brillanten Eigenschaften noch dem Bösen zugelegt werden, so daß er mit diesen brillanten Eigenschaften—jetzt können wir mit Bezug auf Mephistopheles sagen, mit dessen zivilisatorischen Eigenschaften—noch böser ist, als er ohne sie wäre. Er ist also nicht nur der Bösewicht mit einigen guten Eigenschaften, die sozusagen von der Bosheit abgezogen werden (= Typus II), sondern der Bösewicht mit einigen brillanten Eigenschaften, die gerade wegen ihrer Sublimität dem Bösen noch zugelegt werden. Klaus Mann hat in seinem bekannten *Mephisto*-Roman, in dem er ja Gustaf Gründgens als Mephistopheles darstellt, versucht, diesen Typus im diabolischen Zusammenwirken von Goering und Goebbels, zu verwirklichen—sozusagen als eine Trinität des Sublim-Bösen, wie man im einzelnen in dem Roman nachlesen kann.

Ich will aber an dieser Stelle auch darauf aufmerksam machen, daß Thomas Mann bei jener Beschreibung nicht geblieben ist, die ich oben aus seinem Aufsatz über Goethes *Faust* zitiert habe. In seinen *Reden und Vorträgen zur politischen Situation Deutschlands* aus dem Jahre 1945 hat er mit Blick auf Hitler-Deutschland einen ganz anderen Teufel eingeführt, auch mit deutlichem Seitenblick auf den *Faust*. Er hat in diesen Vorträgen gesagt, daß Luthers und Faustens Teufel derjenige Teufel ist, der nun Deutschland geholt hat. Das ist vielleicht zugleich jener banale Teufel, von dem ich eben mit Blick auf Hannah Arendt gesprochen habe.

V

Nun noch zum Abschluß ein kurzer Blick auf Paul Valérys *Mon Faust*, geschrieben 1940 bis 1945, ein Fragment. In gewisser Weise kann man sagen, daß Paul Valéry in diesem Drama, das aus zwei Teilen besteht, alles das an Goethes *Faust* korrigiert hat, was Madame de Staël nicht gefallen hat. Erstens: Es ist ein richtiges Konversationsstück geworden, im vollen und tiefen Sinn des Wortes, den das Wort "Konversation" bei Madame de Staël hat. Es passiert nichts, aber alle reden sehr gut. Zweitens: Der Fehler der Gretchengestalt wird auch korrigiert. An Gretchens Stelle tritt als Fausts Geliebte Mademoiselle Lust. Mademoiselle Lust ist eine gebrochenere, modernere Gestalt. In einem Entwurf Valérys wird vermerkt, sie lasse sich sogar therapieren, und zwar durch Psychoanalyse. Und wer ist der Psychoanalytiker? Mephistopheles! Ein Geniestreich erster Güte.

Auch der Doktor Faust wird bei Valéry modernisiert. Als Wissenschaftler ist er auf der Höhe der Forschung; er ist Physiker und kennt sich bei Einstein und Heisenberg aus. Und dann kommt noch ein typisch französischer Zug hinzu: Faust schreibt ein Buch. Nun, das tun viele, und es ist vielleicht nichts Besonderes. Aber dieses Buch hat's in sich. Faust schreibt nämlich—und da greift Paul Valéry auf einen zentralen Gedanken von Mallarmé zurück—*das* Buch, jenes vollkommene

Buch, nach dem kein weiteres Buch mehr geschrieben und gelesen zu werden braucht: das definitive und letzte Buch. Dieses Buch sollte aber eigentlich die Bibel sein.

Und genau an der Stelle läuft Faust dem Valéry'schen Mephistopheles in die Falle; denn wenn Faust Literat ist, dann ist Mephistopheles Literaturkritiker und Literaturwissenschaftler. Als solcher hat Mephistopheles natürlich seinen Buffon gelesen, den berühmten Vortrag über den Stil nämlich mit dem berühmten Satz, der in der üblichen Zitierform lautet: "der Stil, das ist der Mensch" ("le style c'est l'homme"), und dieser Satz wird jetzt in Bezug auf Fausts Buchprojekt des "letzten Buches" abgewandelt. Mephistopheles hält ihm entgegen: "Der Stil, das ist der Teufel" ("le style, c'est le diable").

JANE K. BROWN
MARSHALL BROWN

Faust and the Gothic Novel

> . . . un vampire, une goule, un homme artificiel,
> une espèce de Faust. . . (H. de Balzac, *Sarrasine*)

OUR AIM IN THE PRESENT PAPER IS TO CONJURE up an unfamiliar vision of *Faust*. So far as we know, our topic is nearly virgin, though Faust's vision of Gretchen appears for a moment at the start of Mario Praz's classic *La Morte, la carne e la diavola*.[1] Since, after all, *Faust* isn't a gothic novel, we are not inclined to call this neglect startling. Goethe's play lacks almost totally the sadistic terror that was the visible hallmark of the gothic, and what motifs it shares with the gothic novel are also Shakespearean or general romantic features. Yet while Goethe was cool toward the fashionable gothic, he was not ignorant about it.[2] Surely, for instance, he knew the work of the Jena professor of philosophy, Justus Christian Hennings, since he attacks Hennings in the "Walpurgisnachtstraum," both by name and as the "*Ci-devant* Genius der Zeit." Writing in the spirit of the Enlightenment about supernatural beliefs in his book of 1780, *Von Geistern und Geistersehern*, Hennings asks derisively, "Vielleicht denkst du, der böse Feind spucke zum Wohl des Menschen?"[3]–a possibility that the more imaginative *Faust* plays with. As Faust says in the last speech before his blinding, "Dämonen, weiß ich, wird man schwerlich los" (11491). Perhaps it isn't so foolish to wonder what the old men– Faust and his creator–thought about ghosts and those who see them.

Early readers of the play clearly perceived its gothic tendencies or potential. Despite their differences, Faust's devilish wager is readily assimilated to demonic pacts in works like Maturin's *Melmoth the Wanderer*.[4] When Balzac's Raphaël starts hallucinating in the old curiosity shop of *La Peau de chagrin*, it was, the narrator says, "un mystérieux sabbat digne des fantaisies entrevues par le docteur Faust sur le *Brocken*."[5] In opera, too, there is no doubt that the Faustian witches' sabbath provided a stimulus for gothic creators. *Der Freischütz*, *La Damnation de Faust*, and *Mefistofele* are likely to leave spectators feeling they have missed something in Goethe's more pedestrian world. Or there is that quintessentially gothic concert piece, the *Symphonie fantastique*, where the hallucinatory witches' sabbath is accompanied by so many other representative features: the dream of an ideal beloved (with its ungrounded or immaterial consciousness evoked by unsupported treble melodies), primitive pastoralism, the dissolution of aristocratic society in a mad waltz that serves as a kind of "Walpurgisnachtstraum," and the concluding march to the scaffold.

A review like this calls to mind how many elements *Faust* really does share with gothic novels dating from before, during, and after its composition. Supernatural figures: devils, angels, witches, hags. Excessively natural figures: the innocent maiden, fatherless and ultimately orphaned, the warrior, the tormented natural scientist and philosopher. Figures of exceptional authority in church and state: rulers and holy men. Plot motifs: dangerous and illicit sexuality (though infanticide replaces the more common gothic incest), disguises and Doppelgänger figures, spying on actions near and far, religious rites and mysteries, political despotism and usurpation, a last-minute deathbed struggle of good and evil. Elements of setting: prison-like enclosures, gothic chambers, churches, and fortresses, vast, moonlit natural expanses through which the characters voyage in space and time. Psychodynamics: a feminine focus, regression to infantile states, haunted reverie, impending doom, with the clock either stopped or moving with unnatural swiftness, helpless unconsciousness. Formal characteristics: most obviously the inserted songs and ballads, but also the multitude of fictional frames, together with the combination of epic sweep and dramatic concentration that makes the gothic novel into its own peculiar kind of *Gesamtkunstwerk*. And, in addition to all these familiar gothic features, an important, but less well recognized one—a certain ambivalence of tone and a self-conscious playfulness that the gothic often reinforced with themes of playing or gambling. Unfamiliar as a Faustian device, wagers and contests are almost inescapable as a gothic one, whether centrally, or else—what is even more revealing—as an almost gratuitous kind of generic tag.[6] In gothic play, it's often not even a step from the sublime to the ridiculous. If critics argue endlessly about how we are supposed to feel at different moments in Goethe's play, perhaps the moral is not the futility of critical analysis, but rather the affinity of the play with a mode in which such things are generically, uncannily undecidable.[7] "Ihr naht euch wieder, schwankende Gestalten."

The wavering visions of the notorious "Proktophantasmist," for example, lead directly to the gothic milieu. Although commentaries correctly identify him as Friedrich Nicolai, Germany's leading rationalist, they do not mention that the story was originally reported (without the name, as in *Faust*) in 1797 by Christoph Wilhelm Hufeland, who at the time was court physician in Weimar and Goethe's family doctor.[8] A delightfully prosaic vitalist, Hufeland was widely known for his lifelong preoccupation with the premature burial of the dead, a topic on which he wrote a book and numerous essays. Faust, like his epigones in the various sections of *Melmoth*, is prone to falling asleep at moments of crisis, in order to revive refreshed. And at the end, when Mephisto is in too much of a hurry to inter him, Faust rises like one of Hufeland's none-too-dead souls to complete the proof that you can't keep a good self down.[9] Flea-bitten rationalism proves to be the nightmare from which even Goethe's gothic is always trying to awaken.

*

Mostly, when *Faust* approaches the characteristic gothic mood of terror, it veers off into satire–"Hexenküche," "Walpurgisnacht" with its dissolve into "Walpurgisnachtstraum," the scene with–or, better, without–the Mothers, "Grablegung." But then, the Burkean terror that is often identified as the defining characteristic of the gothic is, in our view, the least of the genre. Rather, the romantic gothic naturally interrogates or ironizes its worst imaginings. It presupposes Olympian detachment, whether in Goethe's apparent serenity[10] or in the triumph of a demon confronting a shipwreck (*Melmoth*, ch. 4). Hence Radcliffe is full of reverie and reflection, Lewis and Maturin are full of exotic pageantry and meticulous exposition, Hoffmann of witty outrage. Whether underdone or overdone–or, typically, some of each–romantic gothic novels achieve their effects by testing, tantalizing, and teasing their characters and their readers alike. Like *Faust* they offer sophisticated pleasures of crafty, knowing superiority. The true focus is not on the supernatural, but on the human response and resistance to the supernatural. The conclusions, as in *Faust*, are characteristically rapid, and whether the victims *ultimately* triumph or fail, the issue is not so much suffering as survivability.

In their own way, then, romantic gothic novels are as much a critique of gothic terror as *Faust* is.[11] If works like *Dracula* bare the inhuman desires that gnaw at all of us, romantic gothic novels display the human face within their extraordinary events. Poe's "The Pit and the Pendulum" shows how much punishment the human spirit can take; Tieck's "Der blonde Eckbert" or Byron's "Prisoner of Chillon" show how much punishment it takes to overwhelm the human spirit. And though the back cover of our edition of Walpole's *Castle of Otranto* proclaims in red, "A Bleeding Statue, A Praying Skeleton, A Castle of *Horror!*," the author's preface has this to say:

> The author of the following pages. . . wished to conduct the mortal agents in his drama according to the rules of probability; in short, to make them think, speak, and act, as it might be supposed mere men and women would do in extraordinary positions. He had observed, that, in all inspired writings, the personages under the dispensation of miracles, and witnesses to the most stupendous phenomena, never lose sight of their human character.[12]

What Walpole wished in his book never to lose sight of is also what our approach to the gothic aims to keep in view. It is the humanity that matters, not the inhumanity. Consequently, in admitting that *Faust* is opposed to the gothic in its vulgar sense, we are also in a position to claim that it is allied with the deeper tendencies of the mode. Were we given to paradox, we might say that *Faust* is gothic precisely because it is anti-gothic.

Where the supernatural character of events lies in melodramatic externals, the human character of agents might naturally be expected to lie in their inward reserves. The mysterious physical powers of an overwhelming world are encountered by a mysterious spiritual integrity. The best language that we have discovered for analyzing this configuration is that of Kantian philosophy, and it turns out indeed that a direct line leads from Kant's own works to the abnormal psychiatry of high romantic medicine and into the tradition of the gothic itself. As the post-Kantian analysis develops, it relates the supernatural mysteries beyond our knowledge or control to the impenetrable world of things in themselves, and it locates the power confronting that world in what Kant calls the transcendental consciousness. Again, we cannot fully argue this thesis here, which will eventually be developed in a book on the gothic novel. But the terms that generate the analysis—and specifically the notion of a transcendental inwardness as defense against a supernatural outwardness—will provide the framework for our consideration of *Faust*, both in its partial affiliation with and in its distinctive response to the gothic mode.

Here, still as a series of largely undeveloped theses, are the basic features of the transcendental consciousness as they emerge in romantic philosophical and medical discourse, as well as in gothic representations. The first is the unity of the individual, or, as Kant terms it, the transcendental unity of apperception. In contrast to the heterogeneity of experience as envisioned by Enlightenment empiricism, romanticism envisions an integral self whose fundamental character is immutably generated from within. For Kant himself, the unity of the self is a universal phenomenon defined by the laws of experience that all humans share; for those who come after, it often appears as a psychological rather than a logical unity and may differ in character or mood from one individual to another. Second, as the unity of the self is removed from and precedes any possible experience, it cannot be manifested to ordinary consciousness. But those who followed Kant and tried to apply his conceptions to real life looked for the essence of the person in manifestations that lie beyond the conditioning of empirical existence. Specifically, it is in the dream state that we come into contact with our most inward and most fundamental self. Third, however, there also exist waking states in which the core of humanity surfaces. These are the states in which we are least responsive to the world around. Daydreaming and mesmeric states—such as, for instance, Charles Brockden Brown's *Wieland; or, The Transformation* (1798) explores—are borderline conditions where the inward self enters into a kind of contact with the outside world. But most commonly in the romantic period the inner self is brought into view by madness. Those driven beyond the bounds of normal experience are also not vulnerable to the pressures of experience, and they reveal instead the inviolable, transcendental basis of humanity. Hence, in Maturin, the more successful the devil's persecutions are in corporeal terms, the more he frustrates his endeavor to win over the minds of his victims. Fourth, then, there is a fundamental continuity to the self that cannot be broken by any force short of complete annihilation. The inward self reposes on a real, if indeterminate, inner sense of self, in its continuous and unbroken integrity. Kant's name for the inner sense is likewise that of those who come after him—namely, time. Our outer, spatial existence may be broken, fragmented, cut off—may be infringed in countless ways. But our true life is our life in time. So long as our mental existence continues—even in dreams, even in madness—so long do we continue to feel the pulse of existence. Fifth and finally, that pulse then beats through and despite all the forces that would destroy it. In the gothic, life often seems to hang by a thread. Yet the thread persists with a remarkable obstinacy that transcends the mere necessity to keep the narrative going. It becomes hard to keep even the dead down, starting with the ancestral ruler of *The Castle of Otranto*, who rises up after generations to restore his rightful heir to the throne. The gothic, in this period, is one of the most striking manifestations of the pervasive vitalism of the romantic period. There may be nothing else—not wealth, not health, not even sanity—but there is still life. "Des Lebens Pulse," these books keep insisting, "schlagen frisch lebendig."

*

In order to outline Goethe's complex stance toward this complex mode, we propose to scrutinize his use of the typically gothic terms *schaudern* and *Grauen*.[13] "O schaudre nicht!" (3188) Faust tells Gretchen after she has plucked the last petal from the daisy and discovered that Faust loves her. Both recognize in this shudder the doom allegorically executed upon the flower that bears her name. Gretchen had already had a similar moment of premonitory terror in "Abend" (2757), right after Mephistopheles left the first casket of jewels in her cupboard; in "Dom" the evil spirit transforms her into an object of terror for others (3831). Faust also has his moments of terror—when the Erdgeist appears (473) and when he enters the dungeon at the end of Part I (4405), where the phrase "längst entwöhnt" connects his *Schauer* to his response to his study and to the Erdgeist. The conventional gothic sensationalism manifested in such moments is at its height in the prison scene at the end of Part I. "Kerker" predates the gothic fad, which began in the 1780s, yet the early text of the *Urfaust* contains the most explicit mention of terror, "Inneres Grauen der Menschheit," altered in the final version to the more sentimental, "Der Menschheit ganzer Jammer" (4406). And the *Urfaust*'s gothic stage direction, "Er hört die Ketten klirren und das Stroh rauschen," turns into self-conscious discourse: "Sie ahnet nicht, daß der Geliebte lauscht, / Die Ketten klirren hört, das Stroh, das rauscht" (4421–22). Thus, quite apart from the addition of Gretchen's abrupt salvation, Goethe distances himself from the gothic even as its popularity was spreading. And then, just a few lines before Faust terrifies Gretchen for the last time ("Mir graut's vor dir," 4610), Mephistopheles' horses shudder because dawn arrives (4599). Suddenly the supernatural is subject to nature, reversing the gothic norm. Indeed, natural and supernatural complement one another: for the archangels in the "Prolog im Himmel" night is "schauervoll" (254); for the devil day is. The process of terror is reversible; it can be part of building up a consciousness as well as of reducing one to its core.

As Part II unfolds, it becomes increasingly gothic on a cosmic scale. Despite its moments of uncanny terror such as the arrival of Faust's anti-masque or Mephistopheles's reference to the Mothers, Act I hardly evokes a full-scale gothic response. Indeed the gothic Mothers—regressive, awakening shudders—prompt Faust to say, "Das Schaudern ist der Menschheit bestes Teil" (6272), just as he had earlier told Mephistopheles "In deinem Nichts hoff' ich das All zu finden" (6255). Terror evokes the answering assertion of creation from the self. This is more explicit in Act II, where *Schauer* and its compounds occur nine times (of the total of twenty-two occurrences in all of *Faust II*). First, terror is trivialized in a series of elaborate compounds from the beginning of the act ("Schauderfest" 7005, "Schaudergrauen" 7041, "schauderhaft" 7518 and 7788, "schauern" 7798, 7968—notice the progression away from absurd compounds once the point is made). The most specific moment of terror is the eruption of Seismos, who makes the earth itself shake. He unleashes human greed and violence, supernatural forces of destruction (the meteor that destroys the mountain), and dream (we finally learn that the entire affair was an illusion). Other gothic elements around this scene include descent, night, uncertainty, disorientation, and the demonic encounters of Mephistopheles, the Lamien, and the Phorcyads, where sexuality is a constant threat to identity. But the great oddity of these gothic elements is that terror is felt by the supernatural figures who themselves ought to evoke terror—the witch Erichtho, the sirens, Mephistopheles, the dryads, and Homunculus all experience *Schauer*. Whose consciousness is actually being narrated in Act II? Whose dream is it? Stuart Atkins (note 7, 142) has long since asserted that Act II is Faust's dream, but we might go even further. Somehow this is a dream Goethe dreams for the spectator, calling the very boundaries of the individual into question.

Act V is more traditionally gothic. The three mighty men terrorize the world about, especially Baucis and Philemon, who are also terrorized by the mysterious nighttime goings-on at Faust's castle. Here are the evil and violence we conventionally expect from the gothic. Faust himself has become part of this terrorizing mentality, so that the alien shadow of Baucis's and Philemon's trees makes him shudder. A "Schauerwindchen" (11380) brings the four ghosts Death, Care, Want, Need. In a gesture of stripping down to core consciousness Care blinds Faust; as Faust dies, Mephistopheles calls for the clock to stop. Faust's last moments in "Mitternacht" are perhaps the only moments of full gothic horror in *Faust*. Yet they too are soon ironized as angels descend to the rescue. Even here terror is rapidly commuted into play.

Crucial to Faust's death is the experience of time. Gothic time fluctuates between the extremes of frenzied disorientation and empty, rudderless waiting. The most revealing period terms come from Kant's student and close friend, the physician Markus Herz, who in the 1780s wrote a treatise on vertigo. Herz's term for proper time, like Goethe's, is *Weile*; *Schwindel* is the insane pace associated with supernatural action and *Langerweile* the aimlessness found in the demon's lost victims.[14] Clearly Faust suffers at the beginning of the play from boredom; he is desperate to speed time up, to experience *Schwindel* ("das Rauschen der Zeit," "[das] Rollen der Begebenheit," 1754–55.). But the wager as formulated challenges Mephisto to instill in him a healthy, purified temporal *Weilen*. Similarly, though Care claims the power to stop time just before she blinds Faust (11455ff.), the night of his soul approaches apace, without terrifying suddenness (11499: "Die Nacht scheint tiefer tief hereinzudringen"). And though early in the play Care was associated with the shipwreck of hopes in the maelstrom of time (643–44), that is, with arrested time, even earlier yet the Erdgeist had awakened in Faust the courage to overcome shipwrecks (467). It follows, then, that Care now only provokes a counterspirit (11510: "*ein* Geist") into activity. Faust resists Care with his famous speech about slowing down to the pace of nature (11450: "Wenn Geister spuken, geh' er seinen Gang"): his absolute striving yields to a relation to transcendence mediated by his own imaginative consciousness. Thus *Faust* confronts the gothic challenge differently from the gothic novels: in place of a reduction to pure consciousness and internal selfhood, Faust outlines a healthy relationship to time extending beyond the self dynamically into the future.

Such reversals are characteristic of *Faust*'s response to the gothic. In the first line of "Zueignung" wavering forms approach us with their madness (4) and "Zauberhauch" (8), bringing in their train the temporal disorientation of the second and third stanzas. The moment of terror, however, comes only in the second half of the last stanza, "Ein Schauer faßt mich" (29), in the same language as the terror of the Erdgeist (472–74: "Es weht / Ein Schauer vom Gewölb' herab / Und faßt mich an!"). Yet in "Zueignung" the terror brings peace:

> Ein Schauer faßt mich, Träne folgt den Tränen,
> Das strenge Herz, es fühlt sich mild und weich;
> Was ich besitze, seh' ich wie im Weiten,
> Und was verschwand, wird mir zu Wirklichkeiten. (29–32)

The heart softens, consciousness releases its hold, yet what follows is the return of the whole world that had been lost. Gothic nothingness is nowhere to be found, let alone feared.

But if there is no nothingness, there is then no pressing need for the unconditional selfhood explored so intensely by the gothic. Gothic novels usually reach their climax in a prison, but Faust begins in one, feeling imprisoned in his "hochgewölbten, engen *gotischen* Zimmer." We know what the first word of the play proper is not: instead of "ich," Faust has only a depressive and paranoid "ach" to offer. Friedrich Kittler, who has called our attention to these words, sees in this opening a condition of "pure soul" preceding Faust's fall into writing, a change in mode vital to the action of the play.[15] Yet Faust's initial condition of "pure soul" is as much an unhappy limbo as the successor condition is: whatever "pure" means here, it does not include healthy or effective. Suspended in such gothic chambers, "Wandering between two worlds, one dead, / The other powerless to be born" (Arnold, "Stanzas from the Grande Chartreuse"), the continuity of the self is tested and, very often, assured. The gothic novel is, generically, a thought experiment with premature burial, and Faust in his dark and narrow chamber, almost like a figure from Poe, starts off already dead and waiting to be reborn.

What normally symbolizes a late stage in the reduction to pure consciousness is here a starting point Faust rejects with vigor. Consciousness of self is not Faust's defense in the prison; on the contrary, it is itself the very prison to be escaped.[16] Time and again the play unmasks self-consciousness as empty solipsism. Imprisoned Gretchen in her madness is a paradigm of gothic reduction to the essential core of the self: her continuing love for an infant and family and her unstained innocence are unchanged from her earlier, sane moments, and she desires only to return to the past. But in *Faust* this essential self represents the temptation to stasis articulated in the bet—"verweile doch." It must be rejected, and indeed, "Anmutige Gegend" brings growth and change through positive erasure of the past; as Emrich says, "Schlaf und spontan organisches 'Vergessen' sind Funktionen einer Natur, die nur darum 'mildert', versöhnt und 'heilt', weil sie ihren 'Liebling' bis zu den Grenzen des Daseins geführt hat, über die hinaus es nur Entsetzen oder—Vergessen geben kann."[17] Faust's monologue once again contains all the themes of the post-Kantian gothic self. "Des Lebens Pulse schlagen frisch lebendig": the life force is the first thing to impinge on the consciousness of the waking Faust. Next comes continuity in time: "Du, Erde, warst auch diese Nacht beständig." But as Faust's awakening consciousness gathers force, it focuses less and less on a unified self, and more and more on a world that comes into being through the words he utters ("Ein Paradies wird um mich her die Runde"). By the end of the monologue his consciousness extends beyond the earth to the rainbow, a sign that is anchored both in scientific objectivity and in a tradition that evokes not gothic shudders but rather pastoral showers (as "Schauer" must clearly be translated in line 4726).

In such manner *Faust* adds layer after layer until consciousness of self disappears in consciousness of the world. The first three acts of Part II abandon self-absorption for a phantasmagoria of the history of our culture and bring Faust and Helena onto the stage only as literary figures in elaborate costumes, conscious at every moment of themselves as constructs from a long tradition (hence Helena:

"Ich schwinde hin und werde selbst mir ein Idol," 8881). And what then of the apparent return to an authentic self when Faust resists Care? Faust grounds his satisfaction with time and his supposed identity in the labors of others who will do what he has done all through Part II–be conscious not of themselves but of the need to recreate the world each day through their own labor (11575–76).

Faust's death provokes a mock-epic battle in which each side looks gothic to its opponents. "Grablegung" gives us, of course, the devil's perspective.[18] To Mephisto all the wavering rescuers (11723: "Schon schwebts heran"; 11740 s.d.: "Sich mit den schwebenden Rosen herumschlagend"; 11787: "Ihr schwanket hin und her") appear as demons; he calls them "ein überteuflisch Element," "Liebes-spuk," and the like (11754, 11814). But the final scene revives the perspective of "Zueignung," in which wavering and swaying are associated with the uncertain, preconscious reawakening to life. The "Chor und Echo" that open "Bergs-schluchten" begin the last revival of the song whose "erster Widerklang" resonated behind "Zueignung" (20). Answering to the gothic interior of Faust's monologue, the stage now presents a gothic exterior, a mountainous region reminiscent of the landscapes of *The Mysteries of Udolpho*. Yet the setting sheds the contamination by individualized conflict that polarizes the gothic self. Release proceeds in stages, without the cathartic shudder that would memorialize what is to be left behind. Hence, responding to Mephisto's mistaken boast, "Gerettet sind die edlen Teufelsteile" (11813), Goethe produces the following sequence. First angels "schwebend in der höheren Atmosphäre," emit a counterboast, "Gerettet ist das edle Glied / Der Geisterwelt vom Bösen" (11934–35). Next the more perfect angels correct them, complaining, "Uns bleibt ein Erdenrest / Zu tragen peinlich, / Und wär er von Asbest, / Er ist nicht reinlich" (11954–57). And then the purifying Doctor Marianus, "in der höchsten, reinlichsten Zelle," mediates the ultimate release, "Hier ist die Aussicht frei, / Der Geist erhoben" (11989–90), once more evoking "Zueignung," which ends, "Was ich besitze, seh ich wie im Weiten, / Und was verschwand [Faust's body, in the final instance], wird mir zu Wirklichkeiten" (31–32). Redeeming the blinded, haunted Faust, the clarified vision into the distance lifts spirituality to a new and higher level.

At the end gothic conflict gives up the ghost. The younger angels, who were there, appear to speak of victory: "Böse wichen, als wir streuten, / Teufel flohen, als wir trafen" (11947–48). But in truth their attack transformed the nature of the encounter: "Statt gewohnter Höllenstrafen / Fühlten Liebesqual die Geister" (11949–50). War has become passionate love, and the necessary lessons of human violence have forged bonds between individuals. "Und aus ätherischem Gewande / Hervortritt erste Jugendkraft!" (12090–91). Finally Faust is truly born–but not into a merely personal condition of separated consciousness: "Er ahnet kaum das frische Leben [not self-conscious], / So gleicht er schon der heiligen Schar [not personal]" (12086–87). A powerfully active response replaces the spiritual essentialism typical of the gothic, as the blessed youths say, with a circling motion, "Er überwächst uns schon / An mächtigen Gliedern" (12076–77). The professor has become a good learner, and hence a good teacher at last: "Doch dieser hat gelernt, / Er wird uns lehren" (12082–83). But he becomes a good teacher by virtue of confronting his *Unmündigkeit*. A powerful child rather than an independent adult, Goethe's counter-gothic personality does not free himself by force of will, for "Wer zerreißt aus eigner Kraft / Der Gelüste Ketten?" (12026–27). Rather, the gothic manacles lose their terror and become an ecstatic living union transcending any possible individualism. In the penultimate strophe of the play the Doctor Marianus describes the process thus: "Euch zu seligem Geschick / Dankend umzuarten" (12098–99), in a pair of lines whose collective plural is as essential as its perhaps unprecedented verb of communal response, "umzuarten."[19]

Faust, then, preserves the legacy of the gothic in the very process of transmuting it. There is, to be sure, no novelty in contending that *Faust* in some sense transvalues evil and that in some sense it honors collectivities. But it does make a difference if we stress the gothic tonalities that persist into the final scene, even as the play abandons a conventionally gothic vision. The gothic is the realm of the sublime, of the unspeakable and unperformable that the final "Chorus Mysticus" invokes. Consequently, the gothic bequeaths to the play's ideological convictions a sense of urgency and a restless energy beyond conceptual grasp.[20] Because it has passed through the gothic crucible, the world of *Faust* must always view love as passion–a better form of war and not a negation of it. It must always view maturity under the sign of power, breaking the bonds of earth, and not as settled conviction. And it must always view teaching as a stab in the dark: even through the desperate straits of Sorge and her companions men must risk the *Hinanziehen* and *Hinangezogensein* of and by the Eternal Feminine, formerly the spinning Gretchen whose rest is always and forever gone because she does not and cannot hold her beloved firmly on the spot. She knows, as the blessed youths in their blissful ignorance do not, that Faust has not really learned and cannot really teach: she answers them with a reminder that their new teacher is blind, with a blindness carried over from his prior, gothic existence into a new day that can never fully dawn for humans, since humanity lies in acceptance, not rejection, of their gothic fetters: "Vergönne mir, ihn zu belehren! / Noch blendet ihn der neue Tag" (12092–93). That is the sublime condition we transcend exactly to the extent that we learn to submit to it.[21]

What *Faust* rejects, then, is not the gothic as such–not human limitation, not the confrontation with evil, not fatality–so much as the rebelliousness that the gothic novels inscribe into their portrayal of the gothic condition. Gothic rebellion is contaminated by the forces it opposes; as Act V shows, if you command the devil, it is only to become a stronger devil yourself. Resistance is always tainted, whether by the perpetual melancholy of *The Castle of Otranto*, Radcliffe's undercurrents of sexual indulgence, or the recalcitrant monstrousness of Mary Shelley's pure-hearted monster. Like his creators in the "Vorspiel auf dem Theater," Faust begins angry. Unlike his fellows in confrontation with forces of evil–and most unlike the increasingly angry Mephisto–Faust wins by losing, swallowing his pride, and submitting. The gothic mode is divided against itself, and Goethe rectifies it by refusing to bring its dialectic to a standstill.

Amid all the differences, then, *Faust* shares with the gothic a radical dialectic.[22] Indeed, insofar as the gothic novels bring their dialectic to a terminus, *Faust* outdoes their radicalism. It is a dialectic because its values insistently come in competing pairs: good and evil, heaven and earth, man and woman. Its two-souledness is radical in the political sense that human structures will not satisfy its demands; radical in the moral sense that erring, sin, and care, hopeless blindness and the struggle against it remain inevitable; radical in the epistemological sense that mediations are relentlessly excluded or satirized in a series of ever more astonishing dramatic confrontations; and radical in the aesthetic sense that this is all a wondrous spectacle, of value precisely to the extent that it does not touch real–ordinary, petty–life. *Faust* consummates the gothic self-critique not by turning against the gothic but rather by pursuing the gothic impulse to its logical, bittersweet end.

NOTES

1. Mario Praz, *The Romantic Agony*, trans. Angus Davidson (London and New York: Oxford University Press, 1970) 26, following only a long Shelley quote. Other bits of Part I figure very occasionally through the rest of the book as analogies to Maturin's *Melmoth the Wanderer* and to victimized females.

2. Cf. WA I, 42.2:86–88 (Scott, Hoffmann); he made repeated references to Walpole's *Castle of Otranto* (WA III, 2:224; WA IV, 13:91, 343, 361; 14:54; and 15:50), also to Walpole's "Das Geheimnis der Mutter" (WA I, 35:86). He even translated a bit of Maturin's *Bertram* (WA I, 11:353–58) and was aware of Monk Lewis. Closer to home he knew both Tieck's "romantic" writings, as he refers to them (WA III, 2:259), and Schiller's "Geisterseher" (WA III, 3:124). On Kant as an ironist, WA II, 11:54–55 and 13:448.

3. [Justus Christian Hennings], *Von Geistern und Geistersehern* (Leipzig: Weygand, 1780) 368.

4. The most detailed comparison of *Faust* and *Melmoth* can be found in Syndy M. Conger, *Matthew G. Lewis, Charles Robert Maturin and the Germans: An Interpretative Study of the Influence of German Literature on Two Gothic Novels*, Salzburg Studies in English Literature 67 (Salzburg: Institut für englische Sprache und Literatur, Universität Salzburg, 1977) 12–42.

5. Honoré de Balzac, *La Peau de chagrin*, in *La Comédie humaine*, ed. Marcel Bouteron, 10 vols. (Paris: Gallimard, 1950) 9:30.

6. On gothic play see Marshall Brown, "Kant e i demoni della notte," *Studi sull'estetica* 12 (1984): 155–65.

7. See for instance the "quite astonishing" claim by Jane K. Brown that the final moments of Part I derive from the comic-opera tradition (quoted words on p. 111). The more conventional reading can be illustrated with Stuart Atkins's emphasis on the "tragic defeat," "horror," and "tragic dignity" of Gretchen's "secular-sentimental apotheosis": *Goethe's "Faust": A Literary Analysis* (Cambridge, Mass.: Harvard University Press, 1964) 99–100.

8. We quote a sentence to illustrate the tone of Hufeland's narrative: "Es fängt wirklich diesem äußerst aufgeklärten und vorurtheilsfreyen Manne endlich an darüber zu schwindeln; nie allein zu seyn, sich ewig von sonderbaren und immer wechselnden Gestalten umgeben, ja angesprochen zu sehen, dieß raubt ihm endlich alle Gemüthsruhe, ja alle Gedanken, und es versetzt ihn in die peinlichste Agitation." C.W. Hufeland, "Sonderbare Geistererscheinung," in *Kleine medizinische Schriften* 2 (Berlin: G. Reimer, 1823): 378 (originally in Hufeland's *Journal der praktischen Heilkunde*).

9. Emil Staiger mentions Hufeland in connection with Faust's resurrection, 3:451.

10. Matthew Arnold's lines on Goethe in "Memorial Verses: April, 1850," note the gothic ground of his detachment: "And he was happy, if to know / Causes of things, and far below / His feet to see the lurid flow / Of terror, and insane distress, / And headlong fate, be happiness." Wilhelm Emrich (73–74) builds his passing mention of madness on a line from *Egmont*, "eingehüllt in gefälligen Wahnsinn versinken wir und hören auf zu sein"; his Hegelian bias toward redemptive *Gefälligkeit* leads him to slight the significance of *Wahnsinn*, a word that is absent from his index of concepts.

11. See Marshall Brown, "A Philosophical View of the Gothic Novel," *Studies in Romanticism* 26 (1987): 275–301, for a fuller presentation of the way that gothic novels test the limits of terror.

12. Horace Walpole, *The Castle of Otranto*, ed. Marvin Mudrick (New York: Collier, 1963) 19.

13. As part of his demonstration of the thematic unity of *Faust*, Joachim Müller surveys representative occurrences of *schauern* and *schaudern* in the play, without discussing their significance: "Zur Motivstruktur von Goethes 'Faust,' " in: *Sitzungsberichte der sächsischen Akademie der Wissenschaften zu Leipzig: Philologisch-historische Klasse* 116:3 (Berlin: Akademie-Verlag, 1972) 9–11.

14. Herz defines *Langerweile* [sic] as "ein einförmiger Spatziergang oder Reiseweg, auf welchem sich keine abwechselnde Mannichfaltigkeit darbietet," leading to despair; *Schwindel* is "der widernatürlich schnelle Fortgang der Ideen." Markus Herz, *Versuch über den Schwindel*, 2nd ed. (Berlin: Vossische Buchhandlung, 1791) 158–59.

15. Friedrich Kittler, *Discourse Networks 1800/1900*, trans. Michael Metteer (Stanford: Stanford University Press, 1990) 3.

16. See the groundbreaking general discussion of this phenomenon by Geoffrey H. Hartman, "Romanticism and Anti-Self-Consciousness," *Beyond Formalism* (New Haven: Yale University Press, 1970) 298–310.

17. Emrich 71. See further Peter Michelsen's nice analysis of "Anmutige Gegend" in relation to Faust's opening monologue, "Fausts Schlaf und Erwachen," *Jahrbuch des freien deutschen Hochstifts* (1983) 21–61. Michelsen identifies cathartic forgetting as the new motif at this point in the play, and he compares the action here to the procedures "des Experiments in der Naturwissenschaft" (38). For his theory of sleep Michelsen draws on the *Aphorismen aus der Physiologie der Pflanzen* (1808) by Goethe's friend and admirer Dietrich Georg Kieser. The passages he quotes (40–41) were, however, commonplace both among mystics and, in variants, among rationalists like Heinrich Nudow, whose *Versuch einer Theorie des Schlafs* was published by Kant's (and Fichte's) publisher Nicolovius in Königsberg in 1795. For a stronger account of the power of forgetting in the play, see Theodor Adorno, "Zur Schlußszene des Faust," *Noten zur Literatur* (Frankfurt/Main: Suhrkamp, 1981) 129–38. Helmut Schanze presents the final scene as a *theatrum memoriae* in "Szenen, Schema, Schwammfamilie: Goethes Arbeitsweise und die Frage der Struktureinheit von *Faust I* und *II*," *Euphorion* 78 (1984) 383–400; however, Schanze's

thesis differs less from ours than might appear, since he emphasizes collective memory and a transcendence of the individual perspective.

18. On the importance of perspective and point of view in *Faust* see Jane K. Brown, *Faust: Theater of the World* (New York: Twayne, 1992) 26–34.

19. Grimm's *Deutsches Wörterbuch* cites only this passage to illustrate a transitive use of "umarten." Its two prior instances of intransitive "umarten" do not appear to constitute a precedent. In a subsection (145–52) of his essay "Theatrum Mundi: Anfang und Schluß von Goethes 'Faust' " called "Umartung," Hermann Kunisch transmutes the reflexive into a passive, "ein Umgeartetwerden in dem gnadevollen Sichmitteilen der Liebe": *Goethe-Studien*, ed. Franz Link (Berlin: Duncker & Humblot, 1991) 131–58 (quotation is on p. 146).

20. We argue here against the type of idealizing reading canonized by Max Kommerell in "Faust II: Letzte Szene," *Geist und Buchstabe der Dichtung* (Frankfurt/Main: Klostermann, 1956) 112–31. "In Prosa aufgelöst" (116)–which is to say, substituting doctrinal pieties for human feeling–the conclusion seems to Kommerell a "Mysterium" that preaches "eine seraphische Geselligkeit und Kollegialität" (121) and that portrays "die Genialität des Liebeszustands in jener Allgemeinheit, wie sie der Stil des zweiten Teils mit sich bringt" (129). "D'un coup," writes one pygmy working the vein of this generalissimo and oblivious of the Ibycean cranes on the horizon, "les scènes de magie noire, les interminables promenades de la seconde partie à travers les diableries anciennes et modernes, pâlissent devant cette fin d'un centenaire aveugle et visionnaire," Pierre Grapin, "Faust aveugle," *Etudes germaniques* 38 (1983): 146.

21. Jean-François Lyotard has provided the most apposite analyses of the sublime as a darkness that wrings morality out of disintegration. See in particular "L'Intérêt du sublime," *Du sublime* (a collective volume with preface by Jean-Luc Nancy) (n.p.: Belin, 1988) 149–77. In the more concise formulation of another essay, "the sublime is the affective paradox, the paradox of feeling (of feeling publicly) in common a formlessness for which there is no image or sensory intuition," "The Sign of History," trans. Geoff Bennington, *Post-Structuralism and the Question of History*, ed. Derek Attridge et al. (Cambridge: Cambridge University Press, 1987) 176.

22. There are valuable comments about *Faust* as a dialectic in extremis in Jochen Schmidt, "Die 'katholische Mythologie' und ihre mystische Entmythologisierung in der Schlußszene des *Faust II*," *Jahrbuch der deutschen Schillergesellschaft* 34 (1990) 230–56. See particularly the essay's last sentence: "So weitet sich das Spektrum der Entmythologisierung ins Totale, indem nicht bloß eine alte Welt von gestalthaft ausgeprägten Glaubensvorstellungen und Sinn-Figuren, sondern überhaupt die Vorstellung einer allumfassenden Sinn-Figur: die Vorstellung des ganzheitlich geordneten Kosmos als mythologische Vorstellungsform aufgehoben wird in einem Jenseits, das als Sphäre des irreal Gewordenen schon umschlägt ins Nichts" (256). Having let the genie out of the bottle, however, Schmidt simultaneously tries to nail it to the wall, claiming that Dionysius the Areopagite is the secret source that explains all. "Erst damit wird der Sinn der bisher unerschlossenen berühmten Verse [of the final chorus] exakt faßbar" (245)–a claim that would be more persuasive if the "exact" meaning that he finds were more than a conventionally hermetic approximation: "Daher ist Gott nicht in seiner Eigentlichkeit, sondern nur uneigentlich zu erkennen" (246).

MEREDITH LEE

Faust's Harzreise

"WALPURGISNACHT" AND ESPECIALLY THE "Walpurgisnachtstraum" have been a persistent source of irritation for readers of *Faust*. The dilettante theater of the "Walpurgisnachtstraum" seems a most tedious and anticlimactic conclusion to what was supposed to be a night of wild sexual frenzy at a witches' sabbath. Faust appears far too easily distracted—too eager to hike the forested slopes and then too willing to abandon the original goal of the Brocken peak when Mephisto leads him aside into the Small Worlds ("Kleine Welten") of scattered fires and away from the presumed heart of the revels. His attention is finally diverted by an amateur theater performance that lasts until dawn. Most recently Albrecht Schöne has responded to the challenge of the two scenes by banishing the second, the "Walpurgisnachtstraum," from the play altogether and by rewriting the first.[1] Unlike the nineteenth-century opera versions and twentieth-century stagings that have handled the problem by similar revisions and exclusions, Schöne claims a special legitimacy for his rewriting: he asserts he is completing the task Goethe began. Using the preserved fragments and early drafts for the Walpurgisnacht scenes (Paralipomena first fully reprinted by Witkowski in 1894),[2] he attempts a plausible version of the work that he believes Goethe himself would have completed, but did not for reasons of editorial self-censorship when he anticipated reactive and prudish responses in his immediate and wider public.

In Schöne's "Walpurgisnacht" Faust and Mephistopheles join the crowds at the mountain peak. A triumphant Satan receives from his vassals the homage of anal adoration. Faust is in the audience for this solemnly conceived event and Mephisto serves as master of ceremonies. In the climactic black mass Satan holds his anti-Sermon on the Mount before consecrating the eucharistic vagina and phallus. Faust comes to within a hair's breadth of total ruin in his dance with the naked witch. It is all deadly earnest and he escapes with his soul intact because of the intervention of Gretchen's apparition. Schöne understands the Satanic mass to stand in rich and productive opposition to the "Prolog im Himmel," a Manichean counterposing of good and evil. The scene is the apotheosis of evil in the world and thus a profound demonstration of the power of Mephistopheles's world.

In introducing the interpretive problems posed by the Walpurgisnacht scenes, I have outlined Schöne's intriguing reconstruction in some detail because his work succeeds so well, in my judgment, in showing precisely the kind of Walpurgisnacht that Goethe purposefully did not write. While I do not intend in this essay to dispute Schöne overtly or on his own grounds—with an alternative reading of the Paralipomena and a debate on his methodological assumptions—I believe it is useful to stress from the outset some of the differences between the reading offered here and his reconstruction of Goethe's intentions. Quite apart from the methodological issue of when and to what purposes we as readers might favor an author's first sketches over his completed work—a not uninteresting question, actually—his work provides a powerful foil in terms of assessing the basic tenor of the two scenes. I am primarily interested in this essay in identifying a stylistic feature that both underlies and links various components of the scene—a kind of stylistic *basso continuo* of literal and physical reference, at once playful and earnest. I clearly disagree with Schöne on the basic question of how to read the sexual language in the text, and particularly in the Walpurgisnacht songs. Where he has seen a profound demonstration of a dangerously demonic sexuality, I see a kind of bawdiness that is meant to shock and excite, to amuse and finally to disappoint. Stated somewhat reductively: where Schöne asserts that Goethe depicts the apotheosis of evil and its vast dominion in the play, I am suggesting that the two Walpurgisnacht scenes are a dramatic display of a realist, materialist physicality underlying Mephisto's realm that is more revealing of its limits than its glory. (The difference cannot, of course, be explained by self-censorship.)

In reviewing the Faust legend, we realize that Goethe had no obligation to bring Faust into the Harz Mountains, nor any need to raise the spectre of the Witches' Sabbath. Admittedly he had to bridge a time period of some nine months before returning to Gretchen's plight in prison and we could argue he had to do this in a way that did not permanently disrupt the dramatic concern for her fate. But nothing in the Faust legend compelled Goethe to bring Faust to the Brocken on the eve of 1 May. Before Goethe only Johann Friedrich Löwen's mock epic "Die Walpurgis Nacht" (1756) had introduced Faust to the region.[3] In Löwen's poem Faust, invoked as magician and muse, is on the Blocksberg itself, a guest of Belzebub in the night of the revels. While I believe that Goethe's boyhood reading of Löwen is indeed the imaginative point of departure for his placement of Faust at the Walpurgisnacht,[4] the decision to bring Faust into the Harz Mountains in the drama is fully Goethe's own. He appears to do so specifically to counter the expectations about the journey that he himself has introduced into the text.

Furthermore, nothing in either the Faust legend or the Walpurgisnacht legends suggests why he might have identified the environs of the two small villages Schierke and Elend with surprising specificity as the geographic point of departure.

At the beginning of the scene Faust and Mephistopheles are not simply in the Harz Mountains, according to the stage directions, but in the "Gegend von Schierke und Elend" (WA I, 14:195). In a play generally lacking precise geographical settings the designation gives pause.[5] I have taken this small but willful site selection as my entree to the piece by asking what Goethe has gained by naming these two villages and placing Faust nearby. Although Schierke and Elend have neither a role within the Faust legend nor any distinctive identity in the traditional representations of Walpurgisnacht, as named sites they are put to good thematic use in the play. Furthermore, quite apart from the thematic ends, the very specificity of the setting, the exploitation of its literalness in terms physical and geographical as well as linguistic, serves a greater programmatic purpose.

It is well known that Goethe uses names thematically, both in *Faust* and in other works. Even when the names are not of his own creation, he frequently exploits their metaphorical or literary resonance. Examples include Mephistopheles, the spoiler and liar, Margarete, both pearl and flower, and Faust, the happy one, the fortunate one, who is explicitly identified in his distress in Act I of Part II as "der Unglücksmann" (4620).[6]

What of Schierke und Elend? The two villages, located half-way up the Brocken, at approximately 600 meters and 530 meters respectively, are linked by the Kalte Bode which runs through the connecting Elendstal. As early as 1407 the site where Schierke was later established was known as the "Stervedhall" or "Sterbetal"; in the 16th century the designation "uf dem Schiricken" that had referred to a particular stand of oaks was generalized: "dat Stervedhall, itzo das Schiereksche thal gnant. . . ."[7] As commentators have noted, in the opening scene Faust and Mephistopheles are still some two hours away from the top of the Brocken, the site of the revels. In Goethe's stage directions Schierke precedes Elend, but the sequence is misleading. If the path from Schierke to Elend were followed by a Harz hiker, it would lead away from the peak. The naming of Schierke along with Elend serves a purpose other than merely mapping the terrain: namely, to guarantee the geographical specificity for the claim that Faust is in Elend. At the root sense of the word, to be in Elend means to be in exile and Faust is indeed "in exilio": "in fremdem Land, aus dem Frieden der angeborenen Rechtsgenossenschaft ausgewiesen, verbannt."[8] Faust and Mephistopheles were last on stage in the scene that ended with Valentin's death. As Faust and the audience learned in Mephistopheles's final words, Mephisto anticipates a "Blutbann" (3715) will be issued. They must flee from the town and live "in exilio"–"in der Verbannung."

The secondary meaning of "Elend" as *miseria* is derivative. He who lives exiled lives in want, misery, and need. The literalness of Faust's "Elend," as opposed to its figurative meaning, is underscored in the contrast between Faust's fate and Gretchen's. He is "in Elend" only in the sense of physical banishment, as his presence near the village of that name underscores. Elend is a literal state and site. Gretchen, on the other hand, is presented in full-fledged misery. When Faust discovers her plight, her "Elend" is forcefully proclaimed. Although Gretchen's growing estrangement from her community began even before Valentin's death, it is not given its full name until Faust's outburst in "Trüber Tag. Feld." Previously we hear of her "Noth" in the prayers to the Mater dolorosa (3589, 3595, 3619); she decries her plight when she confronts her dying brother: "welche Noth!" (3721), "Welche Höllenpein!" (3770); and in the cathedral her distress is given liturgical formulation: "Quid sum miser tunc dicturus?" (3825, 3833; in German translation: Was soll ich Elender dann sagen?) The line of avowed misery is repeated just before she faints.

But the term "Elend" itself is absent from all these scenes and, apart from the stage direction "Gegend von Schierke und Elend," it is absent from the Walpurgisnacht scene and the Walpurgisnachtstraum as well. "Elend" is all the more vigorously reintroduced in the next scene "Trüber Tag. Feld" (WA I, 14:225–27). Indeed, the scene opens with Faust's angry exclamation: "Im Elend! Verzweifelnd! Erbärmlich auf der Erde lange verirrt und nun gefangen!" (l. 5–6) "Elend" is repeated emphatically three more times as he rails against her fate: "Gefangen! Im unwiederbringlichen Elend!" (l. 12–13) and again in his lament "daß mehr als ein Geschöpf in die Tiefe dieses Elendes versank" (l. 29–30). And finally: "Mir wühlt es Mark und Leben durch, das Elend dieser Einzigen" (l. 32–33). Gretchen has become the embodiment of "Elend."

Why the two contrasting states of "Elend," both linked to civic status of exile, but one decidedly descriptive of physical location and the other psychological trauma? One answer is Goethe's practiced repetitions throughout the play of complementary structures, events, and sequences that are set up to comment upon each other, a device already apparent in *Faust I*, whose full potential is realized in *Faust II*. A second is the irony of it all. Faust, "in Elend," appears to be anything but "im Elend." But his turn will come: "Elend" is, after all, the opposite of "Glückseligkeit," and his moment of misery will follow when he is proclaimed the "Unglücksmann" at the beginning of Part II. Third, the literalness of his "Elend," which contrasts so markedly with the metaphorically rich and fully lived anguish of Gretchen's experience, serves as a linguistic norm for a host of events within the Walpurgisnacht.

This third points demands elaboration. The programmatic purpose of this literalness, I suggest, is the revelation of Mephisto's world as assertively physical and materially bound. Despite its elaborate spectacle and its evocation of mounting excitement (flying witches, light and sound effects, and promise of mountain-top climaxes), the text serves finally as a reminder of the limitations of Mephisto's world. For a spirit world there is not much engaged spirit, indeed very little of anything that constitutes the avowed aims of Faust's quest: direct experience of the world in the fullness of its activity, or a flight to the heights that transcends the earth. Faust anticipates some kind of transcendent revelation at the heights of the revels, as he himself asserts: "Doch droben möcht' ich lieber sein! / . . . / Da muß sich manches Räthsel lösen" (4037, 4040). But he will be disappointed.

What he encounters, finally, is earthbound spectacle, and not very good spectacle, at that, as the dilettante theater of the "Walpurgisnachtstraum" underscores.

Faust's entire journey towards the top of the Brocken is unexpectedly earthbound. We recall from numerous previous passages the privileged metaphor of flight, of soaring, of rising above and Faust's frustrated attempts to experience the transcendence he longs for. The speech on Easter Sunday in the late afternoon in "Vor dem Tor" as he watches the setting sun is explicit (the scene was written at about the same time as "Walpurgisnacht"):

> O daß kein Flügel mich vom Boden hebt,
> Ihr nach und immer nach zu streben! (1074–75)

In the Walpurgisnacht scene the "heben" in question is decidedly more material, more physical in its reference. The witches' song provides multiple examples that introduce a series of sexual puns, double entendres, and innuendoes.

> Wer heute sich nicht heben kann,
> Ist ewig ein verlorner Mann. (4002–3)

A comparison with Dryden is instructive. In one of his dramatic works a character proclaims: "I cannot come aloft to an old woman."[9] And there is a song in *Marriage A-la-Mode*[10] in which the young shepherd Alexis's mounting physical pleasure is likened to a tempest that releases his "soul" in flight (his soul is, of course, not the issue):

> He found the fierce pleasure too hasty to stay,
> And his soul in the tempest just flying away. (Act IV, ii)

We also have Goethe's own example from his poem "Das Tagebuch":

> Doch Meister Iste hat nun seine Grillen
> Und läßt sich nicht befehlen noch verachten,
> Auf einmal ist er da, und ganz im Stillen
> Erhebt er sich zu allen seinen Prachten. (WA I, 5.2:349)

In the Witches' entry song in *Faust* coming aloft is the purpose of the journey up the Brocken. Sexual double entendres fill the presentation of their flight to the mountain peak: flying, soaring, little steps and single spurts.[11]

Der flieget nie, der heut nicht flog. (4011)

Ich tripple nach, so lange Zeit;
Wie sind die andern schon so weit! (4004–5)

The Male Chorus in antiphony:

Wir schleichen wie die Schneck' im Haus,
Die Weiber alle sind voraus.
Denn, geht es zu des Bösen Haus,
Das Weib hat tausend Schritt voraus. (3978–81)

The answering stanza:

Wir nehmen das nicht so genau,
Mit tausend Schritten macht's die Frau;
Doch, wie sie auch sich eilen kann,
Mit Einem Sprunge macht's der Mann. (3982–85)

"So Ehre denn, wem Ehre gebührt! / Frau Baubo vor! und angeführt!" (3964–65). In this landscape of literalness Baubo serves as the physical reduction of "das Ewig-Weibliche." There is no need in this Harzreise for what Theodore Ziolkowski describes as the archetypal *regressis ad uterum*, the Romantic descent "into the tellurian depths of Mother Earth."[12] In the Walpurgisnacht it is all exposed, just like Baubo's signature gesture.[13] Erections and broom sticks, stoppers to plug the open hole—this is the promise of the Walpurgisnacht songs.

But it is all fundamentally ironic, of course, a lot of sound and fury signifying nothing, or at least nothing for Faust. The desire to fly to the peak of the Brocken—even when aided by all the witches' salves, broomsticks and incantations—brings one no farther than one might have laboriously climbed on foot. Once more magic is not supernatural, just a short cut within the natural world, as Jane K. Brown has repeatedly asserted.[14] And as Faust exclaims at the beginning of the scene: "Was hilfts, daß man den Weg verkürzt!" (3840).[15]

Furthermore, once arrived, one is not above the earth at all, but still firmly on it. The notion that one has transcended is illusory. In *Faust II*, Act IV Mephistopheles drives home the point that the highest peaks are but the ruptured ceiling of the Old Hell (10075–94)—in other words, of his world, understood in the most traditional sense. The peak experience provided by this particular landscape is the fulfillment of earthbound pleasure. Underneath the spectacle and mounting excitement it is a world as physical, material and literal as found anywhere in the text.

But a final irony must be noted. Faust does not reach the top; he doesn't go all the way. The scene ends anti-climactically with a piece of dilettante theater.

There is the final insistent substitution of a "Hügelchen" for the Brocken: "Komm doch das Hügelchen heran" (4210). At best he has reached "Heinrichshöhe,"[16] the plateau below the final peak that Goethe has Mephistopheles identify as one of the familiar and stable sites within the Harz Mountains in the midst of his discomfort in the Classical Walpurgisnacht:

> Auf seiner *Höh* wird *Heinrich* munter sein,
> Die *Schnarcher* schnauzen zwar das *Elend* an,
> Doch alles ist für tausend Jahr gethan. (7681–83)

In Part II Goethe makes explicit the kind of geographical punning that runs as a private joke beneath the surface of the opening songs in the Walpurgisnacht. Like "Heinrichshöhe," the "Schnarcher" are there in Part I, too, but not explicitly named. The granite outcroppings with their protruding rock-noses are indirectly evoked in the "Wechselgesang" sung by Faust, Mephistopheles and the Irrlicht: "Und die langen Felsennasen, / Wie sie schnarchen, wie sie blasen!" (3879–80).

Heinrich is, of course, anything but vigorously cheery ("munter") at the heights he achieves. He has to be coaxed repeatedly along the way.

> Komm nur! von Feuer gehen wir zu Feuer,
> Ich bin der Werber, und du bist der Freier. (4070–71)

It is indeed Mephisto's insistent refrain: "Komm, komm."[17]

> 4029 Komm, komm! wir schlupfen da hinein
> 4052 Komm mit! Komm mit! Es kann nicht anders sein
> 4070 Komm nur! von Feuer gehen wir zu Feuer
> 4127 Es geht zum neuen Tanz; nun komm! wir greifen zu
> 4210 Komm doch das Hügelchen heran

"Fassen," "packen," "zugreifen"—Mephisto's imperative is clear:[18]

> 3912 Fasse wacker meinen Zipfel!
> 3938 Du mußt des Felsens alte Rippen packen
> 4127 Nun komm! Wir greifen zu

Nowhere but in the Walpurgisnacht, where he is so decidedly "Herr von Haus" (3866) and able to claim his "Hausrecht" (4022) has the urgent physicality of his invitation been so evident. Correspondingly, it is only here, where he asserts he is "ehrenvoll zu Haus" (4065), that Mephistopheles identifies himself in a literal, physical manner by means of his cloven hoof. (In the "Hexenküche" its absence provokes specific comment [2490] and he merely walks with a limp in Auerbach's Keller [2184].) The physical is proclaimed the real in the Walpurgisnacht.

The linguistic materiality of the scene is initially meant to titillate in its bawdy allusions and to shock in its moments of vulgarity and eventually it bores in its earthbound inability to do little more than distract the senses and lull the mind. In fact, the Walpurgisnacht has proven to be intensely full of very ordinary distracting things, as Mephistopheles makes explicit:

> Man tanzt, man schwatzt, man kocht, man trinkt, man liebt;
> Nun sage mir, wo es was Bessers gibt? (4058–59)

As an awareness of Gretchen's "Elend" dawns, Faust finds his own angry name for the revels: "Und mich wiegst du indeß in abgeschmackten Zerstreuungen" (l. 14–15). By this point the theater audience and the play's reader have also been both distracted by the scene's initial promise and irritated by its diminishing spectacle.

After Faust's ranting and railing against him in "Trüber Tag. Feld," Mephisto asks pointedly: "Willst fliegen und bist vor'm Schwindel nicht sicher?" (l. 39–40) A desire to fly is indeed Mephisto's interpretive summary of all that initially drove Faust from his study and into the Gretchen Tragedy. But like all the verbs with sexual potential—such as "fliegen," "sich heben," "zugreifen"—the terms span the range in the drama from the purely physical and material to the fully spiritual and abstracted. The subsequent repetition of the terms in the Helena scene and the final "Bergschluchten," in particular, gives the lie to the limits set by the celebrations of the emphatically realist world of the Walpurgisnacht. The witches may sing:

> Wer heute sich nicht heben kann
> Ist ewig ein verlorner Mann. (4002–3)

But after metamorphozing into a cloud Helena's clothing does carry Faust aloft. Mephisto himself gives him direction:

> . . . Bediene dich der hohen,
> Unschätzbaren Gunst und hebe dich empor,
> Es trägt dich über alles Gemeine rasch
> Am Aether hin, so lange du dauern kannst. (9950–53)

The Mater Gloriosa directs the Gretchen-penitent at the end of *Faust II*:

> Komm! hebe dich zu höhern Sphären,
> Wenn er dich ahnet, folgt er nach. (12094–95)

The Walpurgisnacht is simply the fullest manifestation of the ascent that is possible within Mephistopheles's world of the real—the physical, sexual, material aspects of existence. It serves as a reminder of Mephisto's limitations; a parody of Dante's Vergil, he is a guide who can only ascend so far. Indeed he never leaves the earth.

Nothing finally is very lofty at the Walpurgisnacht revels. Puck, the phallic nature spirit, plops himself down as the one most at home at the end of the play. The spirits, we are told, need space because they have "plumpe Glieder" (4386). Only Ariel departs, calling to any who might have wings to follow him at dawn to the Rosenhügel, an apparent alternative not only to the Blocksberg, but also the "Hügelchen" that is the theater site for the dilettante performance.

This particular theater offers a slight lift at best. In Löwen's "Walpurgis Nacht" Belzebub proclaims himself patron to a series of marginal authors, "halblahm, zerquetscht und matt," led by "Bav, der Apollen nie gekannt und nie gesehn" and who is unable to ride Pegasus without falling off (he cannot even stay on the goat he is riding to the Brocken ceremonies and arrives with a broken leg).[19] Although not explicitly called "Blocksbergsdichter" in Löwen's text, their ilk are the obvious reference of the term that seems to have entered general literary parlance by the late 1790's. In a letter from Johann Ludwig Gleim to Johann Heinrich Voß (23 January 1798) Gleim writes: "Neulich las ich. . . eine Stelle. . . und fand sie so platt, daß ein Blocksbergsdichter sie hätte machen können."[20] The piece in question is Goethe's *Hermann und Dorothea*, and Gleim, still smarting from Goethe's and Schiller's attacks in the *Xenien*, privately perpetuates the feud. In his dilettante theatrical performance at the close of the Walpurgisnacht Goethe appropriates Löwen's mock heroic representation of such "fiendish" action in the world—a flood of mediocre writing and a spate of literary quarrels is its product.[21] Mephistopheles greets those responsible for the play:

> Wenn ich euch auf dem Blocksberg finde,
> Das find' ich gut; denn da gehört ihr hin. (4221–22)

In his writings with Schiller on dilettantism Goethe is emphatically dismissive of dilettante theater. There is little in it for the performer and absolutely nothing for the audience.[22] Not only is the theater at the Walpurgisnacht revels explicitly identified as dilettante theater: "Ein Dilettant hat es geschrieben, / Und Dilettanten spielen's auch. / . . . / Mich dilettiert's den Vorhang aufzuziehn" (4217–18, 4220); Faust is nothing more than a distracted member of the audience. The problem with dilettante theater, Goethe summarizes, is that it lacks "Idealität": "Zerstörte Idealität der Kunst, weil der Liebhaber, der sich nicht durch Aneignung der Kunstbegriffe und Traditionen erheben kann, alles durch eine pathologische Wirklichkeit erreichen muß" (WA I, 47:316). Within the real-ideal opposition that underlies all of *Faust*, including the fun and seriousness of the Walpurgisnacht, dilettante theater is emphatically of the real, without any "Idealität der Kunst."

The Walpurgisnacht ends not with a revelatory bang but a whimper, fizzling away with the dawn. In one of his early sketches for the scene Goethe considered using a volcanic eruption to disperse the crowd after midnight (WA I, 14:305).

But rather than present an entire landscape in upheaval, in the final version he restricted the flashing display to the opening sequence. Pausing on his climb Faust views the subterranean volcanic seething that objectifies both potential riches and mounting sexual interest.

> Wie seltsam glimmert durch die Gründe
> Ein morgenröthlich trüber Schein! (3916–17)

(Mammon lighting up his palace, Mephistopheles comments, stressing repeatedly the hidden wealth to be disclosed in the night). Anticipating the approach of Walpurgisnacht, Mephistopheles had hinted that the Harz revels would yield both treasure and pleasure—gold and sex in their most fundamental forms. But the flickering light that suggested the buried treasure from afar in "Nacht" (3664–65) proves to be one in a series of enticements that fail to redeem their promise. Just as the sex proves to be innuendo without fulfillment, Mammon's treasure remains pure visual display. Faust may compare the fiery sparks to gold:

> Da sprühen Funken in der Nähe,
> Wie ausgestreuter goldner Sand. (3928–29)

But the only treasure found in the mountains is what Mephisto foresaw with his extended sight and stated with masterful equivocation: "so ein Ding, / Als wie eine Art von Perlenschnüren" (3672–73). They appear on the Gretchen apparition near the end of the scene: "Wie sonderbar muß diesen schönen Hals / Ein einzig rothes Schnürchen schmücken, / Nicht breiter als ein Messerrücken!" (4203–5). Red pearls for Margarete, Faust's final gift to her. There is no rich supply of gold in the Harz Mountains, as Goethe knew, but a lot of mica ("Glimmer") in the granite.[23]

The counterpart of this scene that fades at dawn with all its disappointments is not the "Prolog im Himmel" as Schöne would have it appear in his rewritten text. Rather, its opposite number is the scene "Vor dem Tor," as it now stands, the scene that ended at sunset and introduced Mephisto to Faust's world. There all of Faust's thoughts of rising above the earth, transcending the world that confines him, are confessed to be disembodied cerebral musings: "O daß kein Flügel mich vom Boden hebt / . . . / Ach! zu des Geistes Flügeln wird so leicht / Kein körperlicher Flügel sich gesellen" (1074, 1090–91). Mephisto appears to offer him physical transport, a lift of sorts:

> Ein bißchen Feuerluft, die ich bereiten werde,
> Hebt uns behend von dieser Erde.
> Und sind wir leicht, so geht es schnell hinauf;
> Ich gratuliere dir zum neuen Lebenslauf. (2069–72)

The flight from the prison of the scholar's cell leads to Gretchen's cell—both to her room and her dungeon, to previously unknown pleasures and deepest misery for both of them. All this would have been impossible without Mephistopheles—for better and for worse. His world, as Goethe evokes it in *Faust I*, is essential—anything but demonically evil in a traditional sense. But it is also utterly realist and materialist in its values, occasionally funny and often destructive in its deficiencies. One of the principal consequences of Faust's journey into the Harz Mountains in the Walpurgisnacht is the revelation of its limits in a symbolic patterning that begins with a literal Elend and moves to fully lived misery.

NOTES

1. Schöne 109–230.

2. Georg Witkowski, *Die Walpurgisnacht im ersten Teil von Goethes Faust* (Leipzig: Biedermann, 1894). Paralipomena in Witkowski, 67–88; in WA I, 14:296–311 with some omissions. See also Siegfried Scheibe, "Zur Entstehungsgeschichte der Walpurgisnacht im Faust I" in Scheibe et al., *Goethe-Studien*, Sitzungsberichte der deutschen Akademie der Wissenschaften zu Berlin (Berlin: Akademie Verlag, 1965) 7–61.

3. Johann Friedrich Löwen, "Die Walpurgis Nacht: Ein Gedicht in drey Gesängen," in *Poetische Werke* (Hamburg und Leipzig: Grunds Witwe und Holle, 1760) 1:275–334. I am grateful to Cyrus Hamlin, Yale University, and Christa Sammons, Curator of the Yale Collection of German Literature, Beinecke Library, for making the text available to me. Georg von Gynz-Rekowski, *Brocken: Historie, Heimat, Humor*, ed. Uwe Gerig, Die grüne Reihe (Königstein/Ts.: Gerig Verlag, 1991) 60–61, 139, surveys other tentative connections between Faust and the Harz region. In the *Faustbuch* Faust visits in Halberstadt; in a derivative variant on the legend Wagner makes a pact with the devil on the Brocken. In at least two entries into the *Brockenbuch* (1768, 1776), Harz wanderers evoke Faust.

4. In *Dichtung und Wahrheit*, Book 6, Löwen's poem is used by Goethe's Frankfurt friends, together with Zachariä's *Renommisten*, as a measure of poetic excellence (WA I, 27:38).

5. Only the scene in Auerbach's Keller is sited with similar specificity, a choice motivated by legendary links between Faust and the tavern that enabled Goethe to use the scene to recreate a moment in the formation of the Faust legend and thus describe a scene of origins to mark the beginnings of Faust's adventures in the world.

6. Manfred Beller, "Gretchens Name und die Tradition der 'heiligen Sünderin,' " paper read at "Faust through Four Centuries. Retrospect and Analysis," a 1987 symposium at Indiana University; Hans Arens, *Kommentar zu Goethes Faust I*, Beiträge zur neueren Literaturgeschichte: Folge 3, Bd. 57 (Heidelberg: Carl Winter Universitätsverlag, 1982) 49; Jane K. Brown, "Mephistopheles the Nature Spirit," *Studies in Romanticism* 24 (1985): 481–82.

7. Georg von Gynz-Rekowski, *Schierke: Historie, Heimat, Humor*, Die grüne Reihe (Königstein/Ts.: Gerig Verlag, 1991) 7–11; cf. E[duard] Jacobs, "Zur geschichtlichen Ortskunde des Brockengebiets," *Zeitschrift des Harz-Vereins für Geschichte und Alterthumskunde* 28 (1895): 362–70.

8. "Elend" in Gerhard Wahrig, ed., *Deutsches Wörterbuch* (Gütersloh: Bertelsmann Verlag, 1970) 1064. Cf. "Elend" in Jacob and Wilhelm Grimm, *Deutsches Wörterbuch* (Leipzig: S. Hirzel, 1862) 3: 406–11.

9. R.W. Holder, *A Dictionary of American and British Euphemisms* (Bath: Bath University Press, 1987) 43.

10. *The Works of John Dryden*, ed. Edward Niles Hooker and Hugh Thomas Swedenberg, Jr. (Berkeley: University of California Press, 1956ff.) 11:285.

11. Schöne calls attention to the sexual significance of the "Schritten" and "Sprung" in the Male chorus (135). Harry G. Haile, *Invitation to Goethe's Faust*, Studies in the Humanities, 21 (University, Alabama: University of Alabama Press, 1978) 96 suggests in passing that many of the single-voiced stanzas present examples of sexual psychosis.

12. Theodore Ziolkowski, *German Romanticism and its Institutions* (Princeton: Princeton University Press, 1990) 51.

13. Alfred Zastrau, "Baubo," in *Goethe Handbuch: Goethe, seine Welt und Zeit in Werk und Wirkung*, ed. Alfred Zastrau (Stuttgart: Metzler, 1961) 1:837–39; Maurice Olender, "Baubo," in Mircea Eliade, ed., *Encyclopedia of Religion* (New York: Macmillan, 1987) 2:83–84.

14. Brown 23, 68, 85–86.

15. A similar notion is expressed in the poem "The Perfect Enjoyment" in *The Anthology of Restoration Erotic Poetry*, ed. Ed Cray (North Hollywood: Brandon House, 1965) 98. The lovers mount Pleasure's Hill:

> Still thither our unwearied wishes tend
> Till we that height of happiness ascend
> By gentle steps; the ascent itself exceeds
> All joys, but that alone to which it leads.

16. Heinrichshöhe was named by Count Christian Ernst zu Stolberg-Wernigerode (1710–1771) after his son Heinrich Ernst. See Ed[uard] Jacobs, "Der Brocken und sein Gebiet," *Zeitschrift des Harz-Vereins für Geschichte und Alterthumskunde* 4 (1871): 154.

17. A parallel enticement with new urgency but without success will echo later from Gretchen's cell:

> 4479 Komm mit! Komm mit!
> 4498 Komm! Folge mir!
> 4502 Ich bin's! Komm mit!
> 4506 Komm! komm! Schon weicht die tiefe Nacht.

Physical rescue has little meaning in her anguish. Gretchen cannot simply be led out of her "Elend," as she stresses in her response to Faust:

> Ich darf nicht fort; für mich ist nichts zu hoffen.
> Was hilft es fliehn? Sie lauern doch mir auf.
> Es ist so elend betteln zu müssen,
> Und noch dazu mit bösem Gewissen!

Es ist so elend in der Fremde schweifen,
Und sie werden mich doch ergreifen! (4544–49)

18. Mephisto's terms are echoed and turned back on him in the taunt of the Lamien in the Classical Walpurgisnacht:

Versuch' es doch! sind unsrer viele.
Greif' zu! Und hast du Glück im Spiele,
Erhasche dir das beste Loos.
Was soll das lüsterne Geleier?
Du bist ein miserabler Freier. (7760–64)

19. Löwen, Gesang 2, lines 225–34; Gesang 3, line 347.

20. *Goethe in vertraulichen Briefen seiner Zeitgenossen. Zusammengestellt von Wilhelm Bode*, rev. ed. Regine Otto and Paul Gerhard Wenzlaff (München: C.H. Beck, 1982) 2:124. In conversation with Kanzler Müller 14 December 1808 Goethe indicates that Voß is a possible addition to the group on the Blocksberg. See Ernst Grumach, ed., *Kanzler von Müller: Unterhaltungen mit Goethe* (Weimar: Hermann Böhlaus Nachfolger, 1956) 7. For other "Blocksbergs-Candidaten" see Paralipomenon 47 (WA I, 14:304–5).

21. Löwen, Gesang 3, lines 331–34.

22. The term "Dilettant" has considerable range in the writings of Goethe and his contemporaries, and cannot simply be assumed to be negative. See H[ans] Rudolf Vaget "Der Dilettant: Eine Skizze der Wort- und Bedeutungsgeschichte," *Jahrbuch der deutschen Schillergesellschaft* 14 (1970): 131–58. In their programmatic studies on dilettantism (the portion on amateur theatrics is dated 26 May 1799 and thus provides a judgment more or less contemporaneous with the writing of the "Walpurgisnachtstraum"), Goethe and Schiller have initially placed a "0" under the category "Nutzen" "fürs Ganze" in their evaluation of "Schauspielkunst." Having made this categorical denial of value, they elaborate the circumstances under which some benefit may possibly be derived from amateur theatrics despite the lengthy entry under the rubric "Schaden" (WA I, 47:316). Vaget explores possible reasons for this uncharacteristically sharply negative criticism in *Dilettantismus und Meisterschaft. Zum Problem des Dilettantismus bei Goethe: Praxis, Theorie, Zeitkritik* (München: Winkler-Verlag, 1971) 177–83.

23. Friedrich Leopold von Stolberg's ode "Der Harz" (published in the *Göttinger Musenalmanach auf das Jahr 1774*) specifically commends the region for largely escaping the curse of gold. In particular the area around Schierke, however, was associated with alchemists and treasure hunters, and secret reports purported to describe the location of hidden gold and silver. Cf. Ed[uard] Jacobs, "Johann Christian Ruberg: Ein Beitrag zur Geschichte der Goldmacherei am Harz," *Zeitschrift des Harz-Vereins für Geschichte und Alterthumskunde* 21 (1888): 131–58, esp. 132–35. See also Arens (note 6) 379–80.

SIMON WILLIAMS

Performing Mephistopheles

As a THEATERGOER FOR SOME DECADES in Germany, America and Britain, I have always been struck by two differences between the German and Anglo-American theaters. One is seemingly trivial, the other definitely substantial.

The seemingly trivial difference concerns the programs one buys in the foyer. In Germany such programs are booklets, generally composed of a series of essays—critical, dramaturgical, and philosophical—centered around the themes of the play and the historical context from which they arise. If the patron wishes to discover who is performing, such information will quite likely only be found with difficulty, perhaps in a flyer inserted in an obscure part of the booklet. Information about the performers usually comprises, however, the main content of theater programs in America and Britain. They include primarily detailed biographies of everyone involved in the production from all actors, leading and supporting, to principal and occasionally secondary technicians. Apart from the odd dramaturgical note, essays in Anglo-American programs are as likely to be about wine, fashion, or the condition of local real estate as about the stage-work to be performed.

The substantial difference between the German and Anglo-American theaters concerns Shakespeare. I have often found it disconcerting to attend a performance of Shakespeare in Britain or America soon after seeing his plays performed in Germany. In contrast to the Germans, Anglo-American actors can seem disturbed, embarrassed even, by the stark angularity, extreme psychic states, and strong poetry of Shakespeare's characters. All too frequently, by the exploitation of decorous underplaying and of elegant cadences in their delivery of the verse, Shakespeare in Anglo-American hands can lack theatrical excitement.

After several years ruminating on these differences, the experience of performing Mephistopheles unexpectedly led me toward a deeper understanding of them.

I did not approach the task of performing Mephisto with much assurance. The sheer length of the role is intimidating and its complexity baffling. My confidence was not given much of a boost when, in the course of research on something else, I came across a letter by Josef Kainz referring to Hamlet and Mephistopheles as the two greatest challenges to the actor in world theater. Once engaged in learning and rehearsing the role, doubts as to my capacity increased even further as I realized that what little training I have received in acting would be of virtually no aid at all. The problem was this: In much English-language actor-training, actors are encouraged, for good or ill, to think of dramatic character in the same terms that they think of human beings in everyday life. They search for a psychological consistency that gives the character individuality and are encouraged to create for each character an imaginative past that accounts for that individuality.

But, in the representation of Mephistopheles, and I venture to say of most, probably all other characters in *Faust*, such an approach is distinctly for ill rather than good. In his behavior, Mephisto has no consistency. In the earliest rehearsals I quickly discovered that the character had myriad ways of expressing himself. In speaking to the Lord, the most appropriate tone is defiance and coarse mockery, but in persuading Faust to enter into the wager, Mephisto's sophistry is offset by a strong undertone of existential despair. Throughout Part I, Mephisto assumes in turn the guises of society galant, loyal manservant, *bon viveur*, pious guide and Lord of Misrule. In Part II, the character goes through a medley of even more confusing changes, ending ultimately in a frenzy of nihilistic denial.

Such inconsistency in behavior is not, of course, unusual in drama, as what *are* dramatic characters composed of if not their masks? But unity, one feels, should be found. Accordingly, I read the role for hints that would allow me to reconstruct the past of the character, in the expectation that if that past is coherent and communicated effectively, unity among the disparate masks of the role would emerge. But Mephisto has no past, or rather, if he does have one, it is not a personal one, it is general. It is, in fact, the history of the universe, and that is so immense, it has nothing to offer the actor.

Absorbed as I was with the sheer logistics of learning the role and becoming familiar with its moment-to-moment dynamics, it was not until we were half-way through the six-week rehearsal period that I even started to develop a clear awareness of this problem. Once I had reached this point, the initial step toward reaching a solution struck me as simply to allow the salient features of the role that emerged in our adaptation to rise to consciousness. What first struck me in the adaptation we were using was that our Mephisto did have one character trait that remained consistent throughout Parts I and II, this being his obsession with sex; not with sex in practice, but with sex as a spectator. Mephisto is the voyeur supreme, though while in Part I he positively revels in this prurience, in Part II, faced with a realm of existence that openly acknowledges, even celebrates carnality, he becomes increasingly uneasy. Not only did this perception of warped sexuality provide me with a whole range of attitudes and tones particular to such a personality, ranging from obscene gestures to hideously nasal gibbering, it also invested the role with its basic form. Part I sees the rise of Mephisto to a peak of control; Faust's sexual confusion and the Gothic environment that stands in part as a metaphor for it, provides a milieu in which Mephisto is entirely at home. The chaos he creates by the unleashing of sexuality is complete. In Part II, the classical Walpurgis Night and Helena sequences, which were the central episodes of our version, initiate a decline in the potency of Mephisto's influence over Faust, suitably preparing for his downfall and expulsion by the Lord and his angels. While specific concern with Mephisto's sexuality dissolves at the end of the play—or at least it did in our version as Peter Lackner prudently cut those passages where Mephisto betrays his attraction to the cherubim—the theme allowed me to give clear contours and body to a role that can all too easily lose itself in formlessness and abstractions.

The second salient feature of the role suggested itself through certain lines that, once I had learnt them, haunted me. They are the last words Mephisto speaks to Faust before the seduction of Gretchen and they stand, therefore, as the inciting moment to the main crisis of the play. Mephisto has eavesdropped on Faust and Gretchen and mocks her for telling Faust of her dislike for him, Mephisto.

> Und die Physiognomie versteht sie meisterlich:
> In meiner Gegenwart wird's ihr, sie weiß nicht wie,
> Mein Mäskchen da weissagt verborgnen Sinn;
> Sie fühlt, daß ich ganz sicher ein Genie,
> Vielleicht wohl gar der Teufel bin.

In Stuart Atkins's translation, these lines are imaginatively rendered as follows:

> And what a physiognomist she is!
> My presence fills her with the strangest feelings;
> she reads deep meanings in my ugly face
> and senses that I am some sort of radical,
> perhaps, in fact, the very devil.

The passage ran in my head like a demonic jingle. Perhaps they had a particular appeal because, in my job as a theater historian, I was, and indeed still am, engaged in a study of the Romantic actor as an expression of the revolutionary consciousness of early nineteenth-century Europe. But these lines became vital too to my understanding of Mephisto, as they directed me to a nexus of ideas that could be centered in his character. He embodies the spirit of total disorder, which, when viewed in the context of the decades over which *Faust* was written, manifested itself above all in the French Revolution, an event toward which Goethe expressed the greatest antipathy.

The idea of disorder transforming itself into revolution and Mephisto as the spirit of that revolution was strengthened by one of those felicitous coincidences that occur in most successful theatrical undertakings. Early in rehearsals the costume shop handed me an old hat that was to be used solely in rehearsals. The hat and I instantly became intimate companions. I have never known a hat so easy to handle, nor one that fit so snugly on my head with no danger of ever coming off. Best of all, it was a tricorn, one of the most characteristic pieces of headwear from the French Revolution. So close did we become, I insisted on keeping the hat in performance, though it did acquire a flamboyant red feather that perhaps gave it a quasi-aristocratic air. Nevertheless, whatever confusion this may have caused in the semiotics of the production, the passage on the devil as political radical and my love affair with the tricorned hat encouraged me to consider as crucial structural points in my interpretation all those moments in which Mephisto undermines the *status quo*. As these occur throughout the role, the unity of the character came to reside in his destructiveness as expressed in the revolutionary language of the time. Mephisto as the mocker of the Lord, the scourge of the priesthood, the abuser of the aristocracy, the subverter of family values, established itself as the preeminent image in my imagination. The specifically temporal aspects of this conception pointed constantly to Mephisto's principal function in the action of the play as a whole. For Mephisto, whatever is should not be. As he says to Faust at their first meeting, "This awkward world, this Something. . . confronts as foe my Nothing."

Here lay the ultimate challenge of the role, which is formally impossible for the actor, how to present "Nothing" out of the distinct "Something" of one's body and presence. At this point I realized that the very lack of a past was an asset rather than a liability. Mephisto is nothing but roles, nothing but masks, nothing but the appearance necessary to destroy the actuality, the "Something" of the world. To embody such "Nothing" on stage, one does not need psychological consistency, instead the dramatic truth of each role adopted by Mephisto is determined by the specifically destructive or subversive function it plays in each separate scene, is determined too, one might say, by its very discontinuity. In representing the various masks of the character, one temptation had to be avoided. It was entirely inappropriate to fall back on the cliches of the nineteenth-century stage villain that are so tempting in a role such as Mephisto. Such villainy, after all, implies consistent purpose toward a predefined, tangible goal. Conventional villainy implies substance, something Mephisto does not have. Consequently, the opposite of villainy, good humor, is as germane to the role as villainy. Indeed, in the gap between the masks of good humor and villainy, and between the several other facets of the character, the nothingness, the actuality of Mephisto exists.

As any attitude, from active malignity to the highest good humor could only be a passing mood in the role, the solution to presenting Mephisto's "Nothing" ultimately came to reside in steeping the whole role with the spirit of play. At only one point in the drama does Mephisto express, I think, without irony, a personal truth, and that is in his culminatory outburst of nihilism over Faust's corpse at the end of Part II. Up to this point, everything is a game, a more or less confident playing with appearances as the situation dictates. Such play by its very nature challenges entrenched values and beliefs, lightness suggests the ephemerality of everything permanent.

This concept of Mephisto as the supreme player, the skilled actor, provided me, however, with a very personal challenge. Both on and off stage I am not entirely lacking in a sense of humor, but I am congenitally incapable of playing light comedy—the witty heroes of the comedy of manners from the Renaissance through to Noel Coward and Tom Stoppard elude me entirely. I place a heavy boot where the lightest of footfalls is called for. Consequently, Mephisto as the player of roles, the revealer of the ephemerality of all that exists, was in danger of eluding me.

Goethe, however, came to my rescue. One of the great strengths of *Faust*, both Parts I and II, lies in the boldness of the dramatic writing, in stark stylistic contrasts between different passages, and in the overt theatricality of the whole. I have no doubt that Goethe was right when he claimed, in defiance of most subsequent critical commentary, that he wrote Part II with the theater in mind. Indeed, in both parts, the actor who plays Mephisto is encouraged to adopt broad gestures and strongly defined stances, to exploit his vocal range to the fullest, and to endow the role with a deliberate theatricality. Seamlessness, decorousness, wholeness of characterization, elegance of demeanor and beautiful delivery—all elements of a classical theater—are inappropriate. Vigorous and often rough characterization, a broad and earthy sense of humor, and above all no attempt to make a seamless whole of the role are what Mephisto requires.

I was abetted in my endeavors by the production itself, which was the apogee of rough theater. For us as performers and I think for audiences as well, the great surprise of the production was the range of dramatic modes we discovered in Goethe's text. It displays an extraordinarily varied comedy ranging from the witty repartee of intellectual debate, through harsh social satire to the benign pleasantries of folk comedy and frequently, of course, it spills over into the most supreme comedy of all, blithe revelling in total nonsense. In this drama, which violates all canons of neoclassical decorum, comedy coexists with the pathetic and the two vitalize each other. In the rough theater such a drama invites, no accommodation needs to be made between different modes of dramatic language, indeed their very incompatibility is the life of the performance. The unmediated stylistic contrasts of our production therefore also suited precisely my own conception of the character. Fortunately for me, they mercifully disguised my shortcomings as an actor.

To return to my original observations on the nature of theater programs and Shakespeare in the German and English-language theaters. The focus on biography in Anglo-American programs suggests that performance is to be regarded as an extension of the actor's personality, that the combined personal and theatrical experience of the actor is a vital ingredient in the chemistry of a successful production. It presupposes too that dramatic character by definition projects an illusion of continuity in time, of growth, of personal wholeness. Given such presuppositions which are, I must stress, far from negligible, it is not surprising that the classic dramatists Anglo-American actors seem most at home in are Ibsen, Chekhov and others in a realistic tradition. My experience of playing

Mephistopheles has suggested to me that dramatic character as the nexus of ideas may, when necessary, take precedence over character as recreation of real-life personality. Hence in the German theater, where such a priority is more readily acceptable than in the English-language theater, the tendency to provide audiences with programs that provide detailed documentation and lengthy discussions of the play as historical artifact.

Playing Mephistopheles has enriched my understanding of the German Shakespeare too. *Faust*, like many, perhaps most of Shakespeare's plays, is a work of conflicting modes and these modes are usually most effectively staged when no attempt is made to hide the conflict, when the fissures in the piece are openly acknowledged, even become the subject of representation. Shakespeare's characters are possibly more life-like than Goethe's and they are less schematically an embodiment of ideas or of symbolic experience beyond the purely human. Nevertheless, and this is where I suggest German actors have an advantage over their Anglo-American colleagues, the extreme states of mind—suffering, aspiration, ecstasy, terror, exhilaration—that are the essence of Shakespeare's central characters, cannot easily be realized by an actor concerned primarily with psychological consistency. The German actor, to whom wholeness of character is not always a prime consideration, is freer to leap at once to extremes and can therefore take the Shakespearean character to levels of stimulating excess that the English-speaking actor achieves only with difficulty.

The prime fallacy in the broader reaches of my argument is, of course, that I am proving a point from the example of one character in one play. Not all plays in the mainstream German repertoire require an approach to character such as the one I have outlined—Schiller and Grillparzer for example may well call for a more rounded and consistent approach to characterization; furthermore, the later naturalists obviously require a more psychologically consistent approach. But *Faust* also stands in a distinguishing mainstream of German theater. I will leave it to you to determine what other plays and other roles might support or challenge this personal argument, which arises from the memorable experience of performing Goethe's greatest dramatic creation.

Simon Williams, Mephistopheles; Robert G. Egan as Faust

THE ETERNAL FEMININE

Hannelore Schlaffer

Paradies und Parodie: Die letzten Szenen in
Goethes letzten Werken

Paradise and Parody: The Final Scenes in Goethe's Late Works

*Characteristic of Goethe's works written after 1800 are the blissful conclusions with which the
author ends the sufferings of his figures. Visions of paradise, reconciliation, and the reunion
of lovers frequently read as parody. These astonishingly consistent conclusions are actually the
product of an artistic dilemma: Goethe's recognition that his poetic language belongs to the world
of the senses and thus is incapable of depicting the divine (or the absolute of Platonic origin or
any other metaphysical infinity). Parody functions as a kind of negative theology allowing
expression. In the final lines of Faust II the closing parody takes a confessional turn: in a negative
aesthetic of hope, the parody of paradise is the admission that there would not be a paradise
if poetry were capable of speaking about it.*

Ein Merkmal des Goetheschen Werkes nach 1800 ist das selige Ende, mit dem
der Autor das Leiden seiner Figuren beschließt. Der *Divan*, die *Wahlverwandtschaften*,
die *Novelle*, *Faust II* enden allesamt im Paradies oder in paradiesischen Zuständen;
durch Schuld oder Zufall getrennte Liebende sind wieder vereint, sich bedrohende
Wesen nähern sich einander freundlich. "So ruhen die Liebenden nebeneinander,"
heißt es in den *Wahlverwandtschaften*, nachdem Eduard, der gerade über den
Reliquien Ottilies trauert, ein schneller Tod ereilt hatte, "und welch ein freundli-
cher Augenblick wird es sein, wenn sie dereinst wieder zusammen erwachen"
(HA 6:490). Den ermüdeten Divan-Dichter, der unter den Huris Suleika
wiedererkannte, bettet der Erzengel Gabriel,

> Daß er frisch und wohlerhalten,
> Froh, wie immer, gern gesellig,
> Möge Felsenklüfte spalten,
> Um in Paradieses Weiten,
> Mit Heroen aller Zeiten
> Im Genusse zu durchschreiten. (HA 2:120)

In der *Novelle* kehrt die Menschheit, als hätte sie die Empfehlung von Kleists Marionettentheater gekannt und ernstgenommen, von hinten her wieder ins Paradies zurück, in dem Mensch und Tier friedlich beieinander wohnen. Fast vermeint man da einen lächelnden Löwen zu sehen und einen puttohaften Sieger voll lieblicher Ahnungslosigkeit:

> Ist es möglich zu denken, daß man in den Zügen eines so grimmigen Geschöpfes, des Tyrannen der Wälder, des Despoten des Tierreiches, einen Ausdruck von Freundlichkeit, von dankbarer Zufriedenheit habe spüren können, so geschah es hier, und wirklich sah das Kind in seiner Verklärung aus wie ein mächtiger, siegreicher Überwinder, jener zwar nicht wie der Überwundene, denn seine Kraft blieb in ihm verborgen, aber doch wie der Gezähmte, wie der dem eigenen friedlichen Willen Anheimgegebene. (HA 6:512).

Und schließlich das "Ewig-Weibliche," das Faust zu sich hinanzieht, unterscheidet sich in nichts von der Kraft, mit der Ottilie Eduard und Suleika den Divan-Dichter zu sich erheben. Am Ende sind alle im Paradies untergebracht.

Die so oft zitierte Szene von *Faust II* ist so singulär also nicht: Die Rückkehr ins Paradies ist ein Stilmittel Goethes, mit dem er, über die Gattungen hinweg, dramatische Situationen in eine visionäre Unendlichkeit hinauslaufen läßt. Da Goethe die Sequenz des Erlösungsbildes[1] in den verschiedensten Genres, wenngleich immer am selben Platz, am Ende, einsetzt, tritt ihr gattungsbestimmender Charakter zurück hinter dem thematischen Gewicht, das sie haben.

Erstaunlicherweise variiert die Verwendung in Drama, Erzählung und Gedicht auch die interne Anlage der Sequenz selbst kaum. Außer in der *Novelle* folgt in allen Fällen der Mann einer im Tode vorausgegangenen Geliebten; die Nachfolge verschafft dem Werbungsverhältnis eine metaphysische Legitimation. Dieses zeichnet sich von nun an durch überirdische Dauer aus und schlägt dadurch in sein gerades Gegenteil um: im Diesseits war der Liebhaber schuldig, die Erhebung ist seine Katharsis, der aber Buße nicht vorausgehen mußte, und im Jenseits gelangt der Gereinigte im Chor der Seligen an. Die Himmelfahrt selbst ist schon Seligsprechung. Die Roman- oder Dramenfigur wird zur legendären, ihr Fall zum Exemplum. So leistet also die Erlösungssequenz des Endes eine Auslöschung der Gattungen, der literarische Charakter des Werkes tritt hinter einer alle Fiktionalität überschreitenden Bedeutung zurück. Das mag einer der Gründe sein, weshalb bei Goethe, der wie kein anderer sein Augenmerk auf den Kunstcharakter seiner Poesien gerichtet hat, der Leser fast immer über diese hinwegsieht, um unter der Kunstschicht nach Sinn und Tiefsinn zu graben.

Die Heilige jedenfalls in dieser Legende des Endes ist die Geliebte, die sich in irgendeiner Weise durch Leiden ausgezeichnet hat, und die der Geliebte selbstherrlich zu seinem *imitabile* erhebt. Faust zwar hat Gretchen, das ihn erlösen soll, ganz vergessen, Eduard aber stirbt im Gedächtnis an Ottilie, deren Verehrungswürdigkeit er gerade durch diesen Tod erst bestätigt. Auch die *Novelle*

führt das Verhältnis der Nachfolge vor, wenngleich nicht als *imitatio* einer
Geliebten. Honorio ist der Begeisterte, der auf gerade die künftigen Heldentaten
sinnt, die der Knabe aus der Zirkusgesellschaft ihm in der Löwengrube vorspielt.
Die Mutter des Knaben sekundiert dem Jüngling, der sein Ideal sucht, mit der
Devise, derer jeder Heiligenverehrer bedarf, die freilich Honorio nicht zur Tat,
wohl aber zum Enthusiasmus verführt: " 'Du schaust nach Abend,' rief die Frau,
'du tust wohl daran, dort gibts viel zu tun; eile nur, säume nicht, du wirst
überwinden. Aber zuerst überwinde dich selbst.' Hierauf schien er zu lächeln"
(HA 6:510).

Die Nachfolge, die die Figuren der späten Werke wählen, ist immer mühelos,
selbst bei Eduard, der sich dieselbe Askese auferlegt, an der Ottilie starb. Letztlich
schläft er über seinem Andenken an sie nur ein: "und wie er in Gedanken an
die Heilige eingeschlafen war, so konnte man wohl ihn selig nennen" (6:490),
kommentiert der Erzähler. Ließe sich diese kleine Apathie, an der Eduard
zugrunde geht, gerade noch als Opfer deuten, so gewinnen Faust und der Divan-
Dichter das Himmelreich durch nichts als ein Diktum. Der Divan-Dichter attestiert
sich selbst die Qualität eines Menschen, der himmlischen Lohn verdient habe,
wenn er kurz und bündig der an der Himmelpforte wachhabenden und zögernden
Huri erklärt:

> Nicht so vieles Federlesen!
> Laß mich immer nur herein:
> Denn ich bin ein Mensch gewesen,
> Und das heißt ein Kämpfer sein. (HA 2:110)

Das korrespondiert dem wohlwollenden, aber nicht weniger willkürlichen Urteil
der Engel in *Faust II*: "Wer immer strebend sich bemüht, den können wir erlösen."
Mit diesem Richtspruch sprechen sie eine Figur frei, der vieles einfiel, am allerwe-
nigsten aber, sich zu bemühen. Faust ist eine einzigartige Figur in der Weltliteratur,
die sich immer helfen läßt: selbst den Schlaf, den er in der Eingangsszene sucht,
findet er nur mit Hilfe märchenhafter Elfen und Ariels, den naturmagische Schriften des Mittelalters als Höllengeist kennen.

Mit dieser unverdienten Apotheose eines unheldischen Träumers deutet sich
der parodistische Charakter des verwendeten Sujets an. Archaische Erlösungs-
wünsche und Paradiesesvorstellungen einer mündlichen Kultur übernimmt Goethe
in schriftliche Formen, die selbst das geschlossene Weltbild zersetzt und längst
hinter sich gelassen haben. Seine Figuren glauben nicht, sondern spielen sich als
Gläubige auf: die *imitatio* verwandelt sich in Zitatenkunst.

Dabei muß das Zitat nicht immer, wie etwa in *Faust II* und in der *Novelle*,
sprachlicher Art sein, es kann durchaus auch Spiel und Schauspiel sein. Der *pompe
funèbre* um die verstorbene Ottilie ist durchaus ein Theater, das seine eigene
Kulisse hat. Das Gesellschaftsspiel der lebenden Bilder, das die Figuren der
Wahlverwandtschaften so oft geübt haben und so gut beherrschen, treiben sie auch
im Tode noch fort. Der Architekt fühlt sich, als er ans Grab Ottilies, seiner

Freundin, tritt, zurückversetzt in eine solche Attitüdendarstellung, wie er sie schon einmal, allerdings mit der lauten Luciane, einer aristokratischen und profanen Gesellschaft geboten hat: "Schon einmal hatte er so vor Belisar gestanden. Unwillkürlich geriet er jetzt in die gleiche Stellung; und wie natürlich war sie auch diesmal!" (HA 6:487). Die Rührung, die den Architekten übermannt, wird gar von Nanny, jenem zwergenhaften und unschönen Gegenstück Ottiles, erregt. Sie ist es, die ihn dahinbringt, "daß er, über den Fluß ihrer Rede erstaunt, sich zu fassen vermochte und seine schöne Freundin ihm in einer höhern Region lebend und wirkend vorschwebte" (HA 6:488). Die Ergriffenheit ist eine theatralische Inszenierung seiner Phantasie so gut wie die andächtige Haltung eine seines Körpers ist. Wenn die Szene "auch diesmal natürlich" geriet, so ist der letzte Stil, der in jener Epoche der Kunst Wahrhaftigkeit noch hätte garantieren können, verraten.

Legende und lebendes Bild konvergieren im Gestus der Nachahmung. Der Heilige der Legende verweist zuletzt auf Christus, der Kunstgegenstand aber, der im lebenden Bild wiederholt wird, hat keinen über sich hinausverweisenden Horizont. Eduard stellt, ehe er stirbt, das lebende Bild eines Gläubigen über den Reliquien seiner Heiligen, die Ottilie ist; Ottilie aber stellt das lebende Bild einer toten Heiligen, das auf nichts als auf sich selbst verweist.

Das typische selige Ende von Goethes späten Werken umspielt immer ein ironisches Ambiente. Das Zitat selbst, wie auch das lebende Bild, das ihm als optisches Zitat zuzuordnen ist, sind wesentlich ironisch. Sie werden nur kenntlich, wenn sie mit hör- oder sichtbaren Anführungszeichen gegeben werden. Das Zitat tendiert daher zur Übertreibung des originalen Sprachflusses, entweder also zur Deklamation oder zur Witzelei. Die Haltungen, die diesen rhetorischen Gesten entsprechen, sind überzogene Feierlichkeit oder Albernheit. Beide Weisen der Rede und Selbstdarstellung finden sich in Goethes Schlußszenen der Seligkeit, in der *Novelle* zum Beispiel oder im *Divan*. Der hochtrabende Ton des alten Schaustellers in der *Novelle*, der seine biblischen Gleichnisse mit einem gehörigen "Sehet..." und "Betrachtet..." einleitet, um ihnen die hohepriesterliche Würde zu geben, und die Albernheiten des Divan-Dichters werden dennoch gerne überhört.

Dabei rechnen gerade diese Figuren mit ihrer Wirkung. Alle Zurschaustellung im lebenden Bild und im Zitat, alle Anstrengung, ein Anderer und Besserer zu sein, wären verfehlt, wenn ihr der Zuschauer fehlte. In allen genannten Fällen findet daher die *imitatio* in einer Arena und vor einem Publikum statt. Ottilies Grab zieht die Gemeinde derer an, die auf Glaube nicht verzichten wollen; das Wunder der Löwenbändigung beobachten Fürst und Fürstin samt Gefolge von den Rängen des amphitheatralischen Burghofes herab; der Divan-Dichter rechnet mit einem bewundernden Volk, das seine Lieder tradieren wird, wenn er im Schlußgebet spricht:

> Nun, so legt euch, liebe Lieder,
> An den Busen meinem Volke! (HA 2:120)

Auf dem Theater, wo *Faust II* spielt, kann ein Zuschauer freilich nicht auftreten, sonst wäre es kaum Theater mehr zu nennen. Eine im Stück inszenierte Zuschauersituation braucht es aber auch gar nicht, denn das Parkett hat seine Rolle schon übernommen—und so soll es denn auch genauso genasführt werden, wie die Zuschauer aller anderen Himmelfahrten und Seligsprechungen.

An der Erlösung Fausts besteht für diesen Zuschauer kein Zweifel. Der Schlußvers eines Autors wird allgemein als das Sigel seines Werkes verstanden, mit dem er ihm seine Absicht auf- und einprägt. Das "Ewig-Weibliche" also mußte zum wesentlichen Thema der Tragödie werden. Diese Lesart scheint die Apotheose zu unterstreichen, die—eine Ungewöhnlichkeit in der Tragödie—hier sichtbar vorgeführt wird. Von der Grablegung an flüstern, singen, deklamieren, posaunen Eremiten, Heilige, Büßer und Engel die Vokabel "Liebe" samt ihren Ableitungen vierundzwanzigmal. Sowohl der Wald als auch der Himmel sind nun der "Liebeshort," die Menschen fesseln ein "Liebesband," die "allmächtige Liebe," "die Liebesboten," der "Ewigen Liebe Kern," des "Ewigen Lieben Offenbaren," die "Liebe gar," die "Liebesqualen," die "heilige Liebeslust," die "früh Geliebte," überirdische Regungen jedenfalls, die allerdings von der "fröhlichen Liebe" des "Verliebten" Mephisto und seiner "Liebsten" präludiert wird. Seine Sehnsucht nach "den allerliebsten Jungen," den Engeln, die ihm ganz "lieblich" vorkommen und die ihn in sein "Liebeselement" versetzen, weil sie "liebende Flammen" in ihm entzünden, bis er endlich merkt, daß das ein "Liebesspuk" und eine "absurde Liebschaft" ist, haben von vornherein den hohen Ton der Himmelfahrtsszene herabgestimmt, das hohe Gefühl, zu dem sie erhebt, herabgewürdigt.

Immerhin ließe sich die Erniedrigung der Liebe durch die Lüsternheit des Teufels als Hintergrund verstehen, auf den die Heiligung Fausts in umso himmlischeren Farben aufgetragen ist. Die Glaubwürdigkeit der Szene aus lauter hochgestochenen Worten stiftet ohnehin erst die mystische Metaphysik der Schlußverse. Sie beziehen den Zuschauer in das Geschehen mit ein; letztlich sind diese Worte ad spectatores gesprochen. Sie kommentieren nicht Fausts Erhebung, sie verkünden "unsere" Erlösung: "Das Ewig-Weibliche zieht *uns* hinan." Damit ist—hier wie in den anderen späten Werken auch—der Zuschauer ins Geschehen verwickelt, nur daß er diesmal aus dem Text herausgetreten ist. Der Abgesang, der in die Wirklichkeit hineingesprochen ist, macht das Drama zum Mysterienspiel, an dem die ganze Menschheit teilhat. Fausts *vita* gibt sich zu erkennen als Exemplum zur Erbauung der Gläubigen, die im Zuschauerraum sitzen.

Dem letzten Wort als dem Vermächtnis eines Dichters kann der reale Zuschauer nicht widerstehen. Er hat, im Unterschied zum erzählten Publikum in den anderen Spätwerken, keinen Autor, der ihn ironisiert. Dem schönen Schein der Inszenierung bleibt er ausgeliefert, während in den anderen Fällen der Autor den Leser vor dem Irrtum warnt, der durch das legendäre Geschehen entstehen könnte, indem er ihm ein irregeleitetes Publikum vor Augen führt.

Die Zuschauer der *Novelle* zum Beispiel sind gebannt von dem "seltenen menschlichen Fall" (HA 6:511) eines Schauspiels, das für den Zigeunerknaben—nicht anders übrigens als für seinen Mitspieler, den Löwen—eine alltägliche Pflicht ist. Der Autor paßt sich der Perspektive des von ihm entworfenen Publikums an, wenn er sagt, der Knabe steige *"gleichsam* wie in die Arena des Schauspiels" hinab; die Formulierung gibt vor, der Knabe habe eine einmalige Heldentat zu vollbringen–tatsächlich aber geht er nicht "gleichsam" in die Arena, sondern tatsächlich so wie jeden Tag, nur daß diesmal das Schauspiel unterm Himmelszelt und nicht unterm Zirkuszelt stattfindet. Das Kind vollzieht–geradezu pflichtbewußt und in der gegebenen Situation übertrieben folgsam–all die Gänge und Rituale, die zu seiner Nummer gehören. Auch der Löwe ist bei der Vorführung geradeso willenlos gelangweilt wie jeden Tag, wo er nur mitspielt, weil er weiß, daß die Peitsche droht.

> Er zeigte hie und da Lust, sich niederzulegen; doch der Knabe führte ihn
> im Halbkreise durch die wenig entblätterten, buntbelaubten Bäume, bis
> er sich endlich in den letzten Strahlen der Sonne, die sie durch eine
> Ruinenlücke hereinsandte, wie verklärt niedersetzte. . . . (HA 6:511)

Die Nummer gelingt im Sonnenlicht um so vieles besser als im Rampenlicht, daß die wie immer bänglich beobachtende Mutter, die durch ihr übereifriges Klatschen alltäglich das Publikum zum selben Lob ermuntert, auch diesmal "sich vor Freuden mit ausgestreckten Armen zurückbog und vielleicht *angewohnterweise* Beifall gerufen und geklatscht hätte. . ." (6:512, von mir hervorgehoben).

Nicht der Autor, sondern der gebildete Zuschauer erhebt den Dressurakt zur biblischen Szene, und der Leser springt ihm bei, indem auch er sich angelegentlich an der Deutung beteiligt, wobei er mitten im alttestamentlichen Tableau sogar eine nachbiblische Kirchenväterlegende gelten läßt. Hätte der Autor das Ereignis glaubwürdig in einer biblischen Tradition ansiedeln wollen, so hätte er das Bild vom Dornauszieher vermeiden müssen. Die bewegliche Phantasie des Gebildeten aber, dem mythische Ereignisse mehr Stoff, Bild und ästhetischer Reiz als Sinn sind, erfreut sich geradezu an der originellen Kontamination. Solch geschmäcklerisches Vergnügen beweist, daß die Szene ein gebildetes Arrangement, ein gestelltes Bild ist. Die Bibelszene ist Attitüdendarstellung, nicht Wiederkehr des archaischen Ereignisses. Sie ist, wie in der Schlußszene des *Faust* ohnehin, Stoff für ein Theater, oder, mit Handlung umgeben, für eine Novelle (welcher Gattung denn auch die *Wahlverwandtschaften* zu zählen wären). Kopierter Sinn aber verhält sich immer parodistisch zu seinem Vorbild. Das lebende Bild ist eine falsche *imitatio*, sie ist–um an das für Ottilie vorbehaltene Epitheton zu erinnern–im schlechten Sinne ein "Augentrost"; letztlich ist und bleibt sie ein Theaterspaß für den Augenblick.

Nun geht aber Goethes Absicht nicht dahin, ein Publikum zu verspotten–er ist kein Satiriker. Die Parodie entsteht bei ihm aus einer Notlage und ist geboren aus der Erfahrung, daß die Sprache des Dichters an den Tod nicht heran- und noch viel weniger über ihn hinausreicht. Sie gehört dem Reich der Sinne an, ihre Schönheit ist Sinnlichkeit. Wenn also der Dichter die eigene Sprache beibehält, um das Übersinnliche auszudrücken, so drückt er sich notwendig unangemessen aus, will er hingegen angemessen sein, so muß er seine Sprache vom Priester leihen. In beiden Fällen wählt er den falschen Ton, das eine Mal wirkt seine Sprache–unangemessen, wie sie ihrem Gegenstand gegenüber ist–albern, das andre Mal verlogen. Der eine Fall findet sich im "Buch des Paradieses," der andere in der Schlußszene von *Faust II*.[2]

Das "Buch des Paradieses," das so unsinnig über die Liebe eines alten Poeten zu einer Huri spricht, über Huris, die in Knittelversen dichten und in menschlichen Dialekten kokettieren, über heilige Tiere und was sonst für Neckereien und Skurilitäten, hat sein eigentliches Thema in der Unfähigkeit des Dichters, mit seiner Einbildungskraft an das Überirdische heranzureichen. Die Huri klärt den Divan-Dichter darüber auf, daß es Herablassung von ihrer Seite ist, wenn es dahin kommt, daß er sie überhaupt versteht, denn nur weil sie es gewohnt ist, zu tun, als sei sie eine der irdischen Frauen, kann sich der Dichter ihr nähern:

> So wie ihr dächtet, sollten wir denken,
> Wir sollten euren Liebchen gleichen.
> . . .
> Nun sieht ein jeder, was er sah,
> Und ihm geschieht, was ihm geschah.
> Wir sind die Blonden, wir sind die Braunen,
> Wir haben Grillen und haben Launen,
> Ja, wohl auch manchmal eine Flause,
> ein jeder denkt, er sei zu Hause. (HA 2:113–14)

Das Gedicht "Höheres und Höchstes" (HA 2:116f.) spricht gerade vom Gegenteil dessen, was sein Titel verspricht: davon nämlich, daß ein Höchstes nur in den Bildern einer banalen Alltäglichkeit zu denken sei. Auch im Jenseits sucht der Mensch nichts als irdische Reize, "schöne Gärten, / Blum' und Frucht und hübsche Kinder," nicht die Ruhe in Gott. Vor allem aber reicht die Sprache an das überirdische Vergnügen nicht heran; nicht einmal der Dichter vermag mit himmlischen Zungen zu sprechen. Auch seine Sprache bleibt eine gestammelte Übersetzung:

> Und so möcht' ich alle Freunde,
> Jung und alt, in *eins* versammeln,
> Gar zu gern in deutscher Sprache
> Paradiesesworte stammeln.

Die Resignation malt sich schließlich doch eine blasse Hoffnung an den Himmel:

> Ist somit dem Fünf der Sinne
> Vorgesehn im Paradiese,
> Sicher ist es, ich gewinne
> Einen Sinn für alle diese.

Oberflächlich läßt sich das als eine Satire auf die psychologische Unzulänglichkeit des Menschen lesen, sich das Göttliche vorzustellen. Im Rahmen des
Modells aber, dem die Alterswerke Goethes allesamt unterworfen sind, des
Plotinismus, ist die Sprachunfähigkeit dem Göttlichen gegenüber die letzte Stufe
der Hypostase, die auch der Dichter nicht überwinden kann.[3] Die in die Welt
entlassene Seele, die im Körper wie in ein Grab gebannt ist, schaut in der Schönheit der Geliebten, in Suleika also, die Schönheit der Ideen und kann sie in dieser
sinnlichen Gestalt auch benennen und bedichten. Die Poesie des Divan-Dichters
also ist sinnliches Erscheinen der Idee. Damit aber hat die Katharsis der Weltseele,
die zu ihrem Ursprung zurückkehren will, ihr letztes irdisches Ziel erreicht. Vor
der Beschreibung des Jenseits versagt selbst die poetische Sprache. Die Rückkehr
zum Ursprung ist nur sagbar als Albernheit, als Koketterie mit den orientalischen
Huris oder als Spiel mit christlichem Legendenkitsch. "Nicht zuletzt auf das
Abstruse kam es Goethe an," kommentiert Jochen Schmidt die unzusammen-
passende Verwendung von lateinischen Hymnenformen und christlichen Bildern
in der Schlußszene des *Faust*.[4] Er kommt zu dem Schluß, daß dieses Arrangement
einem philosophischen Konzept des Autors entspringt: "Indem er dieses als das
'Unzulängliche,' das heißt als das mit menschlichen Begriffen nicht Erlangbare
und als das 'Unbeschreibliche' bezeichnet, bewegt er sich ganz im mystischen
Kategoriensystem der Theologia negativa, das gerade im Neuplatonismus... seine
entschiedene Ausprägung gefunden hatte."[5]

Goethe hat dem *Faust II* als seinem letzten Werk einen besonderen Rang
zugewiesen. Während die übrigen Spätwerke die Unzulänglichkeit der poetischen
Sprache dem Unendlichen gegenüber ganz an die Reflektion einer fiktiven Figur
gebunden haben, fehlt diese im *Faust* ebenso wie ein fingierter Zuschauer des
legendären Ereignisses. Goethe bezieht den realen Zuschauer in die Inszenierung
der albernen Apotheose mit ein; dadurch macht er auch sich selbst zum Mitspieler
im Stück: die Verlegenheit des Dichters ist diesmal seine eigene. In *Faust II* hat
der reale Autor die Rolle des Divan-Dichters. Dessen letztem Gedicht, seinem
"Gute Nacht," korrespondieren die letzten Verse des *Faust II*:

> Alles Vergängliche
> Ist nur ein Gleichnis;
> Das Unzulängliche,
> Hier wird's Ereignis;
> Das Unbeschreibliche,
> Hier ist's getan;
> Das Ewig-Weibliche
> Zieht uns hinan. (12104–111)

Sie sind die Abschiedsverse des realen Autors an sein reales Publikum. In ihnen
spricht er so eindeutig, wie einst der Divan-Dichter vor der Himmelspforte: die
Dichterworte versuchen die Tore zu öffnen und sind doch auf die Gnade der
Himmlischen angewiesen, wenn sie überhaupt nur gehört werden wollen. Die

acht Verse des Schlusses resümieren ein ganzes poetisches Leben und sind eine poetische Dichtungstheorie in nuce. Die ersten sechs Verse sprechen von der Unfähigkeit des Wortes dem Unendlichen gegenüber, das im Gleichnis einen höheren Sinn nur anzudeuten vermag, von Ereignissen, die im Unzulänglichen der Poesie und Wirklichkeit ihre Bilder suchen, von dem, was unbeschreiblich ist, und was zu beschreiben der Dichter dennoch übermütig genug ist.

Nach dieser resignativen Einsicht aber unterbricht sich der Autor. Die allerletzten beiden Verse von *Faust II* sind sowohl im Wortfeld wie im Sinn von den vorausgehenden durch eine tiefe Kluft getrennt. Der negativen Ästhetik der ersten sechs Verse folgt eine übervolle Sinndeutung, die für den, der Goethes sprachliche Dezenz kennt, allein schon durch ihre Vollmundigkeit die vorausgehende Skepsis belegt. Das Wechselspiel zwischen diesen sechs und den letzten beiden Verse ist parodistisch. Die Resignation klammert sich an eine äußerste Hoffnung: was Inbegriff der Poesie und Sinnlichkeit war, die Liebe, die Frau, das Gretchen, entleert sie zum Abstraktum und knüpft es mit einem Bindestrich an die Ewigkeit. Der Weg, den das "Ewig-Weibliche," dieser Kentaur aus Sinn und Sinnlichkeit, weist, ist denkbar unbestimmt. "Hinan" immerhin ist das Wort, das Goethe gern für den plotinischen Aufstieg benutzt, so etwa in den "Dornburger Gedichten." "So hinan denn hell und heller," heißt es da von dem Mond, der die Geliebte vorstellt und im Rahmen des Plotinismus der Vorschein der Seele ist.

Sind die Schlußverse von *Faust II* die Abschiedsrede des realen Autors Goethe an sein Publikum, so scheint schließlich auch das gesamte Werk von der Reflexion an die Endlichkeit und Grenze der Poesie getragen zu sein. In den vielen Tönen, die es anschlägt, scheint Goethe noch einmal sein ganzes poetisches Können auszubreiten. Die Absicht dieser ästhetischen Anlage kann nur die Selbstparodie sein. Der Autor spielt mit den eigenen Möglichkeiten genauso wie mit den verbindlichen Sinnkonstitutionen seines Publikums. Goethe führt seine poetischen Fähigkeiten durch den ganzen zweiten Teil des *Faust* hindurch in einer Serie von Kabarettnummern vor: der schnelle Wechsel der Metren, der bunte Zug des Personals, das Spiel mit Glaubenswahrheiten, die längst verlorengegangen sind und einem Bildungswissen, das seine Gültigkeit zu verlieren gerade im Begriffe ist, das Jonglieren mit ernsten Weltentwürfen–das alles sind Charakteristika des Kabaretts. Die Schwierigkeit der Gattungszuweisung von *Faust II*, die seit der Veröffentlichung des versiegelten Werkes besteht, löst sich bei der Einsicht in den parodistischen Charakter des Werkes auf: es ist ein Kabarett avant la lettre. Auch zu Beginn dieses Jahrhunderts, als die Gattung eigentlich erst entstand, gewann sie mit ihren Respektlosigkeiten ein Publikum, das seine Traditionen gerade vergessen wollte und den metaphysischen Horizont schon verloren gegeben hatte. Die kabarettistische Vielfalt und Frechheit des *Faust II* ist die Respektlosigkeit eines Dichters, der diesmal seine eigene Tradition zwar nicht aufgeben will, aber muß.

Die Deutung von *Faust II* als einer bewußten Reflexion auf die eigene Existenz als Dichter mag die Beobachtung stützen, daß Goethe mit dem Werk in vielen

Momenten an Shakespeares *Sturm* anknüpft, jenes Werk, mit dem der englische
Dichter, wie man meinte, sich von der Bühne verabschiedete. Mit Ariel eröffnet
nun auch Goethe nicht zufällig sein letztes Drama, in dem es, wie bei Shakespeare,
Götter, Geister und Menschen bunt durcheinandertreibt. Nicht allein, daß Goethe
mit dieser Allusion einen Bogen schlägt zu den eigenen Anfängen, die im Zeichen
Shakespeares standen. Er hat sich, um seinen Rang als Dichter zu bestimmen,
später auch kleiner als Shakespeare und größer als Tieck genannt. *Faust II* ist die
Referenz an das größere Erbe, der spielerische Umgang mit dem Vorbild, die
darin enthaltene Selbstparodie eine *captatio benevolentiae* an die Tradition. Die
gelegentliche Albernheit des *Faust II* ist die Einsicht in die eigenen Grenzen so
gut wie in die Grenze aller Poesie, und sei sie auch von shakespearischer Größe.
Die metaphysische Welt ist für sie nur ein Spielplatz, und nur die Parodie vermag
diese Einsicht unmißverständlich auszudrücken. Die Parodie des Paradieses ist
das Eingeständnis, daß es ein Paradies nicht gäbe, wenn die Dichtung in der Lage
wäre, von ihm zu sprechen.

ANMERKUNGEN

1. Vgl. dazu Gerhard Wild, *Goethes Versöhnungsbilder: eine geschichtsphilosophische Untersuchung
zu Goethes späten Werken* (Stuttgart: Metzler, 1991).

2. Schon 1956 hat Stuart Atkins eine ironische Lesart der Schlußszene der damals noch
geläufigen emphatischen entgegengesetzt ("Irony and Ambiguity in the Final Scene of
Goethe's *Faust*," in Gottfried F. Merkel, ed., *On Romanticism and the Art of Translation: Studies
in Honor of Edwin Hermann Zeydel* (Princeton: Princeton University Press, 1956) 7–27).
Gegen den Todernst der damaligen Wissenschaft kann Atkins nur einen Vorläufer auf
seiner Seite aufweisen, Kurt May. Nicht allein, daß Atkins den ironischen Ton der Szene
"Bergschluchten" erkennt; er bleibt bei einer oberflächlichen Stilbeobachtung nicht stehen.
Er verweist auf die Bedeutung dieses Stils für Goethe, der damit seine Erfahrung von
der Unzulänglichkeit der Sprache dem Transzendenten gegenüber ausdrücken will.

3. Es würde in diesem Zusammenhang zu weit führen, wollte ich noch einmal diese These
von der plotinischen Thematik des *Divan* beweisen, die ich in einem Aufsatz schon belegt
habe ("Furor poeticus. Die vier Trunkenheiten in Goethes *West-östlichem Divan*," *Poetica*
22 (1990): 303–23. Ebenso hat Jochen Schmidt denselben philosophischen Horizont für
die Schlußszene von *Faust II* belegt: ("Die 'katholische Mythologie' und ihre mystische
Entmythologisierung in der Schluß-Szene des *Faust II*," in Werner Keller, ed., *Aufsätze
zu Goethes Faust II* [Darmstadt: Wissenschaftliche Buchgesellschaft, 1992] 384–417).

4. a.a.O. 389.

5. a.a.O. 395.

Gail K. Hart

Das Ewig-Weibliche nasführet dich: Feminine Leadership in Goethe's *Faust* and Sacher-Masoch's *Venus*

I. "Einführung"

My title, a combination of two well-known *Faust* passages, is intended to provoke reflection on the twisted problem of feminine authority or feminine leadership in Goethe's masterpiece, where there is much talk of leading and following as well as of who should be conducting whom. Whereas Faust is popularly known for his restless movement or striving, the context for this activity is deeply imbued with the problematics of guidance or channeling of such movement by a leader or guide. Faust needs to be shown the way, led to his goals by a series of figures, but this relationship is not framed in conventionally authoritarian terms (with the leader enjoying dominion or superiority over the follower). Rather the partial abdication of authority or self-determination that constitutes 'following' appears to involve a projection of self onto a muse figure, an objectification of self–here as a feminine spirit preoccupied with the education or salvation of the subject.[1] The purpose of my essay is twofold. First I wish to examine this aspect of *Faust* in relation to its own times and tradition, and secondly to explore this externalizing or sharing of prerogative in dialogue with one of the premier students of power relations, Leopold von Sacher-Masoch, who uses Goethe's *Faust* as his authority for the authoritarian posturings of *Venus im Pelz*.

The second of the two passages that form my title (and the first chronologically) is Mephistopheles' stinging reproach to Faust that Gretchen is seducing him into risky theological discussions that may culminate in submission to both divine and feminine authority:

> Du übersinnlicher sinnlicher Freier,
> Ein Mägdelein nasführet dich. (3534–35)

Mephistopheles has already remarked on the connection between conventional piety and apron strings–"[Die Mädels] denken: duckt er da, folgt er uns eben auch" (3527)–and here he establishes his contempt for the idea of feminine leadership as a base reversal of the proper procedure he had recommended to the *Schüler* in "Studierzimmer": "Besonders lernt die Weiber führen" (2023). Faust apparently shares his tempter's contempt for such inversions of leader and follower because he reacts to the charge with obvious spite: "Du Spottgeburt von Dreck und Feuer!" (3536). Clearly, the familiar prohibition against submitting to feminine leadership is in force and the man thus guided is "der Genasführte."[2]

The other excerpt incorporated in the title is, of course, the concluding passage of *Faust II*:

> Das Unbeschreibliche,
> Hier ist's getan;
> Das Ewig-Weibliche
> Zieht uns hinan. (12108–12)

This indicates (we think) that a feminine principle powers the striving that leads "us" to salvation, that we are, in some abstract and indescribable way, saved by the belle. If this is so, then feminine leadership is not as unsavory as Mephistopheles made it out to be–though it is nonetheless unsavory to Mephistopheles. There is, however, an obvious difference between the feminine leaders here (though they are apparently the same person); one is the young Gretchen, living, corporeal feminine matter, and the other is the penitent of the heavenly host, pure spirit, "sonst Gretchen genannt." The subtraction of body–though it does not de-gender the heroine–lends her the massive authority to lead Faust to heaven and his salvation (at the Virgin Mary's urging). She who was misled or seduced in life leads her seducer to glory in the afterlife.

Superficially, this is unproblematic: Gretchen is the errant "carnal" object of seduction on earth and in her heavenly "excarnation" she functions as mediatrix and guiding principle.[3] In this spirit, the two passages illustrate the two dominant modes of representation of the feminine; the actual woman or girl whose will to guide or lead is characterized as "nasführen" and the abstracted ethereal essence of femininity which (as muse, patroness or patron saint) can lead, inspire or attract the active creative man toward ever higher realms of achievement. It has always been the case that the Christian hierarchy of spirit over matter is especially intensive when it is a question of the distinction between female spirit and female matter. Death can only enhance a woman's appeal (and *hinanziehen* means to compel movement in an upward direction by attracting as much as by leading or pulling).

Dead women are the stock in trade of the tradition from which Goethe takes his Gretchen tragedy–namely that of the so-called "bürgerliches Trauerspiel." In these plays, heroines and their mothers are systematically eliminated as a means of securing domestic authority. When the bourgeois man, the object of aristocratic domination, retreats from a public sphere of subjection to traditional authority to the intimate private sphere, the roost he presumably rules, he encounters a challenge to his authority in the form of female relatives. Briefly, these are a wife who may resist his will in domestic matters and a daughter who may also defy him and realize his worst fears by transferring her allegiance to a class enemy—the aristocratic suitor. This suitor is a stock character who invades the inner sanctum to exercise his (inherited) authority even in this last bastion of bourgeois self-determination. (I exaggerate a bit for effect, and to save space, but this is the general framework of these plays.) As Denis Jonnes has noted in his subtle analysis of the father's centrality in bourgeois tragedy,[4] it is necessary that the women in the family be autonomous to a certain degree, so that they may freely choose to submit to the father/husband figure, thus legitimating his authority. However, this autonomy by definition creates the possibility of defiance and defection and hence the need for their elimination.

From poisoned Sara Sampson with her dead mother to poisoned Luise Miller, whose mother simply disappears, to Hebbel's pregnant Clara lying at the bottom of the well after her mother has died of grief, women are banished from the scene of what is supposed to be family drama, and I have argued elsewhere that the elimination of women and the reconstitution of the family under exclusively male (unchallenged) leadership is the *telos* of bourgeois drama.[5] The necessary autonomy of the women in these domestic dramas raises the possibility of their defection and creates "das Unbehagen in der Familie," a need for cathartic relief that comes from the purging of women. Somehow, "bürgerliches Trauerspiel" seems broadly intended to ease the anxieties of an oppressed male middle-class—this could have been its social function—and on the surface it would seem that women (at least autonomous women) cannot be integrated into the solutions it proposes. In other words, they cannot lead, and if they will not follow, they have no function.

This characterization of bourgeois tragedy derives from examination of paradigmatic works by Lessing (*Miß Sara Sampson, Emilia Galotti*) as well as the Schiller, Klinger, H.L. Wagner and Hebbel plays that follow in this mold. Within these parameters, the form is surprisingly regular—with *Miß Sara Sampson* as a norming intertext. Though not all such plays actually realize the deaths of mother and daughter, they do move in this direction.[6] Yet, despite the fact that in the text at hand both Gretchen and her mother die, this pattern of slaughter is not well represented in Goethe's work. As a rule, the dramatist Goethe tends to separate his seduced women from the family, so that his bourgeois tragedies or dramas of seduction, such as *Clavigo* and *Stella*, take place outside the home, where the father is not the central point of reference. Indeed, in Goethe's work, the father is often dead and his representative (Stella's uncle, Marie Beaumarchais' brother or Gretchen's brother Valentin) does not enjoy the central status of Sir William Sampson, who is at all times the real hero of Lessing's play (the action of the play derives significance from the ways in which it affects him).[7] Secondly, in addition to breaking down the father-daughter or father-daughter's seducer relationship as a nodal point, Goethe tends to depict his seducible young women not as autonomous beings, but as creatures determined by nature to be loving and compliant. Consider, for example, Kurt Eissler's description of Gretchen:

[She] is pictured as feminine, soft, surrendering to the man whom she loves, and functioning as the self-sacrificing intermediary between the guilt-laden man and a God-Mother, a sublime symbol of true, most tender femaleness.[8]

Gretchen "chooses" Faust because she is in the grip of a determining passion ("Mein Busen drängt / Sich nach ihm hin" [3406–7]) similar to that which causes Stella's and Cäcilie's total devotion to Fernando. They could not have chosen otherwise. It is their nature and, as Stella puts it, "Wir können ja einmal nichts dafür, daß wir so sind."[9]

This is not the place for a taxonomy of Goethe's heroines or of bourgeois tragedies. For the present I am attempting to locate Goethe's *Faust* with regard to a tradition and to suggest that it observes the conventions of this tradition only up to a certain point. Gretchen is a sweet young bourgeois thing seduced by a powerful exciting stranger whom she reveres as a social superior, but her drama lacks the paternalistic authority figure, the real subject of bourgeois tragedy. Her play is at bottom not a "bürgerliches Trauerspiel," after all, but rather a/the "Gretchentragödie." The strong, central (intra-familial) authority of a Sir William Sampson or Odoardo Galotti is missing here. Though Faust is the declared center of his play(s), he yields center stage to other figures and concerns almost as often as he occupies it—the role of Mephistopheles being far richer than that of Faust, for example—and these secondary plots do not derive their interest primarily from their bearing on Faust. Furthermore, Faust is a follower (rather than a fixed beacon of authority) and his drama does not unfold between the poles of obedience and defiance toward such authority. On the contrary, Faust's path is open as he negotiates a course and a program of guidance.

II. Laß dich führen

As noted, leadership and leading are basic concepts in the vocabulary of *Faust* (I and II). There is ample reference to forward movement with another in tow (leading) and linear progress behind a guide (following), inaugurated by God's remark in the prologue, that, should Faust ever become confused, "So werd' ich ihn bald in die Klarheit führen" (309). Mephistopheles then requests permission to *lead* Faust in another direction: "ihn meine Straße sacht zu führen" (314). Between this exchange and the final "zieht uns hinan" unfolds a tale of leading and following with special emphasis on misleading or seduction—the difference between *führen* and *verführen*. Stasis is death—as Faust implies in his wager with Mephistopheles when he abjures the *Faulbett*—or decomposition, as in the scene in Gretchen's room where Faust, perceiving plenitude or "Fülle" (2693), is initially compelled to stay within the confines of the tiny chamber, where he anticipates such changes of condition as "zerfließen" (2723) and "hinschmelzen" (2728). Thus de-natured, Faust laments that he no longer knows himself: "Armsel'ger Faust! ich kenne dich nicht mehr" (2720). Thus, stasis or the plenitude that appears to inhabit small spaces are non-Faustian environs out of which the hero must be led—and Mephistopheles arrives promptly to fetch him out of Gretchen's room.

From the very first Faust desires a person, spirit or power to direct the restless stirrings of his nature. Philosophy, law, medicine, theology, Nostradamus and the Erdgeist fail to satisfy his need for guidance and he cries out in despair:

> O gibt es Geister in der Luft,
> Die zwischen Erd' und Himmel herrschend weben,
> So steiget nieder aus dem goldnen Duft
> Und *führt* mich weg, zu neuem, buntem Leben!
> (1118–21, my emphasis).

This is, of course, what Gretchen will eventually do, but Faust has yet to meet her. He must first follow Mephistopheles to the "Hexenküche" for a cup of the witches' brew that rejuvenates him and enhances his appreciation of women: "Du siehst, mit diesem Trank im Leibe, / Bald Helenen in jedem Weibe" (2603–4). At the close of "Hexenküche," immediately (12 lines) before they encounter Gretchen, Mephistopheles enjoins Faust, "Komm nur geschwind und laß dich führen" (2593), urging him to give in to the effects of the drink that will direct him to women and love. This particular "lead-in" to the Faust and Gretchen affair properly portends her leadership function, her *führen* as opposed to Faust's *verführen*.

The terms are established in the very beginning of the encounter. Faust attempts to take the lead, but Gretchen refuses to yield it. He takes her arm and asks:

> Mein schönes Fräulein, darf ich wagen,
> Meinen Arm und Geleit Ihr anzutragen? (2605–6)

But Gretchen insists on setting an independent course:

> Bin weder Fräulein, weder schön,
> Kann ungeleitet nach Hause gehn.
> (Sie macht sich los und ab). (2607–8)

Whatever Gretchen does for Faust, she does not ever follow him, not here, not in their courtship interludes in the garden ("macht sich los und läuft weg. Er steht einen Augenblick in Gedanken, dann folgt er ihr" [after 3194]) and not when he attempts to lead her out of her cell to escape execution. Of particular interest with respect to her failure to follow him or even comply with his requests is "Gartenhäuschen," where Faust once again offers to take her home:

> *MEPH*: Es ist wohl Zeit zu scheiden.
> *MARTHE* kommt: Ja, es ist spät, mein Herr.

FAUST: Darf ich Euch nicht geleiten?
MARG: Die Mutter würde mich—Lebt wohl! (3207-8)

It is here that Gretchen's dialogue suggests the contradiction in her character. After firmly and successfully refusing Faust (in the name of the mother), she laments her lack of resistance:

> Du lieber Gott! was so ein Mann
> Nicht alles, alles denken kann!
> Beschämt nur steh' ich vor ihm da,
> *Und sag' zu allen Sachen ja.*
> Bin doch ein arm unwissend Kind,
> Begreife nicht, was er an mir find't. (3211–16, my emphasis)

The shamefaced ingenue expresses her feelings of inadequacy in the presence of her learned acquaintance, but her lament contains a forceful and unmistakable declaration of absolute compliance. Not only does she say that she can only nod in agreement when he displays his erudition; she also says that she grants all of his requests: "Und sag' zu allen Sachen ja." The "Sache" at issue is Faust's attempt to seduce (literally to mislead) her, and though she will eventually agree to drug her mother and leave the door open, she has at this point just finished refusing Faust's attempt at closeness when she reproaches herself for caving in. Gretchen's initial resistance and her wavering contribute to the drama of the seduction, but the contradiction remains. What kind of figure can say no to a crucial request and then describe herself as absolutely compliant?

III. Nasführen

Interestingly, Mephistopheles' taunt, "Ein Mägdelein nasführet dich," was the passage chosen by Sacher-Masoch's Severin in *Venus im Pelz* as a motto for his "Bekenntnisse eines Übersinnlichen," where it appears slightly modified:

> Du übersinnlicher sinnlicher Freier,
> Ein *Weib* nasführet dich![10]

Severin's autobiographical "Bekenntnisse" represent a painstaking study of masculine and feminine authority which follows the hero as he manipulates a woman into exercising authority over him, eventually losing control of the situation and experiencing subjection to a feminine will which is no longer subject to his own. This experience reforms Severin, who vows ever to be the direct and unmediated dominator and who enlists Goethe—the Goethe of *Faust*—as authority for his conviction that one must be either hammer or anvil. Henceforth Severin will be the hammer. As he explains to his interlocutor in the beginning:

Nirgends paßt Goethes "Du mußt Hammer oder Amboß sein" so vortrefflich hin wie auf das Verhältnis zwischen Mann und Weib. . . . In der Leidenschaft des Mannes ruht die Macht des Weibes, und es versteht sie zu benützen, wenn der Mann sich nicht vorsieht. Er hat nur die Wahl, der Tyrann oder der Sklave des Weibes zu sein. Wie er sich hingibt, hat er auch schon den Kopf im Joche und wird die Peitsche fühlen. (16)

Severin later articulates the social basis for his conviction:

Daß das Weib, wie es die Natur geschaffen und wie es der Mann gegenwärtig heranzieht, sein Feind ist und nur seine Sklavin oder seine Despotin sein kann, *nie aber seine Gefährtin*. Dies wird sie erst dann sein können, wenn sie ihm gleich steht an Rechten, wenn sie ihm ebenbürtig ist durch Bildung und Arbeit. (138)

Severin's conclusion that women can only stand above or below, in front of or behind men (never at their side or on their level) bears some resemblance to Georg Lukács's remarks on love in the "Gretchentragödie," which cast lovers in the roles of either dominators or subordinates, never partners or companions:

Die Unmöglichkeit einer realen Gleichheit von Mann und Frau in der bürgerlichen Gesellschaft erscheint [in den Liebestragödien des jungen Goethe] in den mannigfaltigsten Formen. . . . Die vorzeitige Bindung, selbst auf der Grundlage der echtesten und tiefsten Liebe, kann also in der Klassengesellschaft zum Ausgangspunkt unlösbarer tragischer Konflikte werden. Bleibt sie bestehen, so wird der sich bindende Jüngling das Opfer sein, reißt er sich, getrieben vom Drang seiner ungehemmten Entwicklungsmöglichkeiten, los, so muß das Mädchen aufgeopfert werden.[11]

These passages are interpretations or extrapolations from *Faust*, but whereas Lukács's reaction is to some extent predictable (but nevertheless insightful), Sacher-Masoch/Severin's reading of Goethe and *Faust* is intriguing and bears examination. Why, we might ask, does the masochist footnote *Faust*?

Venus opens with the account of an unnamed narrator who finds his way to Severin's parlor, where he reads the latter's "Confessions" and reproduces them for the reader. Immediately previous to this visit, the narrator dreams of the goddess Venus, who explains to him the dynamics of love, a power struggle between man and woman, which can only be won by the woman if she understands how to be *grausam*. He agrees: "Ich kann es nicht leugnen. . . es gibt für den Mann nichts, das ihn mehr reizen könnte, als das Bild einer schönen wollüstigen und grausamen Despotin. . . ." (12). The narrator who has just acknowledged his wish to be the subject or servant of his despotic mistress then feels her marble hand on his arm urging him to wake up. Yet, as he opens his eyes, the hand and voice of the mistress are transformed into those of his Cossack servant, a transformation that suggests the reciprocity of these respective postures as does the servant's (non-servile) reproach to his master:

"Stehen Sie doch auf," fuhr der Wackere fort, "es ist eine wahrhafte Schande."

"Und weshalb eine Schande?"

"Eine Schande in Kleidern einzuschlafen und noch dazu bei einem Buche," er putzte die heruntergebrannten Kerzen und hob den Band auf, der meiner Hand entsunken war, "*bei einem Buche von–er schlug den Deckel auf, von Hegel*–dabei ist es die höchste Zeit zu Herrn Severin zu fahren, der uns zum Tee erwartet" (13, my emphasis).

We never learn which of Hegel's works occasioned the Venus dream, but the master-slave thematics, the fluid transferral of authority from the despot to the servant, who chides the master (and the authoritarian concerns of the novel itself) strongly imply that the narrator may have been reading that section of the *Phänomenologie des Geistes* where Hegel "elucidates" the dialectical relationship of *Herrschaft* and *Knechtschaft*:

Die *Wahrheit* des selbstständigen Bewußtseins ist. . . das *knechtische Bewußt- sein*. Dieses erscheint zunächst *außer* sich und nicht als die Wahrheit des Selbstbewußtseins. Aber wie die Herrschaft zeigte, daß ihr Wesen das Verkehrte dessen ist, was sie sein will, so wird auch wohl die Knechtschaft vielmehr in ihrer Vollbringung zum Gegenteil dessen werden, was sie unmittelbar ist; sie wird als in sich *zurückgedrängtes* Bewußtsein in sich gehen und zur wahren Selbständigkeit sich umkehren.[12]

Leaving aside the intricate relations of reflective self-consciousness to itself and the other (as does Sacher-Masoch), we have not only master-slave reciprocity, but an identification of each with the other, a reassessment of authority as a result of the independent depending on the dependent for their dependence. The allusion is also playful in that it cites (it seems) and subverts Hegel's analysis of authoritarian relations; Hegel has inspired the profound dream in which truths about male-female power politics are revealed, but he has also put the narrator to sleep. If Hegel is indeed the textual prop for the narrator's and Severin's abdication of authority, his doctrine nonetheless needs to be delivered by a more palatable (and less ambiguous) figure.

Guided and prodded by his servant, the narrator/master reaches Severin's parlor and picks up the *Bekenntnisse*. In the beginning of his journal, Severin describes his former, "masochistic" self reading happily in the Book of Judith:

[Ich] beneidete den grimmen Heiden Holofernes um das königliche Weib, das ihm den Kopf heruntertrieb, und um sein blutig schönes Ende. . . . *"Gott hat ihn gestraft und hat ihn in eines Weibes Hände gegeben"* wiederholte ich für mich. Nun, was soll ich etwa anstellen, damit er mich straft? (21)

This is not exactly a Faustian question because it presages the repeated instances of bondage and confinement that cater to the wishes of the decidedly non-expansive hero of *Venus*, but it is similar in spirit to the structure of agency in *Faust* because Severin wishes to be punished by a woman acting on God's behalf, to be dominated and determined by an intermediary (as Faust is led to heaven by a woman). There is a strong analogy between the *Strafen* which Severin so eagerly seeks and the *Führen* which Faust requires.

As noted above, the God of *Faust* (*Der Herr* of the "Prolog im Himmel," who designates Faust his "Knecht" [299]) announces in his conversation with the devil that he will personally lead Faust to salvation. But the large cast of supernatural characters that accompanies Faust's ascension at the end of Part II does not include the deity personified. Never does he personally appear to lead his servant home. Hans Schwerte refers to this inconsistency and asks: "Hat der lenkende Herr des Prologs ("so werd' ich ihn [Faust] bald in die Klarheit führen") diese Lenkung übertragen an das 'Ewig-Weibliche?' "[13] Schwerte's question alludes to a divine example of abdication of authority. Severin's God delegates the punishing function and Faust's delegates the leading function.

But do these women act purely as representatives or messengers of a higher paternalistic authority? They are certainly disguised as such, but the chain of command is open to question. In his influential essay on Sacher-Masoch and Sade, translated as "Coldness and Cruelty,"[14] Gilles Deleuze seeks to drive a wedge between sadism and masochism considered as opposites or complementary positions. In brief, he finds, with Krafft-Ebing, that sadism duplicates (in an intensified fashion) typical authoritarian relations with a monolithic paternalistic authority figure demonstrating his dominion over the victim:

> Sadism is in every sense an active negation of the mother and an exaltation of the father who is beyond all laws. (60)

Masochism, however, is an effort to do away with the father. Against those who would see in the punishing woman with her fetishized adornments a mere mutation of the father and his discipline,[15] Deleuze argues most effectively that masochism (or Masoch's masochism) represents an exclusion of the father:

> The masochist experiences the symbolic order as an intermaternal order in which the mother represents the law under certain prescribed conditions. (63)

The masochistic contract excludes the father and displaces onto the mother the task of exercising and applying the paternal law. (93)

The elimination of the father from the masochistic transaction allows for a reorganization of authority and a conflicted hierarchical configuration. The punishing woman, who commands and humiliates the masochist, does so at his bidding. He dresses her, places the whip in her hand and more or less prescribes her every word and gesture, such that, god-like, he absolutely determines the course of a scenario that will then unfold without further interference from him. (This is the function of the contract.) In other words, the dominatrix is controlled by the man she ostensibly dominates. The servant (Severin assumed the identity of one named Gregor) realizes himself as master and the mistress is in reality a servant. The masochist, for the sake of being answerable to a being outside himself—of indulging his desire for a *Despotin*—projects his own absolute authority onto the woman he manipulates into being his master.

IV. Follow-up

Where does all this lead? Certainly not to the conclusion that Faust is a masochist or even a masochist-in-denial—I can think of few labels that would be less appropriate. Rather these observations, especially Deleuze's comments about the elimination of the father (to the extent that this is conceivable or representable), do, I think, throw some light on both the affinities between Goethe's drama and its unconventional receptor, Sacher-Masoch, as well as the relations between Goethe's plays and the conventions of contemporary bourgeois tragedy. Though Gretchen and Wanda von Dunajew are obviously diverse renderings of the female leader, each is a figure whose authority is a projection of her subject/follower's wishes and each ostensibly substitutes for a divine authority that might otherwise have punished or led the male subject (leading us to the conclusion that divinity may reside in him). Furthermore, the masochistic removal of the father from the punishing scenario has its counterpart in the operations performed by Goethe on the father-centered tradition of bourgeois tragedy in which we are inclined to place his "Gretchentragödie." Against the "sadistic" tendencies of "bürgerliches Trauerspiel" to refer everything back to the father, Goethe, a more "masochistic" sensibility in Deleuze's terms, plays down the role of the father in his seduction drama, featuring the *fatherless* daughter, who is a figure created to advance a compliant Faust toward his heavenly goal. Faust, who had no father before the 1808 version[16] and whose shady progenitor, "ein dunkler Ehrenmann" (1034), merits only very brief mention as a mad alchemist and murderer in "Vor dem Tor," is neither son nor father (both of his children die). He is, rather, the follower of himself, the eternally forward-moving pursuer of "das Ewig-Weibliche," which is ultimately a feminized projection of himself.

NOTES

1. This abstraction of self in order to be answerable to an (imaginary) other recalls Ludwig Feuerbach's critique of Christianity in *Das Wesen des Christentums.*

2. Peter Heller notes that according to standards set in *Faust,* the seducer must eventually leave the woman he has seduced, "wenn er nicht als der Genasführte gelten will." "Gretchen: Figur, Klischee, Symbol," in *Die Frau als Heldin und Autorin,* ed. Wolfgang Paulsen (Bern: Francke, 1979) 183.

3. See also Sandra M. Gilbert, Susan Gubar, *The Madwoman in the Attic* (New Haven: Yale University Press, 1979) 21.

4. Dennis Jonnes, "*Solche Väter:* The Sentimental Family Paradigm in Lessing's Drama," *Lessing Yearbook* XII (1981): 157–74.

5. "A Family Without Women: The Triumph of the Sentimental Father in Lessing's *Sara Sampson* and Klinger's *Sturm und Drang,*" *Lessing Yearbook* XXII (1990): 113–32.

6. H.L. Wagner's Evchen, for example, survives, but she appears to be headed for execution in *Die Kindermörderin* as the play closes. Frau Miller of *Kabale und Liebe* and Claudia Galotti are sent away toward the ends of their respective plays and thus effectively removed from the scene of action.

7. See Michael Schmidt, *Genossin der Hexe: Interpretation der Gretchentragödie in Goethes Faust aus der Perspektive der Kindesmordproblematik* (Göttingen: Verlag Altaquito, 1985) 1–68; André Banuls, "Familienverhältnisse in Goethes Faust," *Orbis Litterarum* 42 (1987): 332–37.

8. Kurt Eissler, *Goethe: A Psychoanalytic Study* (Detroit: Wayne State University Press, 1963) 1:277.

9. *Stella,* HA 4:319.

10. Leopold von Sacher-Masoch, *Venus im Pelz* (Frankfurt/Main: Insel [1980]) 17, my emphasis. Further citations will be given within the text by page number.

11. Georg Lukács, "Die Gretchentragödie," in *Aufsätze zu Goethes "Faust I,"* ed. Werner Keller (Darmstadt: Wissenschaftliche Buchgesellschaft, 1974) 481, (originally published in G.L., *Goethe und seine Zeit* [Berlin: Aufbau, 1953]).

12. Hegel, *Phänomenologie des Geistes,* in *Werke,* ed. Eva Moldenhauer, Karl Markus Michel, 3:152 (Frankfurt/Main: Suhrkamp, 1986; originally published 1970).

13. Hans Schwerte, "Der weibliche Schluß von Goethes 'Faust,' " *Sprachkunst* XXI (1990): 129–43, 138.

14. In Gilles Deleuze, *Masochism* (New York: Zone Books, 1989) 9–138.

15. Especially Theodor Reik, *Masochism in Sex and Society,* transl. M.H. Beigel and G.M. Kurth (Grove Press, 1962). See Deleuze, "Coldness and Cruelty" in *Masochism* 136, n. 14.

16. See Banuls 333.

Herbert Lindenberger

Closing up *Faust:* The Final Lines According to Schumann, Liszt, and Mahler

> Alles Vergängliche
> Ist nur ein Gleichnis;
> Das Unzulängliche,
> Hier wird's Ereignis;
> Das Unbeschreibliche,
> Hier ist's getan;
> Das Ewig-Weibliche
> Zieht uns hinan.

WHAT IS THE APPROPRIATE MUSICAL SETTING TO THE Chorus Mysticus with which Goethe's poem seeks to find closure? For those who, since the time of Monteverdi, have asserted the primacy of verbal text over music, Goethe's own words in these final eight lines should somehow determine their musical embodiment.[1] If we examine the three major settings of the Chorus–those of Robert Schumann, Franz Liszt, and Gustav Mahler–we note a common rhythm that can be explained at once by the rhythm of the words themselves and by the fact that each of the two later composers was familiar with the work of his predecessor(s).[2]

Yet it is difficult to approach these settings in the same way that one approaches the setting for a *Lied* by these same composers. Listening to them in succession, one is less aware here–as one normally is with *Lieder*–of how a particular word or line is being interpreted than one is aware of the composers' attempts to celebrate at once a diverse set of matters–for example, Faust's ascension into the peculiarly baroque heaven that Goethe concocted for the "Bergschluchten" scene; the principle of the eternal feminine as enunciated in the last two lines; the role of Goethe, and of *Faust* in particular, as a cornerstone of German culture; the role that the large-scale musical work came to assume in the course of the nineteenth century. My remarks on these passages will thus not concern themselves with how each composer comes to terms musically with Goethe's individual words but rather with the larger cultural statements suggested by the settings.

But first some historical background about the works within which these settings of the last lines occur. Schumann, like Mahler two generations later, set the whole final scene of *Faust II* to music. Liszt set only the Chorus Mysticus—and then as an afterthought to his otherwise wholly instrumental *Faust* Symphony, composed three years before. Schumann had begun his *Faust* settings in 1844 with the final scene and over the next nine years added selected scenes from both the first and second parts of the drama. Schumann's final scene received its first performance in 1849 at Weimar under Liszt's direction as part of the festivities surrounding the Goethe centennial. Schumann's section on the final eight lines is the longest of these three settings, over nine minutes of choral polyphony in which the various parts interweave to the point that the words are often difficult to discern.

Liszt composed his *Faust* Symphony in a two-month period in 1854 and added his brief choral finale, with tenor solo, in 1857. The first hour of the symphony consists of what are essentially three Lisztian tone poems—character sketches devoted, respectively, to Faust, Gretchen, and Mephistopheles; in view of Liszt's much-advertised literary inclinations, it is no wonder that the Mephisto section consists of musical parodies of the Faust themes. Mahler composed his Eighth Symphony in the summer of 1906, and it consisted of two movements, the first a setting of the medieval hymn, "Veni Creator Spiritus," and the second, much longer part in which, unlike Schumann, Mahler makes several cuts and editorial changes. The last eight lines combine chorus with solo women's voices.

My commentary on the three settings will juxtapose three modes of triumph: first, the triumph of Goethe, in particular as it is embodied in the work we call *Faust*; second, the triumph of the "eternal feminine"; and, third, the triumph of achieving closure on the grandest possible scale.

I start with the triumph of Goethe, who for the purpose of this argument exists within a continuum that includes at once his drama *Faust* and his character Faust. Accompanying the canonization of Goethe as a figure throughout the first half of the century, *Faust*, and distinctly not that early success *Werther*, emerged as the work that counted as the central embodiment of his genius. *Faust* found its way into the European consciousness not only in those objects we today call high art but also in less elevated forms—Gothic novels, thriller operas like Meyerbeer's *Robert le Diable* (a work decidedly more fustian than Faustian), countless Victorian melodramas—in which one can locate distant offshoots of Goethe's characters appearing in guises such as the stupidly idealistic hero, the sneering, often Byronically colored villain, the sweet-tempered girl crushed by forces beyond her control.

But setting the actual drama *Faust* to music constituted a special act of cultural piety, and few composers can be found during the nineteenth century who did not consider some musical embodiment of *Faust*, be it opera, symphony, or simply an overture such as Wagner's. Goethe, who was himself quite conscious of the operatic quality of his work, above all of the second part, even had particular composers in mind for a *Faust* opera—Mozart, if he had not died too soon, and, among living composers, Meyerbeer, who, as a German residing in Italy during the 1820s, struck Goethe, soon after he finished the Helena act, as someone who could mediate between the northern and the classical worlds.[3]

Among the many actually composed *Faust*s, the Berlioz, the Gounod, and the Boito versions are still in the repertory, but the unrealized *Faust*s by famous composers—besides, of course, the Mozart and Meyerbeer versions within Goethe's own imagination—are not so often cited. Rossini, for instance, sketched out a *Faust* scenario in 1830, the year after he completed what turned out to be his final opera, *Guillaume Tell*. And Beethoven discussed a possible *Faust* opera on several occasions. As late as 1823, he could contrast his lofty aspirations for a *Faust* composition with the pieces he had to do for money: responding to a request for an oratorio from a Boston choral society, Beethoven writes, "Ich schreibe nur *das* nicht, was ich am liebsten möchte, sondern des geldes wegen, was ich brauche, Es ist deswegen nicht gesagt, daß ich doch *bloß* ums Geld schreibe—ist diese Periode vorbey, so hoffe ich endlich zu schreiben, was mir und der Kunst das höchste ist—*Faust*."[4]

Of course Beethoven, even if financial pressures had not prevented a *Faust*, could never have given us the final lines, for he died several years before Goethe even wrote them. Indeed, the *Faust* we generally know in other media is the First Part. Those elements that might have made their way into popular art forms were doubtless not evident to contemporary composers in *Faust II*, and certainly not in the final scene. It seems especially appropriate that the first composer of rank to attempt this scene was the avant-gardist Schumann, editor of the *Neue Zeitschrift für Musik*, who remained noticeably reticent about his ability to wrestle with so mighty a text. Long before Liszt coaxed him into allowing a performance for the centennial, Schumann had written to Mendelssohn, "The scene from *Faust* reposes in my desk. I am absolutely afraid to look at it again. The lofty poetry, especially of the final part, moved me so deeply that I ventured to begin. I have no idea whether I shall ever publish it."[5] Composing a *Faust* would be something different in kind from setting an ordinary literary work, for Schumann, in a letter to Clara written in 1838, several years before his decision to embark on the project, viewed Goethe as something much more than simply a poet but as a God-like force who demanded an attitude of awe: "Goethe war ein großer Mann—vor dem hatte die Natur keine Geheimnisse—die Ehrfurcht vor diesem Mann kann gar keine Gränzen haben—und über alles ist er auch noch Dichter."[6]

Liszt's approach to composing a *Faust* was considerably more intrepid than Schumann's. One has doubts about his actual devotion to the text. He has been recorded as expressing a preference for Schiller over Goethe (a common enough matter to argue over at the time).[7] His introduction to *Faust* was not through the German original, but through the Nerval translation, which Berlioz had shown him in 1830. Yet Liszt's actual writings show a good bit of Goethe-idolatry, as in his lengthy proposal of 1850 for a Goethe Foundation to be established to further all the arts in the poet's (and also Liszt's!) adopted town.[8] Earlier, in his famous analysis of Berlioz's *Harold in Italy*, he credits Goethe and Byron with creating a major new genre, the philosophical epic, of which *Faust* becomes the towering example—"jene modernen Dichtungen, die wir in Ermangelung eines anderen Namens 'philosophische Epopöen' nennen möchten, unter denen Goethe's 'Faust' die riesigste ist."[9] In this same essay Liszt celebrates the fact that the new music has been appropriating the great literature of the past: "Die Meisterwerke der Musik nehmen mehr und mehr die Meisterwerke der Literatur in sich auf"[10]—but is it the literature they are appropriating, or simply the great artist-heroes, who for Liszt and many of his contemporaries could not be separated from their creators? Liszt's own tone poems and symphonies are based sometimes on overt literary characters like Faust and Mazeppa and sometimes on authors like Dante and Tasso—though the Dante symphony is a setting of the first two parts of the *Divine Comedy* and the Tasso has already been mediated by Goethe's drama on the poet. In setting the final words of *Faust*, one might add that Liszt is self-consciously making music aspire to the condition of a literature that has already aspired to the condition of music. Liszt's most recent biographer, Alan Walker, attributes the composer's actually getting to work on his *Faust* Symphony to the visit to Weimar of George Henry Lewes, who was researching his biography of the poet and pumping Liszt and his mistress, the Princess Sayn-Wittgenstein, with questions about Goethe: if a noted English critic was worshipping at the shrine, surely it was time, one can imagine Liszt thinking, for a composer to appropriate his work.[11]

By Mahler's time Goethe had not only been long since canonized, but had also become a subject for academic commentary. In a letter written to Alma in 1909, three years after his composition of the Eighth Symphony, Mahler compliments his wife for the good judgment she has shown in choosing to study the lines he had set: "Und daß Du Dir gerade Goethe ausgesucht hast, läßt in Dein Inneres blicken; daß Du kerzengerade in die Höhe gewachsen—so wie außen, auch innen."[12] Goethe evidently provided the authority that could guarantee both his wife's inward growth and the worth of his most grand-scale symphony. In the remainder of this long letter Mahler comments favorably on her own interpretation of the final lines and then himself assumes the role of academic commentator: "Deine Deutung der letzten Verse ist famos," he writes, "und ich bin überzeugt, besser als die der Herren Commentatoren (die ich zwar nicht kenne, aber von denen ich weiß, daß sie sich bald seit einem Jahrhundert die Zähne daran ausbeißen). Nun, mit den Deutungen eines Kunstwerkes hat es seine eigene Bewandtnis, das *Rationale* daran (d.h. das vom Verstand Aufzulösende) ist fast immer das nicht Wesentliche und eigentlich ein Schleier, der die Gestalt verhüllt" (430). Soon after, Mahler begins to explicate the final lines, which he calls "[die] Spitze der ungeheuren Pyramide des ganzen Werkes" (that is, Goethe's whole dramatic poem) in terms of the hermeneutic theory he has just elaborated: "Alles ist nur ein *Gleichnis*, für Etwas, dessen Gestaltung nur ein *unzulänglicher* Ausdruck für das sein kann, was hier gefordert ist. Es läßt sich eben Vergängliches wohl beschreiben; aber, was wir fühlen, ahnen, aber nie *erreichen* werden (also was hier ein *Ereignis* werden kann) eben das hinter allen Erscheinungen dauernd

Unvergängliche ist *unbeschreiblich*" (431). As literary critic Mahler is obviously reworking the characteristic clichés of his time (and this despite his claim not to know the scholarly commentary on *Faust*) as he emphatically did not in his role as composer of the very lines he is here explicating. The distinction he makes in his theory of interpretation between external rationality and inner mystery is paralleled in the dichotomy between the describable temporal world and the rationally indescribable eternal world that he locates in Goethe's lines themselves.

Mahler's commentary to his wife builds up to a lengthy discussion of Goethe's last two lines, but before taking these up I turn to the triumph of the eternal feminine as interpreted by the two earlier composers. Although I have been unable to find any specific allusion to "das Ewig-Weibliche" (outside of his musical setting) in Schumann's writings, throughout his work (not only in his great song cycles about love but above all in his correspondence with Clara) he idealizes the female as a being who, on the one hand, is more naive, passive and self-sufficient than the male and, on the other, someone who soothes him in his restlessness and is necessary for his salvation. Schumann's attitude is epitomized in an analogy he draws from Goethe on several occasions when writing to Clara: he views himself as playing Egmont to his fiancée, whom he decides, after rereading Goethe's text, henceforth to call Clärchen; had Clara Wieck borne the name Margarete, Schumann would doubtless have drawn his analogy from *Faust*.[13]

The classic nineteenth-century view of the eternal feminine principle can be found in a passage that Liszt, in his analysis of *Der fliegende Holländer*, wrote at the very time he was starting his *Faust* Symphony: "Wenn man auf die Grundlage der Wagner'schen Fictionen näher eingeht, so möchte man sie eine Dramatisirung des Cultus jenes 'Ewig Weiblichen' in allen seinen Formen nennen, mit welchem Göthe wie mit einem Schlußstein den gigantischen Bau seines Faust endete. Für Wagner wie für Göthe ist es das Weib, von der Natur als herrlichste Blüthe des *Gefühls* erzeugt, welches den Mann, in dem die *That* als Frucht des *Gedankens* reift, reinigt und heiligt."[14]

Here we note a standard manifestation of nineteenth-century gender ideology—the woman as compliant yet indispensable by virtue of her inspirational and sanctifying power, the man as the one who keeps things going yet is always in need of the purification that his female partner can dispense.[15] The strict demarcation of gender roles evident here can be seen as a relatively new development within nineteenth-century culture, as a recent feminist study of the relationship of Clara and Robert Schumann has shown: this demarcation, according to this study, represents a conspicuous reversal of the blurring of gender roles to be found in the writings of the early Romantics.[16] But Liszt's statement goes back to Wagner himself, who, in discussing the final chorus of Beethoven's Ninth Symphony in *Oper und Drama*, applied the term *ewig-weiblich* to the musical setting, with the poet standing for the male principle that celebrates his own salvation by means of the union of text and sound that Beethoven has accomplished.[17] For Liszt, as later for Mahler, the act of setting the final lines of *Faust* becomes

a means for realizing Wagner's ideal union of words and music with the very
term that Wagner had borrowed from Goethe and transferred from the discourse
of love to aesthetic theory.[18]

By the time Mahler set Goethe's lines, the term *das Ewig-Weibliche* had become
a part of everyday language, often in a jocular way, as when Mahler, in a letter
to Alma, describes Richard Strauß's shrewish wife Pauline as "das ewig
Weibliche."[19] Yet when explicating the final lines to her two years later in the
letter from which I quoted earlier, he presents "das Ewig-Weibliche" with total
earnestness: "Das, was uns mit mystischer Gewalt hinanzieht, was jede Creatur,
vielleicht sogar die Steine, mit unbedingter Sicherheit als das Centrum ihres Seins
empfindet, was Goethe hier—*wieder in einem Gleichnis*—das *Ewig-Weibliche* nennt—
nämlich das *Ruhende*, das *Ziel*—im Gegensatze zu dem ewigen Sehnen, Streben,
sich Hinbewegen zu diesem Ziel—also dem Ewig-Männlichen! Du hast ganz recht,
es als die Liebesgewalt zu charakterisieren" (431). The feminine appears here as
the passive, peace-giving principle—"das Ruhende"—which is the opposite of the
eternal effort and the eternal struggle that constitute the "eternal masculine."

From what we know today of the Mahlers' relationship, it is evident that the
composer prized the role of quiet inspirer that he could read at once into his wife's
personality and into the lines he had set by Goethe, and it must have given him
considerable satisfaction to find her reading the great poet and, even better,
consulting her husband for the interpretive expertise he could bring to her reading.
It is significant, moreover, that a notation on the original sketch for the Eighth
Symphony in effect deifies Alma by echoing the medieval hymn Mahler set for
the first movement with the words "Almschl—creator spiritus."[20] Yet his interpretation ignores the possibility that the eternal woman might be bestowing her
inspiration upon more than one man at a time: a year after Mahler's letter
instructing his wife on the meaning of Goethe's term, indeed, at the very moment
that Mahler was rehearsing the first performance of the Eighth Symphony at the
Neue Musikfesthalle of the Munich Exposition, the symphony's *creator spiritus* was
making love to her recently acquired lover, Walter Gropius, at the Hotel Regina-
Palast.[21] Perhaps Nietzsche should have the last word on the eternal-feminine,
though he spoke out on the matter well over twenty years before these events
in Munich: after exposing the sickness he saw in Wagner's various heroines,
Nietzsche wrote: "Der Mann ist feige vor allem Ewig-Weiblichen: das wissen die
Weiblein."[22]

At this point I turn to the third and last mode of triumph relevant to these
three musical settings, namely the triumph of achieving musical closure in the
most forceful possible way. Only the last two of these versions end with forceful
closure, with the first concluding on a surprisingly quiet note. Yet Schumann must
have felt the need for a more overtly powerful ending, for he later revised the
score to provide some *forte* chords at the end.[23] When Liszt added his tenor-and-
choral finale three years after completing his instrumental movements based on
the three major characters in the drama, he too must have felt the need for a
literally resounding end. For Mahler the quiet, serene endings that mark other

symphonies such as the Third and Fourth and *Das Lied von der Erde* would have seemed inappropriate to a piece with the particular pretensions of the Eighth. (In view of the prevalence of high-volume closure in late-nineteenth-century symphonies, even Mahler's quiet endings, by confounding our expectations of how works in this genre close, work in effect to confirm the norm of loudness.) Adorno, who felt a disdain for the Eighth that he rarely expressed toward any of Mahler's compositions, speaks of it as belonging to "le genre chef d'oeuvre" or "offizielles Hauptwerk." For Adorno, the role of *Faust*, as well as of the medieval hymn with which the Eighth opens, is to provide "sublime objects" to "guarantee the sublime content" of the work.[24] This sublime content is further guaranteed in both Mahler's and Liszt's settings of *Faust* with the introduction, in the final bars, of the organ, which serves at once to add volume and to introduce an overtly church-like dimension.

Within the history of music, the Eighth provides one of the last of the grand-scale endings that mark a multitude of symphonic works beginning with Beethoven's, for instance, the agonizingly drawn-out last pages of the Fifth or the massively celebratory ending of the Ninth, which throughout the nineteenth century counted as so large in its aspirations that composers often expressed inhibitions about writing symphonies in the wake of Beethoven's final symphonic work. The young Mahler had already sought to outdo Beethoven in the choral finale of his Second Symphony, whose protracted and high-volume ending was scarcely to be outdone by his own Eighth. Soon after Mahler, however, the grand-scale symphonic close became antiquated. The massive ending of Schoenberg's *Gurre-Lieder*, begun before, but not completed until after the composer had broken with tonality, provides the coda to a century-long tradition that celebrates by means of massiveness and volume (Mahler's symphony, after all, has been labelled–though not by the composer himself–"The Symphony of a Thousand").

And what, we may ask, is the peculiar triumph these works are celebrating? Mahler would have answered in religious terms–in language such as he employed in a letter to Bruno Walter of 1909 in which the end of Goethe's *Faust* is specifical-ly connected with his own intuitions of personal transcendence: "Ich sehe alles in einem so neuen Lichte–bin so in Bewegung; ich würde mich manchmal gar nicht wundern, wenn ich plötzlich einen neuen Körper an mir bemerken würde. (Wie Faust in der letzten Szene.)"[25] But the triumphs in which these works culminate can also be translated into other terms–the triumph of art, or the triumph of the symphony as a form, or the triumph of the composer himself in his personal struggles, or the triumph of achieving closure, or simply, one is tempted to say, the triumph of triumph as the nineteenth century conceived this term.

Finally, one asks, since Goethe left us no stage directions, as he did with *Egmont*, to indicate what sounds should accompany the last lines of *Faust*, how do these lines function in their own right without the musical and interpretive resources that have been brought to bear on them over the years? Whatever eight lines he might have chosen to end the drama, any of his choices–even perhaps

a set of silent ellipses—would be taken by the reader as some culminating final
statement, a grand closure, to a long uncompleted work that had been part of
the public consciousness for as long as anybody could remember. In their contrast
of two realms, the earthly and whatever one calls that which is above it, they
play upon a traditional dichotomy that runs the gamut of Western culture and
teases us as to whether their proper focus is metaphysics, religion, or art. Above
all, their gnomic quality, together with the inscription "chorus mysticus," tells
us that one of the main things they mean is that they are inviting us to interpret
just what precisely they might happen to mean.

What would a composer of our own time do with them—granted, that is, that
composition by an artist acting as an individual might still be a viable preoccupation and that the setting of hallowed lines can still seem a useful endeavor? I can
imagine a musical collage juxtaposing fragments of these passages in some random,
non-chronological order together with a collage of triumphant *forte* final chords
in major keys appropriated from a myriad of nineteenth-century symphonies,
operas, and choral works. And then, in a characteristic postmodern gesture to
play with the idea of what we mean by final words, one might imagine a weak
voice hidden in the audience piping up, "Mehr Licht!"—at which point the
auditorium in which the music-going public is solemnly gathered would suddenly
light up to remind us that triumphs of the sort we have been hearing have long
been out of date.

NOTES

1. For a discussion of the debate on whether the words or the music is primary, see my
book *Opera: The Extravagant Art* (Ithaca: Cornell University Press, 1984) 108–27.

2. The rhythmic similarities look particularly striking when the three settings are juxta-
posed with one another, as in Donald Mitchell's analysis in *Gustav Mahler: Songs and
Symphonies of Life and Death* (Berkeley: University of California Press, 1985) 583–84.

3. For the comment on Meyerbeer, made 29 January 1827, see Johann Peter Eckermann,
Gespräche mit Goethe. Two years later, on 12 February 1829, Goethe expressed discourage-
ment that Meyerbeer could undertake the task since he seemed too much engaged with
theaters in Italy; in this same conversation he brings up Mozart as the ideal composer
of *Faust* because "die Musik müßte im Character des Don Juan sein." It is ironic that
two years later Meyerbeer *did* produce a *Faust* of sorts, or at least a Faust-inspired,
thoroughly Gothic opera, *Robert le Diable*, which, by a further irony, was neither German
nor Italian but initiated the composer's period as the reigning composer of French *grand
opéra*.

4. Beethoven, *Konversationshefte*, ed. Karl-Heinz Köhler and Dagmar Beck, vol. 3 (Leipzig:
VEB Deutscher Verlag für Musik, 1983) 148.

5. Quoted by Frank Cooper in "[Schumann's] Operatic and Dramatic Music," in *Robert
Schumann: The Man and His Music*, ed. Alan Walker (London: Barrie and Jenkins, 1972)
324. I have not had access to the German original of this letter.

6. Clara und Robert Schumann, *Briefwechsel*, Kritische Gesamtausgabe, vol. 1 (Stroemfeld: Roter Stern, 1984) 98.

7. See the description of his argument with Bettina von Arnim over the respective merits of the two writers in Alan Walker, *Franz Liszt*, vol. 2 (New York: Knopf, 1989) 132.

8. See Liszt, "Zur Goethe-Stiftung," in *Gesammelte Schriften*, ed. L. Ramann, vol. 5 (Leipzig: Breitkopf und Härtel, 1882) 3–109.

9. "Berlioz und seine 'Harold-Symphonie,' " in *Gesammelte Schriften*, vol. 4 (1882) 53.

10. "Berlioz und seine Harold-Symphonie" 58.

11. Walker, *Franz Liszt* 2:327. For additional descriptions of Lewes's visit, including the role played by Lewes's companion, Mary Ann Evans (who had not yet begun her career as George Eliot), see 246–51.

12. Alma Mahler, *Gustav Mahler: Erinnerungen und Briefe* (Amsterdam: Allert de Lange, 1940) 430. Subsequent passages from this letter will be cited within the text.

13. For Schumann's *Egmont* analogies, see Clara and Robert Schumann, *Briefwechsel* 1:73, 97–98, 294. Though Schumann insisted on the Egmont-Clärchen analogy, Clara herself at one point in their correspondence identifies overtly with Gretchen (1:195).

14. "Wagner's Fliegender Holländer," in *Sämtliche Schriften*, ed. Dorothea Redepenning and Britta Schilling, vol. 5 (Wiesbaden: Breitkopf und Härtel, 1989) 100–1.

15. For an excellent analysis of how Liszt's musical style embodies nineteenth-century gender ideology, see the chapter entitled "Liszt, Goethe, and the Discourse of Gender" in Lawrence Kramer, *Music as Cultural Practice, 1800–1900* (Berkeley: University of California Press, 1990) 102–34. Although he does not mention Liszt's use of gender discourse in his prose writings, Kramer makes some useful analogies between the ideas embodied in the *Faust* symphony and in writers such as Keats and D.G. Rosetti.

16. See Beatrix Borchard, *Robert Schumann und Clara Wieck: Bedingungen künstlerischer Arbeit in der ersten Hälfte des 19. Jahrhunderts* (Weinheim: Beltz Verlag, 1985) 87–112. It is ironical that, despite his subscribing to the woman's role as inspirer of male creative activity, Schumann, who had meager financial resources of his own and little hope of income from his compositions, was also eager for the earnings that his wife was able to bring home in her role as one of Europe's most illustrious pianists.

17. As Wagner put it, "Diese Melodie war der Liebesgruß des Weibes an den Mann; das umfassende ewig 'Weibliche' bewährte sich hier liebevoller als das egoistische Männliche." See Wagner, *Gesammelte Schriften*, ed. Julius Kapp, vol. 11 (Leipzig: Hesse und Becker, 1914) 254.

18. For a detailed account of how the concept of the eternal feminine at the end of the drama can be linked to earlier female figures and allusions within the text, see Michael Neumann, *Das Ewig-Weibliche in Goethes 'Faust'* (Heidelberg: Carl Winter, 1985). See also the discussion of earlier commentaries on the last two lines in Hans Arens, *Kommentar zu Goethes Faust II* (Heidelberg: Carl Winter, 1989) 1051–54.

19. In Alma Mahler (note 12) 372.

20. Noted by Donald Mitchell (note 2) 531. The printed score of the symphony contains a more formal dedication: "Meiner lieben Frau Alma Maria." Mahler's use of Alma's middle name in this dedication may have been motivated by the four-hour "psychoanalysis" that he had recently received while walking the streets of Leiden with Sigmund Freud,

who found a confirmation of the Oedipus complex in the fact that this name was the same as that of Mahler's mother (see Henry-Louis de la Grange, *Gustav Mahler: Chronique d'une vie*, vol. 3 [Paris: Fayard, 1984] 770–71).

21. See La Grange 3:777. The encounters at the hotel were first revealed by Reginald R. Isaacs in *Walter Gropius: Der Mensch und sein Werk* (Berlin: Gebr. Mann, 1983) 103–4. Mahler learned of his wife's affair with Gropius earlier in the summer of 1910, and Alma discussed it in a veiled manner and without naming her suitor in her 1940 volume (note 12) 210–19. Yet Mahler apparently had no knowledge that the affair continued into September when the whole musical world of Germany had converged on Munich to hear the premiere of the symphony dedicated to Alma. The shock that Mahler had received on first hearing of the affair evidently motivated a significant series of events: his formal dedication of the long-since-completed symphony to his wife, his seeking out of Freud for counseling, and his publication of Alma's *Lieder*, which, in conformity with nineteenth-century gender ideology, he had forbidden her to continue composing at the time of their marriage (see his letter of 19 December 1901 in La Grange, *Gustav Mahler*, 2 [1979] 187–93).

22. Nietzsche, *Der Fall Wagner* (Section 3) in *Werke*, ed. Karl Schlechta (Darmstadt: Wissenschaftliche Buchgesellschaft, 1966) 2:909.

23. Conductors have traditionally preferred the first version, which is used in both recordings that are currently available.

24. Theodor W. Adorno, *Mahler* (Frankfurt/Main: Suhrkamp, 1960): "Solche Hypostasis betreibt das offizielle Hauptwerk, die Achte Symphonie. Die Worte offiziell und Hauptwerk nennen die Angriffspunkte, le genre chef d'oeuvre. . ." (182). "Die Achte ist angesteckt von dem Wahn, erhabene Gegenstände, jener Hymnus Veni Creator Spiritus, die Schlußszene des Faust, bürgten für die Erhabenheit des Gehalts" (184). One might add that the Eighth is also lacking in the irony that Adorno praises in many other Mahler works.

25. Gustav Mahler, *Briefe*, ed. and rev. Herta Blaukopf (Vienna: Paul Zsolnay Verlag, 1982) 351.

Christoph E. Schweitzer

Gretchen and the Feminine in Goethe's *Faust*

In the following I will pursue an issue in Goethe's *Faust* that seems to me of crucial importance to an understanding of the work. Jane Brown confirmed the importance of the issue when she reported that at the NEH Seminar on *Faust* at Santa Barbara in 1990 the figure of Gretchen caused the most heated debate. The centrality of Gretchen, the strongest character in Part I, has long been recognized.

The ideas in this paper have been sharpened not only from the vast secondary literature but also from the various contributions to the Santa Barbara conference and the discussions that followed them. If there was one theme that prevailed at the conference, it was that there is no *one* way of reading Goethe's *Faust*; any given interpretation must necessarily isolate *one* aspect of the mammoth work and thus do a disservice to the overall significance which at best can be experienced but not stated in words. The presence of irony in all scenes compounds the difficulty of any attempt to pinpoint the work's meaning.

Anyone looking at *Faust* must be struck by the strength of Gretchen's character and must then ask questions about her fate. Mephisto and she are, at least in Part I, the two outstanding figures; they are also the most opposite ones. In a simplified formula one could say both want Faust. Mephisto's aim, though, is a selfish and thus negative one while hers is selfless and thus ultimately the one that prevails.

One can hardly imagine two more contrastive lives than those of Gretchen and Faust. He appears as the prototype male and Gretchen as what from a male point of view can be considered the embodiment of the female, with all privileges and advantages on the side of the male. As the son of a well-to-do physician, Faust achieves prominence as an academician, and then is given the chance, after rejuvenation, to use his persuasive powers and wealth to seduce Gretchen. Soon afterwards he abandons her and yields to his sexual fantasies and then becomes in "Walpurgisnachtstraum" a spectator of a sideshow of arid parodies. He leaves the dead Gretchen behind to enter the world of the powerful, imagines that he has been able to conjure up Helen, the epitome of female beauty, and is finally shown as having conquered a large piece of land from the sea through part of which a long drainage canal is to be dug and where a large community of free

and industrious people are supposed to thrive. And while the text shows that
Faust's so-called "striving" has brought, directly or indirectly, violent death to
Gretchen's mother, brother, and child, as well as to Philemon and Baucis and
their grateful visitor, Faust seems to be able to resist any feelings of responsibility
or guilt. Just the same, after death he is "erlöst" (I will discuss the term below),
supposedly on the basis of his incessant striving, as the angels have it in
"Bergschluchten." Finally, we must assume that the Mater Gloriosa is pointing
to what will happen, i.e., that his spirit is going to follow Gretchen's spirit to the
"higher spheres." After all, he is at this point at the complete mercy of forces
outside himself and thus seems no longer capable of making decisions on his own,
decisions that would counter the upward movement in the wake of Gretchen.
The redeeming aspect of striving was introduced by the Lord, as I will call
Goethe's "Der Herr" of "Prolog im Himmel." According to the Lord it is
Mephisto's role to keep Faust from yielding to sloth ("unbedingte Ruh," 341).
The Lord is even aware of the fact that striving implies erring. He furthermore
claims that while Faust is serving him at this time in a confused manner ("ver-
worren," 308), Faust, "his servant," is basically a good person who knows what
is right and one whom he, the Lord, will soon lead to clarity. There is clearly
an enormous discrepancy between our and the Lord's assessment of Faust.

I do not need to spell out in detail Gretchen's fate.[1] Feminists would call her
falling in love with Faust a typical romantic fantasy and would refer to Faust as
the paternal " 'knight in shining armor' who represents freedom, the outside
world, will, agency, and desire."[2] Gretchen's short period of bliss with Faust is
preceded by many years of daily toil under the watchful eyes of her widowed
mother and is followed by months of terrible suffering during which she gives
birth to an illegitimate child whom she, in despair, kills, a murder for which she
is then executed.

Critics who find in "Prolog im Himmel" the fixed vantage point from which
to view and judge the play proper tend to make neither Faust nor Gretchen
responsible for their actions and the consequences of these actions. For them the
responsibility lies with the Lord or his agent Mephisto. With this way of looking
at Faust it is impossible to speak of him as someone who makes his own decisions.
Ultimately, everyone in the work would have to be considered the Lord's puppet,
an approach to *Faust* that would make it a game of chess in which the Lord is
responsible for all the moves. It is best not to look at the dialogue between the
Lord and Mephisto as containing the key to a correct reading of *Faust*. Even
Werner Keller, whose views on the Faust/Gretchen relationship are more
traditional than mine, shows doubts about the Lord of "Prolog im Himmel" when
he writes that "der Halbernst des 'Herrn' seinem [Faust's] späteren schrecklichen
'Irren' und Mephistos diabolischem Treiben nicht gerecht wird."[3] One thing is
certain: the Lord of "Prolog im Himmel" does not control what happens on earth.

No outside force—not God or the Lord, not Mephisto—need or should be
referred to when explaining Faust's or Gretchen's feelings or actions. That Faust
is sensually attracted to Gretchen and then uses all the means at his disposal—

including his wealth and his facility with words—to seduce her should not come as a surprise to anyone in Goethe's or our time. That Gretchen is impressed by Faust, by his looks, station, experience—Mephisto introduces him to Gretchen as a man who has travelled far (3019), a fact that clearly makes her look at him with awe (3075–78)—and wealth is equally understandable. Gretchen is on the one hand the product of her environment: before meeting Faust she voiced the same conventional moral judgments as other members of the community, as "Am Brunnen" shows. But there is also another side to her. When she sings "Es war ein König in Thule," she subconsciously reveals that other side by choosing a song about a relationship of true love that is not sanctioned by society. One must also not forget that she is on good terms with a woman of such dubious character as Frau Marthe, to whom Gretchen seems to turn when she has something to confide which would not find an understanding ear in her stern mother. She definitely transgresses social norms when she agrees to meet Faust and she subsequently accepts his precious gifts. In so doing she breaks out of her confined situation to risk all for a short period of utter bliss, pushing aside all thought about the consequences.

Gretchen's relationship to Faust develops into one of selfless love, a love that must be considered the only satisfactory explanation for his not going to Hell, a fate that otherwise seems most appropriate for him. Faust, to be sure, believes that he loves her. Gretchen tries to and some critics are inclined to believe that indeed his protestations are truly felt commitments. They are definitely not that. As Gretchen says in prison: "Wo ist dein Lieben / Geblieben?" (4495–96).

As mentioned above, many critics put the blame for Faust's seduction and subsequent abandonment of Gretchen on Mephisto, who for me is nothing more than the visual and vocal representation of Faust's erotic desire for her, a desire that is rekindled at a time of his dissatisfaction with lonely masturbation (3291–96).[4] Other critics see in Faust's vision of the dead Gretchen in "Walpurgisnacht" evidence of his love for Gretchen. If one wants to see in her appearance in "Walpurgisnacht" something other than a projection of Faust's bad conscience, then I would propose that she has followed him to participate in the pursuit of sexual fantasies but then tries in vain to turn him back to her; in vain, since immediately after her appearance he falls silent and allows Mephisto to put on an inane show by dilettantes. Here I cannot agree with Albrecht Schöne, who suggests that Goethe really wanted to have Gretchen appear on the Brocken as a witch: after all, she had killed her baby, something, according to Schöne, not uncommon in the case of witches.[5] I cannot see her being both a witch in Part I and a key agent for Faust's salvation at the end of Part II.

Faust's perjuring himself when he agrees to testify to having seen Herr Schwerdtlein's grave "vorzüglich weil ich muß" (3072) or his less than complete honesty toward Gretchen are not the decisive causes of the ensuing terrible events. All this is understandable in a man/woman relationship. Rather, the fact that Faust's relationship to Gretchen does not develop into one of caring, of faithfulness, of true love brings about her terrible fate. His life, then, is characterized by a series of failures or, at best, of temporary accomplishments of egocentric goals. He abandons learning, teaching, and research, he fails as far as Gretchen is concerned, he is unable to give permanence to absolute beauty, and he dies completely alone in the illusory belief of having conquered land from the sea for a new community when in reality the sea will soon again overrun the land. In view of such a negative overall assessment I again agree with Werner Keller when he says: "Wer Faust versteht, begreift nicht mehr, daß er Generationen von Deutschen als Identifikationsmuster dienen konnte."[6] Benjamin Bennett speaks of Faust's failure on a more philosophical level as being unable both to immerse himself fully in an experience and, at the same time, to be conscious of that experience.[7] Both Faust's constant urge to go one step further and his egocentric philosophizing are aptly parodied by Herr Schwerdtlein's *Wanderlust* (see "Der Nachbarin Haus") and by the student's creation of his own universe (6689–6814).

Kenneth Weisinger, who devalues, as I do, the Lord of "Prolog im Himmel," complains about the "total lack of material within the text to provide adequate grounding for valid judgment."[8] However, he concentrates on the first part and thus does the work an injustice. Actually, the voice from above at the end of Part I ("Ist gerettet!") already provides such material. I take this to be a female voice which thus foreshadows the preeminence of the feminine of "Bergschluchten," a scene in which important clues for the work's ultimate meaning are to be found. I will take up that scene below.

The excitement of Faust's adventurous undertakings is especially attractive to male academicians who, after all, form the majority of the interpreters. Established scholars will yearn, like Faust, to break out of the confines of academia while students will empathize with his disgust with learning and his desire to experience "real life." Thus, one can consider *Faust* a "subversive classic," to use Theodore Ziolkowski's phrase.[9] The fact that so many female readers also have found in Faust, at least in the past, an attractive figure is somewhat more difficult to understand. A thorough explanation would go beyond the limits of this study. That explanation must be found in the traditional self-perception of women. A parallel phenomenon can be seen in the reception of "Heidenröslein," which is, after all, a poem about rape that has been recited and sung with approval by both men and women all over the world. As I see it, the subject matter kept Goethe from publishing the poem for some sixteen years.

One can read, then, *Faust* as the projection of a male point of view of the world in which the male's ceaseless striving and erring is sanctioned by divine authority. Interpreters who follow this line of argumentation often refer to Goethe's maxim: "Der Handelnde ist immer gewissenlos, es hat niemand Gewissen als der Betrachtende" (*Maximen und Reflexionen*, HA 12:251). But even divine sanction does not for most readers go so far as to give a blessing to Faust's killing of Valentin or his ordering the forceful removal of Philemon and Baucis from their land just because on it is the highest elevation of the area where Faust wants to build a tower from which to survey his realm. Just as important is the reader's realization that, regardless of divine sanction, Faust's striving has ultimately resulted in nothing permanent. Rather, his striving has reinforced in the reader's mind the futility of his endeavors. In the end the reader understands that Faust's redemption, as indicated in the last scene, functions as a safety net provided by the female principle, specifically by Gretchen and her selfless love for him.

Here one could refer to cultural and psychological studies such as David Gilmore's *Manhood in the Making* where patterns of masculine breaking away and the "ineradicable fantasy of the return to the blissful experience with the mother" are discussed in detail.[10] Thomas Mann has Adrian Leverkühn revert to complete dependency on his mother after his collapse at the end of *Doktor Faustus*. One can see a similar regressive movement in Goethe's *Faust* when the spirit of the protagonist in the last scene is reduced to "Unmündigkeit," to silence and to complete dependency. He who had been so talkative in his life, especially talkative when it came to persuading Gretchen that he *was* a believer, is now not allowed to utter a single word. Faust had made Gretchen follow him in almost all he wanted her to do for him ("Sonst hab' ich dir ja alles zu Lieb' getan," 4578). The only exception was when she refused to leave prison with him and thus assumed responsibility for her actions and, in so doing, saved herself. Now, at the end of "Bergschluchten," Faust obediently and, we may assume, meekly and happily, follows her who is already moving in an upward direction toward the "höhern Sphären" (12094).

Faust is portrayed as a person who has lived as long and intensely as is humanly possible. Goethe mentioned to Eckermann on 6 June 1831 that Faust is supposed to be one hundred years old when he dies. I have already pointed out the negative and ultimately futile results of his activities. "Bergschluchten" confirms such a judgment: the residues of these activities which cling to Faust have to be removed before he can enter the next phase of his "reorientation."[11] The "erlösen" (11937) of the angels must be read in this sense, i.e., as meaning "freimachen," and not as "redeem." The angels only make possible what is to follow. The actual removal of the dross is undertaken by the "selige Knaben," the stillborn who didn't even have a chance to see the light of day because they were born at midnight. They form the greatest possible contrast to Faust with his extra-long life. Let me mention here that I believe the introduction of so weighty an issue as that of the "selige Knaben" in "Bergschluchten"—an issue that belongs at the very center of theodicy—must mean that in the last scene *Ernst* prevails over *Scherz*, that Goethe tries in "Bergschluchten" to find language, figures, movements, and interrelationships that are suggestive of a possible way of looking at life and death. As came out in the Santa Barbara conference, language must fail here, and the "Unbeschreibliche" (12108) is ultimately left to the "Chorus mysticus," to music.

In contrast to Faust, the "selige Knaben" are given a voice. Between them and Faust a compensatory exchange takes place so that they experience, at least vicariously, life on earth, and so that he profits from their purity. The angels (of indeterminate sex) and the "selige Knaben" form the transition in "Bergschluchten" from the dominance of the male principle to that of the female. It is Gretchen who, already touching the Mater Gloriosa ("sich anschmiegend" before 12069), intercedes on behalf of the beloved of earlier times who now is the "nicht mehr Getrübte" (12074, i.e., "no longer in the dark") and whom she asks the Mater Gloriosa to be allowed to instruct. Clearly, Gretchen's wish is granted, thus emphasizing the predominance of the female at the end of the scene, a predominance that is reinforced by the last two lines of the work. The Mater Gloriosa is, of course, one of the terms used to refer to the Virgin Mary. At the same time, as Hans Schwerte has pointed out, it is completely unorthodox to refer to her as *Königin*, as Queen, as the Doctor Marianus does on three occasions when addressing her in the second half of "Bergschluchten" (11995, 12011, 12102).[12] He also calls her "Höchste Herrscherin der Welt" (11997). I take these terms to be further evidence that in "Bergschluchten" the male principle—let me for the sake of simplicity connect it with *streben*—has receded and yielded to that of the feminine. That principle, in turn, is intimately connected with grace and especially with love, a word that is used either by itself or in a derivative or a compound fifteen times in the 207 lines of the scene. Love, Eros, then, in its most general meanings is the positive force in the universe as evidenced in the glorious festival of the sea that is celebrated at the end of "Klassische Walpurgisnacht," a festival at which Faust is not present and one that leads to life.[13] Faust's two offspring, on the other hand, die young. In *Faust*, then, ultimate values are not established in "Prolog im Himmel" but by what transpires in the last scene. It, like the first scene of the play proper, takes place in a realm of symbols and thus prods us to relate the two to each other. Mephisto obviously does not belong to "Bergschluchten" and the Lord, as I will show below, has yielded to the Mater Gloriosa, at least as far as the final judgment of Faust is concerned, the person about whose ultimate destiny the Lord and Mephisto had had opposing ideas. Gretchen's fate is also decided by the Mater Gloriosa, who thus replaces the Lord as the highest authority when it comes to the assessment of the value of a human life.

Hans Schwerte stresses the presence of God, the Lord of "Prolog im Himmel," as being "unerläßlich zur höchsten Offenbarung 'ewigen Liebens.' "[14] However, even if we assume the Lord's presence somewhere in "Bergschluchten," something for which there is only slim evidence in the text—Schwerte refers to lines 11888 and 11921, both of which passages belong to the first third of the scene—the Lord, like Faust, is kept from saying anything and he is not addressed again in the crucial last part of the scene. Schwerte reads the famous lines 11936–37 as the message the Lord has sent via his angels; thus, according to Schwerte, only "Gott der Herr und/oder sein Sohn, der Miterlöser" can redeem Faust.[15] I claim that, even if lines 11936–37 are to be taken as the Lord's message, they refer only to a first phase of Faust's reorientation. There is not a single reference to the Lord after 11937 in what turns out to be twice as much text as that before that line. Only at the end of the scene is Faust's redemption suggested, a redemption in which the Lord is not involved.

There are two final aspects in connection with Gretchen and the overall meaning of *Faust* that need mentioning. First of all, it has been suggested that "Bergschluchten"–as well as "Prolog im Himmel"–must primarily be considered a travesty on prevailing religious cliches, similar, let us say, to what we have in the ending of *Die Wahlverwandtschaften*. There the very unholy Eduard follows into death his certainly less than saintly Ottilie. While I grant that the narrator of the *Wahlverwandtschaften* is constantly undercutting the happenings of the novel, including the ending, I cannot read "Bergschluchten" in the same manner. I have already mentioned above the weighty issue of the "selige Knaben," who are completely out of place in a travesty. While I see the playfulness of much of *Faust*, I cannot believe that "Bergschluchten," with its elaborate wording, carefully balanced movements, and correspondences, including that of a parody of Gretchen's outcry of despair in "Zwinger," is primarily a travesty.[16] Rather, I think this is Goethe's attempt to express the ineffable in words.

There is another issue, though, that is more bothersome. After all is said about the crucial role of Gretchen and, by extension, the feminine principle, in determining ultimate human values, we still see in Faust's erring on earth something more positive than in Gretchen's suffering. We know that Faust's striving has been the cause of the tragedy, but his long and adventure-filled life is so much more attractive than that of Gretchen, whose short period of bliss with the beloved is surrounded by daily toil and then by the most terrible suffering. I do not find the satisfaction of having their roles reversed in "Bergschluchten" when Gretchen takes over and Faust is at her mercy to be sufficient to turn us away from seeing in his life the better one. The "sweet revenge" that the reader might feel in her having the last word comes at too late a point in the work. We feel that the author, in spite of the various caveats built into Faust's role, favors Faust over Gretchen.

It is clear, at the same time, how much weight is given to the idea of love in the work. That is already apparent in the words of the Lord, who at the end of "Prolog im Himmel" turns away from earthly matters, about which, as I claimed above, he knows little, and turns to "die echten Göttersöhne." The Lord wishes that the eternally becoming, i.e., nature, life, should embrace the true angels–they stand in contrast to Mephisto–within the benign limits of love. And then he wishes that the angels, in turn, should give conceptual permanence to unsteady appearances, i.e., to nature, life. This is the way I read the difficult lines 346–49.[17] The message is a strange one: should the Lord not have instructed the archangels rather to, let us say, prevent Faust's criminal acts and Gretchen's suffering? Obviously, Goethe's Lord is not omnipotent, apparently not omniscient either. What he does tell "die echten Göttersöhne" seems actually not so much directed at them–what is the sense of a loving interpenetration between nature and them, followed by their giving conceptual permanence to ever transitory nature?–but rather a message to the poet, to the author, to Goethe himself. In the relationship between the poet and the world love forms an essential ingredient as it does ultimately in the relationship among people. That Faust was incapable of developing his relationship to Gretchen into one of true love is his tragedy.[18] Goethe, on the other hand, has tried in his *magnum opus* to be sensitive to the love emanating from creation and has tried to give permanence in words to such a loving relationship.

NOTES

1. I profited from the following articles and books on Gretchen: Peter Heller, "Gretchen: Figur, Klischee, Symbol," in *Die Frau als Heldin und Autorin*, ed. Wolfgang Paulsen (Bern and München: Francke, 1979) 175–89. Heller looks at Gretchen and Faust as representatives of their sexes and stresses the ambivalence of the Gretchen figure. Margaret B. Guenther sees Gretchen as primarily the victim of Faust, the "ultimate consumer," in *"Faust*: The Tragedy Reexamined," in *Beyond the Eternal Feminine: Critical Essays on Women and German Literature*, ed. Susan L. Cocalis, Kay Goodman (Stuttgart: Akademischer Verlag Hans-Dieter Heinz, 1982) 75–98. Jane K. Brown devotes a chapter to "The Gretchen Tragedy" in which she asserts that "the principle of love and the principle of striving work in parallel" (103). I fully agree with the assertion except that I see less love in Faust than Brown does. Lilian Furst analyzes the Gretchen of Part I within the literary tradition and the socio-historical context in "The Problem of Gretchen," in *Approaches to Teaching Goethe's "Faust,"* ed. Douglas J. McMillan (New York: MLA, 1987) 48–54.

2. Jessica Benjamin, "A Desire of One's Own: Psychoanalytic Feminism and Intersubjective Space," in *Feminist Studies/Critical Studies*, ed. Teresa de Lauretis (Bloomington: Indiana University Press, 1986) 78–101, here 86.

3. Werner Keller, "Faust: Eine Tragödie (1808)," in *Goethes Dramen: Neue Interpretationen*, ed. Walter Hinderer (Stuttgart: Reclam, 1980) 244–80, here 254.

4. See Peter Heller 177 and Bennett, chapter 4.

5. Schöne 181.

6. Keller 275.

7. Bennett 29–30.

8. Kenneth D. Weisinger, *The Classical Facade: A Nonclassical Reading of Goethe's Classicism* (University Park and London: The Pennsylvania State University Press, 1988) 72.

9. Theodore Ziolkowski, *"Faust* and the University: Pedagogical Ruminations on a Subversive Classic," in *Texte, Motive und Gestalten der Goethezeit: Festschrift für Hans Reiss*, ed. John L. Hibberd and H.B. Nisbet (Tübingen: Niemeyer, 1989) 65–79.

10. David D. Gilmore, *Manhood in the Making: Cultural Concepts of Masculinity* (New Haven and London: Yale University Press, 1990) 26–29.

11. Eudo C. Mason speaks of a "twofold process" Faust's spirit must undergo in order to be reconditioned (*Goethe's* Faust: *Its Genesis and Purport*, Berkeley and Los Angeles: University of California Press, 1967, 365). I would rather posit at least three stages, i.e., the angels' snatching away Faust's soul from Mephisto, the removal of the earthly baseness, and his salvation.

12. Hans Schwerte, "Der weibliche Schluß von Goethes 'Faust,' " in: *Sprachkunst* 21 (1990): 129–43, here 131–34.

13. See the contribution of Cyrus Hamlin in this volume for a thorough discussion of the interrelationship between "Klassische Walpurgisnacht" and "Bergschluchten."

14. Schwerte 137.

15. Schwerte 137–43.

16. Schwerte refers to Heinz Schlaffer as maintaining that "Grablegung" and "Berg-schluchten" are ultimately face-saving solutions ("Verlegenheitslösungen"), that these scenes should not be taken at face value. In Santa Barbara it was Hannelore Schlaffer who spoke of "Bergschluchten" as a parody. Schwerte, " 'Umfass' euch mit der Liebe holden Schranken.' Zum *Faust*prolog, Vers 347," in: *Euphorion* 74 (1990): 417–26, here 425.

17. Schwerte has investigated the meaning of "hold" in line 347 in his *Euphorion* article.

18. Thus I disagree with Stephan Landolt, who maintains that there is "wechselseitige Hilfe und Liebe" between Faust and Gretchen "im 'Jenseits.' " Stephan Landolt, "Goethes 'Faust.' Das Verhältnis von Grablegungs- und Bergschluchten-Szene zur Kirchenlehre," in: *Sprachkunst* 21 (1990): 155–94, here 191.

Cyrus Hamlin

Tracking the Eternal-Feminine in Goethe's *Faust II*[1]

> Das Ewig-Weibliche
> Zieht uns hinan.

THE ENDING OF GOETHE's *Faust* has assumed an independent fame far beyond the limits of the readership for Goethe's drama. The couplet which concludes the Chorus Mysticus at the end of the scene entitled "Bergschluchten, Wald, Fels, Einöde," is well known and often cited without any concern for its context within the strange spirit-festival of a quasi-medieval Catholic mythology that follows the demise of the human character Faust. Even the English translation of the strange neologism which Goethe introduced to this closing couplet: the "Eternal-Feminine," has achieved an independent life in English usage, to the point where its source in *Faust* may often be forgotten entirely. What is at issue in this final couplet for Goethe's drama? and what are the implications of this problematic generic hyphenated adjectival noun?

Of interest with regard to these questions are the comments on this passage, assembled in two recent exhaustive critical studies, the one a monograph by Michael Neumann of more than four hundred pages devoted entirely to the Eternal-Feminine[2] and the other a commentary by Hans Arens of over one thousand pages on *Faust II* as a whole.[3] As indicated by the length of these books, critics are not at a loss for words on the subject.

Arens asserts directly that the Eternal-Feminine must be understood with reference to Faust's all-pervasive will, in particular the power of *Eros*, which motivates his desire toward various women in the drama, Gretchen and Helena above all. He even posits a related counter-principle to define a focus of response in Faust to the Eternal-Feminine, which he labels the Eternal-Masculine (*das Ewig-Männliche*[4]), even though the drama nowhere offers the slightest hint that such a principle might exist. Arens also insists that the plural pronoun which constitutes the object of the final verb: "Zieht *uns* hinan," must be limited to men, thus excluding all women, since the world of *Faust*, he asserts, is essentially masculine: "[eine] wesentlich männliche Welt."

Neumann surveys a wide range of views concerning the Eternal-Feminine both in the context of the final scene and with regard to various female figures who appear throughout the drama. In doing so, he reviews the entire secondary literature on the subject, something for which scholars of Goethe's drama, including myself, can only be grateful. His several concluding points on the question, however,[5] make it emphatically clear that he understands the concept of the Eternal-Feminine exclusively in terms of an idealized erotic love. The term signifies for him a purified form of desire between man and woman, for which he takes the reunion of the souls of Faust and Gretchen in the final scene to be the perfect and exemplary instance. Neumann's conclusion on this point is worth citing, since it carries with it the burden of such wide-ranging evidence:

> Daß Eros Fausts und Gretchens Unsterbliches zur Einheit bindet, befreit Fausts Zerrissenheit zur Ganzheit, und diese Ganzheit tritt damit als in sich geschlossener Teil vollgültig in die Ganzheit des harmonischen Alls ein. In solcher doppelten Vereinigung realisiert sich die Identität von horizontalem Eros und vertikaler Liebe.[6]

There is much to quarrel with in these readings, even though an approximate consensus would seem to emerge from everything that has been argued about the Eternal-Feminine throughout the complex history of the reception of Goethe's cosmic theater.[7] The conclusion would thus seem to be that the Eternal-Feminine is defined by a form of erotic love, however idealized and purified by mythological and spiritual transformations, for which the desire of Faust's soul (as masculine principle) for the penitent soul of Gretchen (as feminine principle), as she hovers in the company of the Mater Gloriosa, serves as the highest instance. The principle of the feminine, however "eternal," may thus be defined as the object of erotic desire, projected upon it by an opposing masculine impulse. The tragedy of Goethe's *Faust*, in other words, no matter how complex and cosmic in the symbolism of Part II, finally collapses into the familiar convention of a seduction, where the woman falls victim to the sexual desire of the man. In the end, through a highly questionable *salto mortale* of ethical values, the destruction of an innocent woman is transformed into a celebration of the erotic desire which destroys her. The reason for this reversal is that the woman, who returns at the end as a penitent spirit ("Una Poenitentium"), through the intervention of the Virgin Mary ("Mater gloriosa"), intercedes for the soul of her dead lover. Gretchen thus becomes for Faust a Romantic version of Dante's Beatrice. In what follows I shall attempt to outline, if only provisionally and very briefly, a revisionary reading of the Eternal-Feminine which opposes such a consensus for the affirmation of erotic desire.

Within the limitations of a short essay it is necessary to select only a few examples from those episodes in the drama which may be argued to manifest the Eternal-Feminine. My central purpose is to support the claim that the fundamental human values, in aesthetic as well as ethical terms, symbolized by these manifestations must be distinguished from, and contrasted with, the basic erotic impulse which motivates Faust's desire for sexual union, first with Gretchen in the scenes of seduction in Part I and later with the spirit of Helena in Act III of Part II. This argument, as already indicated, involves a considerable departure from the consensus of Faust scholarship. I locate the significance of the Eternal-Feminine within a pattern of events in Goethe's drama at the level of symbolic and mythological action, beyond all conventional limits of plot and character.

My claim is as follows: the power of the Eternal-Feminine, which is said to "draw us onward" (*zieht uns hinan*), resides in specific moments of festival epiphany in the drama, which transcend the erotic and need to be interpreted with reference to the aesthetics of the moment (*Augenblick*). The terms for such a model or norm, as every reader of *Faust* well knows, are established initially by Faust in his wager with Mephistopheles in the pact-scene of Part I. He there speaks, though only implicitly, of an ideal of beauty such that in a single moment his fundamental and all-consuming desire or will might be completely fulfilled and satisfied:

> Werd' ich zum Augenblicke sagen:
> Verweile doch! du bist so schön!
> Dann magst du mich in Fesseln schlagen,
> Dann will ich gern zugrunde gehn! (1699–1702)

These privileged moments of festival epiphany assume both a mythological and a religious meaning, which transcends the limits of human experience. They also represent moments of ideal beauty in the drama, where all desire or striving is resolved within a mood or state of universal harmony and reconciliation. As such they fulfill, consciously and intentionally on Goethe's part, the highest norms of the program for art developed within the tradition of philosophical aesthetics and artistic practice in Germany during Goethe's lifetime, from Kant and Schiller, Friedrich Schlegel and Schelling, on to Hegel and Schopenhauer among many others, whose writings on aesthetics were for the most part well known to the poet.

Two supreme and climactic moments of festive epiphany occur in *Faust II* at separate junctures quite removed from one another in the text, but actually written at virtually the same time during the final weeks of 1830.[8] This was also, incidentally, very close to the time at which the final Chorus Mysticus with its allusion to the Eternal-Feminine was formulated. I refer to the Triumph of Galatea, on the one hand, at the end of the "Classical Walpurgis Night" in Act II, the high point of the mythological festival celebrated at the shores of the Aegean Sea in the land of Greece; and to the epiphany of the Virgin, on the other, in the final scene of the drama, where she appears under the title of "Mater Gloriosa." In what follows I will address the aesthetic and ethical significance of the Eternal-Feminine by approaching this final epiphany of the Mater Gloriosa at the very end of *Faust II* by way of the Triumph of Galatea at the end of Act II.

*

Three points of comparison between these two female figures, Galatea and the Mater Gloriosa, as embodiments of the Eternal-Feminine may be considered here. The first concerns the displacement of the erotic within the aesthetics of the moment. The second concerns the reappropriation of a mythical tradition in order to achieve a sense of authenticity for the ritual and specular event through an effect of citation or repetition of what is already known and established. The third point has to do with the hermeneutical implications of the verbal exchange which occurs between both female figures and those who invoke and appeal to them, whereby the aesthetic experience of the moment is translated into a figure of reflected fulfillment and affirmation.

I) Both these mythical figures for the Eternal-Feminine, Galatea and the Mater Gloriosa, enter their respective scenes in festive processions, responding to expectations and desires proclaimed by their several devotees and servants. These several modes of devotion and service articulate a process of sublimation, whereby erotic desire is transformed into ritual celebration, shifting the focus of response to issues of aesthetics and hermeneutics. We may consider each instance in turn.

The festival of Galatea elicits powerful, though quite dissimilar gestures of longing from Nereus and Homunculus, who are the most immediately affected by her appearance. The former, located on the shore as spectator alongside the philosopher Thales, expresses above all the desire to be reunited with his daughter. Ironically, Nereus also receives an appeal from the Dorids, who ride past on dolphins accompanied by young sailors rescued by them from shipwreck in the sea, that these youths may be granted immortality in order to dwell with them in love eternally. Nereus indicates that only Zeus could grant such a request and instructs them instead to nurture the growth of these youths to manhood and to set them safely on land once desire has played itself out (8408–15). Immediately following these, Galatea passes by with a quick greeting to her father before she is gone. The mood of longing in Nereus then shifts to a stance of resigned devotion as he gazes out to sea at the retreating procession. He describes the sight of Galatea's shell in the distance shining like a star:

> Aber Galateas Muschelthron
> Seh' ich schon und aber schon.
> Er glänzt wie ein Stern
> Durch die Menge.
> Geliebtes leuchtet durchs Gedränge!

> Auch noch so fern
> Schimmert's hell und klar,
> Immer nah und wahr. (8450–57)

Nereus thus celebrates the distant sight of the nymph on her shell as an object of beauty, essentially as a work of art, which abides, however distant, as an object which is "clear and bright, near and true." Such an image of ideal beauty recalls, on the one hand, the rainbow created by the refraction of the sunlight through the mist thrown up by the cataract in "Anmutige Gegend," as it also anticipates the remote image of Helena as a cloud formation spread out on the horizon like a distant range of icy mountains at the outset of Act IV.

Homunculus, by contrast to Nereus, gives chase to the nymph, motivated by erotic desire in response to the beauty of Galatea. We hear his voice far out at sea, echoed by that of Proteus, describing the intensity of his spiritual light and musical tone as manifestation of this desire:

> HOMUNCULUS. In dieser holden Feuchte
>   Was ich auch hier beleuchte,
>   Ist alles reizend schön.
> PROTEUS. In dieser Lebensfeuchte
>   Erglänzt erst deine Leuchte
>   Mit herrlichem Getön. (8458–63)

This erotic desire assumes obvious sexual implications when Homunculus shatters his glass against the shell and dissipates himself orgasmically into the ocean. This act of union between the spirit of Homunculus as fire and the water of the ocean as primal element of life (which affirms the teaching of Thales, 8432–43) constitutes an ironic form of immaculate conception, the original act of procreation. Yet equally this moment thematizes an event of self-sacrifice, which transforms and negates erotic desire as it also affirms and fulfills it. Nor does the act impose in any way upon the freedom and autonomy of the nymph Galatea as the object of desire, since there is no indication that she is ever aware of Homunculus's presence. The affirmation of Eros, as celebrated triumphantly at the end by the Sirens ("So herrsche denn Eros, der alles begonnen," 8479), is thus offset by the pattern of dissipation and transformation in Homunculus, an authentic model of death and rebirth, whereby the spirit is disseminated into the elements in order that it may come to be and truly live.

The Mater Gloriosa enters the scene at the end of "Bergschluchten" accompanied by a chorus of penitent female spirits ("Chor der Büßerinnen"). This follows an extensive prayer of devotion and celebration by the Doctor Marianus, "in ecstasy" (entzückt), as he gazes upwards to the heavens from his cell at the extreme highest point of the mountain landscape. This figure of devotion stands in exact parallel, I suggest, to Nereus in his relation to Galatea. Following the epiphany of the Virgin, he prostrates himself in prayer as he calls upon all those who are penitent and responsive to gaze upward toward her gaze of rescue: "Blicket auf zum Retterblick, / Alle reuig Zarten" (12096f.). His final plea in direct address of prayer to the Mater Gloriosa as "Virgin, Mother, Queen, Goddess" is that she remain or abide full of grace ("bleibe gnädig!"). His prayer includes in its emphasis on a reciprocal glance or gaze, "Blicket. . . zum. . . -blick," an oblique recollection of the theme of the moment, or *Augenblick*, just as the appeal to the Madonna that her grace may abide or endure ("bleibe") recalls the terms of Faust's wager with regard to the ideal of fulfillment in the beauty of the moment.

Parallel to the role of Homunculus in response to Galatea, though with significant difference, is that of Faust, or his immortal remains, in response to the spirit of Gretchen, which also appears to thematize longing or desire. Yet that response, only anticipated as an outcome resulting from this spiritual encounter, depends upon the intercession by Gretchen to the Virgin, adapting the words she had earlier spoken in Part I before the statue of the Mater Dolorosa in the city wall, themselves derived by Goethe from the medieval "Stabat Mater":

> Neige, neige,
> Du Ohnegleiche,
> Du Strahlenreiche,
> Dein Antlitz gnädig meinem Glück! (12069–72)

What the spirit of Gretchen requests from the Mater Gloriosa is permission to instruct the soul of Faust in true devotion and penitence. It should also be noted that penitence defines the essential attitude of this spirit figure and also of the other female spirits who accompany the Virgin as chorus: *Magna peccatrix* from the Gospel of Luke (7:36); *Mulier Samaritana* from the Gospel of John (4:1); and *Maria Aegyptiaca* from the *Acts of the Apostles*, all of them victims in their earthly lives of the ravages of desire. Such transformation of desire into penitence appears to constitute what is attributed to the Virgin as the blessing she bestows under the heading of grace.

II) My second point concerns Goethe's use of tradition in both these complex scenes, particularly with regard to the citation of or allusion to specific artistic and literary sources which are appropriated and transformed for the specific context of *Faust*. We recognize, and are intended to do so as readers, that both the triumph of Galatea and the epiphany of the Virgin derive from long and rich traditions of representation. Goethe's particular citation of these traditions, furthermore, includes the explicit application of a single specific source: Raphael's famous fresco depicting the former in the Villa Farnesina in Rome and Dante's evocation of the latter in the final cantos of the *Paradiso*. What precisely is the challenge for interpretation conveyed by such explicit poetic acts of imitation?

In the case of Raphael's "Triumph of Galatea," one of the richest and most frequently discussed works of visual art from the Italian Renaissance,[9] two specific

details of similarity and contrast may be cited. First, following a suggestion by
Jane Brown in her recent book on *Faust*, we may surmise that the figure of
Homunculus in his pursuit of the retreating Galatea is intended as substitute for
the three cherubs hovering in the air above the nymph in Raphael's painting,
taking aim with their arrows of desire.[10] What matters for an intertextual reading
of *Faust*, however, is that the outcome of Homunculus's chase is thematically
opposite to the implied act of erotic aggression by the cherubs in the painting.
This point of contrast has not been recognized hitherto by critics of Goethe.

The second point of intertextual relationship has not, so far as I know, been
recognized in the scholarly literature on *Faust*, and requires a somewhat broader
perspective on Raphael's use of the Galatea myth. A central feature of that myth,
from Theocritus to the Renaissance,[11] is the hopeless love of the ugly giant
Polyphemus, the Cyclops famous from his encounter with Odysseus in Homer's
Odyssey, for the beautiful sea nymph. In the Villa Farnesina, furthermore, just to
the left of Raphael's wall painting is another fresco by the Venetian painter
Sebastiano, depicting the mournful giant gazing toward the nymph. The visual
interaction of desire between the two paintings thus corresponds to the longing
for reunion expressed by Nereus in Goethe's scene with his daughter. The
climactic moment of encounter indicated by their exchange of greetings as Galatea
passes by (8424f.) dramatizes precisely the moment of reciprocal visual contact
between the nymph and the giant represented by the adjoining wall paintings
in the Villa Farnesina. Once again, however, Goethe reverses the erotic implications of his source by presenting the process of transformation for Nereus,
whereby desire for reunion becomes devotion from a distance for the absent ideal
of beauty as Galatea moves on past her father out to sea again.

The debt of Goethe's "Bergschluchten" to Dante's *Paradiso* has likewise not
generally been recognized. Two specific details will demonstrate the kind of
revisionary relationship which pertains between *Faust* and this source text.[12] The
Mater Gloriosa appears on the scene with the significant stage direction "schwebt
einher" (after 12031), and the Chorus of Female Penitents, which accompanies
her, invokes her with the same term: "Du *schwebst* zu Höhen / Der ewigen Reiche"
(12032f.; my emphasis). The iconography for such a *hovering* in the company of
devoted spirits could well include the entire Christian tradition of painting, where
the Virgin is often portrayed suspended (*schwebend*) on high, surrounded by
attendant saints. In Dante's *Paradiso*, Cantos XXXI and XXXII, Maria appears
within the mystical rose, also surrounded by the spirits of blessed women, among
them Dante's own Beatrice (who has at that point in the poem been replaced by
St. Bernard as Dante's guide). Any sense of analogy between Goethe and Dante,
however, with regard to their portrayal of the Madonna could still seem to be
accidental.

What makes the influence of Dante more apparent is the close parallel between
the prayers of the Doctor Marianus in "Bergschluchten" (11988–12031), addressed
in mystical and ecstatic devotion to the Mater Gloriosa, and the great prayer of
St. Bernard in the final canto of the *Commedia* (XXXIII, 1–39), addressed

specifically to Maria in the heavenly rose. Has any commentator on Goethe's *Faust* ever claimed, as I do, that Dante's St. Bernard served as the model for Doctor Marianus? It may incidentally also be noted that Doctor Marianus in his relation to the Mater Dolorosa performs a function exactly analogous to that of Nereus in his devotion to Galatea at the end of the "Classical Walpurgis Night," just as the appearance of the Virgin with her train of penitents recalls the triumph of Galatea with her accompanying Dorids.

The second aspect of this scene which derives from Dante, more persuasive perhaps than the appearance of the Mater Dolorosa and the prayer of Doctor Marianus, is the intercession by the penitent spirit of Gretchen on behalf of Faust. Every reader of Dante's *Divine Comedy* will recall the account given by the spirit of Vergil at the outset of the *Inferno* (II, 43–126) concerning the manner in which he was called by Beatrice to rescue Dante from his erring path in the dark wood. We thus learn at the beginning of the poem how Beatrice interceded with Maria, through the mediation of St. Lucia, on behalf of Dante, requesting permission to send Vergil to his rescue. At the end of the *Paradiso* we finally learn what the full circumstances of mystical relationship had been, within which Beatrice had made her appeal to the Virgin. Precisely that relationship is recreated by Goethe at the end of "Bergschluchten" just after the Mater Gloriosa has entered the scene, where Gretchen as penitent soul intercedes on Faust's behalf, appealing to the Virgin that she be allowed to rescue his immortal remains. Once again, we may ask why scholars of *Faust* have not commented upon such a close intertextual resonance between Dante and Goethe.

Nor should we ignore the close parallels shared by Goethe's two scenes of epiphany with each other, despite the fundamental difference in tone, manner and style between them, where the one derives from a pagan mythological source, though represented in the Renaissance version of it by Raphael, while the other borrows from a Christian mystical tradition as represented by Dante in his *Commedia*. Homunculus, as argued above, is substituted for the cherubs pointing their arrows above the head of Galatea in Raphael's painting and his self-sacrifice signifies a transformation of the erotic into a mystery of procreation and new life. In "Bergschluchten," through the intercession of Gretchen with the Mater Gloriosa, Faust's soul is also rescued and revived to a further, as yet indeterminate mode of existence, "following after" the spirit of Gretchen. The specific appropriations and transformations of traditional sources by Goethe—from Raphael on the one hand and from Dante on the other—establish identical patterns of spiritual and poetic experience with regard to the Eternal Feminine and the fulfillment and sublimation of desire within the moment (*Augenblick*) of epiphany. Homunculus through his self-sacrifice and Faust in his spiritual apotheosis after death signify an identical mode of hermeneutical affirmation for the reader of Goethe's drama. The final couplet of the Chorus Mysticus conveys precisely what this affirmation should be: "Das Ewig-Weibliche / Zieht uns hinan."

III) My third and final point about the comparison of these two scenes pertains to a specific verbal feature of Goethe's dramatization of the respective moments of epiphany, which, so far as I am aware, has not been noticed by critics. Both Galatea and the Mater Gloriosa appear very near the end of their respective scenes after an elaborate preparation and with powerful rhetorical and theatrical emphasis. These are the moments of mythical climax for the respective scenes, which also constitute—let me assert again unequivocally—moments of supreme symbolic significance for the drama as a whole. These moments, if any in all of *Faust*, achieve what may be truly regarded as norms of fulfillment: *erfüllte Augenblicke*. Yet in both cases the figures of the feminine are virtually silent, even inarticulate; each has only two lines to speak, though these lines are central and all-encompassing for any definition of their respective roles. Galatea as she passes by on her shell speaks in immediate reply to a call of recognition from her father, Nereus, who cries out: "Du bist es, mein Liebchen!" (8424). Her answer is: "O Vater! das Glück! / Delphine, verweilet! mich fesselt der Blick" (8424f.). And with that she is gone. The Mater Gloriosa speaks only in reply to the elaborate plea from the penitent soul of the one "formerly called Gretchen" with reference to the "immortal" remains of Faust being carried upward by the angels, surrounded by the chorus of "blessed boys" ("selige Knaben") who died in infancy. Her plea is that she be allowed to teach Faust's soul how to accommodate itself to the bliss of his spiritual condition, to which the Mother responds: "Komm! hebe dich zu höhern Sphären! / Wenn er dich ahnet, folgt er nach" (12094f.). Nothing more is said prior to the final Chorus Mysticus, except that—as noted above—Doctor Marianus, praying prostrate before the Virgin, calls upon all who are truly penitent ("Alle reuig Zarten," 12097) to look up toward her rescuing glance: "Blicket auf zum Retterblick" (12096), with a final appeal to the Mater Gloriosa as Virgin, as Mother, as Queen, and as Goddess that she remain full of grace, presumably toward those who look to her for her blessing: "bleibe gnädig" (12103).

The point I wish to make about these moments of dialogical response by the figures of the Eternal-Feminine is twofold. First, both instances focus thematically, though perhaps only obliquely, on the concept of the moment and the glance, playing on the German term *Augenblick* as *Blick des Auges*. Galatea looks back to her father, appealing in vain to her dolphins to stop their movement because the glance or the sight shared between herself and her father so captivates her. The Mater Gloriosa instructs Gretchen's spirit to ascend with her to higher spheres so that Faust's remains, as soon as her presence is perceived, will follow after. This movement of ascent is precisely parallel to that movement called for by Doctor Marianus in prayer for the eyes of those who look up to the Virgin for their rescue, their grace, their salvation: "Blicket auf zum Retterblick!" In both instances the emphasis is placed upon the moment of reciprocity within the structure of vision, sight, glance, as the means to salvation.

Equally important here—the second aspect—is the verbal form of exchange which establishes the single moment of speech for both figures of the Eternal-

Feminine. It is a response or reply to words spoken to them by another, by Nereus to Galatea and by Gretchen's penitent spirit to the Mater Dolorosa. It is the pattern of a call or a prayer and its appropriate answer. This pattern of exchange thematizes a structure of reciprocal interrelationship, which may be regarded—at least within the fictional aesthetic space of the theater, where these events are realized—as true models for hermeneutical consciousness.[13] We also, as readers and audience of the drama, enter into the shared perspective of such reciprocity, so that implicitly the words spoken by the two female figures reach out to us and gather our own response, figuratively and imaginatively, into the sense of affirmation achieved by these moments of dialogical exchange. Precisely within the perspective of such hermeneutical consciousness, I submit, the meaning of the climactic moments of epiphany is to be found. Here alone we may locate the legitimacy and authority of what, at the very end of *Faust*, the Chorus Mysticus asserts to be true: "Das Ewig-Weibliche / Zieht uns hinan."

*

A number of points may be offered by way of conclusion to this survey of the Eternal-Feminine as it is manifested in these two scenes of festival celebration in *Faust II*. For the purpose of a revisionary polemic directed against the consensus of scholars who discuss the concept of the Eternal-Feminine, as indicated with reference to the studies by Neumann and Arens at the outset, these two scenes: the Triumph of Galatea at the end of the "Classical Walpurgis Night" and the appearance of the Mater Gloriosa in "Bergschluchten," will suffice.

The first point was, in effect, the premise with which my argument began, namely that the Eternal-Feminine as concept or force in the drama should not be identified with any of the actual episodes or experiences of Faust the character, least of all with either Gretchen or Helena. It has become clear that claims for the erotic encounter between male and female, whether it be defined as seduction (in the case of Gretchen) or as visionary-poetic appropriation (in the case of Helena), are too simplistic and reductive for the complex symbolic scope of *Faust II*. More generally, it may be argued that for Goethe at the time of composing the second part of his drama during the last years of his life the issue of character with specific reference to Faust himself had largely been replaced by more universal concerns of theatrical representation. *Faust II* attains the scope of a Theater of the World, where individual experience becomes at most the instance for more comprehensive questions of human, natural, social, political, cosmic and spiritual value. Such scope is achieved above all in the allegorical-festival moments of climax, such as the "Classical Walpurgis Night" and "Bergschluchten," which were both composed essentially in 1830 near the very end of the long history of the poet's work on *Faust*.

Directly related to such general claims for the scope of the drama as symbolic action are the more specific results of my remarks on the three separate aspects of these moments of epiphany for the Eternal-Feminine. The appearance of both figures of feminine agency in these scenes—Galatea as surrogate for the goddess Aphrodite in the context of classical mythology and the Virgin Mother as embodiment of a transcendent spiritual force within a Christian iconographical tradition— is defined above all by moments of dialogical exchange, which are neither of them erotic in any legitimate sense of the term. On one hand, the exchange constitutes a form of reciprocal recognition between father and daughter, where the impulse expressed by Galatea explicitly is to suspend and sustain the moment of encounter and recognition as a *Verweilen*, precisely in the sense originally envisioned by Faust himself in the terms of his wager with Mephistopheles in the Pact Scene of Part I. On the other hand, the Mater Gloriosa responds to the appeal of Gretchen's spirit on behalf of Faust's immortal part in a gesture of affirmation and encouragement, which fulfills the terms of her abiding grace ("bleibe gnädig"), as the prayer of Doctor Marianus articulates it. In both cases, the one involving father and daughter, the other involving the Glorious Mother and one of her penitent spiritual "daughters," no trace of the erotic is to be found. In place of more conventional relations between male and female, as lovers or husband and wife, Goethe substitutes the bond between parent and child. And how splendid to alternate the role assigned to the figure who embodies the Eternal-Feminine: as daughter in the one instance, who is in constant motion from afar to the moment of passing by, and as mother in the other, who essentially does not move, suspended (*schwebend*) in the air!

Even in the modes of response for the male figures of desire in these two scenes—Homunculus in his quest for Galatea, as means to his own procreation and embodiment through the dissipation of the spirit, and Faust's soul in its response to the vision of Gretchen as penitent spirit, where the "following after" is a form of spiritual development—the erotic motive is transformed by sacrifice and by ascension, respectively, into something more universal and all-encompassing within the realms of nature and spirit, as the two scenes represent them symbolically. Nothing of any erotic union between male and female is thus figured at the center of these two moments.

Yet for both scenes, in ways that are indeed central to the poetics of Goethe's *Faust*, the dramatic and theatrical focus of these festive epiphanies is precisely of the *moment*, in accord with the full implications of the term *Augen-blick*. In the case of Galatea, the moment of communication is a form of reciprocal bond, as she herself emphasizes: "Mich *fesselt* der Blick!" In the case of the Mater Gloriosa, the moment of her gift of grace is defined by the ecstatic cry of Doctor Marianus as a reciprocity of the gaze: "Blicket auf zum Retterblick," where the ascent of vision in mystical communion is correlative to the reception of a "rescue" from that very source. It is a form of the gaze where we look upward toward that transcendent power which, by looking back upon us, provides us with the salvation of an abiding grace.

Finally, I have suggested that the two symbolic moments, which Goethe here realizes as dramatic and theatrical events, also establish a pattern of hermeneutical consciousness that is fundamental and all-encompassing for the reader or audience

of *Faust* as a whole. The key to this participatory and interpretive function for
the Eternal-Feminine is found in its simplest form in the use of the first-person
plural pronoun: *wir* or *uns*. Those figures within the scenes of festival who affirm
the symbolic event of the fulfilled moment with greatest authority, namely Nereus
and Doctor Marianus, serve as the vehicles for just such a hermeneutical
consciousness. They both speak *for us* and articulate the mode of cognitive and
collective response to the epiphany, which affirms the realization of the event as
beauty in its visionary fullness for the collective participating, though diverse,
consciousness of audience and readership. *We* are the implied and intended
recipients of the Doctor Marianus's final phrase of address: "alle reuig Zarten."
This sense of community ought presumably to hold true, at least hypothetically,
for an ideal performance, for the audience in the theater, where *Faust II* might
be presented on the stage (however preposterous that would have been in actuality
for theaters in Goethe's lifetime, nonetheless a true possibility in our own time).
Yet equally, such a collective realization of the moment as symbolic beauty would
hold true for the entire tradition of reception, through which the drama has been
received and is interpreted by its readership as a whole. Here precisely may be
affirmed the importance of the cultural and poetic tradition, which provided
Goethe with the specific forms and configurations he appropriated and adapted
to the unique purposes of his drama, as, for instance, in the case of Raphael's
"Triumph of Galatea" in the "Classical Walpurgis Night" and of Dante's *Paradiso*
in the scene "Bergschluchten."

Thus, in concluding, we may refer the concept of the Eternal-Feminine back
to the context of the drama in which the term is uttered, within the sequence of
programmatic, universal truths that make up the four couplets of the Chorus
Mysticus as the last echo of the closing scene. Few readers would doubt that each
of the first three couplets may be referred, not only to the scene just ending, but
back across the drama of *Faust* as a whole. They speak, respectively, about "all
that is transitory" ("Alles Vergängliche"), about "what is unattainable" ("das
Unzulängliche"), and about "what is indescribable," or even un-writ-able ("das
Unbeschreibliche"), as *here* achieved, even if only symbolically (as "Gleichnis"),
as *event* ("Ereignis") and *deed* ("getan," echoing all the way back to Faust's
translation of the *Logos* from the Gospel of John). Only the final couplet, where
the ubiquitous concept of the Eternal-Feminine is named, has caused difficulty
for readers in the history of the drama's reception. Yet here above all, as I have
attempted to show, the moment of epiphany, which we have witnessed and shared
in the full implications of a hermeneutical consciousness of the drama as fulfillment
in beauty, is acknowledged to have been achieved and realized as event. "The
Eternal-Feminine draws us onward." What else could all the effort of our exercise
in *reading*, in *tracking*, in *interpreting* signify other than a response—as a *being-drawn-
onward*—through this all-encompassing power of art and creation from the
beginning to the end of Goethe's *Faust?*

NOTES

1. This paper originated as a presentation for the NEH Summer Institute on Goethe's *Faust* at the University of California, Santa Barbara, in the summer of 1990. It was subsequently delivered as a public lecture at Harvard University in April, 1991.

2. Michael Neumann, *Das Ewig-Weibliche in Goethes Faust* (Heidelberg: Carl Winter, 1985).

3. Hans Arens, *Kommentar zu Goethes Faust II* (Heidelberg: Carl Winter, 1989).

4. Arens 1052.

5. Cf. Neumann 97–102, "Die Dialektik der Liebe"; on the Mater Dolorosa 285–306.

6. Neumann 306. The contrast between a "horizontal" and a "vertical" Eros mentioned here alludes to the two cloud formations observed by Faust in the opening monologue of Act IV, the one (a cumulus cloud) associated with Helena, the other (a cirrus cloud) with Gretchen.

7. The history of scholarly discussion concerning "Bergschluchten" can be conveniently surveyed in the items assembled by Hans Henning in his bibliography to *Faust: Faust-Bibliographie*, bearbeitet von Hans Henning, Teil II, Band 2, Erster Halbband: *Sekundärliteratur zu Goethes Faust* (Berlin and Weimar: Aufbau Verlag, 1970), Nrs. 4372–4424, pp. 250–55. A number of American Germanists have addressed the final scene of *Faust* in separate essays, e.g.: G.C.L. Schuchard, "The Last Scene in Goethe's *Faust*," *PMLA* 64 (1949): 417–44; Harold Jantz, "The Place of the 'Eternal-Womanly' in Goethe's Faust Drama," *PMLA* 68 (1953): 791–805; Stuart Atkins, "Irony and Ambiguity in the Final Scene of Goethe's *Faust*," *On Romanticism and the Art of Translation: Studies in Honor of Edwin Hermann Zeydel*, ed. G. Merkel (Princeton: Princeton University Press, 1956) 7–27; William McClain, "Goethe's Chorus Mysticus as Significant Form," *MLN* 74 (1959): 43–49; Bernhard Blume, "Fausts Himmelfahrt," *Études Germaniques* 22 (1967): 338–45. Virtually all these essays discuss the Eternal-Feminine primarily with reference to the question of Faust's salvation.

8. Precise data concerning the history of composition for these sections of *Faust II* is provided in an essay by Renate Fischer-Lamberg, "Untersuchungen zur Chronologie der Handschriften von Faust II 2 und II 3," *Wissenschaftliche Zeitschrift der Humboldt-Universität zu Berlin, Gesellschafts- und sprachwissenschaftliche Reihe*, Jg. VI (1956/57), Nr. 2, 151–55. This is an "Autoreferat" for a doctoral dissertation submitted to the Humboldt University in 1955.

9. Particularly illuminating on the history of reception for the Raphael painting is the exhaustive study by Christof Thoenes, "Zu Raffaels *Galatea*," *Festschrift für Otto von Simson zum 65. Geburtstag*, ed. Lucius Grisebach and Konrad Renger (Berlin: Propyläen, 1977); cited by Jane Brown 181.

10. This point is made with some emphasis by Jane Brown in her discussion of the scene (186).

11. It is not possible to trace here the complexity of the myth of Galatea in any of its historical delineations. For a useful survey of this history, see the essay by Thoenes cited in note 9 above.

12. Dante's name is barely mentioned in the commentaries by Arens and Neumann. The survey of the entire scholarly literature on the final scene by these studies also yields virtually nothing. The only sustained comparison known to me is an essay of 1923 in

the *Deutsches Dante-Jahrbuch*, vol. VII, by Friedrich Vösching, "Das Paradies bei Dante und im Faust," which offers very little by way of comparative intertextual reading. The most recent discussion of "Bergschluchten," an essay on Goethe's mythological use of Catholic material, by Jochen Schmidt, "Die 'katholische Mythologie' und ihre mystische Entmythologisierung in der Schlußszene des *Faust II*," *Jahrbuch der deutschen Schillergesellschaft* XXXIV (1990): 230–56, likewise makes no mention of Dante as a possible source. Schmidt develops a persuasive argument that Dionysius the Areopagite was Goethe's primary source for the spiritual hierarchy presented in the scene. I see no incompatibility between Schmidt's claim for the influence of Dionysius and my own for Dante. Full justification for the claim of influence which I am making here, however, would require another essay.

13. It is not possible to develop fully the considerations which justify this claim, namely that such a reciprocal exchange in language constitutes the essential form of a hermeneutic consciousness. My thinking on this subject is indebted to the work of Hans-Georg Gadamer, *Wahrheit und Methode: Grundzüge einer philosophischen Hermeneutik* (Tübingen: Mohr, 1960), esp. the discussion of dialogue, the theory of experience (*Erfahrung*), and the essential structure of question and answer as the basis for hermeneutical consciousness in the tradition of Platonic dialogue (324–60).

REPRESENTATION

ULRICH GAIER

Dialektik der Vorstellungsarten als Prinzip in Goethes *Faust*

The Dialectic of Perceptual Modes as a Principle in Goethe's Faust

In the tradition of epistemological and semiotic skepticism, Goethe recognized that conflicting philosophical systems and conceptual modes inform an individual's thinking. This diversity both frustrates and facilitates the attempt to arrive at understanding. Truth cannot be conveyed by any single system or perceptual mode but is discovered by repeatedly combining diverse possibilities, each flawed and each revelatory. In the "Vorspiel auf dem Theater" Goethe adapts this insight to his play: three figures advocate three different and often mutually exclusive positions concerning the constitution, production and reception of text. The activity of interpretation does not demand a resolution of these differences, but a recognition of both their simultaneous incompatibility and legitimacy. The poetics of the scene are programmatic for a reading of the entire Faust text: because no single interpretation can ever be sufficient to comprehension, multiple readings, especially mutually exclusive ones, are the best means to understanding the text.

EIN STÜCK SEINER POETIK HAT GOETHE IN EINEM BRIEF an Carl Jacob Iken vom 27. September 1827 enthüllt:

> Da sich gar manches unserer Erfahrungen nicht ganz rund aussprechen und direkt mitteilen läßt, so habe ich seit langem das Mittel gewählt, durch einander gegenübergestellte und sich gleichsam ineinander abspiegelnde Gebilde den geheimen Sinn dem Aufmerkenden zu offenbaren.

Der Zusammenhang und Kontrast selbständiger, jedoch sich wie Spiegel zueinander verhaltender Gebilde ermöglicht es danach, Unaussprechliches zu offenbaren. Was ist dieses Unaussprechliche?

> Das Wahre, mit dem Göttlichen identisch, läßt sich niemals von uns direkt erkennen, wir schauen es nur im Abglanz, im Beispiel, Symbol, in einzelnen und verwandten Erscheinungen; wir werden es gewahr als unbegreifli-

ches Leben und können dem Wunsch nicht entsagen, es dennoch zu begreifen. (HA 13:305)

Kunst und (poetisches) Symbol sind "lebendig-augenblickliche Offenbarung des Unerforschlichen" (HA 12:471): menschliche Praxis vermag also Göttliches als "Leben" gewahr werden zu lassen, und zwar entweder formal durch die Gegenüberstellung kontrastiver und zugleich zusammenhängender Gebilde oder inhaltlich nach der Aussage des folgenden Aphorismus:

Man sagt, zwischen zwei entgegengesetzten Meinungen liege die Wahrheit mitten inne. Keineswegs! Das Problem liegt dazwischen, das Unschaubare, das ewig tätige Leben, in Ruhe gedacht. (HA 12:422)

Höchstes reines Leben wäre zu erzeugen durch ein Gleichgewicht von Ja und Nein, den "vollkommenen Widerspruch," der "gleich geheimnisvoll für Kluge wie für Toren" ist (*Faust*, 2557f.): ein solches Gleichgewicht läßt sich etablieren bei Aussagen, bei den Figuren, innerhalb der Figuren, bei Werten und Bestrebungen, bei sprachlichen und dramaturgischen Mitteln. Goethe hätte nicht jeweils eines gemeint und intendiert, sondern ein System eines aus horizontalem und vertikalem Widerspruch, d.h. aus Polarität und Steigerung sich fortzeugenden Widerspruchs, der dann das Leben nicht "in Ruhe gedacht" sein, sondern sich als "ewig tätiges" zeigen ließe. So erhielte man einen Begriff von Goethes Poetik und Texten, der ihre Inkommensurabilität plausibel macht, von der Goethe mehrfach spricht.

Vorstellungsarten

Goethe steht hier in einer Tradition der erkenntnistheoretischen und semiotischen Skepsis, für die Erkennungswörter im 18. Jahrhundert die Begriffe "Vorstellungsart" und "Denkweise" waren. Es handelt sich dabei nicht nur um die Anerkennung kulturell verschiedener Denkweisen, sondern auch um philosophische Systeme, die einander bekämpfen, oder um Vorstellungsarten, die sich im Individuum streiten, etwa nach Goethes Wort: "Wir sind naturforschend Pantheisten, dichtend Polytheisten, sittlich Monotheisten" (HA 12:372), oder um naturwissenschaftliche Erklärungen: "Es sind immer nur unsere Augen, unsere Vorstellungsarten; die Natur weiß ganz allein, was sie will, was sie gewollt hat" (HA 12: 399).

Aus der interessanten Geschichte dieser Begriffe wähle ich zwei Beispiele, die Goethe unmittelbar angeregt und in seiner Haltung bestätigt haben dürften. Theoretisch behandelt wurden die Vorstellungsarten von Goethes Freund Friedrich Heinrich Jacobi in einem Aufsatz, den Schiller in den *Horen* veröffentlichte.

Vorstellungsarten und herrschende Systeme—überall weniger Ursache als Wirkung des Geistes der Zeit, den sie jedesmal nur offenbaren, dar-

stellen; freylich auch entwickeln und befördern—gehen auf und gehen
unter vor dem unveränderlichen Geiste der Wahrheit, den sie weder leiten
noch verführen können.[1]

Die Vorstellungsart oder, wie Jacobi bevorzugt sagt, die Meinung, ist jedoch
mit der Wahrheit nicht ohne Verbindung: "Die ursprüngliche Energie der Meynung ist die Energie des Lebens selbst; ihre Gewalt die Gewalt der Wahrheit,
die, in die Zeiten verhüllt, unwiderstehlich die Zeiten regiert" (873). Was den
Meinungen ihren ungereimten, fremden, schädlichen Charakter gibt, ist die
Tatsache ihrer Veraltung, denn jeder solche

> Glaube, wie unsinnig, wie verkehrt er in der Folge auch erscheinen mag,
> ist bey seinem Ursprunge ein wahrer Glaube eine richtige Erkenntniß,
> das ist, ein nothwendiges Resultat der Verhältnisse gewesen, worinn jene
> Menschen, bey denen er entstand, sich gegen Gott, Welt und Mitmen-
> schen befanden. (880)

Die in die Zeit verhüllte und mit der Zeit sich anders ausdrückende Wahrheit
verschwindet aus einer veralteten Meinung und läßt sie "lauter Lüge" werden:

> Wenn Altes untergeht und Neues aufkommt, so entsteht eine andre Mi-
> schung von Wahrheit und Irrthum, von Gutem und Bösem. Die *beste*
> Mischung—wer kann sie bestimmen? Es wäre ungereimt es nur zu wollen.
> —Leider, eine sehr blutig gewordene Schwärmerey unseres Zeitalters! (888)

Vorstellungsarten und Meinungen bilden sich nicht nur für ein ganzes Zeitalter,
sondern auch als "persönliche Meynung." Jacobi gibt dem Satz des Protagoras
vom Menschen als Maß aller Dinge eine neue Interpretation:

> Was seine Vorstellungen von den Dingen enthalten, schreibt er ihnen
> zu; das *sind* die Dinge ihm. Was sie ausser dem seyn mögen, kann er nicht
> erfahren; er kann aus seinen Empfindungen, Wahrnehmungen und Ur-
> theilen nicht herausgehen, und die Gegenstände prüfen ausserhalb seinem
> Verstande, sich selbst ausserhalb sich selbst berichtigen, sich erleuchten
> mit einer Wahrheit, die er nicht verstehen würde. Darum ist überhaupt
> jedem Menschen seine Meynung, mit Recht, die Wahrheit; und er
> behauptet sie mit Recht, weil die Wahrheit jedes Menschen sein Leben
> ist. Hierin: daß jeder Mensch in dem was ihm Wahrheit ist sein Leben
> hat, hat die Gewalt der Meynung ihren Ursprung.

Leben als "bloße leere Form" hätte keinen Wert, Genuß des Lebens entstehe
erst, wenn es einen "Inhalt und Gebrauch" bekomme, dieser werde definiert durch
die Meinungen über die Verhältnisse zu Gott, Welt, Mitmenschen: "Durch
Anwendung, Inhalt und Gebrauch, wird das Leben erst lebendig; es entwickelt

sich in ihm ein *Daseyn*; es entsteht eine Person" (875). Mit der "Gewißheit unseres Daseyns, unserer *Identität* und *Personalität*" ist also die Meinung und persönliche Vorstellungsart untrennbar verbunden. Daraus ergebe sich der

> sehr niederschlagende. . . Gedanke, daß wir nie die Wahrheit selbst, sondern immer nur unser Leben lieb haben; nie recht erfahren können, was nur Wahrheit ist. –Sie ist verborgen in unserm Leben; Geheimes in noch Geheimerem. Doch schimmert hier ein Licht der Hoffnung. Es ist ein Gedanke hoher Ahnung, daß nur Entwickelung des Lebens, Entwickelung der Wahrheit ist; beyde, Wahrheit und Leben, Eins und Dasselbe. (879)

Die Nähe zu Goethe ist unverkennbar. Der Gedanke, daß zwischen entgegengesetzten Vorstellungsarten das Problem, das ewig tätige Leben ruhe, löst sozusagen Jacobis reine Form des Lebens von der zufälligen Hülle, die es sich gibt, um Dasein, Identität und Person eines Menschen zu werden. Der Gedanke, selbständige Gebilde sich ineinander abspiegeln zu lassen, führt den Leser des *Faust* auf den tieferen Sinn, wie er Jacobi anleitet, bei seinen Versuchen der "Übersetzung" von Vorstellungsarten weg vom äußerlichen Buchstaben auf den inneren Sinn vorzudringen und "Proteus, den Wahrsager" zur Enthüllung verborgener Weisheit zu drängen (883f.). Mit Jacobis Gedanken, "daß nur Entwickelung des Lebens, Entwickelung der Wahrheit ist," setzte Goethe sich schon im *Faust*-Fragment von 1790 auseinander, wo Faust erstrebt, was der Menschheit zugeteilt ist, in seinem innern Selbst zu genießen: sein Leben soll an allem Menschenmöglichen teilhaben, damit auch an allen möglichen Vorstellungsarten und Verhüllungen der Wahrheit. Offensichtlich teilte Goethe nicht die Hoffnung Jacobis, denn gerade mit der Planmäßigkeit der allseitigen Entwicklung von Fausts Leben wird die Authentizität durchschnitten, die jede Erfahrung und Meinung zum Ausdruck des Lebens und Anhalt der Persönlichkeit macht. Möglicherweise zur Formulierung dieser Differenz schrieb er am 23.11.1801 an Jacobi von dem "tiefe[n], ruhige[n] Anschauen. . . , in dessen immerwährender synkrisis und diakrisis wir ein göttliches Leben fühlen." Nicht ein Ausdruck höherer Wahrheit entstand für ihn im Zusammenfassen und Trennen der Anschauungen, sondern das Gefühl des ewig tätigen Lebens, also der reinen zeitlosen Form des geheimnisvollen Seins.

Seit Foucault nennen wir Diskurs das Syndrom aus perspektivischem Weltzugang, Erklärungs- und Wertsystem, zugehöriger Sprache und Alleinvertretungsanspruch gegenüber anderen Diskursen. Daß der Begriff "Vorstellungsart" im ausgehenden 18. Jahrhundert genau diese Bedeutung hatte, belegt des Fichte-Vorgängers Karl Leonhard Reinhold *Versuch einer neuen Theorie des menschlichen Vorstellungsvermögens*. In seiner Einleitung behandelt er die "vier metaphysischen Systeme," die sich in seiner Gegenwart gegenüberstehen–Spiritualismus, Materialismus, dogmatischer Skeptizismus und Supernaturalismus[2]–, und beschreibt die

Verwobenheit dieser Philosophien mit dem Leben, der Persönlichkeit ihrer Vertreter:

> Je mehrere Felder der Philosophie [ein Philosoph] bearbeitet hat, desto
> mehr haben seine Principien ihre Fruchtbarkeit und Harmonie vor seinen
> Augen gerechtfertiget, desto inniger sind sie mit seiner gesammten Ideen-
> masse verwebt worden, desto mehr sind sie, wenn ich mich so ausdrücken
> darf, in die Natur seiner Vernunft übergegangen. (38)

Psychologisch bringt er die "Zeit und Mühe" in Anschlag, die die Erwerbung
und Festigung eines philosophischen Systems gekostet hat, und fragt dann:

> Sey auch hier seine Vernunft über allen Einfluß empörter Selbstliebe
> erhaben; wird er auch mit dem besten Willen seiner langgewohnten
> mühsam erworbenen Vorstellungsart auf einmal entsagen können? (28,
> 31)

Die metaphysischen Systeme sind also "Vorstellungsarten." Reinhold schlägt vor,
den Verdrängungskampf der Diskurse durch Anwendung von Kants kritischer
Philosophie beizulegen (die er allerdings selbst auf S. 60 als "Vorstellungsart"
bezeichnet):

> Wenn von jeder Parthey Wahrheit, aber nur *eine* Seite derselben, gesehen
> wird; so zeigt sich diese Seite nur, in wie ferne sie mit einer gegenüber-
> stehenden im Gegensatz, aber nicht wie sie mit der selben zugleich ver-
> einbar, so gar nothwendig verknüpft ist. So lange nun jede Parthey die
> ihr in die Augen fallende Seite für *volle* Wahrheit ankündigt, muß sie von
> der ihr Gegenüberstehenden, die eine entgegengesetzte volle Wahrheit
> im Auge hat, geradezu *widerlegt* werden. Das jeder Sekte einleuchtende
> zum Theil unstreitig Wahre enthält dann den Grund, warum keine von
> allen übrigen verdrängt werden, und das Einseitige im Gesichtspunkte
> einer jeden [den Grund], warum keine auch unter den vortheilhaften
> äussern Umständen einen entscheidenden Sieg über die übrigen davon
> tragen konnte. (43f.)

Es war natürlich die Hoffnung des Kantianers Reinhold, zwischen diesen sich
bekämpfenden Vorstellungsarten, Systemen, Sekten, Parteien, kurz: Diskursen
im kritischen Verfahren die Wahrheit auffinden zu können, von der sie aus ihren
eingeschränkten Gesichtspunkten ein richtiges, aber unvollständiges Bild haben
mußten. Goethe, das haben wir gesehen, war hier weit skeptischer: nicht die
Wahrheit liegt zwischen den entgegengesetzten Vorstellungsarten, sondern "das
Problem..., das Unschaubare, das ewig tätige Leben, in Ruhe gedacht."
    Unsere Aufgabe kann es hier nicht sein, die Frage der bloßen Sprachlichkeit
der Vorstellungsarten, ihrer prinzipiellen Beliebigkeit angesichts eines ohnehin

nicht in Zeichen faßbaren absoluten Seins und Lebens bei den Wissenschaftlern Herder und Goethe zu verfolgen. Dazu müßten wir uns auf ihren kohärenz-theoretischen Wahrheitsbegriff und die von Herder eingeführte Präferenz des "bequemen," d.h. auf möglichst viele Problemfelder sich direkt oder metaphorisch beziehenden Diskurses eingehen.[3] Uns geht es hier um die Dichtung und ihre Aufgabe, lebendig-augenblickliche Offenbarung des Unerforschlichen zu sein. Aufgrund des Blicks in die Geschichte des Begriffs "Vorstellungsarten" können wir nun erkennen, daß Goethe der Dichtung die Funktion zuweist, die Bindung an Vorstellungsarten und Diskurse, der wir als denkende, soziale, religiöse, handelnde Menschen notwendig ausgesetzt sind, durch die Inszenierung einer gleichzeitigen Gültigkeit entgegengesetzter und sich gegenseitig aufhebender Diskurse schlagartig zu negieren, den Menschen ins ewig tätige Leben zurückzu-führen und ihm sozusagen die Wiedergeburt, die Erneuerung seines notwendig eingeschränkten und irrenden Daseins zu ermöglichen.

Dialektik der Poetiken im "Vorspiel auf dem Theater"

Einige Beispiele widersprüchlicher, einander aufhebender Vorstellungsarten aus dem *Faust* habe ich oben schon benannt. Um den prinzipiellen Charakter der behaupteten Dialektik im Sinne von Polarität und Steigerung entgegengesetzter Vorstellungsarten herauszustellen, gehe ich nun auf die drei Poetiken ein, die Goethe im "Vorspiel auf dem Theater" miteinander ins Spiel bringt. Wenn wir annehmen dürfen, daß dieser Text zumindest auch ein Vorspiel zum *Faust* ist,[4] dann bedeutet die Einführung konkurrierender Poetiken, daß möglicherweise im ganzen *Faust*-Text widersprüchliche Prinzipien der Textkonstitution befolgt worden sind. Dies würde natürlich auch die Rezeption und das Verständnis des Textes in entscheidender Weise beeinflussen, nämlich so, daß vielleicht drei partielle Lesungen des Textes jeweils relativ konsistente Verständnis- und Rezeptionsmöglichkeiten erzeugen, daß aber eine vollständige Lesung unmöglich ist, weil sich keine Konsistenzen und Verstehensgrundlagen aufbauen lassen. Intuitiv könnte man sagen, daß sich aus dieser prinzipiellen Unmöglichkeit die von Goethe anerkannte "Inkommensurabilität" des Textes und die Endlosigkeit der *Faust*-Forschung erklären läßt. Es ist diese Unmöglichkeit, die Benjamin Bennett in seinem wichtigen Buch *Goethe's Theory of Poetry* als "antipoetic" bezeichnet: "*Faust* is constructed so as to deny the audience an adequate point of view from which to receive its meaning or accept its teaching."[5] Diese Eigen-schaft des Textes beruhe "on its having the effect, or giving the impression, of anticipating our *every* response to it, of being a mirror by which we view ourselves so completely as to exclude all possibility of ironic distance" (325).

Bennett anerkennt, daß "we cannot read this text against itself, because the text insists on reading itself against itself, in ways that at every turn anticipate our consciousness of it" (292–93); dennoch läßt er die kalkulierten Widersprüche, die der Text aufbaut, stark macht und wieder aufhebt, nicht als Prozeßfiguren wirken, die das Leserbewußtsein jeweils anders okkupieren und z.B. in der

Sukzession mit sich in Widerspruch setzen, sondern beurteilt hinsichtlich dieser Problematik den *Faust*-Text gleichsam von seiner Endsumme her. Diese ist in der Tat, wie auch wir in unserem ersten hypothetischen Gedankengang feststellten, Null oder Unendlich–Null ergibt die Summierung des Mitgeteilten oder der Referenz, Unendlich die Summierung der Referenzakte und -bezüge. Aber in der Staffelung des Textes sowohl in der Folge der Reden, der Szenen und "Gebilde," wie auch in der historischen Staffelung, die im Helena-Akt die Zeit von Troja bis Missolunghi umspannt, wie auch in der wechselnden Konkretheit, Fiktivität oder Abstraktheit der Figuren usw. wird der Leser veranlaßt, im Lesen sich nicht etwa vom Text abzuwenden,[6] sondern sich auf allen Ebenen seiner Rezeptivität zu konstituieren, wieder zu dekonstruieren, mit dem Text ins "ewig tätige Leben" und dessen je notwendige Verfassung in Zeichen, Formen, Vorstellungsarten einzutreten und genau die "synkrisis und diakrisis" zu erfahren, die der Text syntagmatisch und paradigmatisch entfaltet.

Der Mangel an Bennetts Verfahren wird bei seiner Interpretation der Poetik des "Vorspiels auf dem Theater" sichtbar. Nach seiner Ansicht wird der Dichter vom Direktor zu einer übertriebenen Äußerung gereizt, die dann durch die beiden andern Figuren korrigiert wird. Wenn der Dichter das Leben in der ewigen Festigkeit der Wahrheit einsargen wolle, werde er auf etwas ihm längst Bewußtes aufmerksam gemacht, nämlich daß der Dichter nicht Wahrheit sondern Leben, ironische Verhüllung der Wahrheit schaffen müsse (50–55). Obwohl er zwischendurch bei den drei Figuren drei "tendencies" anerkennt, nämlich Pragmatismus beim Direktor, Schätzung der ironischen Subtilität bei der Lustigen Person, Streben nach Wahrheit beim Dichter (60), heißt es am Ende wieder, die drei Figuren "are all in essential philosophical agreement, yet manage to carry on what appears to be a dispute about just what they agree on" (233).

Ich will im Gegenzug skizzieren, daß das "Vorspiel auf dem Theater" drei verschiedene Poetiken exponiert, und zwar, nach der Nennung bestimmter Erfordernisse durch den Direktor, in drei Positionen zur Textkonstitution,[7] drei Positionen zur intendierten Rezeption und drei Positionen zur Charakterisierung des Produzierenden.

Der Direktor stellt anfangs eine Reihe von Forderungen auf, die er durch die gemeinsame "Unternehmung" gern erfüllt sähe, die er jedoch zusammengenommen nur durch ein "Wunder" erfüllbar sieht. Die Forderungen sind: Behagen der Menge, ein Fest, Erzeugung von Erstaunen trotz arroganter Kritikbereitschaft, Versöhnung des "Geists des Volks," Neuheit trotz Belesenheit des Publikums, Gefälligkeit mit Bedeutung, Wunder, das "Wiedergeburt" ermöglicht. Die drei ersten Forderungen zielen auf die Sinne und Affekte, die drei folgenden Forderungen auf die geistigen Ansprüche des Publikums, die letzte Forderung mit ihrer religiösen Bildlichkeit von der Wiedergeburt durch die Gnadenpforte der Kasse in den Himmel des Theaters deutet auf die Schaffung eines neuen Menschen durch die Dichtung, sofern sie sinnlich-affektive und geistige Bedürfnisse nicht nur der einzelnen, sondern "des Volks" in seiner Einheit und Verschiedenheit vereinigt. Die erste, vierte und siebte Forderung zielen auf Vereinigung–das

Behagen auf das "harmonische Spiel" des "ganzen Systems ihrer Empfindungen und dunklen Gefühle,"[8] der versöhnte "Geist des Volks" auf das, was die "Menge" im Herderschen Sinne zur genetisch, kulturell und historisch bestimmten Nation macht, das quasi religiöse Wunder auf die durch die Kunst zu leistende Wiedergeburt im "ewig tätigen Leben." Die Forderungen 2–3 und 5–6 sind je entgegengesetzt und setzen sich den Vereinigungstendenzen entgegen: der sinnliche Genußwunsch beim Fest nimmt aus dem Behagen nur die materiale Komponente heraus, die arrogant gehobenen Augenbrauen setzen dem Genußwunsch Oppositionsgeist entgegen; daß die Kritiker trotzdem erstaunen möchten, zeigt, daß sie an sich gern genießen und behaglich sein wollen, aber sich schuldig sind, ein paar Schwierigkeiten zu machen—bei der dritten Forderung ist also der Widerspruch in die Forderung selbst aufgenommen. Neuheit ist dem zeitüberdauernden Geist des Volks entgegengesetzt, die horazische[9] Forderung "mit Bedeutung. . . gefällig" will mit der Neuheitsforderung nicht zusammengehen ("Wie machen wir's?"), sofern die Lehre immer auf Tradition zurückgeht und nie "frisch und neu" sein kann; sofern aber die dominante Gefälligkeitsforderung wirkt, ist eine Form der Belehrung gemeint, die dem historischen Stand des Volksgeistes entsprechend "frisch" und zeitgemäß ist. Die innere Dialektik und Aufstufung dieses Forderungskatalogs zeigt ihn als strukturiert nach der Herderschen Schöpfungshieroglyphe; was insgesamt vom Direktor damit als Leistung des Unternehmens Theater gefordert wird, ist eine Erneuerung des Publikums als Individuen, als Volk und als Menschheit. Der Direktor formuliert seine Ansprüche nicht im Sinne einer persönlichen Position, sondern im Blick auf die gemeinsame frühere Tätigkeit und den Bestand der beiden andern Figuren.

Der Dichter, die Lustige Person und der Direktor stellen in den folgenden drei Reden (59–103) ihre Positionen unter dem Gesichtspunkt der Textkonstitution gegeneinander, d.h. was wem unter welchen Bedingungen und unter welchen Kriterien zu liefern sei. Der Dichter will in der Einsamkeit unter Freunden für die Nachwelt schaffen; die Lustige Person will vor einem großen Kreis, sich selbst mitteilend, gegenwärtig extemporieren; der Direktor will ein Ragout vorlegen, d.h. Brocken von Vergangenem, in der Gegenwart mit würziger Sauce aufgekocht, und zwar für die Masse, von der sich jeder/mancher nach Belieben etwas auswählen kann. Der Dichter schafft aus dem Herzen (65), die Lustige Person aus der Phantasie, die die übrigen Vermögen mit "Narrheit" hören läßt, der Direktor aus dem Verstand (101). Der Dichter strebt "vollendete Gestalt" des Werks an; die Lustige Person weiß sich "behaglich mitzuteilen," also die "anschauende Erkenntnis einer Fülle von übereinstimmenden Vorstellungen über den Gegenstand" (sich als "braven Knaben") zu geben, die bei den Zuschauern das "harmonische Spiel" des "ganzen Systems ihrer Empfindungen und dunklen Gefühle" erzeugt[10]; der Direktor intendiert ein "Stück. . . in Stücken" als vielseitiges und massenhaftes Angebot zur Auswahl für jeden.

Noch weitere Kontraste wären zu beschreiben: das Echte, das Spaß Machende, das Zufriedenstellende; der Ausdruck des Herzens, das Hör-Spiel der launigen Phantasie, das Schauspiel der kulinarischen Erfindung. Man erkennt, wie genau

Goethe die Vorstellungsarten gegeneinandersetzt, wie verschiedenartig die Produk-
te sein sollen, die nach den Vorstellungen der drei Unterredner die Forderungen
des Direktors erfüllen können. Der Dichter will etwas hervorbringen, welches
das Innerste ganz ins Äußere wendet, erkennbar macht und wie der Christus
ektypus, die vollendete Gestalt des Menschensohns, die Menschheit in ihrer
himmlischen Existenz zeigt. Die Lustige Person will nur einen "ganzen Menschen"
hinstellen, um das Volk zu "erschüttern" und damit in die eigene ganze Menschheit zurückzuführen; der Direktor will unterschiedliche Bedürfnisse der einzelnen
befriedigen, d.h. durch Vervollständigung und Mängelkompensation aus jedem
einen zufriedenen Menschen machen. Der Dichter will ein Werk schaffen, das
einen geistlich wiedergeborenen Menschen hieroglyphisch bildet, die Lustige
Person sich selbst als musterhaft vorzeigen, der Direktor jedem der anwesenden
Menschen die Möglichkeit geben, sich als Individuum momentan Zufriedenheit
zu verschaffen.

   Blickt man nur einmal auf die Konsequenzen, die sich für die Struktur des
Faust-Textes aus diesen Poetiken ergeben, so erstrebt der Dichter "vollendete
Gestalt," die Lustige Person ein unstrukturiertes Bekenntnis, das in Grund und
Wirkung ("behaglich") sowie in der Durchführung ("Chöre") harmonisch sein
soll. Der Direktor endlich verlangt Form und Unform zugleich, Stück in Stücken,
Ragout aus Brocken früherer Texte, gleichmäßig scharf gewürzt.

   Tatsächlich wird der Text des *Faust* allen diesen Strukturkonzepten gerecht.
Er ist ein Stück aus Stücken im Sinne selbständiger Einheiten von Szenen oder
Akten, zwischen denen oft bedeutende Zeit-, Orts- und Handlungslücken klaffen;
er ist ein Stück aus Stücken im Sinne des Ragouts der Weltliteratur durch eine
große Menge intertextueller Bezüge, die oft ganze Lesarten des *Faust* anleiten.
Er ist, wie die "Zueignung" verdeutlicht, Bekenntnis eines "ganzen Menschen,"
"braven Knaben," der sich musterhaft für andere zeigt, das Bild jedoch durch
"Phantasie mit allen ihren Chören" ausgestaltet und durch Narrheit ironisch
verkehrt, das Lied zu Gesängen werden läßt (21, 17); die biographische Forschung
und schon Goethe in seinen Äußerungen haben den Bekenntnischarakter des
Faust wie der anderen Werke Goethes herausgearbeitet, der sich selbst als
Paradigma seiner Zeit verstand und stilisierte. Der Text ist endlich, wie im ersten
Teil dieser Arbeit angedeutet, vollendete Gestalt im Sinne des "vollkommenen
Widerspruchs," der "closure so absolute, so universally satisfying, that it no longer
makes sense as closure."[11] Die Gestalt ist deshalb "vollendet," weil sie nur noch
sie selbst ist und wie Goethes *Märchen* "an nichts und an alles erinnert" (HA
6:209), weil sie im Sinne der Schillerschen Formulierung[12] einen "alles" umfassenden und berührenden Stoff durch die Form vertilgt, sofern jedem stofflichen
Element, seiner Tendenz und seinem Wertanspruch ein anderes polar entgegengesetzt und ihr Patt in einer höheren Steigerungsposition aufgehoben ist. Man
kann das an den Strukturkonzepten beobachten: plastisch vollendeter Gestalt wird
musikalische "Ungestalt" entgegengesetzt, das Ragout aus Festem mit Sauce
kennzeichnet bildlich die aufhebende Verbindung; ihr kann dann etwa eine Helena

als "Gestalt aller Gestalten" (8907) entgegengesetzt werden, die ja auch eine Geburt
aus der Literatur ist.

Gilt also jedes der Strukturkonzepte als Prinzip für die Anlage, den Aufbau,
die Konstitution des Textes, so ist es schlicht unmöglich, sie gleichzeitig zu denken
und wirksam zu sehen. Betrachte ich das "Vorspiel auf dem Theater" als
Aufstellung eines Systems vollkommener Widersprüche zur Poetik des *Faust*, kann
ich nicht gleichzeitig über das Verhältnis dieses Vorspiels zu dem in Kalidasas
Sakuntala oder zu anderen Vorspieltypen in der dramatischen Tradition nachsin-
nen und gleichzeitig Goethe als den eigentlichen Spieler und Bekenner hinter den
Figuren des Direktors, der Lustigen Person und des Dichters bedenken, obwohl
mir dies gerade durch die "Zueignung" besonders nahegelegt wird–der Dichter
verwendet die Stanzen der "Zueignung," die Lustige Person formuliert die Poetik
des Bekenntnisses, das dort angekündigt wird, der Direktor setzt die Unternehmung in die Tat um, auf die die "Zueignung" als Widmungsgedicht hinweist.
Diese Perspektiven des Verstandes, der literarischen Einbildungskraft und der
identifikatorischen Empfindung sind mir alle möglich und bilden, zusammengenommen, nach damaliger Vermögenspsychologie die Totalität meiner Weltzu-
gänge, mich als "ganzen Menschen" ab; die Erfahrung des Lesens führt mich
jedoch immer wieder vor das Eingeständnis, mit der unlösbaren Aufgabe der
Integration meiner selbst als Leser dieses integralen Textes konfrontiert zu sein,
d.h. also mich selbst als "Problem," als "ewig tätiges Leben" durch den Text
zugespiegelt zu erhalten.

Es ist nicht nötig, die Aufstellung der poetologischen Positionen mit derselben
Ausführlichkeit weiter zu verfolgen. Deshalb nur eine Grobskizze der wichtigsten
Unterscheidungskategorien hinsichtlich der drei Reden über die Funktion der
Dichtung (108–83) und der drei Reden über den Produzenten von Dichtung (184–
230), damit nicht wieder der Eindruck entsteht, als herrsche "essential philosophi-
cal agreement" zwischen den drei Poetikern.

Der Direktor will Verwirrung, der Dichter Sinn, die Lustige Person Interesse
stiften, der Direktor wendet sich an eine Menge von oberflächlichen Zerstreuten,
der Dichter an Menschen, die sich als Menschen in ihrer ureigensten Kraft, ihrem
Menschenrecht, offenbart sehen sollen, die Lustige Person an Werdende, die erst
auf dem Weg zum reifen Menschsein sind. Mittel dazu ist für den Direktor die
Redundanz des Angebots–Bennett hat diese Überschwemmung sehr gut her-
ausgestellt–, für den Dichter die rhythmische, harmonische, psychologische,
sozialsystemische, mythologische Ordnung und Zuordnung der Naturelemente,[13]
für die Lustige Person der Roman, der "viel Irrtum und ein Fünkchen Wahrheit"
darstellt, d.h. die oben schon besprochene Exhaustion des Irrtums vorführt und
dem Werdenden damit ein Modell seiner eigenen Bildung an die Hand gibt. Es
braucht nicht gesagt zu werden, daß der *Faust*-Text wiederum diese Leistungs-
richtungen erfüllt; wieder ergeben sich mögliche vollständige Lesungen des Textes,
die jedoch nicht gleichzeitig geschehen können.

Die letzte Trias der Reden handelt von den Voraussetzungen für das Dichten
im Produzierenden. Wenn der Dichter wie von der Lustigen Person gewünscht

dichten soll, möchte er wieder ein Werdender sein, dem Dichtung von selbst
entquillt; wenn die Lustige Person sich einen Dichter denkt, so ist es der alte Herr,
der sich seine Kindlichkeit bewahrt hat und zielbewußt irren kann: jeder von
beiden rekonstruiert in sich anerkennend die entgegengesetzte Dichtungsweise,
das unterschiedene Lebensalter. Die sentimentalische bzw. verehrungsvolle, durch
die Bedingungsform noch weiter vom Dichten distanzierte Rede verwirft der
Direktor als "Komplimente," will Taten sehen, wenn die beiden sich schon als
Poeten ausgeben. Die Poesie kommandieren heißt, die beiden Produktionsvor-
stellungen des Dichters und der Lustigen Person paradox zu verbinden: das
unbewußt Hervordrängende dem fordernden Befehl zu unterwerfen. Es ist nicht
nur ein konstruiertes Paradox, sondern bezieht sich auf den Imperativ, mit dem
die großen Epiker von Homer an ihre Dichtungen begannen—schon Aristoteles
macht darauf aufmerksam, daß Homer der Muse befiehlt "Singe, Göttin den
Zorn. . . ."[14]

Wenn also die beiden Poeten sich als Menschen zu integrieren suchen durch
Sehnsucht nach Verjüngung und Verehrung der Reife, wenn sie das unbewußte
Hervorquellen der Poesie bzw. die bewußte Konstruktion für sich zu erbeuten
suchen, und den jeweiligen Mangel als Einschränkung ihrer universalen Fähigkeit
zu dichten erfahren, ruft der Direktor die älteste und jüngste, Inspiration und
Bewußtsein, Medialität und Tat verbindende Produktionstheorie der Dichtung
auf. Auch diese Produktionsauffassungen haben ihre Konsequenzen im *Faust*-Text
und leiten zu jeweils verschiedenen Lektüren an: Sind die Zufälligkeiten, Will-
kürlichkeiten, Lücken die Arabesken, die sich ein hoher ordnender Geist gestattet,
um anmutig, mit holdem Irren und nicht prosaisch geradeaus zum gesteckten
Ziel zu gelangen? Ist die Unordnung im Text zwischen den klaren Linien und
systematischen Bezügen das Signum der Inspiration durch die Muse, die dem
Befehl Folge geleistet hat, die "schöne Unordnung" des pindarischen Gesangs
und damit die Garantin unerhörter göttlicher Weisheit und Begeisterung? Konkret
am Beispiel: Sollen wir, wie Albrecht Schöne es nahelegt, den "Walpurgisnachtstraum" als willkürlich in den völlig fremden Kontext des *Faust* hineingewor-
fen betrachten und dürfen ihn deshalb auch bedenkenlos wieder hinauswerfen?
Sollen wir ihn als genau kalkulierte Arabeske mit höchst wichtiger Intertextualbe-
ziehung zum *Sommernachtstraum* betrachten, als das Un-Stück neben "Trüber Tag.
Feld," der ebenso genau kalkulierten einzigen unmetrischen Szene? Sollen wir
versuchen, hinter den sich isoliert vordrängenden Einzelfiguren Gruppierungen
von Sinneinheiten, Sinnbezüge zwischen den Gruppen, die dilettantisch aufbereitete
Grundproblematik des *Faust* überhaupt zu fassen versuchen und damit den
"Walpurgisnachtstraum" zum geheimen, inspirierten Schlüssel des ganzen Textes
erheben? Man kann mit gleichem Recht alle drei Lesarten erproben, darf
allerdings keine dogmatisch gegen die andern ausspielen, denn im Prinzip sollen
alle drei gleichzeitig gelten: Wenn der "Walpurgisnachtstraum" Schlüssel des
ganzen sein sollte, bleibt er ein nicht spielbares Un-Stück; wenn er hochkomplexe
Gedankenbezüge enthält, sind sie dilettantisch vorgestellt und von niemandem
rezipierbar. Wieder sollte ich mich als Denkender, Vorstellender und Einfühlender

gleichzeitig integrativ mit dem Text befassen und werde mit der Gespaltenheit meines modernen Bewußtseins konfrontiert. Indem meine Lesarten sich polar neutralisieren und steigernd aufheben, werde ich wieder vor mich als "Problem" gestellt.

Wir haben nun im "Vorspiel auf dem Theater" drei Poetiken, d.h. für den Text des *Faust* generative Prinzipien erkannt, haben ihre deutliche Verschiedenheit, ihre polare und verbindend-steigernde Gegenstellung und damit ihre Gültigkeit bei gleichzeitiger gegenseitiger Neutralisierung und Aufhebung festgestellt und an Beispielen aus dem *Faust*-Text paradigmatisch aufgezeigt. Bei dieser Setzung und Durchstreichung der Poetiken handelt es sich um die Dialektik der Vorstellungsarten, deren erkenntnistheoretische und, für Goethe, metaphysische Problematik wir skizziert haben. Diese Befunde haben für die Interpretation des *Faust* weitreichende Folgen: Der *Faust* zeigt nichts, teilt "unterm Strich" nichts außerhalb seiner Liegendes mit, er zeigt auf *sich*, er teilt *sich* mit. Was der Leser aus ihm erhält, ist er selbst als Aufgabe, ist "ewig tätiges Leben," das durch den "vollkommenen Widerspruch" ewig geheimnisvoll hindurchdringt. Der *Faust* ist andererseits bewußt so angelegt, daß er, als sukzessiver Text betrachtet, unter jedem Thema-Aspekt mehrfach lesbar ist; jede Lesart eröffnet klare und bestimmte Aussagen-Zusammenhänge, die sich über den ganzen Text hinweg entfalten und mannigfach vernetzt sind. Die bestimmten Aussagen werden allerdings durch die zugleich möglichen und nahegelegten Lesarten wieder gestört oder negiert. Es ist also für die Interpretation geboten, mehrere mögliche Lesarten zu einem Themabereich gleichzeitig zu verfolgen, um ihre Bestimmtheit und ihre gegenseitige Auslöschung oder Störung im Blick zu behalten. Die Interpretation des *Faust* wird dadurch nicht leichter, aber genauer, und sie erhält auch den Interpreten im "ewig tätigen Leben."

ANMERKUNGEN

1. Friedrich Heinrich Jacobi, "Zufällige Ergießungen eines einsamen Denkers in Briefen an vertraute Freunde," *Die Horen*, 3. Bd., 1795, 8. Stück (Neudruck Darmstadt: Wissenschaftliche Buchgesellschaft, 1959) 868–90, hier 870. Schiller lobte den Aufsatz in seinem Brief vom 9.7.1795 an Jacobi.

2. Prag und Jena 1789 (Neudruck Darmstadt: Wissenschaftliche Buchgesellschaft, 1963) 21. Weitere Hinweise in Klammern im Text.

3. Dazu vgl. meinen Aufsatz "Literatur und Geschichte bei Johann Gottfried Herder" (im Druck). Kohärenztheoretisch denkt auch Goethe: "Die Theorie an und für sich ist nichts nütze, als insofern sie uns an den Zusammenhang der Erscheinungen glauben macht" (HA 12:443). Das Beharren auf der Licht- und Farbentheorie gegen Newton hat hier m.E. ebenfalls seinen letzten Grund.

4. Die Forschungslage referiert und beurteilt Alwin Binder, *Das Vorspiel auf dem Theater: Poetologische und geschichtsphilosophische Aspekte in Goethes Faust-Vorspiel* (Bonn: Bouvier, 1969)

183–87. Entgegen der von mir vorgeschlagenen Lesung, daß Goethe hier drei distinkte Poetiken konfrontiert, sucht Binder nachzuweisen, es handle sich bei den Äußerungen von Direktor und Lustiger Person um "Antwortversuche auf das. . . Grundproblem, wie sich die Anteilnahme der Zuschauer gewinnen läßt, ohne die Prinzipien des Genies aufzugeben," wobei die Unterredner "fast immer. . . auf die Aussagen des Dichters ein[gehen]" (81). "Im Grunde" (83, 94f.) verfolgten Dichter, Direktor und Lustige Person "das gleiche Interesse" und machten nur der "Art" nach unterschiedliche Aussagen. An den Punkten, wo die Aussagen des Direktors und der Lustigen Person poetologische Ansprüche implizieren, wird Binders Detailkommentar abwegig. So deutet er die Fragmentarisierungspoetik des Direktors ("gebt es gleich in Stücken," V. 99) auf "Repertoirestücke" um (92), und die Romanpoetik der Lustigen Person wird nur als Eingehen auf "reale Verhältnisse" gedeutet, worunter Binder Probleme des "notwendigen Verzichts in sexueller und aggressiver Hinsicht" verstehen will (105f.).

5. Bennett 100, vgl. 291 u.ö. Der Begriff des Antipoetischen scheint mir allerdings widersprüchlich gefaßt zu sein. *Faust* sei "not a work of poetry, at least in Goethe's own understanding of the term. [...] Goethe's idea of poetic tradition implies that a well-conceived work of poetry *must* provide us with a clear relation we may adopt toward it as individuals, for the experience of our individuality is an integral component of the ironic tension poetry must seek to preserve" (290). Nach der von Bennett selbst zitierten Kulturphasentheorie Goethes (252f.) kann es nur eine kultur-relative Definition des Poetischen geben; also ist eine Bestimmung des poetologischen Status des *Faust* nicht auf der Basis von Eigenschaften von Werken der poetischen Tradition zu machen. Ungewollt bestätigt Bennett diese Auffassung, wenn er im Titel und im ganzen Buch von der "Poetik" und dem Poetischen im *Faust* spricht.

6. "The meaning of *Faust* is realized only by our turning away from it" (296). Mir scheint, daß Bennetts Argumentation, mit deren Richtung ich voll übereinstimme, von seiner Bemühung bestimmt ist, ein gewisses empiristisches Vorurteil von der Referentialität poetischer Sprache bei seinen Lesern abzubauen (dazu v.a. 252f.); wer dieses Vorurteil nicht teilt, kann der Rhetorik mancher Formulierungen Bennetts nicht folgen.

7. Die Rede des Dichters 104–7 vermutet eine Position des Direktors und leitet damit zu dessen Antwort und der zweiten Serie von Positionsbestimmungen über.

8. Definition der "Behaglichkeit" von Moses Mendelssohn, *Rhapsodie, oder Zusätze zu den Briefen über die Empfindungen*, in: M.M., *Ästhetische Schriften in Auswahl*, hg. Otto F. Best (Darmstadt: Wissenschaftliche Buchgesellschaft, 1986) 129–36.

9. Die Formel spiegelt den zweiten Teil der berühmten Lehre "Aut prodesse volunt aut delectare poetae, aut simul et iucunda et idonea dicere vitae" (Horaz, *Ars Poetica* 333f.). Nach Fischers Goethe-Wörterbuch hat "Bedeutung" bei Goethe auch die Denotation "Belehrung."

10. Mendelssohn, wie Anm. 8.

11. Bennett 318f.

12. Briefe *Über die ästhetische Erziehung des Menschen*, Nr. XXII.

13. Zur Analyse dieser Wirkungspoetik des Dichters, die wieder präzis im Sinne der Schöpfungshieroglyphe aufgebaut ist, vgl. meinen Aufsatz "Herders 'Aelteste Urkunde des Menschengeschlechts' und Goethe," *Bückeburger Gespräche über Johann Gottfried Herder 1988* (Rinteln: Bösendahl, 1989) 133–50. Der Mangel der Bennettschen Darstellung von

Goethes Poetik im *Faust* ist, daß er diesen Ordnungsaspekt nur als Überschwemmung durch Ordnung liest und den "Roman" der dritten Poetik gar nicht beachtet.

14. Aristoteles, *Poetik* 1456 b (Kap. XIX Schluß).

GERHARD KURZ

Das Drama als Ragout: Zur Metaphorik des Essens und Trinkens in Goethes *Faust*

The Drama as Ragout: Metaphors of Eating and Drinking in Goethe's Faust

Goethe uses metaphors of eating and drinking in his letters and in the work itself to define the dramatic structure of Faust. Examples include the theater director's call for a theatrical ragout (in "Vorspiel auf dem Theater") and the image of a mushroom ring springing up from the earth (in a letter to Schiller). Poetologically these images elaborate a notion of dramatic structure closely aligned with early Romantic aesthetics. Within the text the recurring metaphors of eating and drinking create a metaphorical field of reference that functions structurally to link diverse scenes of the play in variation and contrast.

I

DAS "AUFLEBEN" (24.6.1797 AN SCHILLER) DES *Faust*-PROJEKTS im Jahr 1797, nach der gemeinsamen Balladendichtung, war begleitet von einem intensiven Briefwechsel mit Schiller, den Goethe bat, seine "Träume" und "Gedanken" (22.6.1797) von "außen" zu kommentieren. Schiller hatte Goethe immer wieder gedrängt, die Arbeit am *Faust* aufzunehmen. Diesem Briefwechsel, ein Werkstattgespräch, ist zu entnehmen, wie kühn das Experiment des dramatischen Projekts beiden erschien, wie unterschiedlich aber auch die ästhetischen und poetologischen Aussichten und Überzeugungen waren. Freundschaftlich, aber bestimmt grenzt sich Goethe gegenüber den klassizistischen Forderungen Schillers ab. Seine Konzeption der dramatischen Struktur des *Faust*, wie sie aus diesen—und anderen— Briefen, nicht so sehr theoretisch entwickelt als metaphorisch charakterisiert hervorgeht, bringt das Projekt in eine frappierende Nähe zur frühromantischen Ästhetik und Poetologie, die in diesen Jahren, in unmittelbarer Nachbarschaft, formuliert wurde. Jedenfalls überspielt das Projekt die Demarkationen von Klassik und Romantik.

In der folgenden Skizzierung dieser poetologischen Konzeption konzentriere ich mich vor allem auf die in den Briefen und im Drama selbst verwendete

Metaphorik des Essens und Trinkens und befrage sie auf ihre poetologische Bedeutung.

Auf Schillers Forderung nach einem "poetischen Reif," der die "hoch aufquellende Masse" (26.6.1797 an Goethe) zusammenhalten solle, reagiert Goethe mit der Bemerkung, daß er es sich bei dieser "barbarischen Komposition" bequemer machen wolle und die "höchsten Forderungen mehr zu berühren als zu erfüllen" gedenke (27.6.1797 an Schiller). Die Charakterisierung des "Barbarischen," das Unklassisches, Rohes, "Nordisches" meint, wiederholt Goethe in einem anderen Brief an Schiller (28.4.1798), wo er von einer "barbarischen Produktion" spricht und im Gedicht "Abschied," das als Epilog erwogen wurde:

> Und so geschlossen sei der Barbareien
> Beschränkter Kreis mit seinen Zaubereien.[1]

1800 wird Schiller die Wendung vom Barbarischen aufnehmen und in seinem Sinne gebrauchen:

> Das Barbarische der Behandlung, das Ihnen durch den Geist des Ganzen aufgelegt wird, kann den höhern Gehalt nicht zerstören und das Schöne nicht aufheben, nur es anders spezifizieren und für ein anderes Seelenvermögen zubereiten. [...] Es ist ein sehr bedeutender Vorteil, von dem Reinen mit Bewußtsein ins Unreinere zu gehen, anstatt von dem Unreinen einen Aufschwung zum Reinen zu suchen, wie bei uns übrigen Barbaren der Fall ist. Sie müssen also in Ihrem Faust überall Ihr *Faustrecht* behaupten. (13.9.1800 an Goethe)

Gewiß wird bei solchen Formulierungen Schiller gegenwärtig gewesen sein, daß er Goethe, ohne seinen Namen zu nennen, in den "Ästhetischen Briefen" als einen Künstler apostrophiert, der den "Stoff" zwar von der Gegenwart nehme— die Schiller als "barbarische" (8. Brief) ausmachte und die er, als Ergebnis moderner Kultur, von einer naiven Wildheit unterschied—, der die Form aber aus dem "reinen Äther," aus der "absoluten unwandelbaren Einheit seines Wesens" entlehne (9. Brief).[2] Dem Angebot einer Rettung ins Klassische folgt Goethe jedoch nicht. Er nennt den *Faust* jetzt ein "poetisches Ungeheuer." Er erwidert:

> Der Trost, den Sie mir in Ihrem Briefe geben, daß durch die Verbindung des Reinen und Abenteuerlichen ein nicht ganz verwerfliches poetisches Ungeheuer entstehen könne, hat sich durch die Erfahrung schon an mir bestätigt, indem aus dieser Amalgamation seltsame Erscheinungen, an denen ich selbst einiges Gefallen habe, hervortreten. (16.9.1800)

Amalgamation bezeichnet ein Verfahren, aus Erz Gold und Silber zu gewinnen, indem man das Erz mit Quecksilber versetzt. Die "Erscheinungen," die aus solcher Amalgamation in *Faust* entstehen, bleiben "seltsam."

Daß das "Barbarische" und das "Ungeheure"[3] eine Schlüsselfunktion für Goethes Ästhetik innehat, geht aus einer 1805 verfaßten Anmerkung zu seiner Übersetzung von Diderots Dialog *Le Neveu de Rameau* hervor:

> Wohl findet sich bei den Griechen so wie bei manchen Römern eine sehr geschmackvolle Sonderung und Läuterung der verschiedenen Dichtarten, aber uns Nordländer kann man auf jene Muster nicht ausschließlich hinweisen. Wir haben uns andrer Voreltern zu rühmen und haben manch anderes Vorbild im Auge. Wäre nicht durch die romantische Wendung ungebildeter Jahrhunderte das Ungeheure mit dem Abgeschmackten in Berührung gekommen, woher hätten wir einen Hamlet, einen Lear, eine Anbetung des Kreuzes, einen standhaften Prinzen? Uns auf der Höhe dieser barbarischen Avantagen, da wir die antiken Vortheile wohl niemals erreichen werden, mit Muth zu erhalten, ist unsre Pflicht. . . .[4]

Mit diesen Titeln von Dramen Shakespeares und Calderons sind auch Vorbilder für die dramatische Struktur des *Faust* benannt.[5] Die durch den Namen dieser beiden Autoren markierte Poetik des Theatralischen und des Gattungssynkretismus, so wesentlich für die frühromantische Theorie der Dichtung, gibt auch der Metapher des "Tragelaphen," wieder in einem Brief an Schiller (6.12.1797) die programmatische Bedeutung. Tragelaph kann in der griechischen Literatur ein fiktives Mischwesen aus Bock und Hirsch oder ein Trinkgefäß bezeichnen. Zum Bedeutungskomplex des Barbarischen, Ungeheuren, Zauberischen, Vermischten paßt das Magische und Hexenhafte. An Herzog Carl August (8.12.1787):

> Um das Stück zu vollenden, werd ich mich sonderbar zusammennehmen müßen. Ich muß einen magischen Kreis um mich ziehen, wozu mir das günstige Glück eine eigne Stätte bereiten möge.

Und an Cotta (2.1.1799):

> Mein Faust ist zwar im vorigen Jahre ziemlich vorgerückt, doch wüßt ich bey diesem Hexenproducte die Zeit der Reife nicht voraus zu sagen.

Dazu passen metaphorische Wendungen, die das Veränderliche, Schwankende, Unfeste, Trügerische, Gespenstische, Widersinnige betonen, die "Luftphantome" (1.6.1797 an Schiller), die "nordischen Phantome," die auf einige Zeit durch "südliche Reminiszenzen" zurückgedrängt worden sind, die "Erscheinungen" (16.9.1800 an Schiller). Solchen Wendungen läßt sich Goethes Anmerkung zum "Helena"-Akt im Brief an Wilhelm von Humboldt (22.10.1826) hinzufügen:

Diesem Brief zufolge dauert die Zeiteinheit des "Helena"-Stückes ". . . von Trojas Untergang bis zur Einnahme von Missolunghi," 1826, also auch bis zu Byrons Tod im Jahre 1824. Es trägt den Titel: "Helena. Classisch-romantische Phantasmagorie. Zwischenspiel zu Faust." Die "Phantasmagorie" war ein modernes, seit den späten 90er Jahren des 18. Jahrhunderts zuerst in Paris angewandtes Verfahren, mit Hilfe von Hohlspiegeln und einer magischen Laterne "Erscheinungen" auf der Bühne zu erzeugen.[6] Ein "Hexenproduct" also aufgrund neuester Technik. Dieses phantasmatische Erzeugnis ist Bühnentrick, Sinnestäuschung, show, die eine Pathologie der Moderne aufdecken soll; im Ungenügen an sich selbst erzeugt sie, romantisch, die Antike. Es sind "Possen" (1.7.1797 an Schiller). Noch im letzten Brief zum *Faust* überhaupt, vom 17.3.1832 an Wilhelm von Humboldt, stellt Goethe die ästhetische Abweichung dieses Dramas heraus. Er redet von "diesen sehr ernsten Scherzen" und von diesem "seltsame[n] Gebäu."[7]

Im Brief vom 27.6.1797 an Schiller formuliert Goethe die synkretistische Poetik des *Faust* mit genaueren gattungstheoretischen Bestimmungen. Dabei charakterisiert er das Drama mit einem Begriff, der in dieser Zeit zu einem Schlüsselkonzept der Frühromantik aufsteigen wird, dem des Fragments: "bei dem Ganzen, das immer ein Fragment bleiben wird." Diese Äußerung ist ernst zu nehmen, sowohl was den Anspruch auf ein "Ganzes," als was seine Form des "Fragments" angeht. Nicht nur *Faust. Ein Fragment* von 1790, auch *Faust I* und *Faust II* sind fragmentarische Stücke, wie unmißverständlich aus einem Gespräch mit Riemer aus dem Jahr 1831 hervorgeht: "Der zweite Theil sollte und konnte nicht so fragmentarisch sein, als der erste." Der Unterschied der fragmentarischen Struktur ist nur graduell. Viele "Partien" im zweiten Teil sind nur "angelegt," aber, und darauf komme es an, "der Sinn und die Idee des Ganzen wird sich dem *vernünftigen* Leser entgegenbringen, wenn ihm auch an Übergängen zu suppliren genug übrig bleibt."[8] In dem Brief an Schiller vom 27.6.1797 nennt Goethe auch die Möglichkeit der poetischen Rechtfertigung der fragmentarischen Struktur: "bei dem Ganzen, das immer ein Fragment bleiben wird, mag mir die neue Theorie des epischen Gedichts zustatten kommen."

Diese "neue Theorie des epischen Gedichts" war von Goethe und Schiller Anfang 1797 entwickelt worden. Er führte zu einem gemeinsamen Aufsatz unter dem Titel "Über epische und dramatische Dichtung," der von Goethe 1827 veröffentlicht wurde. Diese neue Theorie wurde im Blick auf Homers Epen formuliert, deren poetische Einheit gerade, 1795, in der sensationellen Abhandlung von Friedrich August Wolf *Prolegomena ad Homerum* in Frage gestellt worden war. Wolf war damit nicht der erste, aber der erste, der mit allen Mitteln philologischer Akribie vorging. Er hatte die alleinige Autorschaft Homers bestritten und die These aufgestellt, daß die homerischen Epen aus von verschiedenen Bearbeitern aufgezeichneten, ursprünglich von Rhapsoden mündlich verbreiteten Teilen bestännden–sie also von disparater Struktur seien: ". . . neque adeo ipsas ἀοίδας, ex quibus. Ilias et Odyssea composita sunt, unum omnes auctorem habere, verisimilibus argumentis et rationibus effici potest."[9] Wolfs *Prolegomena* inspirierten den anfänglich reservierten Goethe nicht nur zu seinem Epos *Hermann und*

Dorothea,[10] wie die Einleitungselegie bekundet, sondern auch, mit Schiller, zu neuen gattungstheoretischen Überlegungen.

In der neuen Goethe-Schillerschen Theorie wird das epische Gedicht bestimmt durch die "Selbständigkeit" und "Substantialität" seiner Teile, in der "alles sich selbst um seiner selbst willen geltend" macht, im Gegensatz zum Drama, in dem alle Teile Mittel für die Folge und das Ende sind und durch das "Retardierende," das "Verweilende," "Breite" des Erzählens (Briefe vom 19.4., 22.4., 25.4.1794). Goethe weist Schiller dabei auf Friedrich Schlegels Abhandlung "Über die Homerische Poesie. Mit Rücksicht auf die Wolfische Untersuchungen" hin, die in Reichardts Zeitschrift "Deutschland" 1796 erschienen war. Auch in dieser Abhandlung liegt die gleiche Methode vor: das Epos wird bestimmt aus den Differenzen von Epos und Drama. Das Epos kennt Schlegel zufolge keine einzige "vollständige poetische Handlung" wie das Drama, sondern eine "unbestimmte Masse von Begebenheiten," die eine "durchaus unbestimmte und also ins Unendliche gehende Erwartung bloßer Fülle überhaupt" erzeugt. Das epische Gedicht ist ein "poetischer Polyp, wo jedes kleinere oder größere Glied. . . für sich eignes Leben, ja auch ebensoviel Harmonie als das Ganze hat."[11] Mit solchen Formulierungen ist für Goethe Schlegel zwar auf dem richtigen Weg, geht aber doch zu weit. Auch das epische "Gedicht" muß eine "Einheit" haben, sonst wäre es keines. So "zerstückelt" die homerischen Epen auch sind, so zeigen sie doch die "Tendenz der poetischen und kritischen Natur nach Einheit." Goethe nennt diese Tendenz sogar "gewaltsam." Die Ausführungen Schlegels lassen freilich die Überlegung zu, daß er der Formulierung "Tendenz" nach "Einheit" zugestimmt hätte.[12]

Die "Selbständigkeit" der Teile, die breite Ausführung und die "Tendenz" zur Einheit machen aus der Struktur des Dramas ein episches oder, wie Goethe im Brief an Schiller vom 11.4.1798 formuliert, ein "rhapsodisches Drama." Es kommt einer Abschwächung seines Vorbehalts gegenüber Schlegel gleich, wenn es in der wohl 1800 gedichteten "Abkündigung" heißt:

> Den besten Köpfen sei das Stück empfohlen,
> Der Deutsche sitzt verständig zu Gericht,
> Und möchten's gerne wiederholen,
> Allein der Beifall gibt allein Gewicht.
> Vielleicht dass sich was Bess'res freilich fände.–
> Des Menschen Leben ist ein ähnliches Gedicht:
> Es hat wohl seinen Anfang und sein Ende,
> Allein ein Ganzes ist es nicht.
> Ihr Herren, seid so gut und klatscht nun in die Hände.

In der ersten Fassung lautet die 6. Zeile: "Des Menschen Leben ist ein episches Gedicht."

Tatsächlich ist ja die Struktur des *Faust* durch einen "fragmentarischen" Zusammenhang, durch die "Selbständigkeit" einzelner Szenen, die "wie eine für sich

bestehende kleine Welt" (Gespräch mit Eckermann, 1831[13]) wirken, gekennzeichnet, durch die Aufhebung dramatischer Sukzession und Zeitenfolge. Die Szenen
werden, vor allem im zweiten Teil, weniger durch eine integrale Entwicklung
von Charakter und Handlung verbunden, wie es dem von Lessing im 18.
Jahrhundert erneuerten aristotelischen Dramenmodell entsprochen hätte, sondern
durch Übergänge und Verwandlungen, durch Gruppierungen und Reihungen.
Eckermann notiert die Zustimmung Goethes zu seiner Äußerung, daß "der
Auerbachsche Keller, die Hexenküche, der Blocksberg, der Reichstag, die
Maskerade, das Papiergeld, das Laboratorium, die Classische Walpurgisnacht,
die Helena lauter für sich bestehende kleine Weltenkreise" seien, "die, in sich
abgeschlossen, wohl auf einander wirken, aber doch einander wenig angehen."[14]
Und schließlich ist das Stück gekennzeichnet durch die Mischung dramatischer
und theatralischer Formen: Tragödie, Komödie, Farce, Oper, Legendenspiel,
Mysterienspiel, Bürgerliches Trauerspiel, Aufzüge, Theater im Theater. Gemischt
werden das Hohe und das Niedrige, das Tragische und das schiere Spektakel,
gemischt werden unterschiedliche Sprachregister vom Zarten, Feierlichen bis zum
Obszönen. Die einzelnen Teile werden jedoch verbunden durch Rekurrenzen,
Korrespondenzen, Varianten und Kontraste von Themen und Motiven, durch
Metaphernfelder, die "anzeigen und andeuten" (am 29.12.1827 an Riemer), als
"gleichsam ineinander abspiegelnde Gebilde" (27.9.1827 an Iken). Solche
Techniken eröffnen im Drama eine Dimension immanenter Reflexion, also eine
Poesie der Poesie[15]—oder, romantisch formuliert, eine Dimension der Ironie.

II

Im Feld der poetologischen Metaphorik Goethes fällt die des Kochens, Essens
und Trinkens auf. Goethe verwendet sie sowohl zur Beschreibung von Produktion
und Rezeption von Dichtung, als auch zur Beschreibung ihrer Struktur. Diese
Metapahorik findet sich, nicht nur auf *Faust* bezogen, bei Goethe schon früh und
geht auf eine lange, auch exegetische, Tradition zurück.[16] Im Mittelalter und in
der Neuzeit bildet diese Metaphorik eine latente eucharistische Bedeutung aus,
die in der biblischen Bedeutung bezogen ist auf den Sündenfall des Essens vom
Baum der Erkenntnis des Guten und Bösen (1. Moses 2 und 3), den sie rückgän-
gig macht. Dieser Bedeutungszusammenhang generiert eine metaphorische
Analogie von Essen, Rede und Reflexion.
Am 8. März 1779 schreibt Goethe an Carl August über seine Arbeit an *Iphigenie
auf Tauris*: "ich [steige] in meine alte Burg der Poesie und koche an meinem Töch-
tergen."[17] In den *Venetianischen Epigrammen* von 1790 wird die Metapher des
Dichters als Koch mit blasphemischer, antichristlicher Bedeutung[18] aufgeladen.
Goethe stilisiert sich im 15. der epigrammatischen Nachträge als "verständiger
Koch," der ein "artig Gastmahl" bereitet, das Heidnisches und Christliches mischt:

Wenn ein verständiger Koch ein artig Gastmahl bereitet,
    Mischt er unter die Kost vieles und vieles zugleich.

> So genießt auch ihr dies Büchlein, und kaum unterscheidet
> Alles ihr, was ihr genießt. Nun, es bekommt euch nur wohl.

Zugleich kann er sich auch als Esser stilisieren, der mit dem "Teufels- und Hexen-
wesen" im *Faust* sein "nordisches Erbteil verzehrt," um sich dann zu den "Tischen
der Griechen" zu wenden (Gespräch mit Eckermann, 16.2.1826).

Im schon zitierten Brief an Schiller vom 1.7.1797 findet sich eine aufschluß-
reiche poetologische Metapher. Dort redet Goethe davon, daß er sich einen
ruhigen Monat erhoffe, und dann "sollte das Werk zu männiglicher
Verwunderung und Entsetzen wie eine große Schwammfamilie aus der Erde
wachsen." Was besagt diese Metapher? Es ist keine eines klassizistischen Programms. Eine Schwammfamilie ist eine Gruppe von Pilzen, die teils oberirdisch,
teils unterirdisch durch ein Geflecht, ein Myzel, verbunden sind. Die Kreise, die
es dabei bilden kann, werden "Hexenringe" oder "Zauberringe" genannt.
Fremdkörper werden in dieses Geflecht integriert. Schwämme sind eßbar–sie
können freilich auch giftig sein. Die Metapher deutet auf das Wachstümlich-
Notwendige der Produktion unter günstigen Bedingungen, auf die Selbständigkeit
der Teile, auf unterschiedlichen, graden oder krummen, unförmigen Wuchs, aber
auch auf ihr teils offenes, teils verborgenes Geflecht von Beziehungen, so daß
die einzelnen Pilze eine "Familie" bilden.

Zugleich drastisch und subtil wird die Kochen-, Essen- und Trink-Metaphorik
im "Vorspiel auf dem Theater" eingesetzt. In diesem "Vorspiel" entfaltet Goethe
eine immanente Poetik des Theaters und seine Wirkungsabsicht.[19] Mit ihr wird
das Publikum, so wie es ist, akzeptiert, der Anspruch der "Menge" auf Unterhal-
tung, ihre Lust auf Effekt und Sensation, am sinnlichen Genuß gerechtfertigt,
jedoch auf "Bedeutung" (48) und moralischen Anspruch und auf beste Kunst
nicht verzichtet. Die Formulierung dieses Programms wird vor allem dem
Theaterdirektor in den Mund gelegt. Ihm entgegengesetzt wird der "Dichter,"
der gegen die "bunte Menge" à la Schiller sich auf den "Geist" (59f.) beruft. Die
lustige Person unterstützt den Theaterdirektor. Sie bestimmt als Gegenstand des
Theaters das Bewußtmachen des "vollen Menschenlebens," das ein jeder "lebt,"
das aber vielen nicht "bekannt" ist (167–68). Die lustige Person vermittelt jedoch
auch zwischen Theaterdirektor und Dichter. Sie redet beide als "alte Herrn" (210)
an, die "uns," das Publikum, als "wahre Kinder" finden (213).

Für den Theaterdirektor hat das Theater eine andere, jedoch keine geringere
Funktion als für den Dichter: Es hat vor allem eine sinnliche Wirkung, die metaphorisch mit einer Nahrungsaufnahme identifiziert wird, mit dem Essen von
"Brot" (55) und einem "Ragout" (100), mit "Trank" (172) und "stark Getränke"
(223). Es hat also auch eine lebenserhaltende Wirkung. Der Theaterdirektor
vergleicht das Drängen der Menge vor der Kasse mit dem Drängen um Brot vor
Bäckertüren:

> Denn freilich mag ich gern die Menge sehen,
> Wenn sich der Strom nach unsrer Bude drängt

Und mit gewaltig wiederholten Wehen
Sich durch die enge Gnadenpforte zwängt,
Bei hellem Tage, schon vor vieren,
Mit Stößen sich bis an die Kasse ficht
Und, wie in Hungersnot um Brot an Bäckertüren,
Um ein Billett sich fast die Hälse bricht. (49–56)

Die Essensmetaphorik nimmt der Theaterdirektor wieder auf, indem er das
Drama ein "Ragout" nennt, also ein Gericht mit Fleisch-, Fisch-, oder Geflügel-
stücken, geköchelt im eigenen Saft, kräftig mit allerlei Zutaten gewürzt, oft mit
Pilzen. Witzig wird dabei mit der Bedeutung von "Stück" gespielt:

Wer vieles bringt, wird manchem etwas bringen;
Und jeder geht zufrieden aus dem Haus.
Gebt ihr ein Stück, so gebt es gleich in Stücken!
Solch ein Ragout, es muß Euch glücken;
Leicht ist es vorgelegt, so leicht als ausgedacht.
Was hilft's, wenn Ihr ein Ganzes dargebracht,
Das Publikum wird es Euch doch zerpflücken. (97–103)

Die Ragout-Metapher akzentuiert wieder die Selbständigkeit, Unterschiede und
Mischung der einzelnen Teile, impliziert jedoch auch, als Zusammen-Gekochtes,
einen Zusammenhang. Der emphatische Anspruch auf ein "Ganzes" ist freilich
illusionär, denn das Interesse des Publikums geht darauf, das Stück in seinen
Teilen zu "essen," es zu zerlegen, zu "zerpflücken." Wer die "Masse zwingen"
will, muß ihr folglich "Masse" (95) geben–die Rechtfertigung der epischen "Breite"
(93) des Dramas. Nicht so sehr der Dichter oder das Kunstwerk verändern das
Publikum. Es kommt darauf an, was das Publikum selbst aus dem, was es sieht
und erfährt, macht.[20] Es ist aber prinzipiell der Wahrheit zugänglich.

Goethe verwendet die Ragout-Metapher auch anderswo. Eine "Zahme Xenie"
lautet:

Gibt's ein Gespräch, wenn wir uns nicht betrügen,
Mehr oder weniger versteckt?
So ein Ragout von Wahrheit und von Lügen,
Das ist die Köcherei die mir am besten schmeckt.[21]

In *Faust* legt Goethe diese Metapher auch Faust in den Mund. In rhetorischer
Selbstgewißheit antwortet Faust auf die Frage Wagners, wie man die Welt durch
"Überredung leiten" solle:

Wenn ihr's nicht fühlt, ihr werdet's nicht erjagen,
Wenn es nicht aus der Seele dringt
Und mit urkräftigem Behagen

> Die Herzen aller Hörer zwingt.
> Sitzt ihr nur immer! Leimt zusammen,
> Braut ein Ragout von andrer Schmaus,
> Und blast die kümmerlichen Flammen
> Aus eurem Aschenhäufchen 'raus! (534–41)

Faust setzt gegen das "Ragout" einer Rede die unmittelbare, arhetorische Kommunikation von "Herz" zu "Herzen" (544–45). Wagners Unterbrechung der Erdgeistszene, "Verzeiht! ich hör' Euch deklamieren" (522), überführt jedoch schon von vornherein diese Absicht der Rhetorik.

Die Metaphorik der Nahrung verwendet auch die lustige Person. Er redet vom "Trank," der aus "bunten Bildern," "wenig Klarheit," viel "Irrtum" und einem "Fünkchen Wahrheit" im "Spiel" gebraucht wird (170–75). Er variiert diese Metaphorik in das "Saugen" von "melanchol'scher Nahrung" aus dem "Werk" (176–77). So verhält sich das erwachsene Publikum als "wahre Kinder" (213).

Zum Schluß fordert der Theaterdirektor vom Dichter und von der lustigen Person:

> Euch ist bekannt, was wir bedürfen:
> Wir wollen stark Getränke schlürfen;
> Nun braut mir unverzüglich dran! (222–24)

Unüberlesbar im "Vorspiel" ist der Gebrauch religiösen Vokabulars: Das Publikum zwängt sich durch die "enge Gnadenpforte" (52). Diese "Enge," die sich auf "Menge" reimt, lehnt der Dichter ab. Er will zur "Himmelsenge" und redet dabei den Theaterdirektor an, als sei er Gott: "Nein, führe mich zur stillen Himmelsenge, / Wo nur dem Dichter reine Freude blüht" (63–64). "Eng" ist auch das "Bretterhaus," in dem der ganze "Kreis der Schöpfung" ausgeschritten werden soll (239–40). Mit dieser Formulierung wird freilich die Bedeutung des Sargs assoziiert. Gegen den Tod, gegen die "enge" Endlichkeit wird sich Faust mit allen Mitteln wehren. Die Endlichkeit des Lebens will er nicht anerkennen. Der Andrang des Publikums zum Theater erscheint als eine Geburt, "mit gewaltig wiederholten Wehen" (51), zugleich als sexueller Akt: das Publikum zwängt sich durch die "enge Pforte" mit "Stößen" (54). Daß so "verschiedne Leute" sich nach dem Theater drängen, ist ein "Wunder" (57), das nur der Dichter bewirkt. Und die lustige Person redet von der "Offenbarung" (175) des Schauspiels. Dieses religiöse Vokabular verleiht der Metaphorik des "Brotes," des "Tranks" und des "starken Getränks" eine eucharistische Bedeutung. Allerdings wird, wie aus der Antithese zum Spiritualismus des Dichters hervorgeht, diese Eucharistie säkularisiert, verkörperlicht. Die "enge Pforte," die nach Matthäus 7:14 zum "Leben" führt, führt wirklich ins volle Leben. Man kann aber auch sagen: das Säkulare, Körperliche wird auch spiritualisiert, denn der Theaterdirektor beauftragt sowohl den Dichter wie die lustige Person, den "ganzen Kreis der Schöpfung" auszuschreiten. Dies bedeutet nicht, daß nun ein christliches Spiel folgt, denn Gott, wie der "Prolog im Himmel" zeigt, ist auch nicht mehr der alte–denn er ist nur noch der "Alte" (350), vergleichbar dem "alten Herrn" des "Vorspiels." Gegen eine Verwandlung ins Spirituelle zumal steht die lustige Person.

Die Metaphorik des Essens und Trinkens zieht sich vor allem durch den ersten Teil: Mephisto will Faust, dessen "Trank und Speise" nach seinen Worten nicht "irdisch" ist (301), dazu bringen, daß er "Staub. . . fressen" wird, und zwar "mit Lust" (334). Fausts Verhältnis zur Welt wird durch diese Metaphorik charakterisiert: Er sucht eine "Speise, die nicht sättigt" (1678); er "nascht" an der Welt ("überall zu naschen," 1761). Am Ende "naschen" (11828) die Engel am toten Faust. "Guts in Ruhe" will er nicht "schmausen" (1691). Für Mephisto ist die Schöpfung eine unverdauliche, harte "Speise" (1777). Eine anti-eucharistische Bedeutung erhält der Trank, wenn Faust am Ostermorgen einen "Saft" (732) aus einer "Schale" (720) trinken will, um seinem Leben ein Ende zu setzen. Das Lied vom König in Thule enthält das Trinken als zentrale Metapher. In "Auerbachs Keller" ist es den Studenten "kannibalisch" (2293) wohl. Der Vers vom "kannibalischen" Wohlsein ist ein gutes Beispiel für die bedeutungsakzentuierende Funktion von textuellen Rekurrenzen und Korrespondenzen. Gretchen singt z.B. im Kerker:

> Mein Vater, der Schelm,
> Der mich gessen hat! (4414–15)

Im 3. Akt des zweiten Teils redet Phorkyas von den Helden der Griechen, die sich als "menschenfresserisch" (9015) erwiesen haben. Dadurch fällt ein scharfes Licht auf das auf den ersten Blick Harmlose des "kannibalischen" Wohlseins.

In der "Sudelköcherei" (2341) der "Hexenküche" erscheint die Metapher schon im Titel der Szene. Der Titel verweist auch–durch den historischen Zusammenhang von Hexenglauben und schwarzer Magie begründbar–auf die "schwarze Küche" (1039), in der Fausts Vater der schwarzen Magie nachgeht. Die "Hexenküche" enthält neben der erotischen, blasphemischen und politischen–und vermutlich vielen Anspielungen auf die zeitgenössische Literaturszene–auch eine poetologische Bedeutung.[22]

Faust sucht eine erotische Verjüngungskur. Der Teufel kann den "Trank" der Verjüngung nicht selber "brauen" (2367), dies kann nur die Hexe, das "alte Weib" (2366). Sie ist im "Prozeß der Zivilisation" zurückgeblieben, denn sie erkennt den zivilisiert gewordenen Teufel nicht wieder. Es handelt sich um "Zauberei," so Mephisto, "tolles Zauberwesen" (2337), so Faust. Dessen Elemente aber sind unzauberische: "Kunst," "Wissenschaft," "stiller Geist" und, was sowohl Mephisto als auch Faust völlig abgeht, "Geduld." Freilich auch "wunderbare Sachen" (2370–75). Zugleich wirkt sie närrisch. Romantisches und Klassisches werden in ihr verbunden, insofern sie Hexe und "Sibylle" (2577), eine wahrsagende Frau, genannt wird. So erscheint die Hexe einerseits als archaische, andererseits als moderne Figur, einerseits als Zauberin und Närrin, andererseits als "Wissenschaftlerin" ("Die hohe Kraft / Der Wissenschaft. . . ," 2567ff.). Mephisto mahnt

Faust, in den zauberischen Zeremonien und Deklamationen der Hexe nicht das
Eigentliche zu sehen. Es sind "Possen" (2536), "Hokuspokus" (2538), den sie als
"Arzt" (2538) veranstalten muß, damit der "Saft" Faust "wohl gedeihen" (2539)
kann.[23]

Der "Trank" der Hexe wird von Mephisto ein "Werk" (2371) genannt, zu
dem Kalkulables, Geduld, Wissenschaft, Kunst, stiller Geist, und Inkalkulables,
wunderbare Sachen, beitragen, Rationalität, Erfahrung, archaische Praktik und
närrischer Hokuspokus. Solche Eigenschaften suggerieren, in dieser "Sudelköchin"
eine allegorische Verkörperung von Poesie zu sehen. Sie bietet Mephisto ihren
"Saft" mit den Worten an:

> Hier ist ein Lied! wenn Ihr's zuweilen singt,
> So werdet Ihr besondre Wirkung spüren. (2591–92)

Was bewirkt jedoch ihr Trank bei Faust? Er verjüngt ihn, macht ihn liebeskrank–
und realitätsblind. Er verstärkt und verfestigt, was sich in Fausts Blick in den
"Zauberspiegel" (2430) schon ereignete: die Verfallenheit in einer narzißtischen
Situation an ein erotisch-ästhetisches Objekt, an das "schönste Bild von einem
Weibe" (2436). Er läßt ihn nun bald in jedem Weibe "Helena" sehen (2604). Faust
verfällt dem, was an Poesie zauberisch ist, der Möglichkeit der Verwechslung
von Schein und Sein, Bild und Wirklichkeit. So muß er über die wirkliche Existenz
des individuellen Lebens–Gretchen–hinweggehen. Nach jenem "schönen Bild"
(3248) taumelt er von Begierde zu Genuß, von Genuß zu Begierde.

Auch mit den Meerkatzen, "Magd" und "Knecht" der Hexe, wird eine poeto-
logische Bedeutungsebene aufgebaut. Traditionell symbolisieren Affen das Ver-
mögen und den Zwang der Nachahmung. Traditionell symbolisieren sie auch
Sexualität, Körperlichkeit und die *vanitas mundi*. Der Meerkater spielt mit einer
Kugel, der "Welt." Sie glänzt, ist aber inwendig hohl und zerbricht bald. (Ein Bild
von Teniers d.J., "Affenküche," stellt Affen in einer Küche dar, die mit einer
Weltkugel spielen.) Das Steigen und Fallen der Kugel parodiert textimmanent
Fausts Vision der Harmonie des Alls (447–53). Die Meerkatze schäumt einen
Kessel ab und sorgt dafür, daß er nicht überkocht. Im Dampf des Kessels zeigen
sich "verschiedene Gestalten" (Regieanweisung, vgl. *Macbeth*, I,1). Die Tiere
kochen "breite Bettelsuppen," wozu Mephisto sagt: "Da habt ihr ein groß
Publikum" (2392–93). Nicht nur fällt "Publikum," sondern auch "breit" als
abweichende Formulierungen auf. Sie ergeben Sinn, wenn man sie auf den Satz
des Theaterdirektors bezieht: "Wer vieles bringt, wird manchem etwas bringen"
(97). Liegt darin eine Selbstpersiflage, wonach epische Breite zu einer "Bettelsuppe"
führt? Aber "Bettelsuppe" kann nicht nur dünne Suppe, sondern auch eine Suppe
bedeuten, die man erbettelt. (Goethe hat im Brief an Schiller vom 26.7.1797 am
Beispiel eines literarischen Werkes von der "Bettelsuppe" gesprochen, wie sie
das deutsche Volk liebe.)

Mephisto nennt die Meerkatzen "aufrichtige Poeten" (2464)–aufrichtig wohl
deshalb, weil ihnen nur etwas im Denken und Reden glückt, nicht in der Wirk-

lichkeit. Sie trennen Schein und Sein. Im 26. seiner "Ästhetischen Briefe" schreibt Schiller: "Nur soweit er *aufrichtig* ist (sich von allem Anspruch auf Realität ausdrücklich lossagt), und nur soweit er *selbständig* ist (allen Beistand der Realität entbehrt), ist der Schein ästhetisch."[24]

Die Krone, die die Meerkatzen in einem närrisch-höfischen Spiel bringen, zerbricht, weil sie mit ihr ungeschickt umgehen. Die Passage dürfte neben ihrer möglichen satirischen Beziehung auf die vorrevolutionären Monarchien–die Szene ist 1788 entstanden oder begonnen worden–eine grotesk-blasphemische Bedeutung haben, die sich in der Szene auch sonst findet, etwa in:

> Es war die Art zu allen Zeiten,
> Durch Drei und Eins, und Eins und Drei
> Irrtum statt Wahrheit zu verbreiten. (2560–62)

Im Spiel weisen die Meerkatzen Mephisto die Rolle des Königs zu, die mit den Attributen des gekreuzigten Jesus ausgestattet wird. Die brüchige Krone, die er "leimen" soll, zerbricht. Die Meerkatzen reagieren freudig und wie befreit: "Nun ist es geschehen!" Denn das Scheitern des wirklichen "Leimens" unter religiösen Vorzeichen ist, wenn die Meerkatzen für die Poesie stehen, die Bedingung der Möglichkeit des aufrichtigen Scheins, des ästhetischen Spiels. Seine Logik ist die einer Inversion: Das Leimen kommt vor dem Zerbrechen, das Reimen vor dem Gedanken[25]:

Die Tiere:

> O sei doch so gut,
> Mit Schweiß und mit Blut
> Die Krone zu leimen!
> . . .
> Nun ist es geschehn!
> Wir reden und sehn,
> Wir hören und reimen–
> . . .
> Und wenn es uns glückt,
> Und wenn es sich schickt,
> So sind es Gedanken! (2450–60)

III

In der "Hexenküche" wird das Trinken mit dem großen metaphorischen Feld des Feuers und der Flamme verbunden, das geistige und natürliche Kreativität, Liebe, Gewalt und apokalyptische Zerstörung bedeuten kann.[26] Die Hexe kommt durch eine große Flamme, unter dem Kessel brennt das Feuer; als Faust die Schale an den Mund führt, entsteht eine "leichte Flamme" (Regieanweisung). Flammen

sind Attribute auch der Dichterfiguren des zweiten Teils, von Knabe Lenker und
Euphorion. Die Metaphorik des Essens und Trinkens nicht mehr! Sie geht bei
Knabe Lenker zurück und verschwindet bei Euphorion ganz. Knabe Lenker ist
die Personifikation der "Verschwendung" und der "Poesie" (5573). Poetische
Kreativität wird verstanden als Überfluß und Verschwendung. Sie belebt und
schmückt das Leben, "Tanz und Schmaus" (5578). Knabe Lenkers Gegenfigur
ist der Geiz, eine von "Hunger" und "Durst" abgemagerte Person (5643). Auch
Knabe Lenker macht Hokuspokus, er verteilt, "umherschnippend," goldene
Glitzerdinge, die sich als Schein erweisen. Die Menge, die wirkliches Gold will,
ist enttäuscht. Als "größte Gaben" (5630) spendet er "Flämmchen" (5633), die
bei manchen aufflammen, bei vielen verlöschen. Mit der Metaphorik des Feuers
wird in dieser Figur das Moment des Spirituellen hervorgehoben (vgl. auch
5623ff.).[27]
    Gesteigert wird diese metaphorische Bedeutung noch in der Figur Euphorions.
Er ist jugendlich, knabenhaft, bezaubernd, hermaphroditisch, gauklerisch (vgl.
9626, 9753) wie Knabe Lenker. Beide haben die Tendenz zum Ätherischen, zum
Transzendieren des Irdischen. Wenn jedoch Knabe Lenker die "Räume" der
Gegenwart und Wirklichkeit zu "ehren" (5525) weiß, so verachtet Euphorion
(wie Faust, vgl. 2364) ihre "Enge" (9813). Er will nicht "am Boden stocken"
(9724). Auf den Ruf zur Mäßigung antwortet er mit:

> Immer höher muß ich steigen,
> Immer weiter muß ich schaun. (9821–22)

Der Chor apostrophiert ihn als "Heilige Poesie, / Himmelan steige sie!" (9863–64).
"Heilige Poesie" ist eine Formel, die Klopstock in das zeitgenössische Dichtungs-
verständnis einführte.[28] Mit dem Tod von Euphorion ist die "Flamme" (9956)
verschwunden. Euphorion, dem bekanntlich Byron Modell stand, verkörpert
die ikarische Poesie der Moderne,[29] die ganz Geist, Innerlichkeit ("Seele," 9692)
und "Flamme" sein will–und die gerade deswegen von Gewalt und "Krieg" (9837)
fasziniert ist. Diese ästhetische Faszination des Krieges läßt sich in der Zeit bei
Novalis, Friedrich Schlegel, Adam Müller, Kleist, Hölderlin und Körner nachwei-
sen. Sie setzt sich fort im europäischen Ästhetizismus des späten 19. und des 20.
Jahrhunderts, von Thomas Manns Essay "Bruder Hitler" von 1938 scharf
diagnostiziert.
    Mit Euphorions Katastrophe geht, wie Phorkyas sagt (9955ff.), diese Poesie
und die Verbindung von Antike und Moderne unwiderruflich zu Ende. Nicht
dauerhaft vereinen sich "Glück und Schönheit" (9940). Nach dieser Kunstperiode
bleibt die Möglichkeit "neuer Lieder" (9935), vom "Boden" (9937) gezeugt. Mit
ihr aber auch der ganze Zauber der Poesie: vom "Lied" spricht auch die Hexe
und das poetische Ich der "Zueignung."

ANMERKUNGEN

Die Äußerungen zu *Faust* werden der Einfachheit halber nach Gräf (II/2) zitiert. Dorothea Hölscher, Ritchie Robertson, Wolfgang Braungart und Manfred Koch danke ich für kritische Anmerkungen.

1. *Faust*, Paralipomenon 97. Zitiert nach Gräf 88.

2. Friedrich Schiller, *Sämtliche Werke*, hg. v. Gerhard Fricke u. Herbert G. Göpfert, 4. Aufl. (München: Carl Hanser Verlag, 1967) 5:593 u. 591.

3. Zum Begriff des "Ungeheuren" bei Goethe vgl. Wolfgang Binder, *Das Ungeheure und das Geordnete: Die Schweiz in Goethes Werk* (Zürich und München: Artemis-Verlag, 1979) 27ff.

4. WA I, 45:176f.

5. Vgl. Stuart Atkins, "Goethe, Calderon, and *Faust. Der Tragödie zweiter Teil*," *Germanic Review* 28 (1953): 83–98; Swana L. Hardy, *Goethe, Calderon und die romantische Theorie des Dramas* (Heidelberg: Winter, 1965); Ulrich Gaier, *Goethes Faust-Dichtungen: Ein Kommentar*, Bd. 1: *Urfaust* (Stuttgart: Reclam, 1989) 239ff.

6. Vgl. Helmut Schanze, *Goethes Dramatik: Theater der Erinnerung* (Tübingen: Niemeyer, 1989) 179ff.; T. Castle, "Phantasmagoria: Spectral Technology and the Metaphorics of Modern Reverie," *Critical Inquiry* 15 (1988): 26–61. Castle weist darauf hin, daß Anfang des 19. Jahrhunderts Phantasmagorie (Phantasmagoria, Phantasmagoriana) als Titel für "literary works of a miscellaneous or feuilletonistic nature" diente (55, Anm. 54).

7. Vgl. Herman Meyer, *Diese sehr ernsten Scherze: Eine Studie zu Faust II* (Heidelberg: Lothar Stiehm, 1970).

8. Gräf 600f.

9. Friedrich August Wolf, *Prolegomena ad Homerum, sive de operum Homericorum. . .*, Bd. 1 (Halle, 1795) XXXIX. Zur Bedeutung der *Prolegomena* vgl. Manfred Fuhrmann, "Friedrich August Wolf. Zur 200. Wiederkehr seines Geburtstages am 15. Februar 1959," *DVjS* 33 (1959), bes. 206ff.

10. Vgl. Joachim Wohlleben, *Die Sonne Homers: Zehn Kapitel deutscher Homer-Begeisterung von Winckelmann bis Schliemann* (Göttingen: Vandenhoeck & Ruprecht, 1990) 46ff.

11. Friedrich Schlegel, "Über die Homerische Poesie. Mit Rücksicht auf die Wolfischen Untersuchungen," zitiert nach: *Deutschland. Eine Zeitschrift*. Herausgegeben von Johann Friedrich Reichardt. Auswahl, hg. v. Gerda Heinrich (Leipzig: Reclam, 1989) 278ff., hier 287. Schlegel bezieht sich dabei auf Aristoteles, *Poetik*, Kap. 26.

12. "Tendenz" ist bekanntlich ein zentrales Konzept frühromantischer Theorie. Nach Friedrich Schlegels Athenäums-Fragment 116 kann romantische Poesie "ewig nur werden, nie vollendet" sein. Der Begriff der Einheit wird dabei nicht aufgegeben. Im Lyceums-Fragment 103 redet er z.B. vom "Trieb nach Einheit."

13. Gräf 564.

14. a.a.O.

15. Zur Frage der Struktur des Dramas vgl. z.B. Max Kommerell, *Geist und Buchstabe der Dichtung: Goethe, Schiller, Kleist, Hölderlin*, 5. Aufl. (Frankfurt/Main: Vittorio Klostermann, 1962) 9ff.; Dorothea Hölscher-Lohmeyer, *Faust und die Welt. Der zweite Teil der Dichtung: Eine Anleitung zum Lesen des Textes* (München: Verlag C.H. Beck, 1975); Werner Keller, "Faust. Eine Tragödie," in Walter Hinderer, Hg., *Goethes Dramen: Neue Interpretationen*

(Stuttgart: Reclam, 1980) 244–80; Victor Lange, "Faust. Der Tragödie zweiter Teil," in Hinderer, Hg., 281–312. Fruchtbar finde ich den Vergleich mit der musikalischen Struktur "Thema mit Variationen" bei Bennett, 19ff.

16. Vgl. z.B. Ernst Robert Curtius, *Europäische Literatur und lateinisches Mittelalter*, 9. Aufl. (Bern und München: Francke, 1978) 144ff.; Klaus Lange, "Geistliche Speise. Untersuchungen zur Metaphorik der Bibelhermeneutik," *Zeitschrift für deutsches Altertum* 95 (1966): 81–122; Hubert Gersch, *Geheimpoetik: Die "Continuatio des abentheuerlichen Simplicissimi" interpretiert als Grimmelshausens verschlüsselter Kommentar zu seinem Roman* (Tübingen: Niemeyer, 1973) 84f. u. passim; *Warum lesen?* Hg. v. Christiaan L. Hart Nibbrig (Frankfurt/Main: Suhrkamp, 1983) 195ff.; Gerhard Neumann, "Das Essen und die Literatur," *Literaturwissenschaftliches Jahrbuch* 23 (1982): 173–90. In der Gegenwart nimmt diese Metaphorik bei Böll und Grass eine zentrale Bedeutung ein. In der Tradition der Alchemie ist die Essensmetaphorik für Sublimierungsprozesse ebenfalls verbreitet, vgl. Hans-Georg Kemper, *Deutsche Lyrik der frühen Neuzeit*, Bd. 5/I (Tübingen: Niemeyer, 1991) 112ff.

17. WA IV, 4:21.

18. Vgl. dazu Jochen Hörisch, *Brot und Wein: Die Poesie des Abendmahls* (Frankfurt/Main: Suhrkamp, 1992) 156.

19. Zum "Vorspiel auf dem Theater," vgl. Alwin Binder, *Das Vorspiel auf dem Theater: Poetologische und geschichtsphilosophische Aspekte in Goethes Faust-Vorspiel* (Bonn: Bouvier, 1969); Bennett 40ff.; Brown 35ff.; Keller, a.a.O., 272ff.

20. Vgl. Brown 215.

21. WA I, 3:239.

22. Vgl. Alwin Binder, "Hexenpoesie. Die 'Hexenküche' in Goethes 'Faust' als Poetologie," *Goethe Jahrbuch* 97 (1980): 140–97. Der Aufsatz enthält treffende Vermutungen, jedoch auch viele problematische Begründungen.

23. Zur "dramentechnischen" Funktion von Magie und Zauberei im Stück vgl. Brown 86.

24. Schiller, *Sämtliche Werke* 5:659.

25. Vgl. Harvey Dunkle, "Monkey Business in Goethe's *Faust, Die Wahlverwandtschaften*, and Science," in: *Goethe Yearbook* 4 (1988): 123–35.

26. Vgl. Brown 153ff.

27. Vgl. Johannes Anderegg, "Knabe Lenker," in: Anselm Maler, Hg., *J.W. Goethe: Fünf Studien zum Werk* (Frankfurt/Main, Bern: Peter Lang Verlag, 1983) 85–114.

28. Vgl. seine Abhandlung "Von der heiligen Poesie" von 1756.

29. Vgl. Felix Philipp Ingold, "Ikarus novus. Zum Selbstverständnis des Autors in der Moderne," in Harro Segeberg, Hg., *Technik in der Literatur: Ein Forschungsüberblick und zwölf Aufsätze* (Frankfurt/Main: Suhrkamp, 1987) 269–350. Ingold geht nicht auf Goethe ein. Er arbeitet an Beispielen des 20. Jahrhunderts den ikarischen Typ heraus, im Gegensatz zum daedalischen. Ikarus gilt als Prototyp des ekstatischen Künstlers, gerade weil er kein Werk hinterlassen hat.

CLARK S. MUENZER

Goethe's Gothic Classicism: Antecedents to the
Architecture of History in *Faust II*, Act III

Der aus der Kindheit aufblickende Mensch findet die Natur nicht etwa rein
und nackt um sich her: denn die göttliche Kraft seiner Vorfahren hat eine
zweite Welt in die Welt erschaffen. Aufgenötigte Angewöhnungen, herkömm-
liche Gebräuche, beliebte Sitten, ehrwürdige Überlieferungen, schätzbare
Denkmale, ersprießliche Gesetze und so mannigfache herrliche Kunster-
zeugnisse umzingeln den Menschen dergestalt, daß er nie zu unterscheiden
weiß, was ursprünglich und was abgeleitet ist.[1]

JANE K. BROWN'S METICULOUS AND INSIGHTFUL elaborations on the third act of
Faust II as "The Spirit of Poetry"[2] begin by situating the marriage of Faust and
Helena as "the last of those great high points in the play we always feel we have
been waiting for."[3] According to Brown, "the power of poetry" here expresses
the mediating power of the mind "to know the world and to know the Absolute."[4]
Furthermore, while "the essence of Goethe's classicism"[5] takes shape upon an
Arcadian stage of Faust's own creation, the magical transformation of setting has
actually been grounded in the *visionary* capacity of Lynkeus, who serves the
northern magus as an " 'eye' for ancient beauty."[6] Lynkeus's conflation of the
sun and Helena—"most beautiful woman who ever lived and most beautiful
woman of antiquity"—leaves no question, Brown argues, that Faust's paramour
"represents one manifestation of spirit in the world, perhaps the ultimate one in
our culture."[7]

My own approach to Act III is similarly concerned with its complex situation—
not only within the play, but also within Goethe's creative life. Like Brown, I
want to understand the problem of *Faust's* third act in terms of its "classicism."
Yet I am not inclined to ground Goethe's northern, or modern classicism in the
way that Lynkeus gazes upon Helena, or to equate it with an aesthetics of
completion (however momentary!) that finally brings into sharp relief "the
synthesis of real and ideal."[8] Indeed, Brown's synthesizing perspective, with its
utopian rhetoric of incarnation, integration, and theodicy, ultimately suppresses

the informing confusions of Act III—including those felt by and embodied in the dazed Lynkeus figure. As Brown herself notes, Faust and Helena focus in their marriage "not on themselves or one another, but on space (here) and time (moment)."[9] Accordingly, when I refer to the problem of "situation" in *Faust*'s third act, I mean to focus on Goethe's attentiveness to times and places outside his own time and place. This attentiveness in turn defines the standpoint of his present moment as replete with history. Along these lines, Brown appropriately goes on to consider a crucial "historicizing tendency"[10] that is ruthlessly at work (as parody) in Act III: "Just as Helen is separated in this scene from the historical and cultural context that brought her into being, tragedy too is untied from its original cultural moorings and set loose in the sea of history."[11] Goethe's "classicism," it appears, makes no normative claim. It cannot be contained by systematically configuring Helena's "ideal beauty"[12] in timeless terms. Hence my point that Act III purposefully confounds and confuses more than it clarifies.

The sweeping scan of the act, which moves along with blurring speed between the Trojan War and the Greek War of Independence, has in fact been calculated to inhibit any sustained focus. As the framing failures of both Helena's initial vision of idyllic return and Euphorion's final vision of heroic conquest together suggest, Goethe refuses the self-centeredness and isolation of all Arcadian projects. Indeed, the genuine site of his characteristically scandalous classicism is, I suggest, the oddly gothic castle of the act's interior scene, "Innerer Burghof," where Faust and Helena exchange their odd vows. From this setting, where an alternative emerges to the timeless and utopian sites of all distant pasts ("Vor dem Palaste des Menelas") and all distant futures ("Schattiger Hain"), the challenge of history is felt as the complex fullness of the present moment: "Nun schaut der Geist nicht vorwärts, nicht zurück, / Die Gegenwart allein—ist unser Glück" (9381–82). By reading the puzzling structure of the *Faustburg* in terms of Goethe's "gothic," or historically situated, classicism, then, I will be linking this architectural representation upon the *Faust* stage to questions of aesthetic structure. By way of introduction, however, I want to offer a series of reflections on the "situation" of Act III by considering other similarly dynamic locations where, according to Goethe, modern culture responded to the challenge of history. Beyond the Helena figure and *Faust* in its entirety, these include the *Ausgabe letzter Hand* and his representations of the gothic cathedrals in Strasbourg and Cologne. In each such project Goethe saw an opportunity to locate what Bakhtin would call the "historical multitemporality"[13] of contemporary life. Within each he imagined his particular historical situation through a temporal organization of space that allows "remnants of the past, and rudiments and tendencies of the future"[14] to emerge into view.

"Wieder an deinem Grabe und dem Denkmal des ewigen Lebens"[15]

To begin, let me suggest a way of rethinking the term "classicism" as it pertains to *Faust*. Clearly, Goethe's *Faust*-work has survived a long and at times contradictory reception, as we expect of a "classic." Furthermore, it is a place where other, older works have similarly survived, including works of "classical" antiquity. Yet in both instances endurance suggests process and not product—a stolen "survival as" rather than an heroic "survival of." Classical works in this sense do not simply offer timeless norms to embrace. Instead, their dominating presence challenges us, in the manner of monuments, to acknowledge an enduring insistence in life that is often inscrutable in its strangeness and paradoxical in its connection with the "dead." Along these lines the monumental quality of Goethe's classicism in *Faust* involves at least two considerations that are not readily compatible. As an incommensurable object, the work requires us to read it for meanings that it always refuses to secure. Its long genesis and unruly massiveness preclude our containing it within any system of transcendent principles. But readers have also long evoked "dieses seltsame Gebäu"[16] canonically—as a highly articulated structure and a stable point of reference through which their culture defines itself.[17] In both cases *Faust* compels attention—either as a hermeneutic challenge of intractable largeness and temporal scope or as a key to the foundational *ethos* that has indelibly inscribed the structure of German (or European) modernity.[18] The question remains, however, whether we may properly evoke only one aspect of *Faust*'s monumentality and ignore the other. While the irony, parody, and anachronism in Goethe's *Tragödie* undermine any claim it would make, in the mode of "classical" tragedy, to foundational values or stable truths,[19] its thematic insistences and overarching symbolic design appear to memorialize it as a unified composition.[20]

My own account of Act III, which is part of a larger study on Goethe's dramas of history, construes the classicism of the *Faust*-work as monumental by acknowledging both its scope and articulateness. Its preliminary focus falls on the stage setting at the center of Goethe's play within a play, where the confusion of romantic and classical motifs defines the contradictory multiplicities of historical representation. Hence my interest in Bakhtin's "chronotope." Like the Goethean monuments I consider, "chronotope" refers to the temporally organized space of the worlds that we construct to occupy and live in, or that we represent in art as the site of cultural production.[21] *Faust*, I am saying—which became Goethe's crowning architectural achievement—may be fruitfully understood as a complex chronotopical monument.

Within this interpretive frame, we can understand the play's abruptly changing stage, especially through Part II, as the key to its essentially *historical* aesthetic. Goethe has layered the *Faust*-stage temporally, so that each of its transformations actualizes "visible vestiges of man's creativity," to borrow from Bakhtin's description of the interrelatedness of time and space in other Goethean works.[22] Like the "cities, streets, buildings, artworks, technology, [and] social organizations" in which Goethe, according to Bakhtin, perceived "the most complex designs of people, generations, epochs, nations, and social and class groups,"[23] the *Faust*-edifice has been structured to respond to the challenges of time and temporality. Any reading adequate to its architecture must therefore locate a privileged interpretive standpoint within the work that is historically charged. Like Brown,

I would situate this "high point" within Act III, where an elaborate confusion arises through the long-awaited reemergence of antiquity's Helen on a northern stage. By connecting this creative event with Goethe's recurrent fascination with gothic architecture,[24] I want to indicate how the aging writer's acute experience of the passing of time came to ground an aesthetic that could visualize the similarly creative fullness of his own moment in history.

My remarks on Act III at the Santa Barbara *Faust* Conference began, as do many treatments, with an attempt to work through to a simple chronology of its composition.[25] I gradually abandoned the chronological perspective, however, because its abstract logic of sequential moments ultimately distorted the act's driving interest in the kind of layered historicity that Goethe felt challenged to express. "Eine Chronik schreibt nur derjenige, dem die Gegenwart wichtig ist," we are reminded in one of the "Maximen und Reflexionen."[26] Because the chronicler is situated close to the events that he records, his account remains rooted in the irredeemable pastness of particular moments in time. By implication, then, chronicles will be of only secondary interest to later generations of readers, if they are likewise rooted in their own (contemporary) worlds. The chronicle does not extend into a present moment other than its own.

When Goethe talked about gothic architecture–"eine alte Überlieferung" that had remained silent to most of his generation[27]–he was able to identify an alternative to chronological recollection that would allow him to reconfigure its disconnected points contemporaneously. Medieval antiquities like the cathedrals in Strasbourg and Cologne could actually fill and expand the present moment into a *threshold space* between the past and the future, Goethe gradually discovered. These minsters did not simply loom in ghostly silence within the modern world; they embodied an ancestral challenge to an avantgarde community of "artisans" to keep their collective past alive. Along these lines, the survival of ancient (medieval) monuments, which is tantamount to their translation into the future, would be guaranteed by re-presenting them again and again in art.[28] The "ruins" of the unfinished cathedrals in Strasbourg and Cologne, which initially evoked in Goethe a profound sense of human insufficiency and anxiety about temporal loss,[29] then, could also be redeemed in new and unforeseeable ways, as his collaboration with the Boisserée brothers would help demonstrate many years later.[30] Accordingly, when gothic-like structures such as the fantastical *Faustburg* of Act III appear in Goethe's own writings, we, too, should feel ourselves challenged to see in them "second, created worlds within the world." As a monumental (or classical) representation of all historically charged places, this complex edifice emerges within the iconography of *Faust* as a special site for the creative translation-work that shapes the cultural life of the community. Here we find one of those privileged places in Goethe where, according to Bakhtin, "the past itself [can] be creative."[31] Like Helena–whose marriage to Faust takes place within it, or like the play in its entirety–which surrounds it–the *Faustburg* is a chronotopical figure, in the Bakhtinian sense.[32] It is an animating structure through which the dramatist could imagine keeping his collective past alive by linking it to both present and future.[33]

25 January 1827

Goethe notes in his diary:

Helena eingepackt. Mit den Kindern im Schlitten nach Belvedere gefahren.[34]

The extensive chronology of Act III approaches its first major conclusion in succinct understatement–whereupon one of the old writer's favorite "daughters" begins her slippery ride into the future.

26 January 1827

Goethe ships off a manuscript packet to his Stuttgart publisher:

Nebenstehendes, zugleich auch manches geordnet, geheftet mundirt und vorbereitet: Herrn v. Cotta, Manuscript der *Helena*, nach Stuttgart.– Mein Sohn hatte einen neuen Schlitten gekauft.[35]

Intermittently dormant and hauntingly awake for some half century, *Helena* begins circulating through the world. Goethe had only recently unearthed and "unpacked" the "fünfzigjährige Gespenst,"[36] but even now, upon its completion, the stubborn stuff of antiquity remains a torso of what might or might not yet become *Der Tragödie zweiter Teil*, where it would serve as *Zwischenspiel*. The unpublished draft of the Cotta "Ankündigung" further indicates that the public's first solemn glimpse into Goethe's *sanctum sanctorum* will reveal a new and fantastic piece of *Faust*-ornamentation.[37] Following the author's bidding, Cotta enticingly attaches the intermezzo to volume four of the monumental *Ausgabe letzter Hand*.

"Bewundert viel und viel gescholten, Helena" (8488)

How oddly Helena first appears on Goethe's stage–as a rhetorical topic. His long-awaited synthesis of ancient and modern models has been published, true to her own turbulent history within the community, as the *locus* of an extensive tradition of public contestation. The chronology here arches back to Schiller in 1797 and again in 1800–still another ghost–whose friendly mediations over a quarter of a century earlier had challenged Goethe spiritually and intellectually to renew his work on "dieser barbarischen Composition."[38] The vision, "daß, von diesem Gipfel aus, sich erst die rechte Aussicht über das Ganze zeigen wird,"[39] is a conceptual inspiration that he already shares with his friend on 23 September 1800. Will the world soon be able to stand upon *Helena's* peak, then–as if atop some high mountain–to view the surrounding *Faust*-world in its entirety and against the background of a vast and diverse horizon? From the 1826 vantage point the question lingers. The public might find itself in awe of the grandeur of his work–"eine ernsthafte Tragödie"[40]–and admire Goethe as another Aeschylus. But the impossible union he has contrived could also evoke censure of a "barbaric" grotesque–"eine Fratze."[41] Whether *Helena* will become a self-contained artistic composition of classical proportions or remain part of the massive and unfinished *Faust*-torso has not yet been settled. Perhaps the play will never serve as anything more than the ornamental advertisement to the final and authoritative edition of the old writer's literary testament: a phantasmal *agora* of classical-romantic intercourse. Schiller, we recall, served as a first intermediary with the publisher Cotta, above whose market place in the years following 1827 Goethe's readers would see loom the fantastic tower of his language edifice–including the finished *Faust* and other literary remains: another "Babelgedanken in der Seele."[42]

Ausgabe letzter Hand

This last Goethean language-handiwork, which the writer began in 1820 as a concluding *addendum* to the 1815–1819 Cotta edition of his *Werke* and which he continued in 1822 as a chronological accounting of his personal archives,[43] would itself have remained, like Erwin von Steinbach's cathedral in Strasbourg, an unfinished building without the later help of other friends. But Sulpiz Boisserée (who in 1826 handles the last negotiations with Cotta) and Eckermann-Riemer (who after Goethe's death continue assembling what he began) become the master's young "Gesellen." Curious, though, how our chronology records a recurring insinuation of Helena and Faust into the (posthumous) completion of Goethe's monument of *Weltliteratur*. The gothic minster, *Faust, Goethes Werke*: each achievement is *Denkmal*. Each becomes massive through its passage across time, and each bears the characteristic marks of incompletion, death, inscription, and survival.[44] Each structure, that is, reveals an open site where the endless befores and afters of chronology have been superseded by the multi-temporality of historical time. As Bakhtin convincingly argues,

> the simple spatial contiguity (*nebeneinander*) of phenomena was profoundly alien to Goethe, so he saturated and imbued it with *time*, revealed emergence and development in it, and he distributed that which was contiguous in *space* in various *temporal* stages, epochs of becoming. For him contemporaneity–both in nature and in human life–is revealed as an essential multitemporality: as remnants or relics of various stages and formations of the past and as rudiments of stages in the more or less distant future.[45]

Goethe's success as a writer, according to this view, lay in his ability to overcome "the ghostly (*Gespenstermäßiges*), the terrifying (*Unerfreuliches*), and the unaccountable (*Unzuberechnendes*), which were strong in his initial feeling of a merged past and present."[46] The past, then, should neither simply dissolve in the face of the present moment, as it does in "naked chronologies," which Goethe once called "skelett-artig"[47]; nor should it hauntingly unsettle the present by disengaging from man's constructive desires. Instead, visualized as *Denkmal*, the past can retain a significance in the present by tensing itself toward the future. Monuments, according to this view, may be thought of as inscribed markers upon graves that allow the dead to survive. Through the transgressive work of their perpetual translations across temporal boundaries, they become sources for experiencing the creative fullness of time, which Bakhtin and Goethe both understand as authentic historicity.

24 June 1826

"Völliger Abschluß der Helena, durch Umschreiben einiger Bogen."[48]

22 October 1826

In separate letters to Wilhelm von Humboldt and Sulpiz Boisserée Goethe offers exciting news. His *Helena* has been finished! The Humboldt letter frames a substantial reflection on the lifelong genesis of his composition by prominently mentioning the *Ausgabe letzter Hand* twice:

> Ich habe den ganzen Sommer zu Hause zugebracht und ungestört an der Ausgabe meiner Werke fortgearbeitet.[49]

That the writer requires no transition between this opening sentence, which highlights his pressing editorial task, and his account of the work on the *Helena*-Act indicates that each project has long been implicated in the other. The precise terms of Goethe's almost habitual conflation[50] clearly emerge in the passage to Humboldt that follows:

> Erinnern Sie sich wohl noch, mein Theuerster, einer dramatischen Helena, die im zweyten Theil von Faust erscheinen sollte? Aus Schillers Briefen vom Anfang des Jahrhunderts sehe ich, daß ich ihm den Anfang vorzeigte, auch, daß er mich zur Fortsetzung treulich ermahnte. Es ist *eine meiner ältesten Conceptionen*, sie ruht auf der *Puppenspiel-Überlieferung*, daß Faust den Mephistopheles genöthigt, ihm die Helena zum Beylager heranzuschaffen. Ich habe von Zeit zu Zeit daran fortgearbeitet, aber abgeschlossen konnte das Stück nicht werden, als in der *Fülle der Zeiten*, da es denn jetzt seine volle 3000 Jahre spielt, von Troja's Untergang bis zur Einnahme von Missolunghi. Dieß kann man also auch für eine *Zeiteinheit* rechnen, im höheren Sinne; die Einheit des Orts und der Handlung sind aber auch im gewöhnlichen Sinn auf's genaueste beobachtet. Es tritt auf unter dem Titel:

Helena
classisch-romantische
Phantasmagorie.
Zwischenspiel zu Faust.

Das heißt denn freylich wenig gesagt, und doch genug, hoff ich, um Ihre
Aufmerksamkeit auf die erste Lieferung lebhafter zu richten, die ich von
meinen Arbeiten zu *Ostern* darzubieten gedenke.[51]

Helena, it seems, has been Goethe's companion through literature from the
start. And as one of his very oldest conceptions, this piece of folkloric *Überlieferung*
appears in the letter to carry the weight of her antiquity like some great burden.
After all, she became currency for the aspiring poet not on the stage of ancient
tragedy, nor as the timeless idea of beauty, but rather on the bawdy puppet-theater
stage, where she had appeared in the service of Pluto as evil enchantress. Helena
was thus born for Goethe, Humboldt learns, in the subversive folk imagination
of late medieval Europe—along with other popular confounders like the
Hanswurst. And she has now returned from that marketplace, phantasmagorially,
to circulate again. Goethe's publication date, which his letter takes special care
to note, is of particular significance in this regard. For with the *Zwischenspiel* and
some other literary remains, he envisions a resurrection. In her Easter incarnation,
his Helena will answer the special challenge that the writer feels to speak with
the dead.[52] Furthermore, her emergence through speech in Act III
paradigmatically demonstrates that in order to animate, language must resonate
with the strange inflections of otherness. Authentic art, we learn there, creates
"a second world in the world" only by overstepping the boundaries of its original
setting through resonant translation.[53] Faust's barbarian tongue thus compels
Helena to seek her survival in the metaphoric substitutions of rhymes. If language—as the preeminent source of our collective life—is to be productive, it must
embrace derivation and resonate with the sound of ancestral words.

"War ich das alles? Bin ich's? Werd' ich's künftig sein?" (8839)

According to Chapter 21 in Lessing's *Laokoon*, Homer's Helen teaches that
human beauty may be properly grasped in literature only by narrating the sequence of its effects upon the beholder: "Was Homer nicht nach seinen Bestand-
teilen beschreiben konnte, läßt er uns in seiner Wirkung erkennen."[54] Phorkyas-
Mephisto, the creative mediator (or *Schaffnerin*) to another Helen, has learned this
Homeric lesson well. Thus, (s)he attaches herself to the Spartan queen as an "Ur-
Urälteste" (8950) who constitutes Helena for Helena as her private history's long
and world-shaping duration of transgressive acts (8843–79). But to articulate
beauty as a transformative idea is, for Goethe, also to acknowledge the fullness
of its effects across time:

Denn eigentlich unternehmen wir umsonst, das Wesen eines Dinges auszudrücken. Wirkungen werden wir gewahr, und eine vollständige Geschichte
dieser Wirkungen umfaßte wohl allenfalls das Wesen jenes Dinges.[55]

Helena, of course, as Goethe's "Gestalt aller Gestalten" (8907), is such a primal
form, "die alle Formen in sich begreift."[56] She therefore traces a reception history
of transgressive events, which have always taken shape on thresholds and which
have always exceeded the borders of the familiar: "Vom Strande komm' ich"
(8489), she appropriately announces as Act III begins, "noch immer trunken von
des Gewoges regsamem Geschaukel" (8490–91). Stepping toward the "hochge-
türmtes Fürstenhaus" (8549) of her father and her husband after the traumas of
Troy, she can physically feel her historicity in the same way that she could still
feel the sea's unsettling motion when she first stepped onto the beach. But Helena
does not yet grasp the significance of her trauma as a (re)turn into history itself.
Hence, she initially expects the ancient housekeeper to show her, in her husband's
words, "der Schätze reiche Sammlung vor, / Wie sie dein Vater hinterließ" (8552–
53). She still believes that patrimony is coterminous with immutability:

> Das ist des Fürsten Vorrecht, daß er alles treu
> In seinem Hause, wiederkehrend, finde, noch
> An seinem Platze jedes, wie er's dort verließ.
> Denn nichts zu ändern hat für sich der Knecht Gewalt. (8556–59)

What Helena finds instead of ordered domesticity, of course, is the hermaphrodite
Phorkyas, her guide and companion into Faust's gothic palace, where Homer's
barbaric patrimony of pillage and rape still appears to survive:

> Man schilt das Volk Barbaren, doch ich dächte nicht,
> Daß grausam einer wäre, wie vor Ilios
> Gar mancher Held sich menschenfresserisch erwies. (9013–15)

And like Phorkyas, this issue of Leda and the Jupiter/swan occupies in her own
lineage, conception, and Überlieferung the wild and shifting territory of the
impossible Both/And: illicit/divine; animal/god; mortal/immortal; body/spirit;
destructive/creative; ghost/person; death/life. Beauty, Phorkyas proclaims in one
of her many sententious jibes, has no shame!

> Alt ist das Wort, doch bleibet hoch und wahr der Sinn,
> Daß Scham und Schönheit nie zusammen, Hand in Hand,
> Den Weg verfolgen über der Erde grünen Pfad. (8754–56)

Authentic "Schönheit," as preserved in folkloric wisdom, staves off death by
remaining "frech gesinnt, / Bis sie zuletzt des Orkus hohle Nacht umfängt, / Wenn
nicht das Alter sie vorher gebändigt hat" (8761–63). Helena's "shamelessness,"

which profoundly expresses itself as her stubborn survival, is therefore also the
source of her chronotopical association with the space of historical time:

> Wer aber seiner Schwelle heilige Richte leicht
> Mit flüchtigen Sohlen überschreitet freventlich,
> Der findet wiederkehrend wohl den alten Platz,
> Doch umgeändert alles, wo nicht gar zerstört. (8978–81)

Goethe's *Zwischenspiel*, which he first called a "satyr-play," emerges in this context
upon a terrifying strand between worlds that lies just beyond the idyllic confines
of patrimonial immutability. Within the constantly shifting threshold regions of
the *Faust*-stage, the decorous limits of theater and poetry are repeatedly challenged
and overstepped in order to open new space for the creative work of the
community's living traditions. Every culture—even modern ones—must conserve
and celebrate such special aboriginal sites, where the governing forms of creative
expression are negotiated. Goethe's *Zwischenspiel* compresses three thousand years
of history as an idealized moment, in order to represent this ur-locality of historical
emergence as a vast duration of time. But such irreverent work cannot be
accomplished without sacrifice. Wrought over and over again in Phorkyas's
powerful accounting of (her) beauty's effects, Helena becomes overwrought by
all the divisions and divisiveness and faints (8881).[57]

"Time and space merge here into an inseparable unity, both in the plot itself and in its individual images"[58]

Curiously, Goethe's 22 October letter to Boisserée uses words nearly identical
to those in the letter of the same day to Humboldt in order to relate the successful
concluding of the *Zwischenspiel*. The phrase "in der Fülle der Zeiten," which Goethe
repeats here to capture his play's three-thousand-year "Zeiteinheit," is again cited
as the phantasmagorial basis of its completion "mit reinster Einheit des Orts und
der Handlung."[59] By saturating the space of his stage and the action upon it with
questions of time and temporality, the work promises to achieve a resonance of
detail that will secure its unique wholeness at some future time. Furthermore,
a number of motifs that occur in both letters combine to establish the act's
compelling necessity as an historically charged aesthetic object. These include
its long genesis within Goethe, its touching implication in an awareness that even
his days were numbered,[60] its repeated and urgent insinuation into the construction of his *Ausgabe letzter Hand*, its filiation with an arch of history extending from
the Trojan War to the Greek War of Independence, and its extended life in
classical mythology and northern folklore. The "fullness of historical time," in
Bakhtin's sense of the phrase, appears to ground "the pure unities of plot and
place" in Goethe's *Helena* as the communal challenge of its interpretive work.

August 1831

Goethe seals the completed *Faust*-work in its shrine. He persistently refuses to show it even to his closest associates. Helena will reemerge as part of its complex totality only after his death, when the entire poem is published in the first volume of Goethe's literary remains. The tower of the *Ausgabe letzter Hand* will rise, appropriately, upon the foundation of its architect's grave.

April 1770 until August 1771 and 3 May 1811

The chronology's arch now sweeps us back some sixty years. Goethe arrives in Strasbourg and sees another tower that rises above another architect's grave. The twenty-one-year-old poet secures accommodations from where he can propitiously approach the minster—in the Hotel "Zum Geist." When he subsequently recounts the events of this period in 1811 for his autobiography, he relives and expands his experience of gothic architecture. That year also introduces him to Boisserée, his "romantic" pendant to the "classical" Humboldt (the translator of Aeschylus's *Agamemnon*) in the two 1826 letters. Now Boisserée's plans to complete the Cologne cathedral further inspire a revisitation of the gothic, which in the *Dichtung und Wahrheit* account increasingly emphasizes such inherently classical elements as the building's order, its proportion, its pleasurable beauty, its unity, its harmony, and, most importantly, its fundamental connection to the surrounding landscape.[61] In this context, Cologne emerges as a second privileged site for Goethe,

> wo das Altertum eine solche unzuberechnende Wirkung auf mich ausüben konnte. Die Ruine des Doms (denn ein nichtfertiges Werk ist einem zerstörten gleich) erregte die von Straßburg her gewohnten Gefühle.[62]

But precisely what does Goethe's "Altertum" intend? After all, Cologne would become an archaeological site where classical and medieval antiquities lay buried together. Perhaps an answer lies in construing the two cathedrals, "deren Sinn *babylonisch* in den Himmel strebte,"[63] archi-*text*-urally: in terms of their critical "situatedness" and their monumentality. As ruins and as challenges to completion, both *Denkmäler* implicate historicity in a creative process of collective survival that tenses them toward the future.

"Nicht gescheiter als ein Volk, das die ganze fremde Welt barbarisch nennt, hieß alles Gotisch, was nicht in mein System paßte"[64]

Goethe himself establishes the connection between building and text in the 1772 essay "Von deutscher Baukunst," where he first suggests replacing the word "gothisch," typically misunderstood as "barbarisch," with "Deutsch" and "charakteristisch." He offers his revisionist reading, we discover, to define an aesthetic rooted in communal translation and survival. From this standpoint, "German" identifies a locality of characteristic and intractable uniqueness that has collectively emerged over time. The exemplary gothic site—here the Strasbourg cathedral, including its urban and rural surroundings—thus expresses the chrono-topical connectedness of time and space. A detailed analysis of Goethe's essay in the context of Herder's anthology *Von deutscher Art und Kunst* and his own autobiographical revisitation would further reveal this site, in Bakhtin's sense, as a chronotope of historical time. For Goethe's gothic also privileges an aesthetic in which "man's individual emergence is inseparably linked to historical emergence."[65] By recapitulating the subjective and private in collective and public terms,[66] it, too, emphasizes the "*necessity* of the past" and its "*creative effectiveness*"[67] for the future.

Goethe's rhapsodic essay on Erwin von Steinbach begins, symptomatically, by attacking the systematizing compulsion of Laugier's neoclassical architectural theory, which reduced the beauty of classical columns to the incessantly repeated intercolumnar wall:

> Und doch, dünkt mich, lieber Abt, hätte die öftere Wiederholung dieser Unschicklichkeit des Säuleneinmauerns, daß die Neuern sogar antiker Tempel Interkolumnia mit Mauerwerk ausstopften, dir einiges Nachdenken erregen können. Wäre dein Ohr nicht für Wahrheit taub, diese Steine würden sie dir gepredigt haben.
>
> Säule ist mit nichten ein Bestandteil unsrer Wohnungen; sie widerspricht vielmehr dem Wesen all unsrer Gebäude. Unsre Häuser entstehen nicht aus vier Säulen in vier Ecken; sie entstehen aus vier Mauern auf vier Seiten, die statt aller Säulen sind, alle Säulen ausschließen, und wo ihr sie anflickt, sind sie belastender Überfluß. . . .
>
> Eure Gebäude stellen euch also Flächen dar, die, je weiter sie sich ausbreiten, je kühner sie gen Himmel steigen, mit desto unerträglicherer Einförmigkeit die Seele unterdrücken müssen![68]

Ironically, Goethe condemns Laugier's systematic incorporation of classical architectural features into modern buildings with an appeal to "appropriateness"—itself a classical principle. Art, he asserts, must be produced *in accordance with* local exigency. Upon considering the northern wall in Laugier's terms, as intercolumnar, however, he has discovered that the French would now use this inherently northern form to imprison the sacred column of antiquity, which they thereby abstract from all local context. At this juncture, an unmistakable political critique reverberates in Goethe's condemnation of the disciplining and domesticating abstractions of neoclassical theory. And as if to counteract the leveling monotony and oppressiveness of the neoclassical school, he next celebrates the colossal fullness of the surging cathedral wall in Strasbourg—which he pictures, significantly, through the variety of its fanciful and detailed ornamentation.[69] Thus, Goethe imagines the genius of gothic art as it might have addressed Erwin with the secret of the wall's perfection:

> Vermannigfaltige die ungeheure Mauer, die du gen Himmel führen sollst, daß sie aufsteige gleich einem hocherhabnen, weitverbreiteten Baume Gottes, der mit tausend Ästen, Millionen Zweigen und Blättern wie der Sand am Meer ringsum der Gegend verkündet die Herrlichkeit des Herrn, seines Meisters.[70]

A messianic rhetoric here enables the aesthetician to introduce the future into a "naturalized" monument of past greatness. Moreover, by comparing gothic architecture to a divinely foliating tree,[71] Goethe introduces horizontality into its structure. He thereby subverts the steep verticality of its height (and depth) and opens the possibility of a gothic classicism, where the vertical aspiration toward timeless hierarchies is counterpoised by the horizontal aspiration toward temporal diversity.[72] Accordingly, the cathedral's observer should not only direct his gaze upward and out of the world toward the heavens, which mark an impassable border, or downward and into the abstract self. He should also look outward toward the horizon and into the surrounding world—as Goethe recalls having done himself in the ninth book of his autobiography, where we find him mounting the platform between the cathedral's towers in order to enjoy the commanding view.[73]

Early in his panegyric, Goethe dubs Erwin's unfinished cathedral "einen Babelgedanken in der Seele,"[74] thereby configuring the legitimation discourse of his *Sturm und Drang* youth as part of a linguistic-aesthetic project of edification. He would restate this configuration in 1811,[75] and we might apply it again—to the lifelong *Faust*-monument and to his work on an *Ausgabe letzter Hand.* For within the Goethean gothic, understood as a post-babelian challenge, a locality emerges that recognizes history's painful transgressions—its thefts and its threshold achievements. Here creative individuals—like Goethe's renegade Prometheus—can mobilize others to construct distinctive cultures after failing to reach the throne of the Gods.[76] These illicit labors of history, however, cannot be accomplished without recognizing the formative power of historically and geographically determined communities—and their fruitful reciprocity across space and time. In short, all individuals are weak in themselves and must *pass away.* Accordingly, Goethe begins his essay by describing his own futile search for the ruins of Erwin's grave and by counting the genial architect among the elect, to whom it was given

> auf tausend bietende Hände zu treffen, Felsengrund zu graben, steile Höhen drauf zu zaubern, und dann sterbend ihren Söhnen zu sagen: Ich bleibe bei euch in den Werken meines Geistes, vollendet das Begonnene in die Wolken.[77]

Instead of the grave, however, Goethe reports finding Erwin's *Denkmal*—in the unfinished cathedral. To survive, then, the architectural *Genie* had to *pass (something) on.* What remained after his death was both his edifying definition of a living community, or *Überlieferung,* and his challenge to take up and take over what he had begun, or *Übertragung.* This, I am suggesting, is also the challenge of Helena: an *Überlieferung* that must pass away in order to be passed on and be taken over as *Übertragung.*

According to Lenardo in the *Wanderjahre,* God scattered the human race throughout the world to thwart the illicit desire to construct the Tower of Babel. Subsequently, however, man's dispersion into time and history proved highly productive: "Daß wir uns in ihr zerstreuen, / Darum ist die Welt so groß."[78] Throughout his own creative lifetime Goethe similarly imagined a post-babelian aesthetic that celebrates the grandeur and fullness of the created world in the formative power of its vast and varied language traditions. His evolving interest in gothic architecture, however, taught him that the specifically historical sources of human creativity, from which art draws, must be conserved in their aboriginal vitality. If his Helena was to mature into such a source, she could not be contained and imprisoned by a normative aesthetic. Hence, she is dragged across time and space as *Übertragung* into Faust's palace with the help of Phorkyas-Mephisto, who as an "Ur-Urälteste" (8950) embodies the ancient challenge of Helena's unfinished project, or *Überlieferung.* The latter, as one ground of her classicism, is also the source of her beauty. But, as we have noted, Goethe's folkloric monument also appropriately emerges in threshold regions of transgressive desires and anxieties. Her classicism, therefore, has always also implied *Übertragung,* or the kind of translational work through which an emerging community speaks historically. And it is in this sense that I am calling Helena's classicism gothic. As both *Überlieferung* and *Übertragung,* she is the complex fullness of historical time, the perpetual insistence of a shared past and its future-directedness.

"Und seine Burg! die solltet ihr mit Augen sehn!" (9017)

Every artist works within the context of specific social and historical settings. Situated within the massive reality of his own temporal-spatial location in the world, like Goethe in front of the Strasbourg minster, the historically aware artist must feel the totality of its resonant relationships as the parameter of his own creative possibilities. When Helena stands at the threshold of Faust's palace, therefore—"der wundersam aus vielen einsgewordnen Burg" (9146)—we sense in Phorkyas's description a place—both of and for her gothic beauty—that properly sets her phantasm-agorial reemergence:

> Das ist was anderes gegen plumpes Mauerwerk,
> Das eure Väter, mir nichts dir nichts, aufgewälzt,
> Zyklopisch wie Zyklopen, rohen Stein sogleich
> Auf rohe Steine stürzend; dort hingegen, dort

Ist alles senk- und waagerecht und regelhaft.
Von außen schaut sie! himmelan sie strebt empor,
So starr, so wohl in Fugen, spiegelglatt wie Stahl.
Zu klettern hier—ja selbst der Gedanke gleitet ab.
Und innen großer Höfe Raumgelasse, rings
Mit Baulichkeit umgeben, aller Art und Zweck.
Da seht ihr Säulen, Säulchen, Bogen, Bögelchen,
Altane, Galerien, zu schauen aus und ein,
Und Wappen. (9018–30)

Phorkyas's almost satiric denunciation of a primitive Greek wall as chaotic and irregular and her privileging of the perfect symmetries of a modern gothic building are, of course, odd in their initial characterizations. In light of my reading of Helena as a Goethean chronotope of historical time, however, the idea of a structure, such as Faust's palace, that visualizes multi-temporality as contradictory detail should no longer perplex. For the classical and the romantic—in Goethe's evolving sense of those terms—have always inhabited each other. Like the "Gestalt aller Gestalten," or the Strasbourg cathedral, where all is emerging "Gestalt,"[79] Faust's pleasure dome presents itself to view, out of the fog and the mist (9123ff.) of the future, as a fully emergent form. Only now the seamless "fitting" of its contending elements into a living totality may be viewed classically, from without, while the variegated detail of its ornamentation appears, gothically, from within.

In the same spirit, Goethe's stage has located the (northern) *wall* of the 1772 essay with classical antiquity and the (ancient) *column* with the barbaric conquerors. However, even within Phorkyas's exterior and interior descriptions of the *Faustburg*, gothic and classical structures involve and implicate each other. For outside, the palace surges steeply upward—like the fantastic postmodern skyscrapers of our own day. Its mirror-like walls must surely also reflect the surrounding world, though, thereby interrupting all efforts to complete the vertical trajectory. Similarly, when Phorkyas's attention moves inside the palace, we find multiple and varied structures that extend it horizontally and around, to complete a site conducive to "classical" circumspection. Yet the scale of this site appears as unmanageable as the unscalable walls outside. For the space has been packed by Faust's men—in "Sälen, grenzenlosen, wie die Welt so weit" (9043)—with the colorful emblazonry of their "Ur-Urahnen" (9038), thereby extending the long heraldic tradition that Phorkyas initiates with her account of the insignia on the shields of Ajax and the Seven against Thebes. The emphatic use of historical citation here is, of course, not simply confounding. As we are reminded, it is "reich bedeutungsvoll" (9033) as well—and so possibly a key to the historically informed architecture of the Faust-work itself. "Da könnt ihr tanzen!" (9044), Phorkyas cries out to Helena, bidding her to enter the *Faustburg*. As readers, we are similarly beckoned to enter—in Goethe's language edifice—one of those "treasured monuments" ("Denkmale") to which my essay's motto refers. As the supreme challenge of Goethean monumentality, *Faust* celebrates the destiny of our own historical moment by asserting the indeterminability of nature ("ursprünglich") and culture ("abgeleitet"). It thereby also continues to envelop us in its confusing dance ("umzingeln").

NOTES

1. Goethe, "Kunst und Altertum am Rhein und Main," HA 12:162.

2. Brown 198–215.

3. Brown 198.

4. Brown 207.

5. Brown 208.

6. Brown 207.

7. Brown 200.

8. Brown 198.

9. Brown 204.

10. Brown 205.

11. Brown 205.

12. Brown 199.

13. M.M. Bakhtin, "The *Bildungsroman* and Its Significance in the History of Realism (Toward a Historical Typology of the Novel)," in *Speech Genres and Other Late Essays,* ed. Caryl Emerson and Michael Holquist, transl. Vern W. McGee (Austin: University of Texas Press, 1986) 26. Hereafter abbreviated BR.

14. BR 26.

15. Goethe, "Dritte Wahlfahrt nach Erwins Grabe im Juli 1775," HA 12:28.

16. In Goethe's last letter, written to Wilhelm von Humboldt on 17 March 1832, WA IV, 49:283.

17. Cf. Martin Esslin, "Goethe's Faust: Pre-Modern, Post-Modern, Proto-Postmodern," in this volume.

18. Cf. Karl Robert Mandelkow, "Wandlungen des *Faust*-Bildes in Deutschland," in this volume.

19. The increasingly large body of literature on irony in *Faust* is well-known, and I cannot cite it here. Benjamin Bennett (143–44) has offered illuminating ideas on anachronism. For more on parody as a survival mechanism in Goethe and in *Faust* cf. Hannelore Schlaffer, "Paradies und Parodie: Die letzten Szenen in Goethes letzten Werken," in this volume. Cf. here also Gerhard Kurz's essay on metaphors of eating and drinking in *Faust,* which connects Goethe's search for an open structure to certain poetologically informed metaphors, and Christoph Jamme's " 'Alter Tage fabelhaft Gebild. . .': Goethes Mythen-Bastelei im *Faust II.*"

20. The poem, according to this view, paradigmatically demonstrates how form and content can still unite to quiet the din of history by articulating a language in harmony with the natural order of things. For the canonical presentation of such a view, cf.

Wilhelm Emrich, *Die Symbolik von Faust II: Sinn und Vorformen*, 2nd. rev. ed. (Bonn: Athenäum Verlag, 1957). In this volume, Mandelkow discusses Emrich's place within the history of *Faust* reception, while Hans Rudolf Vaget, "Act IV Revisited: A 'Post-Wall' Reading of Goethe's *Faust*," criticizes Emrich's sublimation of history in nature.

21. Cf. Michael Holquist, *Dialogism: Bakhtin and his World* (London and New York: Routledge, 1990) 105–48.

22. BR 25.

23. BR 25.

24. The literature on Goethe's complicated reception of gothic architecture is extensive. Cf. Emrich 328–31; Ernst Beutler, *Von Deutscher Baukunst. Goethes Hymnus auf Erwin von Steinbach: Seine Entstehung und Wirkung* (Munich: F. Bruckman, 1943); Herbert von Einem, *Goethe-Studien* (Munich: Wilhelm Fink Verlag, 1972); Harald Keller, *Goethes Hymnus auf das Straßburger Münster und die Wiederentdeckung der Gotik im 18. Jahrhundert* (Munich: Verlag der Bayerischen Akademie der Wissenschaften, 1974); Norbert Knopp, "Zu Goethes Hymnus *Von Deutscher Baukunst. D.M. Ervini a Steinbach*," *Deutsche Vierteljahrsschrift* 53 (1979): 617–50; Reinhard Liess, *Goethe vor dem Straßburger Münster: Zum Wissenschaftsbild der Kunst* (Leipzig: A. Seemann Verlag, 1985); Ernst Osterkamp, *Im Buchstabenbilde: Studien zum Verfahren Goethescher Bildbeschreibungen* (Stuttgart: J.B. Metzlersche Verlagsbuchhandlung, 1991); Regine Otto, "*Von deutscher Art und Kunst*: Aspekte, Wirkungen und Probleme eines ästhetischen Programms," *Impulse* 1 (1978): 67–88; W.D. Robson-Scott, *The Literary Background of the Gothic Revival in Germany: A Chapter in the History of Taste* (Oxford: The Clarendon Press, 1965), especially 76–95 and 153–224; and Werner Schultheis, "Goethe: *Die natürliche Tochter*. Gotisch und modern," *Euphorion* 80 (1986): 326–39.

25. Cf. Joachim Müller, "Faust und Helena: Der arkadische Traum. Genese und dramatisches Medium," *Jahrbuch des Wiener Goethe-Vereins* 86–88 (1982–84): 199–227.

26. HA 12:390.

27. "Standen aber diese Gebäude Jahrhunderte lang nur wie eine alte Überlieferung da, ohne sonderlichen Eindruck auf die größere Menschenmasse, so ließen sich die Ursachen davon gar wohl angeben." Goethe, "Von deutscher Baukunst (1823)," HA 12:178.

28. Goethe's characterization of this cultural avantgarde establishes its reception of the gothic cathedral as a communal process of chronotopical construction: "Jüngere und Ältere beiderlei Geschlechts waren von solchen Eindrücken übermannt und hingerissen, daß sie sich nicht allein durch wiederholte Beschauung, Messung, Nachzeichnung daran erquickten und erbauten, sondern auch diesen Stil bei noch erst zu errichtenden, lebendigem Gebrauch gewidmeten Gebäuden wirklich anwendeten und eine Zufriedenheit fanden, sich gleichsam urväterlich in solchen Umgebungen zu empfinden." The characterization of the community a few lines later in terms of its ability "historisch zu fühlen und zu erkennen" further suggests that the cathedral is a chronotope of historical time itself (HA 12:178).

29. Cf. both *Dichtung und Wahrheit*, Book 14, and "Von deutscher Baukunst (1823)," HA 10:32–33 and 12:180.

30. Cf. HA 10:32–33, 12:179.

31. BR 34. In his seminal essay on Goethe, Bakhtin analyzes the time-space relationship in literature by noting Goethe's "ability. . . to *see time*, to *read time*, in the spatial whole of the world and. . . to perceive the filling of space. . . as an emerging whole, an

event. . . ." Goethe's works, according to Bakhtin, are replete with "complex visible signs of historical time in the strict sense of the word," BR 25. In the spirit of Bakhtin's assessment, I have identified Goethe's literary imagination with such signs. If, as I am suggesting, Goethe structured Act III of *Faust* by deploying a motif that is "monumental," the text should display compositional complexity in its dual orientation toward the past (as vestige) and the future (as design). It should also feature communal transmission as the source of its vitality and represent the world as an emerging totality of discrete languages in conversation with one another.

32. M.M. Bakhtin, "Forms of Time and the Chronotope in the Novel," in *The Dialogic Imagination: Four Essays,* ed. Michael Holquist, transl. Caryl Emerson and Michael Holquist (Austin: University of Texas Press, 1981) 84. Hereafter abbreviated FT.

33. According to Bakhtin, "Goethe's mode of visualizing time" involves "the merging of time (past with present), the fullness and clarity of the visibility of the time in space, the inseparability of the time of an event from the specific place of its occurrence (*Lokalität und Geschichte*), the visible *essential connection* of time (present and past), the creative and active nature of time (of the past in the present and of the present itself), the necessity that penetrates time and links time with space and different times with one another, and, finally, on the basis of the necessity that pervades localized time, the inclusion of the future. . ." (BR 41–42).

34. WA III, 11:12.

35. WA III, 11:12.

36. In a letter to Zelter on 29 March 1827, WA IV, 42:105.

37. The draft characterizes the interlude as both complete in itself and a continuation–over many years–of the *Faust*-fragment. Goethe concludes by noting his intention to offer the *Helena* to his public "mit allen Vorteilen der Dicht- und Redekunst ausgeführt und ausgeschmückt," HA 3:446.

38. In Goethe's letter to Schiller on 27 June 1797, WA IV, 12:169. He had already redefined the "barbaric" in relation to the "gothic" in his 1772 panegyric "Von deutscher Baukunst." Cf. HA 12:10ff., as well as Kurz's essay in this volume for more on this metaphor in relation to *Faust.*

39. WA IV, 15:112. Cf. note 44 for connections between the *Faust* composition, gothic architecture, and granite mountains in Goethean iconography.

40. In Goethe's letter to Schiller on 12 September 1800, WA IV, 15:102.

41. Loc. cit.

42. "Von deutscher Baukunst (1772)," HA 12:7.

43. Cf. Goethe, "Archiv des Dichters und Schriftstellers" and "Lebensbekenntnisse im Auszug," HA 10:532–35.

44. In his 1784 fragment "Über den Granit" (HA 13:253–58) Goethe similarly addresses an island chain of granite mountains as the "älteste, würdigste Denkmäler der Zeit" (255). Already the ancient Egyptians, he points out, had used "die ungeheuren Massen dieses Steines. . . zu ungeheuren Werken" such as "Sphinxe" and "Memnonsbilder" (254). Like Erwin's cathedral, which he had once likened to God's mountains (HA 12:7), these natural monuments provide a summarizing vantage point for his retrospective and prospective reflection on human history as a process of both loss and survival (255). It is interesting to note in these connections that Goethe introduces his hymn by

configuring granite–through a brief history of its scientific reception–as a discursive tradition, or "Überlieferung." This "Grundfeste unserer Erde," which occurs both high above and deep beneath its surface (254), has stubbornly resisted classification. It therefore has the same "barbaric" quality that Goethe notes of *Faust* in the letter to Schiller and that he notes of the gothic minster in Strasbourg: "Nicht gescheiter als ein Volk, das die ganze fremde Welt barbarisch nennt, hieß alles *Gotisch*, was nicht in mein System paßte. . ." (HA 12:10).

45. BR 28.

46. BR 36.

47. HA 10:535.

48. WA III, 10:208.

49. WA IV, 41:202.

50. Cf. Gräf II/2:343–50 for a collection of comments that connect the two projects.

51. WA IV, 41:202–3. Emphasis added.

52. Cf. Stephen Greenblatt, *Shakespearean Negotiations: The Circulation of Social Energy in Renaissance England* (Berkeley and Los Angeles: University of California Press, 1988) 1–20.

53. In this connection, the rhyme-discovery scene in Part II echoes the rhyming Logos-*Übertragung* in Part I (1224–37). The earlier scene also serves to introduce the poodle Mephistopheles into Faust's study, thereby underscoring the transgressive dimension of his translating work.

54. *Laokoon oder über die Grenzen der Malerei und Poesie*, in *Lessings Werke*, ed. Kurt Wölfel (Frankfurt/Main: Insel Verlag, 1967) 3:123.

55. Goethe, "Vorwort" in *Zur Farbenlehre*, HA 13:315.

56. HA 12:22.

57. Another, more subtle indication that Act III takes place upon an irregular and therefore "irreverent" stage lies in Goethe's own characterization of it as "Zwischenspiel." Not only does *Helena* interrupt the action between the first two and the last two acts of *Faust*'s second part as an interlude. Its "illicit" action also threatens to confound any normal sense of temporal sequence. Cf. Goethe's letter to Boisserée on 29 September 1826, where he complains about rumors of an illegal agreement between Cotta and a Vienna publisher to publish his *Werke* as "ein leidig *Zwischenspiel*," WA IV, 41:182. Emphasis added.

58. Bakhtin on Goethe's "Pyrmont" fragment, BR 49.

59. WA IV, 41:209.

60. Goethe concludes the letter to Boisserée with the following, nostalgic glance back at his youthful sense of idyllic time: "Und so thu ich vielleicht mehr und vollende sinnig in zugemessenen Tagen, was man zu einer Zeit versäumt, wo man das Recht hat, zu glauben oder zu wähnen, es gebe noch Wiedermorgen und Immermorgen," WA IV, 41:209.

61. Cf. HA 9:357–85.

62. HA 10:32.

63. HA 9:388, emphasis added.

64. HA 12:10.

65. BR 23.

66. A complete analysis of the "barbaric" form of *Faust II*, I should add, might reveal the basis of its historicity in terms of analogous recapitulations with respect to Part I.

67. BR 36.

68. HA 12:9–10.

69. Cf. note 37 for Goethe's characterization of Act III as a piece of *Faust*-ornamentation. Anthony Vidler, in *The Writing of the Walls: Architectural Theory in the Late Enlightenment* (Princeton: Princeton Architectural Press, 1987) 133, has noted Winckelmann's interest in architectural ornament in terms of both its function (to relieve monotony) and its history: "[ornamentation] emerged with the taste for variety, movement, and diversity." A possible connection between Winckelmann and Goethe's discussion of ornamentation in the Erwin von Steinbach essay has never, to my knowledge, been noted.

70. HA 12:10.

71. Fifty-five years later, on 14 November 1827, Goethe would also liken his *Helena*, in a letter to Carl Ludwig von Knebel, to an ancient tree. He appreciates his friend's interest in Act III, he reflects, "da dieses Werk, ein Erzeugniß vieler Jahre, mir gegenwärtig eben so wunderbar vorkommt als die hohen Bäume in meinem Garten am Stern, welche, doch noch jünger als diese poetische Conception, zu einer Höhe herangewachsen sind, daß ein Wirkliches, welches man selbst verursachte, als ein Wunderbares, Unglaubliches, nicht zu Erlebendes erscheint," WA IV, 43:166.

72. Cf. Bakhtin on Dante, FT 157–58, for a discussion of the horizontal and vertical dimensions in relation to time.

73. HA 9:356–57.

74. HA 12:7.

75. HA 9:388.

76. Cf. the concluding paragraph to "Von deutscher Baukunst (1772)," where Promethean survival is evoked, HA 12:15.

77. HA 12:7.

78. HA 8:392.

79. HA 12:12.

CHRISTOPH JAMME

"alter tage fabelhaft Gebild":
Goethes Mythen-bastelei im *Faust II*

Goethe's Use of Myth in Faust II

Faust II is in large part a criticism of the overweening claim of modern scientific method, which thinks itself superior to the wisdom Goethe felt to be transmitted symbolically in mythological form, to grasp the verities of the universe. He uses myth in the work as an element of that criticism of those who hope to grasp the truth of the universe autonomously and "scientifically," without resort to intuitive wisdom. Parallels to Wilhelm Meisters Wanderjahre are touched on.

IM ZWEITEN TEIL DES *Faust* BEGEGNET CHRISTLICHE, jüdische und antike Mythologie, wobei wir uns hier auf letztere beschränken wollen.[1] Fausts Suche nach und seine Begegnung mit Helena, die "Axe, auf der das ganze Stück dreht" (Gräf II/2:380), läßt sich insgesamt als Versuch lesen, den antiken Mythos wiederzubeleben, und zwar über die äußerste Skepsis. Wie die Farbenlehre mit dem Sehen anfängt, und nicht mit dem Licht, so ist der Mythos bei Goethe–nicht nur hier in der *Faust*-Tragödie–je schon ein durch Deutung gebrochener. Gebrochen in Goethes Verhältnis zum antiken Mythos allein schon wegen seiner bewußten Relativierung der antiken Klassik durch ihre Gleichordnung mit nordischer und orientalischer Klassik. Versteht man ferner unter "Mythos," wie gängig geworden, die Erzählung von Göttern oder Halbgöttern, dann wird es überhaupt schwer, im zweiten Teil des *Faust* Mythen zu finden (von den olympischen Göttern ist nicht die Rede, höchstens–und auch dies selten–von Heroen wie Herakles). Zu diesem Fehlen des sozusagen klassischen Mythenarsenals kommt hinzu, daß Goethe spezifische Deutungsmethoden bzw. Rezeptionsweisen von Mythen vorführt, die die Brechung gleichsam verdoppeln. Vor allem werden die (neben der euhemeristischen) beiden ältesten und wirkungsmächtigsten Erklärungsmodelle vorgeführt, nämlich die Naturmythologie (die die Götter als personifizierte Naturmächte verstand) und der (in der Antike bei der Interpretation der Homerischen Epen entstandene) Allegorismus.

Theagenes von Region erkannte in dem Namen einer Gottheit entweder ein Element der Natur oder einen Zustand der menschlichen Seele. Noch das 19. Jahrhundert hat die naturmythologische Deutungsmethode weitgehend benutzt, während die Allegorese zunehmend der Kritik verfiel: die Romantik zum Beispiel machte einen Unterschied zwischen Symbol und Allegorie und schob die Allegorese dem aufklärerischen Rationalismus zu. Goethe benutzt die Ergebnisse der in der Romantik beginnenden historischen und vergleichenden Mythenforschung, ironisiert sie aber zugleich, weshalb sich sein Umgang mit der Mythologie auch als Karikatur zeitgenössisch-romantischer Bestrebungen deuten läßt. Im Gegensatz zu vielen seiner Zeitgenossen ist Goethe kein Fortsetzer der mit ihren Wurzeln weit ins 18. Jahrhundert zurückreichenden romantischen Forderungen nach einer "neuen Mythologie," er ist vielmehr Erbe der Renaissance und ihres–in einer Flut mythographischer Handbücher dokumentierten–Eklektizismus bei dem Umgang mit antiken Mythen, innerhalb dessen nicht (nur) die prominenten olympischen Götter Karriere machten, sondern vor allem die kleinen, "unreinen" Gottheiten (wie etwa Fortuna).

In jedem Fall ist der Goethesche Mythos schon ein in Rezeption, ja sogar in Theorie übergegangener. Dazu im folgenden einige wenige, notwendig oberflächliche Hinweise.

I

Der antike Mythos ist im *Faust II* vor allem zitathaft präsent, er begegnet zuerst als Dekor des gebildeten Diskurses, d.h. in vornehmlich metaphorischer Funktion. Schon der den zweiten Teil der Tragödie einleitende Gesang Ariels (dieser Luftgeist aus Shakespeares *Sturm* erscheint hier als Symbol der Natur und gewinnt somit pseudo-mythische Funktion) enthält zentrale Beispiele für diese Art der Bildersprache: so wird "Lethe" (4629), ursprünglich der Fluß in der antiken Unterweltssage, bei Goethe zum Bild des Vergessens; die "Horen" (4666), ursprünglich Töchter des Zeus und der Themis, Beweger der den Olymp umgebenden Wolken, werden bei Goethe zum Symbol der Geburt eines neuen Tages. Dieses mythologische Ornament ist gut aufklärerisch: zum Beispiel erschien Hederich die Mythologie als für Künstler, Gelehrte und alle Gebildeten nützliches, lexikalisch inventarisierbares Wissen. Dies führte dann zu dem Streit zwischen Herder und Klotz um die Frage, ob mythologische Namen in einem Gedicht der Neuzeit Platz haben können. Goethe hat zeitlebens die Position Herders verteidigt, wobei er sich der Hilfe von Karl Philipp Moritz versichern konnte. Mir will es allerdings scheinen, als spiele hier im *Faust II* die wesentlich in Italien gewonnene Überzeugung von der Ästhetizität des antiken Mythos (der Mythos als Dichtung, als "Sprache der Phantasie") weniger eine Rolle als die–vor allem an Werken der bildenden Kunst geschulte–Auffassung von der allegorischen Funktion des Mythos (die Moritz eigentlich überwunden geglaubt hatte). So bedeuten "Phöbus" und die "Horen" (4666ff.) die *Allegorie* der Geburt eines neuen Tages, an dem

Faust aus seinem Heilschlaf erwacht–wobei Goethe sich durch Guido Renis Ge-
mälde "Aurora" hat inspirieren lassen.

Ein Bündnis schlossen Mythologie und Allegorik vor allem in der (bildenden
Kunst der) Renaissance. Der–für den Handlungszusammenhang durchaus
entbehrliche–Maskenzug der dritten Szene des ersten Aktes ist deshalb von hoher
Bedeutung, weil er die allegorische Interpretation der Mythologie unterstreicht
("wir sind Allegorien," 5531). Innerhalb des Festzuges zum Fastnachtsfest ruft
der Herold neben verschiedenen Poeten usw. auch "die griechische Mythologie"
auf, "die, selbst in moderner Maske, weder Charakter noch Gefälliges verliert"
(5299ff.). Es treten nacheinander auf die Grazien, die Parzen (wobei Klotho und
Atropos die Rollen getauscht haben), die Furien (hier höfisch-festlich gezähmt),
Viktoria (Nike), Plutus (Faust), Avaritia (Mephisto) und schließlich der große
Pan (Kaiser), umgeben von Satyrn und Nymphen–sie alle begegnen als Allegorien
(der sinnvollen Tätigkeit, des Reichtums, des Geizes und schließlich des "Alls
der Welt," 5873).

Als Vorbild diente Goethe Andrea Mantegnas Zyklus *Julius Cäsars Triumphzug*,
der Goethe durch neun clair-obscur-Holzschnitte, die Andrea Andreani 1598/99
nach dem Zyklus geschaffen hatte, bekannt war und über den er auch 1823 in
einem eigenen Aufsatz gehandelt hat. Goethe stellt hier den *Triumphzug* Blatt für
Blatt in geordneter Folge von der Spitze des Zuges bis zum zehnten Bild dar, das
die auf den Triumphwagen folgenden Sekretäre Cäsars darstellt, wobei er an
Vasaris Beschreibung des Triumphzuges Kritik übt. Goethe geht es nicht so sehr,
wie Vasari, um die Dekorationselemente, sondern vielmehr um die "vollkommene
Symbolik" der Darstellung. Mit dem indirekten Verweis auf Mantegnas Bild spielt
Goethe auf einen Prozeß an, innerhalb dessen im 15. Jahrhundert die Allegorie
und die Mythologie zu einer öffentlichen Angelegenheit wurden. Die Florentiner
Festkultur kannte im Quattrocento Trionfi, für die prunkvolle Wagen und Karren
ausgestattet wurden, auf denen Mimen im Maskenspiel agierten, begleitet von
neben den Wagen schreitenden, laufenden, hüpfenden und springenden Vor-
läufern, Begleitern und Nachfolgern. Die im Umzug–meist in einer Gruppe–
auftretende allegorische Gestalt trug keine Erläuterung mit sich, höchstens die
Triumphpforten oder -wege waren mit lehrhaften Sprüchen versehen. Das
Aussehen der *mythologischen* Gestalten wurde gemäß den antiken Quellen rekonstruiert; die humanistischen *Allegorien* hingegen, die nur selten auf einer
bildlichen Tradition aufbauen konnten, vielmehr ausschließlich auf die antike
und mittelalterliche Dichtung angewiesen waren, mußten immer präziser
formuliert werden, um innerhalb eines Umzuges erkennbar zu bleiben. Mit der
Übernahme der Trionfi Italiens durch die Herrschereinzüge in Frankreich (unter
den späten Valois) wurden Mythologie und profane Allegorie zur Domäne des
höfischen Festes; ihre Fortsetzung fanden sie dann in den Festen der Revolution.
Vor diesem Hintergrund, nämlich der fast direkten Weitergabe der mythologischen Überlieferung der Renaissance an das 19. Jahrhundert durch die französischen Revolutionsfeste, die eine auffallende Konstanz der mythologischen Bilder
und Formeln von der Renaissance bis ins 19. Jahrhundert erklärt, muß die

Goethesche Verwendung der Mythenallegorese im *Faust* verstanden werden, wobei eben zu beachten bleibt, daß die Tradition einer allegorischen Gestalt schon für die Renaissance nicht mehr selbstverständlich gewesen ist. Bei Goethe meinen die mythologischen Masken die in der Gesellschaft herrschenden Mächte, wobei innerhalb des Festzuges eine strenge Hierarchie herrscht. Am Schluß steht der Schwarmzug der *Natur*-Geister (der große Pan in spätantiker Bedeutung). Es soll hier nicht entschieden werden, ob die Mummenschanz eine Selbstrepräsentation der allegorischen Struktur von *Faust II* darstellt; soviel nur scheint gewiß, daß die hier auftretenden Figuren der Illustration von Abstrakta dienen und Goethe mithin an dem seit Mantegna virulenten Problem arbeitet, für ein Abstraktum ein bildliches Korrelat zu finden, und dies zudem in einer Zeit, der—noch viel mehr als in der Renaissance—die Tradition einer allegorischen Gestalt nicht mehr selbstverständlich war.

II

Im *Faust* spielt Goethe nicht nur mit traditionellen Mythen, vor allem der Antike—wobei die Grenzen zur Magie (5970ff., 6315f., 7005ff. bis zum Widerruf der Magie 11404f.), zu den Mysterien (vgl. 62429f.) und zu den Sagen (vgl. 7660ff. und 7606ff.) fließend sind—, aber auch mit denen des nordischen Sagenkreises (vgl. die Rede Fausts von Berggeistern und Wichtelmännern 10425ff. sowie die Rede Mephistos von den "Undinen," d.h. den Elementargeistern des Wassers in den Bergseen). Neben diesem Spiel mit vorhandenem Mythen-Material ist Goethe auch selbständig mythenbildend tätig. Auf beide Verfahrensweisen paßt das von Lévi-Strauss entwickelte Modell des "bricolage," das eine neue Kombination der in den Mythen vorfindlichen alten Elemente impliziert.

Paradigma für Goethes Umgang mit der überlieferten Mythologie ist die Gestalt der "dreitausendjährigen Helena. . . , der ich," wie Goethe am 25. Mai 1827 an Nees von Esenbeck schreibt, "nun auch schon sechzig Jahre nachschleiche" (Gräf II/2:397). In der Tat umfaßt der Helena-Akt bei Goethe dreitausend Jahre Kulturgeschichte: von der Zeit des Trojanischen Krieges bis zu Goethes eigener Zeit. Was man auf den ersten Blick für die ureigenste Erfindung Goethes halten könnte, nämlich die Begegnung zwischen Helena und Faust, ist in Wahrheit durch die von Goethe benutzten Quellen vorgegeben. In der im Dezember 1826 niedergeschriebenen "Ankündigung" *Helena, Zwischenspiel zu Faust* verweist Goethe selbst auf "die alte Legende" und "das Puppenspiel," die nicht verfehlten, "die Scene vorzuführen, daß Faust in seinem herrischen Übermuth durch Mephistopheles den Besitz der schönen Helena von Griechenland verlangt und ihm dieser nach einigem Widerstreben willfahrt habe" (WA I, 41.2:291f., Gräf II/2:364). Der Helena-Akt entstand dann 1825–1827, als die Hauptarbeit an *Faust II* begann, als erster. Er hat sein Zentrum in der geschichtsmetaphysischen Versöhnung von Antike und Moderne (wobei die Moderne hier das umfaßt, was Hegel unter "romantischer Kunstform" begreift, nämlich das Mittelalter und die Romantik). "Es ist Zeit," schreibt Goethe am 17. September 1827 an Iken, "daß der leidenschaftliche Zwiespalt zwischen Classikern und Romantikern sich endlich versöhne. [...] Lernen wir nicht auf dieser hohen Stelle alles in seinem wahren, ethisch-ästhetischen Werthe schätzen, das Älteste wie das Neuste!" Die Zusammenführung von Faust und Helena im dritten Akt besiegelt das Einswerden des Nordisch-Mittelalterlichen mit dem Antik-Griechischen oder des—wie Goethe sagt—"romanti-schen" mit dem "klassischen" Geist. Goethe spricht auch von einem "classisch-romantisch-phantasmagorischen Zwischenspiel zu 'Faust' " (Gräf II/2:374). Bei der angestrebten Synthese zwischen Antike und Moderne, Süd und Nord, Sinnlichkeit und trockener Gelehrsamkeit, Schönheit und Häßlichkeit, geht es nicht nur um eine Synthese zwischen Natur (vgl. 9560f.) und Kultur, sondern auch und zutiefst um den Ausgleich zwischen einer—mythenproduzierenden und-ermöglichenden—Götterverehrung und einer Innerlichkeit, die an die Stelle einer mythisch-objektiven eine zutiefst subjektive Kunst setzt (die ihr Paradigma in der Musik findet, vgl. 9679ff.). Daß eine solche angestrebte Synthese nicht ohne Gefahren ist, verdeutlicht Goethe an der Gestalt des Euphorion. In der griechi-schen Mythologie ein Sohn des Achill und der Helena, ein geflügelter Knabe mit übernatürlichen Kräften, der schließlich von Zeus aus enttäuschter Liebe mit einem Blitzstrahl getötet wird, erscheint er bei Goethe als ein "allegorisches Wesen" (Goethe zu Eckermann, 20.12.1829), als Personifikation der Poesie (5573). Er begegnet zuerst als Knabe Lenker (5521ff.), der in die Einsamkeit als seine eigentliche Region verwiesen wird, und wird dann im dritten Akt in der arkadi-schen Grotte geboren. Sein Tod konnotiert den Ikaros-Mythos, zur warnenden Versinnbildlichung des Schicksals des Nur-Künstlers (9901–2). Neben dieser allegorischen Synthese zwischen Antike und Moderne gibt es bei Goethe auch eine räumlich-geographische: Faust und seine Mannen aus dem Norden siedelten sich während der Raubzüge des Menelaos (d.h. während Paris Helena entführte) in einer Burg in einem Gebirge Spartas an (8994ff.). Eine dritte verbindende Klammer zwischen Antike und Moderne schließlich darf nicht übersehen werden, die Omnipräsenz des Teuflischen nämlich: "Vom Harz bis Hellas immer Vettern," freut sich Mephisto (7743), und: "Absurd ist's hier [im Süden, C.J.], absurd im Norden" (7792).

Wichtiger als eine punktuelle Auflösung der Querelle war Goethe aber wohl eher eine prozeßhafte Anverwandlung von Antike und Moderne. Diese Anver-wandlung beschreibt er im Bild einer zur Kunst werdenden Natur, d.h. mit Hilfe des in der *Italienischen Reise* entwickelten Modells der "zweiten Natur." Helena ist zu Beginn ganz Mythos, und zwar im Sinne wiederum der Naturmythologie. Sie ist Urbild der Natur, höchste Hervorbringung der (griechischen) Natur, und zwar einer Natur als *natura naturans*, einer *bildenden* Natur, die das Schöne hervorbringt. Sie ist angesiedelt in einer dorisch-arkadischen Landschaft nach dem Vorbild Poussins und Lorrains, wo Pan lebt und wo die Nymphen in der Natur wohnen (9538–41). Daß Helena in der ersten Hälfte des dritten Aktes Angehörige des göttlichen, d.h. also des mythischen, Zeitalters ist (9565), wird von Goethe schon im zweiten Akt vorbereitet, wo nämlich Faust die Zeugung der Helena im Bild des Mythos von dem sich Leda in Gestalt eines Schwanes vermählenden Zeus träumt (6903–20). Weil es Goethe von Anfang an um die Naturmythologie oder um die religiöse Naturbetrachtung geht, ist wohl auch die in der ursprünglichen Konzeption vorgesehene Szene weggefallen, in der Faust in die Unterwelt hinabsteigt und von der Unterweltgöttin Proserpina die Losbittung Helenas erwirkt.

Doch auch der Mythos Helena ist von Anfang an ein gebrochener. Helena weiß nicht nur um ihre hohe Schönheit, sondern gleichzeitig um die Tragik ihrer Schönheit (8839ff., 9246ff.), selber Göttin, göttlich, gleich dem Göttlichen (9237, 9257, 9345), ahnt sie, daß sie doch dem Orkus angehört und erinnert sich daran, daß sie einst aus ihm heraufgeholt worden ist (8836f.). So lebt sie auf der einen Seite in idealer Zeitlosigkeit und ist doch geschichtlich (vgl. 9414–16). Sie glaubt aus Troja zu kommen, weiß aber gleichzeitig, daß sie "Sage" und "Dichtung" ist (vgl. 8488–8515); Phorkyas' Bericht von der Achilleus-Episode macht dann ihre Zeitrechnung endlich hinfällig (8876ff.). So wird sie sich am Ende selbst "Idol" (8881). Das aber heißt nichts anderes, als daß sie letztlich ein Kunstwerk ist, und wie ein Künstler geht Faust auch mit Helena um. Wenn Helena in die abendländische-christliche Welt hineinwächst, indem sie den Reim lernt, d.h. die fremde Klang-Welt adaptiert (9367ff.), indem sie die nordische Sprechweise im Dialog einübt (9375ff.), so ist mit Recht darauf hingewiesen worden, daß Helena jetzt ihre mythische Gebundenheit aufgibt, aber nicht um "Person," sondern um vielmehr endgültig zu der Gestalt zu werden, in der der Mythos unter den Bedingungen der Aufklärung einzig fortleben kann: zum Kunstwerk. Der Bestimmung des Mythos als "liebliche Lüge, / Glaubhaftiger als Wahrheit" (9642f.) im *Faust* entspricht die berühmte Bestimmung des Mythos als "schöner Schein" in *Dichtung und Wahrheit* (WA I, 27:312). Diese Deutung des Mythos als Kunstwerk bestimmt–über Friedrich Max Müller und E. Cassirer–die Mythosdebatte bis zur Gegenwart (zu erinnern ist an Blumenbergs These von der Depotenzierung der Angst). Die Götter sind heute, was auch Inhalt der *Iphigenie* gewesen war, zu einem *innerpsychischen* Geschehen geworden (vgl. 9679–86; 9661–64).

Am deutlichsten wird dieser ästhetisch-produktive Charakter des Mythos an den Stellen von *Faust II*, wo Goethe selbst den Versuch unternommen hat, neue Mythen zu schaffen.

III

Für den Mythenforscher Kerényi stellen der Mythos der "Mütter" und das Ägäische Fest die "bedeutendsten mythologischen Schöpfungen der neuzeitlichen Literatur" dar.

Der Mythos der "Mütter" (6213ff.) kommt beim ersten Versuch Fausts ins Spiel, sich Helena zu nähern: will er doch ihren Schatten von den Müttern holen, wozu er den Dreifuß (das Symbol der Prophetie) entführt und Helena und Paris beschwört, ehe er das Bild mit Gewalt zu ergreifen sucht, was nur zum Scheitern führt. Erst im zweiten Akt holt er die wirkliche Helena aus der Unterwelt (7435, 8876ff.). Goethe selbst hat darauf verwiesen, daß dieser Mythos seine ureigenste

Die Emphase, mit der Goethe die Dichtung als den wahren Ort des Mythos unterstreicht, hat eine Spitze auch gegen die Wissenschaft. Die philologische Mythenforschung der (romantischen) Zeit verfällt der Ironie, vor allem an der Stelle, wo es um die Berechnung des Lebensalters Helenas geht. Diese Berechnung, etwa auf zehn Jahre (Theseus hat die Zehnjährige geraubt), wird als Selbstbetrug der "Philologen" gebrandmarkt, dergegenüber die Alterslosigkeit Helenas, ihre ewige Jugend ins Feld geführt wird. Dieses Mysterium der Zeitlosigkeit ist nun einzig das Produkt dichterischer Arbeit (7429): "Den Poeten bindet keine Zeit" (7433). Diese Ironie gegenüber der aufkommenden wissenschaftlichen Mythenforschung seiner Zeit–Goethe spricht einmal gegenüber Eckermann von "Piquen," die er "so von den besonderen Gegenständen abgelöst und in's Allgemeine gespielt [habe], daß es zwar dem Leser nicht an Beziehungen fehlen, aber niemand wissen wird, worauf es eigentlich gemeint ist" (Gräf II/2:548)–ist auch bei der Schilderung der Kabiren am Werk, indem hier die Philologie mit dem olympischen Sein konfrontiert wird (bisher bekannt sind nur sieben, so bei Creuzer und Schelling, der achte "west im Olymp," 8196–99). Das Wesen der Mythologie, nämlich die Verwandlungsfähigkeit und ständige Umgestaltung (auf die heutzutage auch Blumenberg das Gewicht legt), ist nicht wissenschaftlich, sondern einzig mit den Mitteln der künstlerischen Produktivität adäquat zu erfassen. "Weder Mythologie noch Legenden," so Goethe, "sind in der Wissenschaft zu dulden. Lasse man diese den Poeten. . ." (HA 8:301). Eine Wiederbelebung mythischer Gestalten und Geschehnisse ist nur auf dem Wege über die dichterische Einbildungskraft möglich. Goethe sieht es als unveräußerliches "Recht des Dichters" an, "Geschichte in Mythologie zu verwandeln" und "Mythologie nach Belieben umzubilden" (Gedenkausgabe 14:838).

Liest man den *Faust* insgesamt als Kritik des neuzeitlichen Menschen, der autonom, voraussetzungslos die Wahrheit der Dinge begreifen zu können glaubt, und sieht man die symbolische Form des zweiten Teils als Medium der Kritik dieser Faustischen Unmittelbarkeit, so läßt sich auch die Behandlung des Mythos als ein Element dieser Kritik verstehen. Das Göttliche wird dem späten Goethe zum großen Leitthema seines dichterischen Forschens: die Welt wird in ihrer Gleichnishaftigkeit erkannt; für des späten Goethe sinnbildliches Welterleben kann die Wahrheit nur vermittelt ergriffen werden: die Welt fordert Beschränkungen, der Mensch ist auf das Zwischenreich des Trüben und Farbigen angewiesen (4727). Dieses Angewiesensein spiegelt sich auch in der Symbolstruktur des zweiten Teils, in dem Faust nicht mehr der Mittelpunkt ist, sondern dessen Bilder jeweils das Wesen eines Weltkreises widerspiegeln. Hier bilden Mütter-Mythos, Leda-Traum und Meerfest sowie Helena eine große Symbolreihe, in wechselseitiger Spiegelung verbunden. Nehmen wir noch den Schluß der *Faust*-Dichtung (der nicht zur ursprünglichen Konzeption gehörte) hinzu, der eine eigenständige Betrachtung verdiente, so ließe sich die gesamte Dichtung als ein großer Mythos verstehen, dem in *Wilhelm Meisters Wanderjahren* der Makarien-Mythos entspricht, in dem Goethes Forderungen nach "Verselbstung" und "Entselbstung" versöhnt sind.

Erfindung ist: "Ich kann Ihnen weiter nichts verraten," sagt er zu Eckermann am 10. Januar 1830, "als daß ich beim Plutarch gefunden, daß im griechischen Altertume von *Müttern* als Gottheiten die Rede gewesen. Dies ist alles, was ich der Überlieferung verdanke, das übrige ist meine eigene Erfindung." Ob man von einem wirklichen "Mythos" sprechen kann, ist zweifelhaft; in jedem Falle hat Goethe einen Teil seiner (kunst-)religiösen Überzeugungen gestaltet, indem er Anleihen sowohl bei der Mystik wie bei den antiken Mysterien (vgl. 6249f.) gemacht hat. Als Göttinnen, Urbilder alles Lebens sind die "Mütter" Frucht von Goethes Naturphilosophie: diese Urbilder werden entweder unmittelbar lebendig oder sie werden geistig beschworen: "Die einen faßt des Lebens holder Lauf, / Die andern sucht der kühne Magier auf" (6435f.). Diese Parallelsetzung der Metamorphose der Natur und der der Kunst macht deutlich, daß es Goethe hier um die *religiöse* Haltung des Künstlers geht, was auch durch Fausts Lob des "Schauderns" (das antike "thaumazein"!) bekräftigt wird (6271f.). In vielem entspricht der Mütter-Mythos dem Makarien-Mythos in *Wilhelm Meisters Wanderjahren*. Goethe hat dort versucht, den platonischen Schöpfungsmythos im *Timaios* wiederzubeleben: im Irdischen ist das Göttliche möglich; Makarie ist zugleich die Selige, die sich als Gestirn des Sonnensystems spiralförmig in den Kosmos hinausbewegt, und gleichzeitig die Welt-zugewandt Tätige.

Goethe macht an dieser Stelle aber auch deutlich, daß wahre (Kunst)Schöpfung mittels einer bloß magischen Geisterbeschwörung notwendig unvollkommen bleibt: der Schemen von Helena, den Faust hier geschaffen hat, bleibt wortlos (6479ff.), und Faust wird beim Versuch, den Schemen zu ergreifen, "paralysiert" (6568). Er liegt schlafend, bis er in Hellas wiedererwacht. Symbol für die wahre Schöpfung des Schönen ist dann die Klassische Walpurgisnacht im zweiten Akt: nicht Nachahmung der Antike, sondern Neuproduktion aus einem schöpferischen Mythos. Die–dem *Märchen* verwandte–Symbolsprache der Klassischen Walpurgisnacht läßt sich entschlüsseln als geistiger Weg zu Helena, weil in Helena Naturwerdung und Kunstschöpfung zusammengehören. Goethe selbst sprach von diesem Akt als von "Helenas Antecedenzien" (Gräf II/2:375). Wort und Sache sind von Goethe selbständig erfunden, obwohl man inzwischen das antike Fest, das Goethe gemeint hat, identifiziert hat: für den ersten Teil stand das thessalische Fest der Peloria (vermittelt über Athenaeus via Barthélémy) Pate, für das Meerfest im zweiten Teil vor allem Barockopern, was schon Eckermann aufgefallen ist, der den opernhaften Charakter dieses Teils stets betont hat (in der Tat ist Helena in der Szene "Schattiger Hain" in eine Oper übergeführt). Der Unterschied zur Walpurgisnacht des ersten Teils ist offenkundig: verarbeitete Goethe in den Brocken-Szenen jenen uralten Kult, nach dem am Vorabend vor dem großen Fest zum Frühlingserwachen die bösen Mächte noch einmal alle ihre Kräfte aufbieten, Hexen und Druden in dieser magischen Nacht darauf aus sind, der Frühjahrsgöttin den Einzug zu verderben, so erfindet Goethe hier das Fest einer einmal im Jahr stattfindenden Versammlung der antiken Geister. Zu Eckermann sagte er am 21. Februar 1831: "Die alte Walpurgisnacht. . . ist monarchisch, indem der Teufel dort überall als entschiedenes Oberhaupt respectirt wird. Die classische aber ist durchaus republicanisch, indem alles in der Breite neben einander steht, so dass der Eine so viel gilt wie der Andere, und niemand sich subordinirt und sich um den Andern bekümmert" (Gräf II/2:567f.).

Mit dem Ort, dem Schlachtfeld von Pharsalos, steht das Thema des Verhältnisses von Geschichte und Mythologie zur Diskussion. Es geht, wie schon der Eröffnungsprolog der Hexe Erichtho deutlich macht, um die Wiederbelebung eines Mythisch-Vergangenen. Die Geschichte selbst hat mythische Strukturen: "Wie oft schon wiederholt' sich's! wird sich immerfort / Ins Ewige wiederholen. . ." (7012f.) Zwar gehört die mythische Urzeit (so hat Eliade immer wieder betont) einer anderen Ordnung an als die chronologisch ablaufende "Weltzeit," stellt einen anderen "Zeittypus" dar. Doch beide Zeittypen existieren gleichzeitig, durchdringen sich und überschneiden sich an bestimmten Punkten. Diese Überschneidungspunkte markiert der Mythos. Durch den Wechsel der Zeitdimensionen erzielen Erzähler und Hörer des Mythos magische Wirkung. Darauf deuten auch die Worte des Chores in der Szene "Schattiger Hain" des dritten Aktes:

> Dichtend belehrendem Wort
> Hast du gelauscht wohl nimmer?
> . . .
> Nie vernommen auch Hellas'
> Urväterlicher Sagen
> Göttlich-heldenhaften Reichtum?
>
> Alles, was je geschieht
> Heutigen Tages,
> Trauriger Nachklang ist's
> Herrlicher Ahnherrntage. (9631–40)

Eine magische Welt ist es dann auch, die das antike Fest ermöglicht, das seinen Höhepunkt im Meeresfest findet. Nicht die olympischen Götter versammeln sich hier, sondern die antiken Geister (von Ameisen und Greifen bis zu den Kabiren und Galatee), und diese mythischen Geister sind Teil der wirkenden, bildenden Natur, d.h. der Mythos wird als ein Erzeugnis dieser Natur, der (griechischen) Erde verstanden (weshalb D. Hölscher-Lohmeyer sehr treffend von der "Naturgenese des Mythos" gesprochen hat). Gleichzeitig wird der Mythos aber auch verzeitlicht; so wird bei der Gestalt Chirons neben den alten Motiven des Mythos das entscheidende Moment der kreisenden Zeit neu erfunden (vgl. 7426ff.: Mysterium der Wiederholungen). Zu Eckermann sagte Goethe am 24.1.1830: "Der mythologischen Figuren, die sich hiebei zudrängen, sind eine Unzahl." Deshalb mußte er eine Auswahl treffen, und es ist höchst aufschlußreich, daß statt der olympischen Götter selbst nur dämonische Wesen auftreten; wie schon Kerényi beobachtet hat, ist von den Olympiern nur ihre *Idee* geblieben. In der Tat begegnen Faust und Mephisto Sphinxe und Sirenen, Nymphen und Kentauren wie Chiron, Ameisen und Pygmäen, Lamien und Kabiren. Statt Aphrodite erscheint die in ihrem Muschelwagen über das Meer dahinfahrende Galatea, die schöne Nereide, deren Verspottung des verliebten ungeschlachten Kyklopen Polyphem in der hellenistischen Literatur ein beliebtes Thema war. Auch Neptun nimmt selbst am Meerfest nicht teil, nur sein Dreizack ist präsent. An seine Stelle ist der Meergreis Nereus getreten, umgeben von seinen Töchtern und den Tritonen, seinen Söhnen. Das Fest insgesamt ist damit sehr elementisch–das *Göttliche* ist nur durch Zeichen präsent. Das Leitsymbol dieser magischen Welt ist der Mond, der von Szene zu Szene heller scheint, bis er schließlich bei dem Fest der Seegötter "im Zenit verharr[t]." Auch in dieser Szene dominiert letztlich wieder der allegorische Sinn, denn die Elementargeister, besonders aber die auftretenden beiden Naturphilosophen Thales und Anaxagoras, werden zu Allegorien von Goethes eigener naturphilosophischer Aussage (vor dem Hintergrund des zeitgenössischen Streites zwischen dem "Neptunismus" Werners und Okens und dem "Vulkanismus" von Buchs und Alexander von Humboldts). Die schon angesprochene Euphorionszene fügt sich bruchlos in diese Allegorik ein, ehe am Ende mit den Dionysos-Dithyramben wieder an die Mysterien-Religion erinnert wird, deren Elemente schon beim Festzug von Nereiden und Tritonen eine beherrschende Rolle gespielt haben (zum Beispiel in der Betonung des Hochzeitlichen).

Insgesamt gesehen haben wir es hier also mit einem mehrfach gebrochenen Mythos zu tun, mit einem Mythos, der durch die Mythenkritik der Aufklärung hindurchgegangen ist, der in nachantike (= mittelalterliche) Zeiten transponiert ist. Helena stellt ja nicht die historische Gestalt dar, wie sie die Sage überliefert, vielmehr begegnet sie in der Gestalt, die ihr das späte 18. Jahrhundert gegeben hat (was Goethe 1803 in seinem Aufsatz "Polygnots Gemählde" dargelegt hat).

Diese anachronistisch gebrochene Zwitterstellung des Mythos wird deutlich auch an der Gestalt des Homunculus, von dessen "historisch-mythischem Naturell" (Gräf II/2:366) Goethe bewußt paradox spricht. Für Kerényi gehört Homunculus "zu jenen mittelalterlichen Formen, in die sich unterdrückte urmythologische Gestalten gerettet haben." In ihm verkörpert sich die Lebens- und Natursehnsucht des einseitig verstandesorientierten abendländisch-christlichen Menschen. Er verkörpert den wissenden *Geist*, der den Weg zu Helena weisen kann, geschaffen vom fleißigen Gelehrten, der aber nur dann vollständig Mensch werden kann, wenn er sich mit dem Eros des organischen Lebens, mit dem feuchten Element verbindet. Er wird von Proteus, einem der bedeutendsten Meergötter, in das Gestalten und Umgestalten alles Lebendigen mit einbezogen (vgl. 8225ff.). Sein Abenteuer ist mithin das der "reinen Entelechie," wie Goethe sie selbst beschrieben hat.

IV

Nicht kausal folgt Helena auf das Werdefest des Homunculus, sondern dem Natur- und Kunstschönen liegen die gleichen Gesetze der Mütterwelt zugrunde. In der Klassischen Walpurgisnacht wird dargestellt, wie in Helena Naturwerdung und Kunstschöpfung zusammengehören. Natur und Kunst—so war ja die Einsicht der *Italienischen Reise* gewesen—verfahren nach den gleichen Gesetzen; der Künstler verfährt wie die Natur. Unter diesem Blickwinkel betrachtet wird die Mythologie selbst zur Allegorie, zur Allegorie nämlich der schöpferischen Produktivität an sich, ja der Selbstreflexion der Kunst. Im Kult des Werdens, der Vereinigung aller Elemente (8480ff.) geht es um nichts anderes als um das Problem des Bewußten und Unbewußten im Schöpferischen. Faust, "der kühne Magier" (6436), der das Helenabild schafft, steht für die Welt des Produzierens; er will "ins Leben ziehn die einzigste Gestalt" (7439). Kabiren und Galatea stehen in Beziehung zum Eros, der alles durchwaltet (8479), die Telchinen künden vom Kunstwerk (8301–2). Daß die Helenagestalt selber als Modell für eine Geschichte der Kunst gelesen werden kann, hat jüngst Cyrus Hamlin dargestellt, und es verwundert unter dieser Perspektive nicht. Goethe selbst hat in einem Aufsatz in *Über Kunst und Altertum* (Bd. 6, H. 1, 1827) den Gebrauch der griechischen Mythologie damit gerechtfertigt, daß es "dem Dichter erlaubt sein [müsse], auch aus einem solchen Element *Stoff zu seinen Schöpfungen* zu nehmen, welches Recht er sich auf keine Weise wird verkümmern lassen" (66f.; Hervorhebung von mir, C.J.).

Wo Goethe den Mythos aufnimmt, ist er selbst schon Kunst geworden; die Hauptquellen für seine mythologischen Bilder bilden nämlich neben Lexika wie Hederich und Reiseberichten wie jenen des Abbé Barthélémy, neben der Orphik und Homer vor allem Ovid und die antike Tragödie, hier besonders Euripides, von Goethe selbst im Helena-Akt nachgeahmt (z.B. im Gebrauch des Chores, der allgemeingültig-mythisch ist, z. B. den Götterpreis sagt). Eine besondere Rolle spielt die bildende Kunst. "Ohne eine lebenslängliche Beschäftigung mit der bildenden Kunst," sagt Goethe am 21. Februar 1831 gegenüber Eckermann, "wäre es mir nicht möglich gewesen," nämlich das Altertum in dieser Weise wieder lebendig werden zu lassen (Gräf II/2:568). So benutzte er etwa für die Gestaltung des Erdbebengeistes Seismos den Kupferstich "Paulus zu Philippi" nach Raffael, für die Lemuren bildliche Grabdarstellungen, für die Nereidenzüge schließlich römische Sarkophage. Doch höher noch als die bildende Kunst rangiert für Goethe die Dichtung; sie ist der letztlich einzig adäquate Aufbewahrungsort des Mythos in der Moderne. Am Beispiel des Einschmelzens der antiken Götterstatuen aus Gold und Bronze beklagt Goethe durch den Mund des Proteus, daß den "toten Werken" der Kunst nur ein kurzes Leben beschieden sei (8305–12). Im Medium der (nur an die unvergängliche Schrift gebundenen) Dichtung vermag der Mythos dauerhafter zu überleben als in Statuen, wofür Goethe auf ein schon früher öfter benutztes (und von Hegel geliebtes) Symbol zurückgreift: als Helena, das Urbild des Mythos ("das ewige Wesen, Göttern ebenbürtig," 7440), entschwunden ist, bleibt ihr Gewand als Wolke zurück, Zeichen für das Göttliche im Irdischen.

Die Emphase, mit der Goethe die Dichtung als den wahren Ort des Mythos unterstreicht, hat eine Spitze auch gegen die Wissenschaft. Die philologische Mythenforschung der (romantischen) Zeit verfällt der Ironie, vor allem an der Stelle, wo es um die Berechnung des Lebensalters Helenas geht. Diese Berechnung, etwa auf zehn Jahre (Theseus hat die Zehnjährige geraubt), wird als Selbstbetrug der "Philologen " gebrandmarkt, dergegenüber die Alterslosigkeit Helenas, ihre ewige Jugend ins Feld geführt wird. Dieses Mysterium der Zeitlosigkeit ist nun einzig das Produkt dichterischer Arbeit (7429): "Den Poeten bindet keine Zeit" (7433). Diese Ironie gegenüber der aufkommenden wissenschaftlichen Mythenforschung seiner Zeit—Goethe spricht einmal gegenüber Eckermann von "Piquen," die er "so von den besonderen Gegenständen abgelöst und in's Allgemeine gespielt [habe], daß es zwar dem Leser nicht an Beziehungen fehlen, aber niemand wissen wird, worauf es eigentlich gemeint ist" (Gräf II/2:548)—ist auch bei der Schilderung der Kabiren am Werk, indem hier die Philologie mit dem olympischen Sein konfrontiert wird (bisher bekannt sind nur sieben, so bei Creuzer und Schelling, der achte "west im Olymp," 8196–99). Das Wesen der Mythologie, nämlich die Verwandlungsfähigkeit und ständige Umgestaltung (auf die heutzutage auch Blumenberg das Gewicht legt), ist nicht wissenschaftlich, sondern einzig mit den Mitteln der künstlerischen Produktivität adäquat zu erfassen. "Weder Mythologie noch Legenden," so Goethe, "sind in der Wissenschaft zu dulden. Lasse man diese den Poeten. . ." (HA 8:301). Eine Wiederbelebung mythischer Gestalten und Geschehnisse ist nur auf dem Wege über die dichterische Einbildungskraft möglich. Goethe sieht es als unveräußerliches "Recht des Dichters" an, "Geschichte in Mythologie zu verwandeln" und "Mythologie nach Belieben umzubilden" (Gedenkausgabe 14:838).

Liest man den *Faust* insgesamt als Kritik des neuzeitlichen Menschen, der autonom, voraussetzungslos die Wahrheit der Dinge begreifen zu können glaubt, und sieht man die symbolische Form des zweiten Teils als Medium der Kritik dieser Faustischen Unmittelbarkeit, so läßt sich auch die Behandlung des Mythos als ein Element dieser Kritik verstehen. Das Göttliche wird dem späten Goethe zum großen Leitthema seines dichterischen Forschens: die Welt wird in ihrer Gleichnishaftigkeit erkannt; für des späten Goethe sinnbildliches Welterleben kann die Wahrheit nur vermittelt ergriffen werden: die Welt fordert Beschränkungen, der Mensch ist auf das Zwischenreich des Trüben und Farbigen angewiesen (4727). Dieses Angewiesensein spiegelt sich auch in der Symbolstruktur des zweiten Teils, in dem Faust nicht mehr der Mittelpunkt ist, sondern dessen Bilder jeweils das Wesen eines Weltkreises widerspiegeln. Hier bilden Mütter-Mythos, Leda-Traum und Meerfest sowie Helena eine große Symbolreihe, in wechselseitiger Spiegelung verbunden. Nehmen wir noch den Schluß der *Faust*-Dichtung (der nicht zur ursprünglichen Konzeption gehörte) hinzu, der eine eigenständige Betrachtung verdiente, so ließe sich die gesamte Dichtung als ein großer Mythos verstehen, dem in *Wilhelm Meisters Wanderjahren* der Makarien-Mythos entspricht, in dem Goethes Forderungen nach "Verselbstung" und "Entselbstung" versöhnt sind.

ANMERKUNG

Dieser Essay ist eine Fortführung früherer Studien des Verfassers; vgl. "Vom 'Garten des Alcinous' zum Weltgarten. Goethes Begegnung mit dem Mythos im aufgeklärten Zeitalter," *Goethe-Jahrbuch* 105 (1988): 93–114; *Einführung in die Philosophie des Mythos: Neuzeit und Gegenwart* (Darmstadt: Wissenschaftliche Buchgesellschaft, 1991). Angesichts der Fülle der Forschung und des beschränkten Raumes wird im folgenden Text auf eine Auseinandersetzung mit der Forschung bewußt verzichtet; dankbar sei aber verwiesen auf den neuen Sammelband: *Aufsätze zu Goethes "Faust II,"* hg. v. Werner Keller (Darmstadt: Wissenschaftliche Buchgesellschaft, 1991).

Martin Esslin

Goethe's *Faust*: Pre-Modern, Post-Modern, Proto-Postmodern

IF, AS THE TITLE OF THIS PAPER INDICATES, I shall try to look at *Faust* in the light of one of the currently fashionable terms—the postmodern—it is not because I am much inclined to the use of such concepts. Yet I do think that in this case looking at it in relation to some of the ideas connected with the postmodern might open up a slightly different perspective on the subject of *Faust*.

All terms including the prefix post- or pre-something are by their nature highly relative; they merely describe a temporal relationship (the same applies to terms like *avantgarde*), they thus contain no truly descriptive element. That something came after something else cannot define its nature. How long is a piece of string? Moreover—and that seems to me a more dangerous aspect of the matter—the very use of such prefixes implies a linear view of history, implies also that what comes after replaces something else and, by very strong implication, is better than what it replaces, so there is a built-in ideology of relentless progress in the use of such terms. They also emphasize that there is an element of fashion in their use. You wear today's fashion not because it is an advance on the previous one, but simply because it is different. The newest is seen as the best, even in some academic quarters. And yet, paradoxically, it is the old that lasts longest that has the best chance to become part of the canon, the standard for value judgments.

And, of course, history does not proceed on linear trajectories, what was in existence today is never wholly replaced by what comes after; this is particularly true in the field of art, where different styles and forms coexist side by side for centuries. Recourse to the argument: "that was yesterday's style," or in scholarship "that was yesterday's truth or theory," seems to me exceedingly foolish.

In fact, of course, what is nowadays cried up as the very latest thing is most frequently as old as the world itself. Indeed, as Mephistopheles himself remarks:

> Wer kann was Dummes, wer was Kluges denken,
> Das nicht die Vorwelt schon gedacht? (6809–10)

And as the semiotician Umberto Eco–by no means a *laudator temporis acti*–has pointed out:

> I believe postmodernism is not a trend to be chronologically defined, but, rather, an ideal category–or, better still, a *Kunstwollen*, a way of operating. We could say that every period has its own postmodernism, just as every period would have its own mannerism. . . .
>
> The postmodern reply to the modern consists of recognizing that the past, since it cannot really be destroyed, because its destruction leads to silence, must be revisited: but with irony, not innocently. [...] If "postmodern means" this it is clear why Sterne and Rabelais were postmodern, why Borges surely is. . . .[1]

In that sense, I believe, it is of some interest to look at a work like Goethe's *Faust* with these considerations in mind; such a perspective might shed some light on some of its aspects. Of course, the term postmodern itself is extremely vague and shifting; yet it does circumscribe a certain bundle of characteristics. As one of the chief originators of the present currency of the term, Jean-François Lyotard has it, its main characteristic is a deep suspicion of systems for explaining the workings of the world, of what he calls "metarécits," attempts to present the essence of the world in one all-embracing, totalizing narrative: "on tient pour 'post-moderne' l'incrédulité a l'égard des métarécits."[2] Instead of attempting to encompass the world in one narrative–whether ideology, cosmology, philosophical or religious system–the postmodern confines itself to treating separate aspects of reality, each through its own Wittgensteinian "language game":

> Il y a beaucoup de jeux de langage différents, c'est l'heterogénie des éléments. Ils ne donnent lieu à l'institution que par plaques, c'est le déterminisme local.[3]

Renunciation of totalizing system-building and rejection of attempts at over-arching consistency of language, tone or style is clearly one of the most important characteristics of the concept. Combine this with the tendency to ironize the past and to parody its manifestations, and we get the amalgam of different tendencies enumerated by the editor and compiler of an anthology of modernist and postmodernist essays:

> Postmodernism, we can say, splices high with low culture, it raids and parodies past art, it questions all absolutes, it swamps reality in a culture of recycled images, it has to do with deconstruction, with consumerism, with television and the information society, with the end of communism. . . . (Brooker 3)

In the light of these approaches towards a delimitation of the vague and shifting field covered by the concept of the postmodern, Goethe's *Faust*, it seems to me, finds its secure place among the past masterpieces that Eco refers to in his evocation of something like the postmodern as a timeless phenomenon in the history of literature.

That *Faust* presents an image of heterogeneity of styles is self-evident and goes without saying. Goethe himself refers to it as "diese Amalgamation"[4]; and that it eschews any abstract meta-narration or moral lesson is equally clear. As Goethe said to Eckermann on 6 May 1827:

> Aber denkt auch nicht immer, es wäre alles eitel, wenn es nicht irgend abstrakter Gedanke und Idee wäre!

> Da kommen sie und fragen, welche Idee ich in meinem *Faust* zu ver-körpern gesucht. Als ob ich das selber wüßte und aussprechen könnte! *Vom Himmel durch die Welt zur Hölle*, das wäre zur Not etwas; aber das ist keine Idee, sondern Gang der Handlung. . . .

> Es war im Ganzen, fuhr Goethe fort, nicht meine Art, als Poet nach Verkörperung von etwas *Abstraktem* zu streben. Ich empfing in meinem Innern *Eindrücke* sinnlicher, lebensvoller, lieblicher, bunter, hundertfältiger Art, wie eine rege Einbildungskraft es mir darbot; und ich hatte als Poet weiter nichts zu tun, als solche Anschauungen und Eindrücke in mir künstlerisch zu runden und auszubilden und durch eine lebendige Dar-stellung so zum Vorschein zu bringen, daß Andere die selbigen Eindrücke erhielten, wenn sie mein Dargestelltes hörten oder lasen.

Nor can there be the slightest doubt that *Faust* raids and parodies past art. Goethe himself referred to his borrowings repeatedly. And that such citations and references were introduced with conscious irony is repeatedly made clear in the text itself, as in Mephistopheles's comment on Faust's destruction of Philemon and Baucis's domain:

> Auch hier geschieht, was längst geschah,
> Denn Naboths Weinberg war schon da. (11286–87)

Self-reflexive playfulness—one of the main characteristics not only of postmodern literature, but above all also of postmodern architecture—is one of the chief characteristics of *Faust*. In a late letter to Sulpiz Boisserée (24 November 1831) Goethe referred to the play as a series of "ernstgemeinte Scherze." Nor is it a coincidence that in the "Vorspiel auf dem Theater" the actor who is clearly meant later to play Mephistopheles appears as "Lustige Person." It is Mephistopheles who introduces the self-reflexive and parodistic tone to much of the "tragedy" (in which connection it will perhaps be legitimate to raise the question whether, in spite of the subtitles of both parts, the play fits into a rigorous definition of "tragedy" at all. I'll come to that in due course).

The frequent shifts in the text from high comedy to great poetic seriousness are just one aspect of the proto-postmodern heterogeneity of the work. Much more to the point is its approach in mixing elements of high and low culture, great poetry with strong elements of "Trivialliteratur," that is, above all vulgarisms, and a whole series of forms that come from the areas of daily literary consumerism, occasional verse, topical allusions, etc.

In a work that has acquired—largely also by highly selective use of extracts in school curricula—the aura of being the pinnacle of "high" literature, this aspect, at least in the popular consciousness, is frequently overlooked. But, of course, in the work itself it is very prominently stressed, above all in the "Vorspiel auf dem Theater," which promises not only high poetry but in many ways more strongly stressed, spectacle and entertainment. This prologue is a veritable catalogue of highly relevant proto-postmodern ideas, it even anticipates such contemporary critical trends as *Rezeptionsästhetik*. And it clearly, in enlisting an idealistic poet and a crowd-pleasing comedian to collaborate with an entrepreneur bent on making the maximum amount of profit, embodies the postmodern tendency towards obliterating the dividing line between high and trivial art, between Pindar and the Marx Brothers.

In Goethe's *Faust*, for example, the emphasis on sheer spectacle seems to me to point in this direction. Even though the play may perhaps have been conceived as a *Lesedrama*, there certainly is a great deal of effort in it to create spectacular images in the reader's imagination. As the theater manager puts it in the "Vorspiel auf dem Theater":

> Besonders aber laßt genug geschehn!
> Man kommt zu schaun, man will am liebsten sehn.
> Wird vieles vor den Augen abgesponnen,
> So daß die Menge staunend gaffen kann,
> Da habt Ihr in der Breite gleich gewonnen,
> Ihr seid ein vielgeliebter Mann. (89–94)

Much happening, much to be seen, these are clearly elements of low rather than high art doctrine. But even more in line with postmodern tendencies of today is the theater manager's emphasis on heterogeneity, a mixture of styles and genres, the very postmodern mixing of heterogeneous elements, the abandonment of a unified "meta-narrative," artistic style or ideological party line:

> Die Masse könnt Ihr nur durch Masse zwingen,
> Ein jeder sucht sich endlich selbst was aus.
> Wer vieles bringt, wird manchem etwas bringen;
> Und jeder geht zufrieden aus dem Haus.
> Gebt Ihr ein Stück, so gebt es gleich in Stücken!

Solch ein Ragout, es muß Euch glücken;
Leicht ist es vorgelegt, so leicht als ausgedacht.
Was hilft's, wenn Ihr ein Ganzes dargebracht,
Das Publikum wird es Euch doch zerpflücken. (95–103)

And, as though he might be thinking of the present-day audience of the mass media, the theatrical entrepreneur develops a picture of the lack of concentration and varied conditions under which the audience approaches the spectacle:

Und seht nur hin, für wen Ihr schreibt!
Wenn diesen Langeweile treibt,
Kommt jener satt vom übertischten Mahle,
Und, was das Allerschlimmste bleibt,
Gar mancher kommt vom Lesen der Journale.
Man eilt zerstreut zu uns, wie zu den Maskenfesten,
Und Neugier nur beflügelt jeden Schritt;
Die Damen geben sich und ihren Putz zum besten
Und spielen ohne Gage mit.
Was träumet Ihr auf Eurer Dichterhöhe?
Was macht ein volles Haus Euch froh?
Beseht die Gönner in der Nähe!
Halb sind sie kalt, halb sind sie roh.
Der, nach dem Schauspiel, hofft ein Kartenspiel,
Der eine wilde Nacht an einer Dirne Busen.
Was plagt ihr armen Toren viel,
Zu solchem Zweck, die holden Musen?
Ich sag' Euch, gebt nur mehr und immer, immer mehr,
So könnt Ihr Euch vom Ziele nie verirren.
Sucht nur die Menschen zu verwirren,
Sie zu befriedigen, ist schwer– – (112–32)

The Herr Direktor thus is an exponent of the philosophy of the moguls of the mass media of our own time. There is satire in this, but there can be little doubt that Goethe himself was not disinclined to regard his own efforts in this light; he clearly endeavored in the vast plan for his work (which was ripening at this period, when he was preparing the text of Part I for publication) to provide the maximum of variety, elevated thought but also ribald humor and a good deal of sheer spectacle, eternal ontological problems mixed with bitter contemporary satire and barbed comment on literary and scientific controversies. And although the idealistic and high-flown poet makes a good case for high and pure art, the general verdict of the prologue seems to me to be in favor of spectacle, humor, and crowd-pleasing variety:

Drum schonet mir an diesem Tag
Prospekte nicht und nicht Maschinen. (233–34)

This stress on the heterogeneity of levels of seriousness, style, elements of high and low culture, embodies a definite desire to please a large mass audience as much as an elite stratum of high intellectuals. Here Goethe was following in the footsteps of those great masters of the past who had managed to combine the highest and the lowest aspects of the tastes of their times–Shakespeare, Cervantes, Lope de Vega, Rabelais–and thus avoided the–to my mind–very dangerous separation between highbrows and lowbrows in a culture.

If Part I takes its material from the most popular of popular forms, the *Volksbuch* and the *Puppenspiel,* and in its verse form consciously aims for the doggerel meter of *Knittelvers,* if it descends to low clowning in Auerbach's Keller and to pageantry and some obscenity in the Walpurgisnacht, and to topical almost cabaret forms in the intermezzo of Oberon's and Titania's golden wedding, Part II goes in for even more radical shifts, producing not only in the Helena episode a work that, in Eckermann's words (with which Goethe agreed), "als Tragödie anfängt und als Oper endet" (25 January 1827). What strikes me as the most outstanding element of "popular" low culture in Part II is the great influence which Goethe's activity as master of the revels at Weimar has had on its form: much of Part II echoes the form of the *Maskenzug,* allegorical procession, *fête champètre, tableaux vivants* which, though of course mainly part of court amusements, still clearly fall into a category of "low" culture, pure entertainment; witness the remark by the Direktor in the "Vorspiel auf dem Theater," who, to characterize the low receptivity of some of the spectators, mentions that "man eilt zerstreut zu uns, wie zu den Maskenfesten" (117). This type of presentation, between the masked ball and a theatrical performance, might be compared to the processions of floats in a Mardi Gras parade, but also to the dance and production numbers in present-day musicals.

Much of Part II from the big masque at the Emperor's court to the classical Walpurgisnacht (which is clearly greatly influenced by allegorical pageants and processions) to the allegorical figures of the three wild men entering in procession, even to the comical combat between angels and devils at the very end, derives from this form of popular entertainment. This form of spectacle in which emblematic costumes and equally emblematic verses are used to characterize a multitude of apparitions whose nature the spectator has to use his ingenuity to guess, does tend towards opera and ballet: the Euphorion episode in the Helena tragedy clearly falls under this heading, while the final scene of the ascent of Faust's soul comes from oratorio.

The presence of such popular, low-art forms does, of course, not imply that the whole of *Faust* was designed for a mass taste. Indeed, at the period concerned, the very idea of mass taste was as yet inconceivable. The reading public, for whom *Faust,* clearly a *Lesedrama,* was originally conceived, comprised only the relatively small literate public. But even within that circle there were elements more interested in the more entertaining, the more topical aspects of a work—and *Faust* provided a very judicious mixture of all these elements.

There remains from the list of characteristics that I have quoted and which attempts to map at least the vague contours of what could be termed "the post-modern" the equally vague term "deconstruction," another concept highly fashionable today, and used in a multitude of contradictory applications. One of these starts from the insight that any text merely receives meaning from the consciousness of its reader, that there is no such thing as an abstract, "metaphysical" and ultimately uniquely valid interpretation. The heterogeneity and stylistic variety of the text thus serves to produce a multitude of individually different responses:

> Dann wird bald dies, bald jenes aufgeregt,
> Ein jeder sieht, was er im Herzen trägt. (178–79)

Goethe has expressed this proto-postmodernist idea elsewhere, notably in a passage at the beginning of Book 16 of *Dichtung und Wahrheit* which describes his reaction to reading Spinoza:

> Denn daß niemand den andern versteht, daß keiner bei denselben Worten dasselbe was der andere denkt, daß ein Gespräch, eine Lecture bei verschiedenen Personen verschiedene Gedankenfolgen aufregt, hatte ich schon allzu deutlich eingesehen. . . . (HA 10:78)

Moreover, as I understand it—and I am of course subject to correction—the essence of the deconstructive method lies in discovering the contradictions immanent, inevitably immanent, within any text. That, of course, is a hermeneutic method reserved for the critic approaching that text. Yet at times the text itself already displays and proclaims its own deconstructive process. I believe that *Faust*, with its vast span of sections originating at different periods of its author's long life-span, and with the presence of the "Geist, der stets verneint" as one of its protagonists, presents a brilliant example of a self-deconstructing text. The contradictions are planted there by the author himself, quite apart from those that may have escaped his own intention or notice.

The genre definition of the title as a tragedy is itself a contradiction in terms: God, in seeming to accept Mephistopheles's bet at the outset, already guarantees the happy outcome; from the very beginning we must know, God being omnipotent, that Faust will be saved. "Du darfst auch hier nur frei erscheinen," thus Faust's redemption is guaranteed from the outset. Nor do Faust's own attitudes or his own actions make him a true tragic hero; in fact, he appears throughout as a very passive figure, allowing himself to be manipulated in the most blatant manner. Gretchen, who might be seen as the tragic heroine of Part I, also never actually confronts the deep moral choice that characterizes the classical concept of the tragic hero. The same applies to the heroine of what is usually termed the

Helena tragedy in Part II—she too is wholly passive and, although her story here too is sad because she too loses her child, that does not make her fate a tragedy.

Even more openly contradictory are the metaphysical premisses of the play: Faust himself does not have very deep religious beliefs in the God of the "Prologue in Heaven." His real objective throughout is to comprehend and be equal to the *Erdgeist*, the personified embodiment of a pantheistic concept of Nature. But this secondary deity gradually departs from the scene. On the other hand the whole pantheon of Greek classical mythology is resurrected and treated as real in Part II, albeit in an ironic self-reflexive and "postmodern" manner.

Indeed, the whole metaphysical framework of the play is more than once shown up as a mere external scaffolding onto which to hang the varied images that the play conjures up. The very concept of the immortality of the soul, on which the pact that sets it all in motion hinges, is very clearly called into doubt. As Mephistopheles remarks after Faust's death when the chorus exclaims, "Es ist vorbei":

> Vorbei! ein dummes Wort.
> Warum vorbei?
> Vorbei und reines Nicht, vollkommnes Einerlei!
> Was soll uns denn das ew'ge Schaffen!
> Geschaffenes zu nichts hinwegzuraffen!
> "Da ist's vorbei!" Was ist daran zu lesen?
> Es ist so gut, als wär' es nicht gewesen,
> Und treibt sich doch im Kreis, als wenn es wäre.
> Ich liebte mir dafür das Ewig-Leere. (11595–11603)

And yet, immediately afterwards, he is engaged in battle to catch the soul whose survival after death he has just denied.

Pointing to these inconsistencies is not meant as a criticism of the work. On the contrary: it is to emphasize its richness and its profundity, precisely because it recognizes the coexistence of different cosmologies, ideologies, explanations of the world, and sets them up in a fruitful dialectic of contradictions which each individual reader or spectator has to come to terms with on his own. The coexistence of contradictory ideas and explanations mirrors the situation in the real world as seen in post-modernist discourse; different language games exist next to each other and interact, each of them remaining, however, self-contained. What is true within the language game initiated by Aquinas and Dante, and which underlies Faust's final apotheosis, is completely different from the language game that Mephistopheles uses in his conviction that "alles, was entsteht, / Ist wert, daß es zugrunde geht; / Drum besser wär's, daß nichts entstünde," and different again from the ambit of mythological allegories of all kinds.

Goethe himself was very conscious of this, and in that sense very much on the lines of the "postmodern." As he himself put it in his epilogue, "Abkündigung":

Den besten Köpfen sei das Stück empfohlen!
Der Deutsche sitzt verständig zu Gericht.
Wir möchten's gerne wiederholen,
Allein der Beifall gibt allein Gewicht.
Vielleicht, daß sich was Beßres freilich fände.–
Des Menschen Leben ist ein ähnliches Gedicht:
Es hat wohl Anfang, hat ein Ende,
Allein ein Ganzes ist es nicht.
Ihr Herren, seid so gut und klatscht nun in die Hände![5]

And indeed *Faust*, which mirrors a whole life's experience stretching from that of a tempestuous iconoclastic youth to the serenity of old age, derives its greatest strength from the wide variety of styles, genres, mythological systems, poetical discourses and language games which it accommodates in its intricate structure of dialectically opposed and yet stimulatingly coexisting frameworks. The true insight, the ultimate message is the ultimately unsayable and ineffable which emerges at the interstices and intersections of these multiple language games. Goethe's *Faust* thus presents a very "post-modern" type of structure in which different metaphors for human existence and the world interact, overlap, and stand side by side. And that, in itself, is a powerful metaphor for the complexity, impenetrability, and mystery of a world that defies all attempts to reduce it to a single system or story.

Alles Vergängliche
Ist nur ein Gleichnis.
Das Unzulängliche
Hier wird's Ereignis.

NOTES

1. Umberto Eco, "Postmodernism, Irony, the Enjoyable," in *Modernism/Postmodernism*, ed. Peter Brooker (London, New York: Longmans, 1992) 226–27.

2. Jean-François Lyotard, *La Condition Postmoderne: rapport sur le savoir* (Paris: Les Editions de Minuit, 1979) 7.

3. Lyotard 8.

4. Letter to Schiller of 10 September 1800.

5. Quoted according to Berliner Ausgabe 8:549.

personified usage; and avoided target-language equivalents naively literal or inappropriately connotative.

For the most part, then, I have found that recent translations are reasonably accurate, and I agree with the clear majority of reviewers of those I have seen reviewed that most convey with remarkable faithfulness, and often, like that of the distinguished Romanian poet Doinaş, with great felicity, what Goethe says in *Faust* and the various ways in which he does so (although, as I shall explain, they do not necessarily convey it fully, or convey only it, even when they purport to do so). This success is best explained, I believe, by the fact that recent translators—all but three of the thirty-six whose careers I have been able to identify—have been not amateurs (as were the majority of *Faust* translators until the middle of this century) but professionals, two-thirds being already experienced translators, Germanists (most often Goethe specialists), and comparatists, and one-third well-established men and women of letters. The remarkable exactness achieved by Scandinavian and Balto-Slavic translators seems to reflect a still traditional emphasis on thorough philological training, but that scholarly competence of any kind is no hindrance to excellent literary translation must also be recognized, as it is, for example, by the French poet Eugène Guillevic in supplementary matter (p. 207) of the chiefly prose Benoin translation to which he, however, contributed especially felicitous verse passages.

The century and a half old ideal of translating *Faust* "in the original meters" (by which the now "classic" late Victorian translator and extremely minor poet Bayard Taylor meant also keeping the rhyme schemes of the original, although even he took liberties with both), has continued to have orthodox adherents—most consistently in Walter Arndt, with the consequence that his 1976 English version reminded Harry Levin "of Ben Jonson's remark about *The Faerie Queene*: 'Spenser writ no language.' "[2] Other translators who claim to be metrically orthodox prove on inspection to take more liberties with rhyme and meter than did less recent translators, with David Luke even deliberately abandoning Goethe's basically linear rhythmic pattern—skillfully kept by transposition of textual elements in many recent versions—for the more "modern" effect that enjambement can add. Metrical orthodoxy has, however, recently had proportionally fewer adherents than hitherto for two very simple reasons: the first, beyond the translators' control, is the fact that they represent target languages without proper equivalents for Goethe's verse forms and metrical systems (i.e., even less properly equivalent than English, French, Spanish, or Italian); and the second, more specifically of interest to readers, writers, and speakers of almost all Indo-European languages, is the fact that in most of them (I believe) contemporary feeling no longer equates poetry or the poetic with metrical virtuosity—indeed, in some languages serious drama and drama in verse are no longer identical, while rhymed drama in particular has to all intents and purposes ceased to be a viable literary form (especially in English, where it seems to have survived only in the so-called lyrics of popular music-theater).

The first translators of *Faust* used prose, some recognizing that Goethe's verse forms would be incongruous in their own language, others simply despairing of their successful imitation, and still others—most notably Coleridge—considering Goethe's rhymes and meters so unfunctional as to be best simply ignored. It was not long, however, before rhymed-verse translations inspired by such Romantic examples as those of Shelley and Nodier became the norm, and it was only toward the middle of this century that unrhymed translations enjoyed a resurgence of popularity—at first in prose (Italian, American English, French, Spanish) and then in metered verse, like that of Randall Jarrell's *Faust I*, which often reproduce the many-faceted poetic-stylistic richness of Goethe's text far more faithfully than does verse scrupulously imitating its incidental formal features. Of the three recent French *Fausts* two are in prose, with one of these using metrically non-traditional verse for sung texts; of the eight recent English *Fausts*, only four are in rhymed verse—that of the orthodox Arndt, those of Prudhoe and MacDonald (who openly take great liberties with its use), and that of David Luke with its deliberate updating of and improving on Goethe's metrics. Of the three recent Spanish *Fausts*, that of the Uruguayan writer and teacher Galmés is in prose—a prose, incidentally, that captures the stylistic and tonal variety of *Faust I*, I think, better than do any of its verse or prose predecessors in Spanish known to me—while those of Gálvez and Valverde are in verse that is almost always unrhymed.

Translation into astonishingly exact equivalents of Goethe's verse forms continues to be the practice when the target languages—e.g., the Balto-Slavic or Romanian—are syntactically freer than those just mentioned; the consequent versificatory virtuosity nevertheless still often entails a loss of Goethean ease of expression. Accordingly, the faithful reproduction of Goethe's prosody in Antochewicz's extraordinarily accurate—in good part, thanks to sacrificing rhymes—*Faust* of 1978 has been blamed for an artificiality of syntax and unnaturalness of expression that makes it inferior to the older Polish translation of Konopka,[3] and although Stanišev's *Faust* of 1980 has despite an un-Goethean overuse of enjambement been hailed as the best in Bulgarian to date, it has been found flawed—but to a much slighter degree—for the same reason.[4] Certainly Sandauer's adherence to original rhyme schemes makes for diminished semantic accuracy in his 1987 Polish *Faust I*.

No less potentially inhibitory to satisfactory translation than prosodic accuracy is—and this assertion may surprise those who know that I, like Randall Jarrell and Eugène Guillevic, believe that a modern *Faust* must be in free or metered verse—the ideal of semantic accuracy: the temptation to try to convey in the target language every shade of tone and meaning of the original text. With either verse or prose the inevitable consequence is extended periphrase, semi-reduplication, qualifying modification—in short, diffusive expansion that makes *Faust* in translation poetically more dilute and (to the extent that it is in form a tragedy) dramatically less concentrated than in its original German. Only translators deliberately shortening Goethe's text to produce workable stage versions—e.g., Benoin and MacDonald, or less recently (and less obviously) Barker Fairley—avoid such diffuseness almost entirely, although then almost always with a regrettable loss of poeticality or poetic intensity and of that tonal equivalency considered by Malaplate any good translation's *sine qua non.*

In the *Faust* of Malaplate, hailed I think rightly by our late Germanist colleague André Banuls (whose clever fragmentary 1980 translation of "Prolog im Himmel" into medieval Latin many will no doubt know) as the best French translation of the entire–actually a few verses are inadvertently omitted–text to date, the principle of line-for-line equivalency is almost always strictly followed–in good part, in fact, as Malaplate explains, to force him to be poetically concise. Nonetheless, in his French Goethe's tetrameters usually become deca- or hendecasyllabics (though apparently never *vers communs*), pentameters expand into alexandrines, and iambic trimeters metamorphose into amorphous lines with as many as twenty syllables–a textual expansion by twenty or twenty-five percent that is characteristic of all verse-for-verse translations I have seen (e.g., that of David Luke, which lacks the concision of his translations of Goethe's lyrics) except those in Lithuanian (a Latinately terse language), Romanian (also somewhat Latinate), and the richly monosyllabic modern Scandinavian languages. A more solidly printed verse page than that of Goethe's German text is thus the commonest evidence of non-concision, but even when verses are not longer in the target language than in the original German a line-for-line translator will occasionally expand one verse into two (Malaplate not infrequently, Stanišev occasionally, Luke once). The most deceptive printed page of any translation I have seen is that of Živojinović's Serbo-Croatian (Ekavian) version of *Faust I*: only by being some 222 verses or almost five percent longer than Goethe's German is simultaneous semantic and prosodic equivalency with it achieved; that Živojinović himself subsequently came to recognize that diffuseness mars translation may be inferred from what he published of *Faust II* five years later, where his text is only one percent longer than Goethe's. Sëmucha too becomes terser as he translates Part II into Belorussian, and an analogous development is discernible in the fact that, in contrast to his earlier almost exactly verse-for-verse-equivalent *Faust I*, André Bjerke's recent Norwegian *Faust II* exhibits a possibly unique phenomenon: the not infrequent substituting of shorter verses for ones longer in the original, so that any expansions at some point for semantic or prosodic accuracy are balanced out by laconism elsewhere. All too often, however, the compulsion to be accurate results only in needless expansion, as comparison of F.H. Schaefer's 1974 and 1983 Low German *Faust*s demonstrates: "Dat is doch nett vun so en groten Herrn / sölvst mit den Düvel sich so minschlich to besnaken" now ends with an alexandrine instead of the simpler original pentameter "so minschlich mit den Düwel sölvst to snaken," and in the scene "Doom" Gretchen now hears not "de du hest inslapen laten"–half the length of the alexandrine of Goethe it nonetheless adequately translates–but "de dörch dien Schuld in den Dood rinsleep" (which has lost *inslapen*, the exact modern Low German equivalent of the eighteenth-century euphemism for "die," viz. *hinüberschlafen*).

Never has recent translational expansion been as immoderate as it was when John Anster, whose version of *Faust I* appeared in 1835, could gracefully expand seven German verses to fifteen English ones. Some expansions are meant to be, and possibly are, helpful, like the addition of "De diamante ou" before "de asbesto" when the Brazilian Haroldo de Campos, a Walter Benjaminian self-proclaimed laconizer, turns "wär' er von Asbest" into Portuguese—and unlike his tautological "hippopotomo do Nilo" for *Nilpferd.* A similar addition—less useful, but perhaps making the passage more meaningful to people today—is Sëmucha's turning (in his excellent Belorussian translation) of the "Gar mancher" of the verse "Gar mancher kommt vom Lesen der Journale" into "tretsi–krytyk-šarlatan–" and so creating, with an introductory conjunction "A," a whole new line of text. Discreet modernization is absolutely essential if a translation is not to be stillborn, but almost all translators avoid it when its consequence will be a drastic change of tone. Occasionally, however, a shift from simplicity to sophisticated refinement—a relative intratextual modernization of tone—will occur with an unfortunate result, as in David Luke's version of "Es war ein König in Thule," which opens

> There once was a king of Thule,
> Of the far north land of old;
> His dying lady he loved so truly
> She gave him a cup of gold.

Apparently delighted with what seems to me the unhappy and hardly naive-sounding inner rhyme *lady/truly* (demanded by his *Thulè*), Luke transmutes what follows from *Volkslied* into an art song replete with verses like "There was no thing so dear to the king," "And at last, they say, on his dying day" ("they say" is a filler also added, for rhyme with "clay," in v. 2415), "And his son and heir got all his share," "The old man still drank as his life's flame sank," and, finally, "And the sacred cup he raised it up."

Abridged *Faust*s, whether minor reworkings of pre-recent translations like the 1975 "Faust-Salpêtrière" (Part I from Nodier, Part II after Lichtenberger) or new versions like that of Benoin and Guillevic (the former occasionally tricked by his assumption that being a modern Alsatian guarantees correct understanding of Goethe's German), tend to be terse and lively, although when rhyme is used, as in MacDonald's *Part One and Two* of 1988, some translational expansion seems unavoidable. The effectiveness of such abridgements, and of quasi-complete versions whose translators have not pedantically expanded their *Faust*s for the sake of semantic completeness and prosodic accuracy, have persuaded me that the ideal of maximal inclusiveness is self-defeating and results in translations, whether in prose or verse (rhymed *or*—here *mea culpa*—unrhymed verse), so overburdened with poetic data so carefully qualified that they fail more often than they should to convey what, for lack of a better phrase, I would call the feeling of direct immediacy that is the distinguishing feature of so much of Goethe's tragedy.

RECEPTION

Stuart Atkins

Goethe's *Faust* at the Hands of Its Translators:
Some Recent Developments

IN 1949 I REVIEWED THE FIRST INSTALLMENT of Carlo Rudino's Italian-prose version of *Faust,* and since then I have had occasion to comment on dozens of *Faust* translations, chiefly into English. Of all translations to date of *Faust* into Germanic, Balto-Slavic, and Romance languages, one quarter are English, and English continues–this holds true world-wide–to be the language into which *Faust* is most frequently translated. Although it should therefore be possible to generalize validly about recent developments in *Faust* translation with the use of English versions only, I have hesitated to do so because in recent years–which for convenience I arbitrarily took to be the two decades beginning with 1972–there has been a slight decrease in the proportion of English to other new translations. Accordingly, I have examined translations in over a dozen other languages (but not those in eight Eastern ones, in which I have no competence), so that the findings here reported are actually based on a sample comprising well over half of all "recent" *Faust* translations into all languages and should have fairly high statistical validity. In addition, since it is impossible to treat recent developments without some knowledge of what preceded them, the generalizations I offer about new trends are in turn based on close examination of dozens of earlier translations of *Faust* (above all, but by no means exclusively, into English and French) and on considerable familiarity with what critics and scholars have written about them (not infrequently, by the way, in discussions of recent translations too).

But first a word about non-developments. The best or best-known pre-recent *Faust* translations continue to be published with unabated frequency, with nineteenth- and twentieth-century versions in the same language often reappearing almost simultaneously–e.g., Nodier and Lichtenberger, Pelayo Briz and Roviralta-Borrell, Kholodkovskii and Pasternak, Bayard Taylor and Alice Raphael–and with women continuing to constitute fewer than five percent of the translators. Except for Russian and Swedish, the existence of earlier translations, good or bad, has not deterred translating *Faust* anew into any given language, and there have been first translations recently into Belorussian, Chuvash, Malayalam, Low German, and–via a Russian version–Uzbek, to list only non-Far Eastern languages. Although economic factors may explain why earlier translations are often reprinted to the neglect, at times, of superior subsequent ones, there is no doubt that in many countries a goodly segment of the reading public prefers to read older "poetic" texts in more or less old-fashioned versions. However this may be, all the evidence indicates that recently, as earlier, *Faust* continues to become known to an ever greater and broader public and to attract new translators more frequently (averaging figures for the last twenty years against the average for all translations to date) than ever before.

How good is the work of recent translators compared with that of their predecessors? The answer to this question will of course depend upon what the questioner considers good, which in turn will normally mean that a given translation conveys adequately in the target language what the questioner believes to be the sense of the original—that, in other words, the translator has not been guilty of careless omission or ignorant distortion of any important aspect of the text translated. If we momentarily ignore the disputed matter of whether rhyme (which is unmentioned in Goethe's general theory of poetry[1]) is an important feature of *Faust* as a whole, I would answer my question by saying that recent translations are rarely inferior to earlier ones—are, in fact, usually more adequate in most respects and, almost without exception, marred by far fewer elementary errors (something in good part explained, as we shall see, by who recent translators have been, but also importantly contributed to by the availability apparently everywhere of *Faust* in reliable texts with commentaries alerting readers to what are or have become linguistic and lexicographical traps for the unwary; most frequently cited by the translators here discussed is the *Faust* edition of Erich Trunz). Most reviewers of translations are—properly—first and foremost concerned with how idiomatically they read in the target languages; even specialists in the original language rarely examine a translation for elementary errors (the notable exception to this generalization are Slavic Germanists), while men and women of letters (favored by editors of belletristic journals for translation reviewing) often hardly know the original text's language well enough to evaluate accuracy at even the most elementary level. My own generally favorable conclusion about the basic linguistic competence of recent translators is based not on random sampling of familiar or favorite passages of *Faust*, but on systematic examination of twenty-five translation cruxes in Part I, and thirty-five in Part II, from the some twenty versions of it available for autopsy—unfortunately, especially with Part II, ones occasionally omitting either just the crux or else the whole dramatic unit in which it appears, in which cases, however, I always read with particular attention to accuracy other parts of the translations. My samplings enabled me to determine if a translator recognized when *da* means "then" and not "there"; distinguished indicatives from imperatives and subjunctives, and past from present or future tenses; was not misled by now archaic forms, idioms, or meanings; knew the difference between adverb and noun, and adverb and interjection; correctly identified pronoun referents; kept Goethean differentiation between literal and

Despite occasional exceptions, then, recent developments in the history of *Faust* at the hands of its translators seem to suggest that its translations are more exclusively than ever before the work of competent scholars and able creative writers, sensitive to the publics for whom they intend their work and sufficiently appreciative of Goethe's unique achievement to devote years—and sometimes, like Malaplate, almost a lifetime—to a task that is notoriously never properly rewarded, rarely properly acknowledged, and to all intents and purposes unrecognized as even having been done so far as this is—perhaps rightly—of little interest to its beneficiaries if it has been done well.

NOTES

1. See Dorothea Kuhn, "Zu Goethes Theorie der Künste. Mit einem unveröffentlichten Schema Goethes," in: *Goethe Jahrbuch* 78 (1961): 31–48.

2. Harry Levin, review of the Arndt translation, *New York Review of Books* 23 (1976), No. 25.

3. See Grażyna Perepeczo, "Możliwości przekładu dzieła literackiego na przykładzie wybranych tłumaczeń 'Fausta' Goethego," in: *Nurt* (Posen, 1983), No. 3, 34–36.

4. See Žana Nikolova-Gulubova, " 'Faust' na G'ote v prevoda na Krŭst'o Stanišev (Ideĭno i mirogledno osmisliane na legendata za Faust i tragediiata: ot stremežkum delo i ot 'iskam' kum 'triabva')," in: *Literaturna misŭl* 26, No. 4 (1982): 102–21.

FAUST TRANSLATIONS

Translations of *Faust I* and/or *II*, 1972–1990 by language, with translators' names and first publication date; parentheses indicate that Part *I* or *II* is greatly abridged or represented only by one or more excerpts, and asterisks a translation that I have been unable to examine:

I-II Belorussian, Vasil' Sëmucha, 1976.
I-II Bulgarian, Krŭst'o Stanišev (with Simeon Chadžosev), 1980.
*I-II Chinese, Tung Wên-ch'iao, 1982.
*I-II Chinese, Ch'ien Ch'un-ch'i, 1982.
*I Chuvash, N. Andreev-Urchi, 1979.
I-(II) Czech, Olga Mašková, 1985.
I Danish, Jørgen Gustava Brandt, 1984.
II Danish, J.G. Brandt, 1990.
I English, John Prudhoe, 1974.
I-II English, Walter Arndt, 1976.
I English, Robert Lowell, 1976.
I-II English, Stuart Atkins, 1984.

I English, David Luke, 1987.

(I-II) English, Robert D. MacDonald, 1988.

I-II English, John Roth, 1988.

(I-II) French, Nodier's version of *I* and Lichtenberger's of *II* revised by Klaus Michael
    Grüber and Bernard Pautrat, 1975.

(I-II) French, Daniel Benoin and Eugène Guillevic, 1982.

I-II French, Jean Malaplate (with Albert Fuchs for *I*), 1984.

*(I and/or II) Georgian, G. Džordžaneli, 1974.

*I-II Hebrew, Yizhak Kafkafki, 1975.

I-(II) Icelandic, Yngvi Johannesson, 1972.

*I-II Italian, Marcello Veneziani, 1984.

*I-II Italian, R. Hausbrandt, 1987.

I-II Italian, 1988ff. (for and with Giorgio Strehler).

*II Japanese, Tomio Tezuka, 1975.

*I Japanese. Shôzô Inoue, 1976.

*I Japanese, Shô Shibata, 1977.

*I or I-II Korean, Choe Hyeon, 1974.

*I or I-II Korean, Lee Yeong Gu, 1978.

*I Korean, Chong-so Pak, 1982.

(I) Latin, André Banuls, 1980.

*I Latvian, Fedor Poluėketovič Fedorov, 1976.

II Lithuanian, Aleksys Churginas, 1978.

(I) Low German, Friedrich Hans Schaefer, 1974 (revised 1983).

*I-II Malayalam, Mattur Govinda Panikkar, 1983.

II Norwegian, André Bjerke, 1983.

I Polish, Bernard Antochewicz, 1978.

II Polish, B. Antochewicz, 1981.

I Polish, Artur Sandauer, 1987.

I-II Portuguese (Brazil), Silvio Augusto de Bastos Meira, 1976.

(I-II) Portuguese (Brazil), Haraldo de Campos, 1981 (in his volume *Deus e o Diabo no
    "Fausto" de Goethe*, São Paulo).

I-II Romanian, Ştefan Augustin Doinaş, 1982.

*I Serbo-Croatian, Dušan Tomovski, 1977.

*I Serbo-Croatian, Ognjan M. Radović, 1979.

I Serbo-Croatian, Branimir Živojinović, 1980.

(II) Serbo-Croatian, B. Živojinović, 1985.

I Spanish (Uruguay), Hector Galmés, 1972.

I-II Spanish, José María Valverde, 1980.

I Spanish, Pedro Gálvez, 1983.

*I-II Turkish, Hasan Izzettin Dinamo, 1983.

*I-II Uzbek, Erkin Voqhidov (translator from Russian translation), 1972.

Karl Robert Mandelkow

Wandlungen des *Faust*-Bildes in Deutschland

Changes in the Image of Faust in Germany

Hardly any of the great works in world literature has provoked so many con-tradictory interpretations, imitations and parodies as Faust. Surprisingly, no interpretations were published in Goethe's lifetime. But the foundation for later responses was laid in the Romantic search for a modern nationalist myth to express the essence of a new age. The cult of the Faustian that flourished after 1870 as well as the new positivist interest in textual studies were fueled by the discovery of the Urfaust text in 1887. Not until after World War I did scholars focus on aesthetic constellations within the text; after World War II the division of Germany was reflected in the contrasting ideologies informing the text's reception. In recent studies the emphasis has been on the text's distance from all that is modern.

KAUM EINES DER GROSSEN GIPFELWERKE DER Weltliteratur hat derart viele sich widersprechende Deutungen provoziert, wurde zum Anlaß einer so reichen Zahl von Nachahmungen, Nachdichtungen und Parodien wie Goethes *Faust*. Bereits am Ende des 19. Jahrhunderts bildete die schier unübersehbare Flut der *Faust*-Literatur eine eigene Bibliothek, die zu überblicken oder auch nur systematisch zu ordnen die Möglichkeiten eines einzelnen Forschers überfordert hätte. Ange-sichts dieser Situation wurde auf einer Philologentagung 1906 in Hamburg beschlossen, ein enzyklopädisches *Faust*-Werk zu erarbeiten, in dem zu jeder Detailfrage jede bisher vorgeschlagene Antwort erfaßt werden sollte. Das Werk hätte sieben Bände in Lexikonformat umfaßt, kein Verleger fand sich jedoch bereit, sich auf dieses Abenteuer einzulassen, und so blieb der Nachwelt dieses Unikum erspart.[1] Verglichen mit dieser ausufernden Deutungswut des 19. Jahrhunderts, die im 20. Jahrhundert noch um ein Vielfaches übertroffen werden sollte, mag es überraschen, daß zu Goethes Lebzeiten keine einzige Interpretation des Werkes erschienen ist, die noch heute der Beachtung wert gefunden wird oder zum Anknüpfungspunkt späterer Auslegungen hat dienen können. Während für den *Werther* eine reiche Zahl kontroverser Rezeptionszeugnisse vorliegen, die auch heute noch die Diskussion beschäftigen, haben auch die Romane *Wilhelm Meisters Lehrjahre*, die *Wahlverwandtschaften*, *Wilhelm Meisters Wanderjahre* und das Epos *Hermann und Dorothea* in den Abhandlungen von Friedrich Schlegel, Karl Wilhelm Ferdinand Solger, Heinrich Gustav Hotho und Wilhelm von Humboldt Basisdokumente der Rezeption erhalten, die auch der gegenwärtige Interpret mit Gewinn studieren wird und muß. Für den *Faust* fehlt ein solcher Anknüpfungspunkt, genauer gesagt für den ersten Teil, hat Goethe doch bekanntlich den zweiten seinen Zeitgenossen nicht ohne Hintergedanken vorenthalten.

Diese bemerkenswerte Lücke in der sonst so reich dokumentierten Rezeptionsgeschichte Goethes zwischen 1773 und 1832 bedeutet natürlich nicht, daß der erste Teil des *Faust* unbeachtet geblieben ist. Auffällig allerdings ist, daß die bedeutendsten Zeugnisse zur *Faust*-Deutung sich in Briefen, Gesprächsaufzeichnungen und in den großen philosophischen und ästhetischen Werken der Zeit finden, wennschon hier zumeist in kurzen, oft verschlüsselt prophetischen Hinweisen. Die inhaltschwersten Aussagen finden sich in Schellings *Vorlesungen über die Philosophie der Kunst*, die er im Winter 1802/03 an der Universität Jena und im Winter 1804/05 an der Universität Würzburg gehalten hat. Diese Vorlesungen wurden erst 1859 aus dem handschriftlichen Nachlaß des Philosophen veröffentlicht, lagen also als traditionsbildender Text den Zeitgenossen nicht vor! Hier heißt es mit Bezug auf den historischen Faust des Volksbuchs, er sei "unsere mythologische Hauptperson." "Andere teilen wir mit anderen Nationen, diesen haben wir ganz für uns allein, da er recht aus der Mitte des deutschen Charakters und seiner Grundphysiognomie wie geschnitten ist." Über das 1790 erschienene Goethesche *Faust*-Fragment heißt es: "Soweit man Goethes Faust aus dem Fragment, das davon vorhanden ist, beurteilen kann, so ist dieses Gedicht nichts anderes als die innerste, reinste Essenz unseres Zeitalters: Stoff und Form geschaffen aus dem, was die ganze Zeit in sich schloß, und selbst dem, womit sie schwanger war oder noch ist. Daher ist es ein wahrhaft mythologisches Gedicht zu nennen."[2]

Drei Momente sind es, die diesen knappen Bemerkungen eine kaum zu überschätzende Bedeutung für die weitere Geschichte der *Faust*-Rezeption verleihen: 1) der Hinweis auf den Fauststoff als einen spezifisch nationalen; 2) die Behauptung, Goethes *Faust* sei die "innerste, reinste Essenz unseres Zeitalters"; 3) die Überhöhung des Werkes zu einem "wahrhaft mythologischen Gedicht." Das Gewicht dieser Bezeichnung wird nur verständlich, wenn wir sie in den Kontext der Suche der Frühromantik nach einer neuen Mythologie stellen, ein Mythologie-Programm, das das bisherige mythologische Fundament der Dichtung in Antike und Christentum durch einen universalen und zugleich modernen Begründungsrahmen zu überbieten suchte. Dem Fauststoff und seiner Goetheschen Adaption im ersten Teil liege—so Schelling—weder die antike noch die christliche Mythologie zugrunde. Dennoch wird ihm das Prädikat eines "wahrhaft mythologischen Gedichts" zuerkannt. Goethes Gestaltung sei die "reinste Essenz unseres Zeitalters," gleichwohl handelt es sich um einen vormodernen Stoff im strikten Gegensatz zur modernen bürgerlichen Welt der Goetheschen Romane

vom *Werther* an. Mit diesen Paradoxien wird von Schelling, prophetisch aus-
greifend bis in unsere Gegenwart, der poetologisch-geschichtsphilosophische
Sonderstatus des Goetheschen Hauptwerkes begründet. Es ist kein Zufall, daß
diese Basisthesen der gesamten späteren *Faust*-Deutungen im akademischen Milieu
Jenas entwickelt und formuliert worden sind. Will man dem von dem Historiker
Heinrich Luden in seinem Werk *Rückblicke in mein Leben* (1847) mitgeteilten
bekannten *Faust*-Gespräch mit Goethe im August 1806 Glauben schenken, so
hat bereits das in der öffentlichen Kritik weithin unbeachtet gebliebene *Faust*-
Fragment unter den damaligen Jenaer Studenten größte Beachtung gefunden und
zu weitreichenden Spekulationen über eine mögliche Fortsetzung Anlaß gegeben.
In Ludens Bericht finden sich schon Formulierungen, die in der Folgezeit zum
festen Bestand jeder *Faust*-Deutung gehören sollten:

> In der Anschauung dieses Geistes aber erkenne man und müsse man
> erkennen, daß dieses Fragment, Faust genannt, ein Bruchstück aus einer
> großen, erhabenen, ja göttlichen Tragödie sei. In dieser Tragödie, wenn
> sie einst vollendet erscheine, werde der Geist der ganzen Weltgeschichte
> dargestellt sein; sie werde ein wahres Abbild des Lebens der Menschheit
> sein, Vergangenheit, Gegenwart und Zukunft umfassend. In Faust sei die
> Menschheit idealisiert; er sei der Repräsentant der Menschheit.[3]

Auch für den *Faust* bestätigt sich die Tatsache, daß das Goethebild der
Folgezeit wesentlich ein Produkt aus dem Geist der romantischen Poetik und
Geschichtsphilosophie ist. Goethes Faust der "Repräsentant der Menschheit":
diese hier zuerst belegte Formel begleitet als Dominante in zahllosen Variationen
sämtliche *Faust*-Deutungen bis heute. Mit ihr reiht sich das Goethesche Werk
ein in die wenigen großen Archetypen der Weltliteratur, in denen die *condition
humaine* überzeitlich-gültigen Ausdruck gefunden hat. Daß der Stoff zu diesem
Werk nach Meinung Schellings "recht aus der Mitte des deutschen Charakters
und seiner Grundphysiognomie" geschöpft sei, nach Ursprung und Herkunft
nicht mehr den großen Traditionslinien der Antike und dem Christentum ver-
pflichtet, machte den Goetheschen *Faust* zugleich zum idealen Identifikationswerk
für die Deutschen auf ihrem wechselreichen Weg zu einer einheitlichen Nation.
Das am *Faust*-Fragment und am ersten Teil der Dichtung orientierte Deu-
tungsmuster, das vor allem durch die zentrale Stellung der Gretchentragödie für
viele handlungsgehemmte deutsche Intellektuelle ein zusätzliches Moment der
Identifikation mit der Faustfigur wurde, geriet ins Wanken durch die Veröffent-
lichung des zweiten Teils der Dichtung 1832 im ersten Band der *Nachgelassenen
Werke* des Dichters. 1827 war bereits der Helena-Akt im 4. Band der *Ausgabe letzter
Hand* erschienen und ließ etwas von der grundsätzlichen stilistischen Anders-
artigkeit, ja Fremdheit des zweiten Teils der Goetheschen Faustdichtung erahnen.
Der zentrale und am meisten umstrittene Punkt der Auseinandersetzung um
Goethes *Faust* im Zeitraum zwischen 1832 und 1870 wurde die Frage nach dem
Verhältnis des ersten zum zweiten Teil des Werkes, eine Frage, bei der es nur

vordergründig um Probleme der ästhetischen Wertung ging, die vielmehr ins
Zentrum der ideologischen Auseinandersetzung mit dem Dichter führte. Das
Todesjahr Goethes war Kulminationspunkt einer politischen Opposition gegen
den Dichter, der Heinrich Heine 1831 das Schlagwort vom "Ende der Goetheschen Kunstperiode" gegeben hatte.[4] Diese Kritik richtete sich nun auch gegen
den zweiten Teil des *Faust*, dessen esoterisch verschlüsselte Symbolsprache dem
Verständnis der meisten Interpreten verschlossen blieb und dessen Antwort auf
die Fragen und Probleme, die der erste Teil aufgegeben und unbeantwortet
gelassen hatte, den Erwartungen der Zeitgenossen nur höchst bedingt entsprach.
Der Goetheschen Problemlösung antworteten die Dichter und Kritiker des
Vormärz, wie Heinrich Heine, Friedrich Theodor Vischer u.a., mit Alternativ-
konzeptionen, die einer unverhohlenen Mißbilligung der Faustfigur des zweiten
Teils gleichkamen. Erst die Reichsgründung 1870/71 brachte hier die entscheidende Wende. Mit der Einheit der deutschen Nation wurde auch–so kann man
es metaphorisch formulieren–die Einheit der Goetheschen Faustdichtung wieder
hergestellt. Die Goethephilologie des Wilhelminischen Zeitalters schuf ein neues
Interpretationsmodell, das Goethes Version und Gestaltung des Fauststoffs in
beiden Teilen der Dichtung unter dem Aspekt der Problemhomologie als kano-
nisch erklärte und jede Alternativkonzeption und damit auch jede *Faust*-Kritik
für erledigt und unzulässig bezeichnete. Das neue Faust-Bild des Bismarckschen
Reiches hatte Legitimationsfunktion für das neuerwachte und neuerstarkte
Nationalbewußtsein der Deutschen. Die alte Formel, Faust sei der "Repräsentant
der Menschheit," verband sich jetzt mit spezifisch gründerzeitlichen Tugenden
wie entsagungsvolle Arbeit, Tüchtigkeit, unendliches Streben und gesellschaftliche
Tätigkeit. In einer bahnbrechenden Untersuchung zur Wirkungsgeschichte von
Goethes *Faust* im 19. Jahrhundert (1962)[5] hat Hans Schwerte überzeugend
dargelegt, wie seit 1870 die Idee des "Faustischen" und des faustischen Menschen
zur dominanten ideologischen Inanspruchnahme des Goetheschen Werkes wurde,
um dann über Oswald Spenglers *Untergang des Abendlandes* in die *Faust*-Inter-
pretation des Nationalsozialismus einzumünden. Prämisse dieser gründerzeitlichen
Faust-Adaption war die These, daß der Weg der Faustfigur ein Weg fortschreiten-
der Höherentwicklung sei, eine Deutung, die durch ein fast völliges "Verschweigen
der Schuld Fausts" (Schwerte) erkauft war. Die Verdrängung des schuldhaften
Handelns Fausts in der Gretchentragödie und der Philemon-und-Baucis-Szene
im Schlußakt des zweiten Teils wurde vor allem von seiten der christlichen *Faust*-
Kritik geltend gemacht. Dieser Aspekt sollte in der Rezeptionsgeschichte nach
1945 noch einmal eine entscheidende Rolle spielen. Neben der christlichen, vor
allem der katholischen *Faust*-Kritik hat nonkonformistisch Friedrich Nietzsche
seine Stimme gegen den *Faust*-Kult des neuen Reiches erhoben. In bewußter
Trivialisierung und Banalisierung jeglicher mythischer Überhöhung der Faustfigur
heißt es in *Der Wanderer und sein Schatten* (1880):

> Eine kleine Näherin wird verführt und unglücklich gemacht; ein großer
> Gelehrter aller vier Fakultäten ist der Übeltäter. Das kann doch nicht mit

rechten Dingen zugegangen sein? Nein, gewiß nicht! Ohne die Beihülfe des leibhaftigen Teufels hätte es der große Gelehrte nicht zustande gebracht. Sollte dies wirklich der größte deutsche "tragische Gedanke" sein, wie man unter Deutschen sagen hört?[6]

Das wissenschaftliche Interesse der positivistischen Faustphilologie war im Zeitraum zwischen 1870 und 1914 vorrangig an der Entstehungsgeschichte der Goetheschen Faustdichtung interessiert. Dieses Interesse fand durch die Entdeckung des "Urfaust" durch Erich Schmidt (1887) neue Nahrung und ein breiteres Fundament und führte zur Entdeckung der Brüche und Widersprüche eines Textes, der Goethes Leben fast sechzig Jahre lang begleitet hatte. Damit drohte auch die These von der Einheit der beiden Teile des Werkes ins Wanken zu geraten, die jetzt nicht mehr primär in der Werkstruktur selbst, sondern in der Person des Autors, Goethe, gesucht und gefunden wurde. Die Faustdichtung geriet so zum widerspruchsreichen Dokument und Abbild der Biographie Goethes. Dieses autorzentrierte Verfahren korrespondierte mit dem inflationären Aufschwung der Goethebiographien im Kaiserreich. Die Person Goethes wurde zum eigentlichen Identifikationszentrum der Goetherezeption in dieser Epoche, die Werke dienten vornehmlich zur Illustration eines Olympierkults, der bis heute das populäre Bild des Dichters bestimmt.

Die Wendung von einer autorfixierten, die Faustdichtung in "Schichten" der einzelnen Entwicklungsstufen Goethes zerlegenden positivistischen Philologie zur ästhetischen Interpretation des *Faust*-Textes verdanken wir der 1917 erschienenen Abhandlung *Faust, der Tragödie zweiter Teil: Studien zur inneren Form des Werkes* von Helene Herrmann.[7] Ihre subtile, vom Geist des Ästhetizismus des Fin-de-siècle inspirierte Analyse löste den Text des zweiten Teils weitgehend von den Vorgaben des ersten und interpretierte ihn als ein autonomes Gebilde. Die phänomenologische Reduktion ihres Verfahrens auf den Kunstcharakter der Textstruktur blendete alle Bezugnahmen auf biographische, zeitgeschichtliche und soziale Bedingungen aus und vermied auch die Perspektivierung ihrer Untersuchung auf die Entwicklung der Faustfigur. Nicht mehr die Faustfigur als Verkörperung einer "faustischen" Weltanschauung und Weltauslegung standen im Mittelpunkt des Interesses, sondern ästhetisch vermittelte Problemkonstellationen, die das Individuum Faust und dessen psychologischen und gedanklichen Horizont weit hinter sich ließen. Mit dieser Relativierung der Bedeutung der Faustfigur und der Hervorhebung der überindividuellen, transpersonalen Textstruktur des Werkes rückte der zweite Teil des *Faust* in die Nähe einer Entwicklung, die auf dem Gebiet des modernen europäischen Romans zum "Verlust des Helden" führte, eines Romans, der nicht mehr auf die Gestaltung der Geschichte individueller Schicksale gerichtet war sondern auf die Analyse überindividueller Weltauslegungsmuster. Es sollte allerdings noch geraume Zeit dauern bis diese "moderne" Lesart des Werkes sich durchsetzen konnte. So veröffentlicht der Neukantianer Heinrich Rickert 1925 eine einflußreiche programmatische Abhandlung *Die Einheit des Faustischen Charakters: Eine Studie zu Goethes Faustdichtung*,[8] die bereits im Titel die traditionelle Fixierung auf die Person Fausts dokumentiert. In seiner umfassenden Gesamtdeutung des *Faust* von 1932[9] versucht Rickert die Einheit des Werkes aus der Einheit des individuellen Charakters der Faustfigur abzuleiten. Die sogenannte "Einheitsthese," begründet in einem zu diesem Zeitpunkt bereits anachronistischen psychologisch-charakterologischen Individualitätsbegriff, wurde zur polemischen Folie einer in den dreißiger Jahren sich durchsetzenden neuen *Faust*-Deutung, die durch die Namen von Max Kommerell, Kurt May, Dorothea Lohmeyer und Wilhelm Emrich repräsentiert ist. Der avancierteste und für die Folgezeit einflußreichste Versuch in dieser Richtung war das 1943 erschienene monumentale Werk *Die Symbolik von Faust II: Sinn und Vorformen* von Wilhelm Emrich.[10] Es hat die Faustforschung nicht nur, sondern die Goetheforschung insgesamt für mehr als zwei Jahrzehnte bestimmt und beschäftigt. Eine auch nur annähernd zureichende Charakteristik dieser vielschichtigen und voraussetzungsreichen Untersuchung ist im Rahmen dieses Vortrags nicht möglich. Nur einige wenige Stichworte mögen hier genügen. Gegenüber der Einheitsthese von Rickert wird von Emrich, wie vor ihm schon in Ansätzen bei Kommerell und Lohmeyer, eine strikte Trennung zwischen dem ersten und dem zweiten Teil des *Faust* vorgenommen. Der zweite Teil ist für Emrich das Produkt der nachklassischen Kunstpraxis und Kunsttheorie Goethes, die nach 1805 einsetzt und zu einer grundsätzlichen Neuorientierung in ästhetischer und weltanschaulicher Hinsicht führt. Diese "gegenklassische Wandlung" (Hans Pyritz)[11] findet im zweiten Teil des *Faust* ihren kennzeichnendsten Ausdruck in einer konsequenten Entsubjektivierung und Entpsychologisierung der Faustfigur. Das Interesse, das im ersten Teil auf die Faustfigur gerichtet ist, verlagert sich im zweiten auf eine hochkomplexe Struktur der Vernetzung von Symbolketten und Symbolschichten, deren Genese Emrich im Gesamtwerk Goethes aufzuweisen sucht. Ein solches Verfahren würden wir heute als intertextuell bezeichnen. Die Grenzen und Begrenzungen des einzelnen Werkes werden durch eine solche symbolgenetische Interpretation gesprengt zugunsten einer "wechselseitigen Spiegelung" (Goethe) aller Spätwerke Goethes. Es geht Emrich um die Rekonstruktion einer polyphonen Symbolstruktur, die ihr gedankliches Gravitationszentrum in der Dialektik der beiden zentralen Begriffe Natur und Geschichte hat. Für Emrich ist der zentrale Gegenstand von *Faust II* nicht mehr der faustische, in welteroberndem Handeln gipfelnde Titanismus, wie ihn die gleichzeitige faschistische Faustdeutung propagierte, sondern die Selbstreflexion der Kunst im Medium ihrer unterschiedlichen historischen Vorformen seit der Antike.

Mit dem Werk von Emrich hatte die Faustinterpretation den Anschluß an Denk- und Erfahrungsmuster der Moderne im Bereich der Literatur und der Philosophie gefunden, und es war kein Zufall, daß er dem Faustbuch 1958 seine Kafka-Deutung folgen ließ,[12] der das gleiche Verfahren der Symbolinterpretation zugrunde lag.

Mit der Spaltung Deutschlands nach dem Zweiten Weltkrieg und der Errichtung zweier deutscher Staaten im Jahre 1949 verläuft auch die Faustinterpretation in getrennten Bahnen und wird Teil der ideologischen Auseinandersetzungen in den folgenden Jahrzehnten. Während im Westen, nach einer kurzen Phase der kritischen Auseinandersetzung mit dem "Faustischen," die Problemvorgaben der Forschung der dreißiger und vierziger Jahre aufgenommen und weitergeführt wurden und in den beiden für die Nachkriegszeit repräsentativen Faustkommentaren von Erich Trunz (1949) und Ernst Beutler (1950) ihre wirkungsmächtigste Verbreitung fanden,[13] wurde im Osten im Rückgriff auf die *Fauststudien* von Georg Lukács (1940)[14] der Versuch einer radikalen Umwertung der "bürgerlichen" Faustbilder unternommen. Der "Elementarhorizont" der westdeutschen Faustdeutung nach 1945 wurde die These, daß der *Faust* als Tragödie ernst zu nehmen sei und daß Goethes Lösung des tragischen Problems ein dezidiert religiöses und nicht ein gesellschaftlich-politisches sei. Demgegenüber erklärte Lukács unter Rückgriff auf Karl Marx die aus "sich selbst schaffende Tätigkeit" des von allen religiösen Bindungen befreiten Faust zum zentralen Thema des Werkes. Ein entscheidender Differenzpunkt im Vergleich der west-östlichen Faustbilder nach 1945 wurde die Deutung der tragischen Schuld Fausts. Spielte diese Frage in der westdeutschen Forschung eine erhebliche Rolle, so wurde das Schuldproblem in der marxistischen Forschung als historisch bedingte und darum untragische Notwendigkeit neutralisiert und in das positive Bild der Faustfigur als Leit- und Vorbildfigur integriert. Großen Einfluß erlangte die von Lukács begründete und von Ernst Bloch weiterentwickelte These der geschichtsphilosophischen Parallelität von Goethes *Faust* und Hegels *Phänomenologie des Geistes*.[15] Goethe als Dichter und Hegel als Philosoph wurden damit die beiden Säulen der späteren Erbetheorie in der DDR.

Der Weg Fausts als Verkörperung des "unaufhaltsamen Fortschritts im Makrokosmos der Gattung" (Lukács)[16] wurde zur ideologischen Basis der zahlreichen *Faust*-Aufführungen in der DDR, die dieser geschichtsoptimistischen Deutung zu breiter Popularität verhalfen. In Widerspruch zu diesem Faustbild stand die berühmte Aufführung der beiden Teile des *Faust* 1957 und 1958 im Deutschen Schauspielhaus in Hamburg unter der Regie von Gustav Gründgens. In ihr wurde die Faustfigur mit Distanz und Skepsis dargestellt. Eine deutliche Aufwertung dagegen erfuhr die Figur des Mephistopheles, die durch Gründgens ihre kongeniale Realisation fand. In dieser Akzentverlagerung kündigte sich eine folgenreiche Entwicklung in der Geschichte der Klassikeraufführungen in der Bundesrepublik an: die Freiheit des Regisseurs im Umgang mit dem Text, die seit Mitte der sechziger Jahre das sogenannte Regietheater beherrschte und auch Einfluß gewann auf die akademische Klassikerinterpretation. Es ging darum, die alten Texte im Horizont ihrer gegenwärtigen Aktualität zu lesen und zu rezipieren, eine "Faust für uns" zu schaffen, wie es der Theaterkritiker und Theaterwissenschaftler Siegfried Melchinger im Titel seines Kommentars zur Gründgens-Aufführung formulierte.[17] Diese adaptive Wendung von einem "Faust an sich" zu einem "Faust für uns" verteidigte wenige Jahre später auch Richard Friedenthal in seiner vielgelesenen Goethebiographie von 1963 mit dem lapidaren Satz: "Der 'Faust' hat den Sinn, den der Betrachter ihm verleiht."[18] Mit der Unbekümmertheit des philologischen Außenseiters stellte Friedenthal die verbindliche Autorität

des Goetheschen Textes in Frage und verwies auf die Freiheit des Rezipienten,
im Dialog mit der Textvorgabe einen neuen Text zu schaffen, der dem Sinnver-
langen und dem Sinnbedürfnis der eigenen Gegenwart entsprach. Die Rezeptionsästhetik der siebziger Jahre hat dieser immer schon praktizierten, jedoch offiziell
nie eingestandenen Form der Textauslegung einen theoretischen Legitimations-
rahmen zu geben versucht.

Daß die Interpretation eines so komplexen Textcorpus wie die Goethesche
Faustdichtung immer von einer interessengeleiteten Selektion bestimmt ist, wird
im Vergleich zwischen den westlich-bürgerlichen und den östlich-marxistischen
Faustdeutungen besonders deutlich. Stand die bürgerliche Goethedeutung–abstrakt
und verallgemeinernd formuliert–seit der Jahrhundertwende unter dem Primat
des Leitbegriffs "Natur," so die marxistische seit Lukács unter dem der "Geschichte."[19] Emrich hatte als erster die Verbindung und dialektische Verschrän-
kung beider Begriffe zur Achse seiner Faustinterpretation gemacht, wobei die
Transformation von Geschichte in Natur für ihn der Sinn des Werkes und damit
sein überzeitlicher, jedem historischen Relativismus überlegene Geltungsanspruch
war. Der Begriff Natur als primärer Auslegungshorizont des zweiten Teils der
Faustdichtung führte notwendig zur Konzentration des Forschungsinteresses auf
jenen Textbereich, in dem Natur und die mit ihr konnotierten Begriffe wie
Polarität, Entelechie und Steigerung der Goetheschen Naturphilosophie im
Mittelpunkt stehen: den Helena-Akt und die Klassische Walpurgisnacht. Die
Altphilologen Karl Reinhardt und Wolfgang Schadewaldt und die Literaturwissenschaftler und Komparatisten Oskar Seidlin, Horst Rüdiger, Herman Meyer und
Katharina Mommsen haben diesem Textbereich Untersuchungen gewidmet, die
zum bleibenden Ertrag der Faustforschung der letzten fünfzig Jahre gehören. Ein
wesentliches Moment der Faszination, die die Klassische Walpurgisnacht und
die Helena-Handlung auf die westliche Faustforschung ausübte, lag in der
Entdeckung der durch die Leitbegriffe Spiel, Ironie, Reflexivität und Heiterkeit
bestimmten Ästhetik des späten Goethe, in diesen "sehr ernsten Scherzen," wie
Goethe in seinem vermächtnishaften letzten Brief an Wilhelm von Humboldt
den zweiten Teil des *Faust* bezeichnet hat.[20] Diese Poetik des intellektuellen Spiels
wurde zugleich zum Kontrapunkt der pathetisch-ernsthaften, von Ideen und
ethischen Postulaten geleiteten, vergrübelten *Faust*-Deutungen und *Faust*-Inter-
pretationen, die mehr als ein Jahrhundert wie ein Alp auf den Gemütern der
Deutschen gelastet haben. Auf dem Theater erfuhr diese von einer Ästhetik
komödienhafter Heiterkeit bestimmte Deutung des *Faust* ihre spektakuläre
Realisation in der Stuttgarter Aufführung des Werkes 1977 unter der Regie von
Claus Peymann.[21]

Im Unterschied zur Bundesrepublik blieb in der *Faust*-Rezeption in der DDR
die Orientierung am philosophischen Gehalt der Faustdichtung maßgebend,
gipfelnd in der optimistisch gedeuteten Perspektive der Vision des sterbenden
Faust "vom freien Volk auf freiem Grund" am Schluß des Werkes. Dies schloß
die Rechtfertigung der gewaltsamen Liquidierung der Hüttenidylle von Philemon
und Baucis ein, die als historisch notwendiger Sieg der aufstrebenden bürgerlichen

Klasse über einen "religiös-romantischen Konservatismus" (Gerhard Scholz) im Einklang mit der Bodenreform in der DDR bezeichnet wurde.[22] Die Landgewinnungspläne Fausts waren Teil einer selbstverständlich akzeptierten "Beherrschung der Natur," ein Naturverhältnis, das in der DDR noch bis Ende der siebziger Jahre unkritisiert in Geltung stand. Ein erstes Wetterleuchten am bis dahin intakten erbepolitischen Himmel der DDR brachte die Aufführung von *Faust I* am Deutschen Theater in Berlin 1968 in der Inszenierung durch Wolfgang Heinz und Adolf Dresen.[23] Die Vorbildlichkeit und der Repräsentanzcharakter der Faustfigur wurden hier relativiert durch das neue Losungswort "Selbstverwirklichung." Aus dem gefeierten Repräsentanten der Gattung Mensch im Übergang vom Kapitalismus zum Sozialismus wurde das um seine Selbstverwirklichung ringende Individuum Faust, ein Identifikationsangebot an eine Gesellschaft, in der berechtigte Zweifel aufkamen, noch immer Sieger der Geschichte zu sein.

Jede Rezeption klassischer Werke der Weltliteratur vollzieht sich im Spannungsfeld zwischen der Vergangenheit des Textes und der Gegenwart seiner Interpretation. Dieses konstitutive und unhintergehbare Verhältnis drohte in den siebziger Jahren in beiden Teilen Deutschlands in eine einseitige Bevorzugung der Kategorie Gegenwart umzuschlagen. Das Lesen und die Aufführung alter Texte wurde zum Experimentierfeld der Erprobung und Bestätigung neuer Erfahrungen. Damit drohte die Gefahr, die Gegenwart zum alleinigen Maßstab der Vergangenheit zu machen und dem alten Werk die Möglichkeit der Kritik und der Infragestellung der Gegenwart zu nehmen. Eine Revision dieses ungleichgewichtigen Verhältnisses von Gegenwart und Vergangenheit im Umgang mit klassischen Texten war unvermeidlich, und so können wir seit Beginn der achtziger Jahre eine entschiedene Hinwendung zur Historizität der alten Texte beobachten, die gepaart ging mit einer Abkehr von der destruktiven Klassikkritik und bestimmten Auswüchsen der Rezeptionsästhetik. Diese Wende war zum einen Ausdruck eines neuen Traditionsbewußtseins, stand jedoch auch in Zusammenhang mit der Fundamentalkritik an dem Programm einer Moderne, die sich einem rationalitätsorientierten Fortschrittspathos hingegeben hatte, für das in der Geschichte seiner Rezeption auch Goethes *Faust* als Paradigma hatte dienen müssen.

Beispielhaft für den hier skizzierten Prozeß einer Umwertung und Neufassung des Verhältnisses von Gegenwart und Vergangenheit im Umgang mit klassischen Texten ist das 1982 erschienene Buch des Göttinger Literaturwissenschaftlers Albrecht Schöne *Götterzeichen, Liebeszauber, Satanskult.*[24] Es trägt den bezeichnenden Untertitel *Neue Einblicke in alte Goethetexte*, mit dem es sich in den genannten Diskurszusammenhang hineinstellt. "Neue Einblicke" heißt bei Schöne, in deutlicher Abgrenzung gegen die Rezeptionsästhetik, nicht mehr ein aktualisierendes Auslegungsverfahren, das den alten Text den neuen Erfahrungen entsprechend verändernd affirmiert, sondern den Versuch, das Neue, das den Werken "selber innewohnt," in neuer Lesart, herauszuarbeiten. Dieses Neue jedoch, so Schöne in dem *Faust*-Abschnitt seines Buches, ist der vormoderne

Gehalt des *Faust*, dessen Sprengkraft Goethe in der Selbstzensur der ursprüng-
lichen Fassung der "Walpurgisnacht" sekretiert und abgeschwächt habe. Schönes
Faust-Interpretation ist der Versuch einer Rekonstruktion der ursprünglichen
Intention des Dichters, die durch die bisherige Rezeptionsgeschichte entstellt,
verdunkelt und verzerrt worden sei. Die Analogie zur Rückübersetzung des *Faust*-
Dichters in die Welt der Ketzer- und Hexenverfolgung des Mittelalters im
"Walpurgisnacht"-Aufsatz und Schönes neuem Buch über Goethes *Farbentheologie*
(1987) liegt auf der Hand, wenn wir hier lesen: "Von weit her, aus altorientali-
scher, antiker und biblischer, aus gnostischer, kabbalistischer, mittelalterlich-
scholastischer Lichtmetaphorik, Lichtmetaphysik und Lichttheologie kommen
die Gottesvorstellungen, die dieser Farbenlehre zugrunde liegen, in sie eingegangen
sind oder ihr entsprechen."[25] Schönes Versuch, Goethetexte aus der Vorgeschichte
der Moderne zu erklären und zu enträtseln folgt einem Trend, den wir auch bei
anderen Interpreten beobachten können, so bei Rolf Christian Zimmermann,
der *Das Weltbild des jungen Goethe* (2 Bde., 1969/79) aus der hermetischen Tradition
des 18. Jahrhunderts entschlüsseln zu können glaubt oder bei Heinz Schlaffer,
der in einem programmatischen Aufsatz von 1987 von "Goethes Versuch, die
Neuzeit zu hintergehen" spricht.[26] Allen diesen Ansätzen gemeinsam ist das
Bestreben, die "Fremdheit" der Goethetexte gegenüber voreiligen und unhistori-
schen Annäherungsversuchen wiederherzustellen, um ihnen ein Kritikpotential
zurückzugewinnen, das ihnen in der rezeptiven Affirmation an die Moderne drohte
verloren zu gehen. Ob damit eine neue Ära einer postmodernen Goethe- und
Faust-Interpretation eingeleitet ist, möchte ich an dieser Stelle in berechtigter
Berührungsangst gegenüber dem modischen und diffusen Etikett "Postmoderne"
dahingestellt sein lassen.

   "Ein Buch, das große Wirkung gehabt hat, kann eigentlich gar nicht wahr
beurteilt werden." Dieser Satz Goethes, überliefert vom Kanzler von Müller in
dessen *Unterhaltungen mit Goethe*,[27] artikuliert eine Grunderfahrung im Umgang
mit jenen epochalen Werken der Weltliteratur, deren Wirkungsgeschichte den
unmittelbaren und ungetrübten Blick auf sie verstellt, modifiziert und verändert
hat, so daß sich, wie Goethe mit Bezug auf die Rezeptionsgeschichte Walter Scotts
1827 schreibt, "zuletzt alles in Zweifel" auflöst. Der Dichter selbst hat sich gegen
einen solchen historischen Relativismus und Skeptizismus energisch ausgesprochen und in dem obengenannten Gespräch mit von Müller bündig formuliert:
"Man lese ein Buch und lasse es auf sich wirken, gebe sich dieser Einwirkung
hin, so wird man zum richtigen Urteil darüber kommen."[28] Die Utopie einer
solchen individuellen Unmittelbarkeit in der Begegnung mit den wirkungs-
mächtigen Werken ist die fast notwendige Reaktion auf die Übermacht der
Geschichte, die als Tradition ihrer wechselreichen Auslegung ihr historisches
Überdauern und ihre stets wieder erneute Aktualität begleitet und begründet.
Diese Tradition mit Nietzscheschem Pathos im Handstreich zu negieren hieße
zugleich auf die Erfahrungen zu verzichten, die in ihr aufbewahrt und versammelt
sind. Der französische Philosoph Emmanuel Lévinas hat in einem 1980 geführten
Gespräch die Notwendigkeit der Integration der Geschichte der Textauslegung

in den Prozeß jeder neuen und produktiven Textauslegung in unübertroffener Klarheit formuliert:

> Der Kommentar, das ist das Leben des Textes. Wenn ein Text heute lebt, dann weil man ihn kommentiert. Die Bedeutungen erschöpfen sich nicht in der Interpretation. Und das stimmt für den "Talmud," aber auch für Platon oder für Goethe. Wenn man Goethe liest, liest man auch den Kommentar des "Faust," da gibt es unzählige Leben des Textes. . . . Nur weil es eine Vielzahl von Menschen gibt, kann der Text alle diese Bedeutungen haben. Wenn einer fehlt, ist ein Sinn verloren.[29]

ANMERKUNGEN

1. Vgl. Ernst Beutler, "Der Kampf um die Faustdichtung," in Beutler, *Essays um Goethe*. 3. verm. Aufl., Bd. 1 (Wiesbaden: Dieterich, 1946) 384.

2. Friedrich Wilhelm Joseph Schelling, *Philosophie der Kunst* (Darmstadt: Wissenschaftliche Buchgesellschaft, 1966) 82, 90.

3. *Goethes Gespräche*. Eine Sammlung zeitgenössischer Berichte aus seinem Umgang. Auf Grund der Ausgabe und des Nachlaßes von Flodoard Freiherrn von Biedermann. Ergänzt und herausgegeben von Wolfgang Herwig. Band 2: 1805–1817 (Zürich und Stuttgart: Artemis, 1969) 89.

4. Heine, *Französische Maler* (1831), in Heinrich Heine, *Sämtliche Schriften*, hg. von Klaus Briegleb. Band 5: *Schriften 1831–1837*, hg. von Karl Pörnbacher (München: Hanser Verlag, 1976) 72.

5. Hans Schwerte, siehe "Bibliographical Note."

6. Nietzsche, *Der Wanderer und sein Schatten* (1880). Hier zitiert nach Mandelkow I, 3:28f. Der Ironisierung der "Faust-Idee" in *Der Wanderer und sein Schatten* steht Nietzsches grandiose Charakteristik von Goethes Spätstil im ersten Band von *Menschliches, Allzumenschliches* (1878) gegenüber (Abschnitt "Die Revolution in der Poesie"), die–ohne ihn zu nennen–zentrale Strukturmerkmale des *Faust II* zuerst hellsichtig analysiert und beschreibt. Vgl. Mandelkow I, 3:24f.

7. *Zeitschrift für Ästhetik und allgemeine Kunstwissenschaft* 12 (1917): 86–137, 161–78, 316–51. Auszugsweise wieder abgedruckt in Mandelkow I, 3:461ff.

8. In: *Logos* (1925): 1-63. Wiederabgedruckt in Werner Keller, Hg., *Aufsätze zu Goethes "Faust I"* (Darmstadt: Wissenschaftliche Buchgesellschaft, 1974) 247–309.

9. Heinrich Rickert, *Goethes Faust: Die dramatische Einheit der Dichtung* (Tübingen: J.C.B. Mohr, 1932).

10. Berlin, 1943. Seit der 2. Auflage (1957) ist der Verlagsort Bonn (Athenäum). Vgl. meine Analyse des Werkes in Mandelkow II, 2:108–17.

11. Vgl. dazu Hans Pyritz, "Humanität und Leidenschaft: Goethes gegenklassische Wandlung 1814/1815. I. Teil: Voraussetzungen" (1939–1945). In Pyritz, *Goethe-Studien*, hg. von Ilse Pyritz (Köln/Graz: Böhlau, 1962) 97–191.

12. Wilhelm Emrich, *Franz Kafka* (Bonn: Athenäum, 1958).

13. Der Faustkommentar von Erich Trunz erschien zuerst in Band 3 der von ihm herausgegebenen Hamburger Ausgabe von Goethes Werken (Wegner). Er wurde in der Folgezeit zum Erfolgsbuch der Goetheforschung par excellence und erreichte in der Sonderausgabe eine Auflage von über 300000 Exemplaren. Der Faustkommentar von Ernst Beutler erschien 1950 in Band 5 der von ihm herausgegebenen Artemis-Gedenkausgabe von Goethes Werken und Briefen. Ihm vorausgegangen war Beutlers Faustkommentar in der Sammlung Dieterich, zuerst 1940 in Leipzig erschienen.

14. Die Fauststudien von Georg Lukács erschienen zuerst in seinem Aufsatzband *Goethe und seine Zeit* (Bern: A. Francke, 1947) 127–207.

15. Der für die Goetheaufsätze von Lukács konstitutive Parallelismus Goethe-Hegel ist in seiner 1938 abgeschlossenen, jedoch erst 1948 in Zürich erschienenen umfangreichen Darstellung "Der junge Hegel" klar ausgesprochen. Ernst Bloch widmete dieser Konstellation im Goethejahr 1949 seinen Aufsatz "Das Faustmotiv in der Phänomenologie des Geistes," der die Reihe der *Faust*-Kommentare eröffnet, die Bloch in *Das Prinzip Hoffnung* (1959), in der *Tübinger Einleitung in die Philosophie* (1963) und in *Experimentum mundi* (1975) fortsetzte.

16. Lukács (Anm. 14) 147.

17. *Gründgens Faust* (Frankfurt/Main, 1959; enthält Melchinger, "Faust für uns," Rosemarie Clausen, "Bilder der Hamburger Aufführung," Gründgens, "Meine Begegnung mit Faust"). Hier zitiert nach dem Wiederabdruck (Frankfurt/Main: Suhrkamp, 1982) 7–62 (= suhrkamp taschenbuch 838).

18. Richard Friedenthal, *Goethe: Sein Leben und seine Zeit* (München: Piper, 1963) 683.

19. Vgl. dazu meinen Aufsatz, "Natur und Geschichte bei Goethe im Spiegel seiner Rezeption im 19. und 20. Jahrhundert," in Klaus-Detlef Müller, Gerhard Pasternack, Wulf Segebrecht et al., Hg., *Geschichtlichkeit und Aktualität: Studien zur deutschen Literatur seit der Romantik.* Festschrift für Hans-Joachim Mähl zum 65. Geburtstag (Tübingen: Niemeyer, 1988) 69–96.

20. Brief an Wilhelm von Humboldt vom 17. März 1832. Vgl. Herman Meyer, *Diese sehr ernsten Scherze: Eine Studie zu Faust II* (Heidelberg: Stiehm, 1970) (= Poesie und Wissenschaft XIX).

21. Vgl. *Faust. Der Tragödie Erster und Zweiter Teil: Die Aufführung der Württembergischen Staatstheater Stuttgart.* Eine Dokumentation von Hermann Beil, Achim Freyer, Bernd Mahl et al. Fotos von Abisag Tüllmann (Zürich: Belser Verlag, 1979).

22. Vgl. vor allem Gerhard Scholz, *Faust-Gespräche* (Berlin: Verlag Junge Welt, 1967). 15. Gespräch, "Philemon und Baucis," 176–88. Ähnlich auch Peter Hacks in seinen "Faust-Notizen" (1962), in Hacks, *Maßgaben der Kunst: Gesammelte Aufsätze* (Düsseldorf: Claassen, 1977) 91.

23. Vgl. dazu meine Darstellung in Mandelkow II, 2:215ff..

24. Albrecht Schöne, siehe "Bibliographical Note."

25. Albrecht Schöne, *Goethes Farbentheologie* (München: C.H. Beck, 1987) 86f.

26. In Paolo Chiarini, Hg., *Bausteine zu einem neuen Goethe* (Frankfurt/Main: Athenäum, 1987) 9–21.

27. Kanzler von Müller, *Unterhaltungen mit Goethe*. Kleine Ausgabe, hg. von Ernst Grumach mit Anmerkungen von Renate Fischer-Lamberg (Weimar: Böhlau, 1959) 51 (Gespräch am 11. Juni 1822).

28. Ebenda.

29. In Peter Engelmann, Hg., *Philosophien*. Gespräche mit Michel Foucault, Kostas Axelos, Jacques Derrida, Vincent Descombes, André Glucksmann, Emmanuel Lévinas, Jean-François Lyotard, Jacques Rancière, Paul Ricoeur und Michel Serres (Wien/Graz: Böhlau, 1985) 111f. (= Edition Passagen 6).

PETER LACKNER

Directing *Faust* in America Today

WHILE INTERPRETING A TEXT FOR STAGE PRODUCTION, a director may strive to communicate the playwright's vision with utmost fidelity or may use the text merely for inspiration, as a basis for a concept that has much more to do with his own artistic expression than that of the author. These extremes and any approach on the spectrum between them might be as valid as the aesthetic and intellectual experience they afford an audience, but one might argue that some dramatic works simply merit a greater degree of conservational respect than others. A stage director mounting *Faust* in a German speaking country can fairly safely assume that his public is familiar with the play; a radical divergence from the author's vision can then create a deliberate friction between the expectations of the audience and the director's concept, a dialectic that in itself makes a new statement relevant to a new era and societal situation. Furthermore, in a cultural milieu where such a play has a rich performance history, a director might feel obliged to give his interpretation a different bent simply for the sake of originality.

When producing *Faust* in Southern California, one can safely assume that the vast majority of spectators hardly know the drama; a rebellious interpretation would neither stand out as being particularly original nor would it find a resilient surface of "traditional" treatment against which it could rub in creative friction. In this situation a director's main responsibility should probably be to introduce the drama to this audience as clearly and comprehensively as possible. While developing the English-language production of both parts of *Faust* for the Theatre Artists Group affiliated with the University of California, Santa Barbara,[1] I discovered that, paradoxically, the spirit of the original could be better communicated by taking relatively great interpretive liberties with the text than by trying to "stage" it in some literally conservative manner.

This process, however, involved more than a dramaturgical task: in order to create an organic whole that might communicate to a modern American audience as many facets of Goethe's original as possible while remaining within frighteningly concrete production limitations—including a three-and-one-half-hour performance length for both parts together—my functions as stage director and as adaptor/editor of the text became inseparable; the production concept and the script evolved as a single entity.

The motives for producing both parts of *Faust* in the United States included a trust in the inherent theatricality, stageability and playability of much of the entire work; despite evidence suggesting that Goethe meant it to be treated as a "Lesedrama," Goethe's vision has an inherently theatrical plasticity that immediately liberates—as well as challenges—the theatre practitioner's fantasy. The obvious clues about Goethe's visualization of a concrete performance situation lie in the outer frame structure of Part I and in copious references in Part II to actual attributes of a theatre space—such as Mephistopheles "popping up in the prompter's box," Phorkyas "sitting down beside a column of the proscenium," or a chorus appearing behind the audience. But beyond such concrete references to elements of a theatre space, the writing itself cries out for live performance before a very diverse audience, in that it embodies an incredibly wide spectrum of "entertainment" values, from the sublimely poetic, philosophical and spiritual to the topical and humorous. With the anticipated audience for the TAG production ranging from professional Goethe experts to non-drama majors attending the performance as a homework assignment and non-university community members going to the theatre purely for diversion and pleasure, I felt the assistance of Goethe himself in presenting the drama to such a diversity of viewers, because he had written a play capable of addressing them all.

A major factor in the feasibility of any English-language production involves finding a suitable translation—a choice involving considerations of fidelity to the original, poetic mastery of language and imagery on many levels of meaning, clarity of content, and the facility with which actors might speak the text. Although we knew before the first rehearsal that the Stuart Atkins translation[2] fulfilled these criteria "par excellence," only later in the process did we realize with what ease his phrasing and choice of words allowed the actors to reach the pinnacles of intense feeling created by Goethe, for the text truly embodied the momentum and power of the original in words obviously meant to be spoken or almost sung. The only disadvantage of choosing a basically non-rhyming translation was a partial loss of some of the humor and playfulness arising from Goethe's merging simple "folk" rhyme with profound philosophical and poetic wisdom, but we attempted to convey this synthesis of "low" and "high" art in the visual style of our staging devices. Moreover, we emphasized certain fundamental comic elements conceived by Goethe that verge on literary parody and absurdist humor—for example, in the ironizing of Helen as self-consciously trying to live up to her image, or in Mephistopheles being out of his element in the pre-Christian world.

The remaining, albeit formidable, obstacles to staging both parts of the work— its sheer volume and the difficulty of mounting so many highly spectacular scenes on a moderate budget—were tackled in the process of preparing the text, through major and minor cuts and occasional rearrangement of passages. Part I was kept largely intact, but a few entire or major portions of scenes, as well as segments of individual dialogues and isolated phrases, had to be omitted. For Part II the editing approach was actually reversed: instead of segments being "cut" away from the whole, scenes relevant to the main action or of unusual thematic value were picked out and assembled into a cohesive plot structure. Although one might question the ethics of radically cutting this drama as being similar to bulldozing a mountain to make it easier to climb, my own pangs as adaptor were assuaged by the hope that the presentation of major portions might at least serve as an enticement for a subsequent reading of the complete work. It was further hoped, especially in the case of Part II, that a pruning process might make the main branches of dramatic action more visible and therefore the entire work more accessible to the non-specialist viewer.

Generally, the editing involved the streamlining of central actions while respecting Goethe's non-linear plot structure and avoiding overt didacticism or reductionism. Part I was slightly re-shaped—while care was taken to maintain the integrity of the tragic plot—to create a contrast between Faust's secluded life and his immersion in worldly currents. In Part II, many scenes were selected to sustain the plot line involving Faust's (and Mephistopheles') pursuit of the "Eternally Feminine," in various forms ranging from the idealized love for Helen to the compulsive containment of the oceans. The "Hauptmotiv" forging both parts into a continuum was defined as the principle of Faust's striving—with the object of desire taking various forms, but the main drive itself remaining constant.

Beyond mere cutting of the text, certain events and images were combined and compressed. Since Goethe himself created the model for this technique in his brilliantly poignant distillation of the evolution of Euphorion into Icarus, he might have approved of condensation efforts such as the following: the first Witch transforms into, rather than conjures, a vision of Helen, who later is played by the same actress; the costume and movement of Homunculus, as if floating in a subjective ether of an inner-space womb, suggests that he is the embryo of Euphorion (later played by the same actor); the Mighty Men double as Lemure Grave Diggers; after the final battle between Heaven and Hell, all devils become angels, with semi-transparent robes thrown over their red costumes—as though a truly magnanimous god had decided to "save" all creatures, whether deserving of salvation or not. The all-too-transparent reason for this last choice was pragmatic as well as thematic: to let the devils change roles very quickly and thus allow the entire ensemble to people heaven for an impressively grand finale.

In any production of a play with so many levels, certain themes must be given an interpretive emphasis, while others necessarily fall by the wayside. Although *Faust* is not truly a morality play in the sense that the dramatist intends to transmit a dualistic message about salvation and damnation, the incorporation of that structure as a metaphor demands a special treatment for a modern audience. It was my conviction that, although the characters and stories of Faust and Gretchen might not be considered to be truly tragic in the Aristotelian sense, their plights can at least be taken very seriously. The TAG staging allowed Faust and Gretchen to be tragic heros existing within the fairy-tale structure of Christian mythology— that is, the objective surroundings being fantastic, but the human situations having the validity of any universal parable. Furthermore, the respect for tragedy within and beyond the Christian moral system can best be evoked in a modern audience not by emphasizing the guilt induced by God's accusing finger but by focusing on the problem of accepting personal responsibility for one's actions—for example, in love relationships. To deal with the Christian elements as a fairy tale also allows a degree of levity that may trigger the release of stronger serious feelings; for example, Gretchen's being "saved" by being lifted on a trapeze swing out of the prison courtyard and up into heaven has the intended humor of an obvious "deus ex machina" while still allowing emotions of genuine relief and elation. At the end of Part II the angels shooting at the devils with plastic roses as arrows should evoke the modern equivalent of what one might associate with heaven: a joyous feeling of release supplementing the rather solemn feelings of reverence and grandeur.

Another interpretive principle involved avoiding antiquated cliches in dealing with the "Eternally Feminine," by clearly depicting male and female attributes as metaphors for personality traits rather than absolute gender definitions—for example, the masculine as "restless striving," the feminine as daring to "tarry" in the fullness of life and feeling. In the TAG production, the Theatre Manager was played by a woman (inspired by the famous 18th-century actress and manager Caroline Neuber) who in turn insists on playing most of the major female roles in the inner drama. The result of Helen being played by an actress too old for the part is intended humorously (Helen and/or the Manager trying to fight her years, maintain her image), but suddenly reveals the potential of ageless and timeless beauty in women of any age—indeed, in all human beings.

Other themes I felt worth stressing as topically relevant for a modern audience included: personal responsibility in love relationships; guilt-engendering mechanisms in moral belief systems leading to increased human injustice and self-destruction; the invention of paper money with the resulting birth of inflation and national debt as a curse put upon mankind by the devil; the creation of Homunculus suggesting the issues of gene manipulation, artificial life, and dominance of the computer over human intelligence; the Euphorion/Icarus complex as a brilliant metaphor for man's reckless evolution from an egotistical personal "id" to the idealist whose striving for progress culminates in the glorification of war and self-annihilation; the potential of false altruistic intentions for resulting in the destruction of other human beings; the power of isolated wealth as the root of modern international industrial imperialism. Although such a listing of themes suggests a very moralistic reading of Goethe, in the production these ideas were imbedded not only in entertaining spectacle but also in Goethe's own non-causal ethical structure which precludes simple didacticism.

One conceptual nexus for the interpretation was the large theatre wagon, rolled by the ensemble onto the main stage at the outset to provide a variety of playing areas throughout the performance. It ideally embodied those aspects of Goethe's sense of theatricality which I felt important to introduce to the American audience, and it solved a great number of practical staging problems. With its side opening as a small apron stage, this raised "inner" location was often transformed by means of painted backdrops and property shifts to serve for all interior scenes demanding a feeling of confinement or seclusion (Faust's study, Gretchen's room, the prison, the Emperor's throne room, Wagner's laboratory, Helen and Faust's bridal canopy bed, Faust's modern office, etc.). In deliberate contrast, the more expansive scenes demanding open space and wide horizons (encounters in the street, countryside, Walpurgis Night, Hades, etc.) unfolded on the wide, empty stage surrounding the wagon, with scenic elements such as Dame Martha's hedge being obviously painted flats visibly unloaded from the wagon by the actors. The editing process was used to strengthen a convenient pattern in the original—a rough alternation between exterior and interior scenes—so that scene changes could be swift and even overlapping, without blackouts, thus keeping the action going forward and decreasing the total performance time.

The idea of a "Wandertruppe" visiting the area where the real audience has gathered obviously has its foundation in the original Prelude, in which the Manager's skepticism about the new audience and location implies he is head of a touring company rather than one with a permanent home. The concept of a travelling troupe also allows for a stronger feeling of ensemble unity, a festive atmosphere with circus-like levity, as well as suggesting a sense of romantic adventure which Goethe might have felt—and even envied—while experiencing various mobile companies touring Germany.

Further, the wagon, while serving as a frequent reminder that the main body of the drama is a play-within-a-play, allowed for an eclecticism of theatre devices which might have been collected or developed by the travelling company both out of financial necessity and in a light-hearted spirit of "primitive" folk enter-tainment. These included elements of mystery and pageant drama, baroque staging, melodrama and puppet theatre. For example, the poodle appeared first as a somewhat silly hand puppet with red button eyes; then in a puff of smoke the actor playing Mephistopheles, who had also manipulated the puppet, emerged from behind the oven wearing a black clown nose and floppy dog ears, which he then took off to reveal himself as an elegant traveller. Such deliberate artificiali-ty culminated in additional levels of interior theatrical illusion, as when Mephis-topheles and Faust present the pageant play for the court, using two balloons on long sticks with flowing cloth to represent Paris and Helen in a love chase. When Faust loses control of himself and tries to grab Helen, the balloon pops in his grasp, as dreams and visions tend to do when one tries to possess them.

Another major function of the wagon was to provide both metaphorical and literal support for the religious symbolism in the drama. It created a pageant play setting, with a usable "upper" platform for heaven, built solidly enough to hold at least eight angels shooting roses as arrows at the devils below; it was bordered by painted clouds that even folded down when appropriate, suggestive of heaven "opening up" in moments of annunciation or salvation. Such moments were both grand and deliberately amusing in their makeshift quality, reinforcing Goethe's use of the heaven/hell format as a metaphor seen from a humanistic point of view.

On the basis that the medium conveys at least part of the message, the super-natural realms described in the original text—such as magic, alchemy, transmutation/transformation and travel through time and space—were synthesized with the pragmatic and real magic of effective illusion on the stage. That Mephistopheles enjoys performing minor miracles much like a salon magician is obvious from his wine trick in Auerbach's cellar. Combining this with his passion for leading Faust from one adventure to another like a travel guide—except that he does not even need a means of transportation—Mephistopheles becomes the "conferencier" helping Faust jump into a new situation by signaling, with the sweeping gesture of a grand magician, a set change, new lighting effect or entrance of new characters. His final trick, of course, is conjuring the "hell mouth," complete with devils tumbling out of it onto the stage—again similar to a circus master starting the grand finale with a wave of his wand.

This convention also facilitated some major cuts in both parts of the drama, in that abrupt jumps into new scenes were justified by "magic leaps" in the space/time journey under Mephistopheles' guidance. For example, after Faust is given back his youth with the help of the witch, Mephistopheles conjures an entire village square peopled with townsfolk and, of course, the girl Faust then wishes to meet. Another example is the abrupt arrival back upon the earth's surface after the disappointing end of the affair with Helen in Hades, which Mephistopheles again conjures with a few relaxed words that evoke the new space and atmosphere. Generally this staging device not only underscored the experience of the audience accompanying Faust as seen from his subjective point of view, but it allowed for fluid transitions of a filmic nature, even including cross-fades, and helped reduce the playing time by precious moments.

Mephistopheles is a passionate transformation artist who loves to create new parts for himself—from poodle, fashionable traveller, court fool/magician, to ship's captain, and, finally, a classical Satan in his full demonic glory. One might say that the passion for role-playing that this character exhibits is a part of this drama's life force, the vital energy that makes this masterpiece of Goethe truly theatrical, begging to be staged.

In the TAG production Mephistopheles leads Faust upon a magical journey through time as well as space. Although the external frame suggests a contemporary group of actors in modern clothing, their rustical wagon gives them a mysteriously timeless, Pirandellan character. But the interior play begins with a definite plunge into a collage of historical theatre elements—developing from the medieval mystery play and street theatre into Baroque, Renaissance, and Romantic drama (Mephistopheles' guise suggesting a French revolutionary), and continuing in Part II with visual imagery from silent film (Wagner as a "mad scientist"), and modern realistic drama. Although this sequence of stylistic elements is by no means historically accurate or complete, it serves to create the impression of a journey through theatre history. For example, in the first act Faust is shown in a medieval study wearing a robe and hat of that epoch as well as a beard and wig that are obviously fake and theatrical; the bold, somewhat presentational acting suggests a folk style of theatre. When Faust grows into old age in the last act, the actor plays in a more naturalistic fashion, without fake hair and beard, and wearing a contemporary house coat; he is isolated in a modern high-rise office like a lonely Howard Hughes, an intercom on his sleek desk, which he uses to communicate with the "rent-a-cop" watchman on his roof. Near his mansion, Philemon and Baucis staring at the transforming landscape somewhat resemble the farmer pair in the painting "American Gothic." Faust's journey through time suggests something deeper than mere jumps in life style: as he encounters new character challenges in each life role—for example, truly opening up to new experiences such as love, power, and accepting responsibility for his actions—he grows in character depth through the hard school of experience. This progression of the theatre style as moving from the very artificial to the more natural suggests the alchemical transmutation of knowledge into wisdom, Faust's human qualities gaining in ripeness and substance.

Generally, this rough chronology of theatre style itself is intended to function as a poetic stage metaphor contributing to a broadening of the significance of the Faust character. Allowing his life span to extend from medieval Europe to the present in the United States should suggest at least on a subliminal level that the story of Faust is actually that of the cultural evolution of Modern Western Man per se. Ultimately, a production of this masterpiece in the United States can contribute to a transcendence of the nationalistic definition of *Faust* as "das deutsche Drama" by underscoring the true universality of its main character, as well as by sharing with a new audience the wealth of Goethe's poetic and philosophical brilliance.

NOTES

1. The Theatre Artists Group (TAG) received funding from the UCSB Interdisciplinary Humanities Center and the National Endowment for the Humanities to mount this production for the 1990 summer institute on "Goethe's Faust and the Humanities Curriculum," sponsored by the IHC. It featured Simon Williams as Mephistopheles, Robert G. Egan as Faust and Ann Ames as Theatre Director, God, Helen, etc.

In 1992 a multi-media event based upon this production, combining staged reading and video excerpts, was presented at the international conference, "Interpreting Goethe's *Faust* Today," sponsored at UCSB by the IHC.

2. *Faust I & II*, edited and translated by Stuart Atkins (Boston: Suhrkamp/Insel Publishers, Inc., 1984).

Simon Williams, Robert G. Egan

Ann Ames, Emperor; Simon Williams as Mephistopheles;
Robert G. Egan, Faust

Ann Ames, witch; Simon Williams; Robert G. Egan

C. Bernd Sucher

Faust-Inszenierungen in Deutschland, Frankreich und Italien seit 1980

Ihr wißt, auf unseren deutschen Bühnen
Probiert ein jeder, was er mag.

Faust Productions in Germany, France and Italy since 1980

Those Faust productions of the past two decades which can be said to have altered our understanding of the work continue the post-war deflation of the Faust figure and the pointed removal of the Faustian from the play. With the exception of the work of Klaus Michael Grüber and Jürgen Flimm (with their radically personal statements based on fragmented reductions of the text) most productions of the past two decades have proven, at best, to be interesting failures.

Das subventionierte Staats- und Stadttheatersystem macht's möglich. Das Zitat aus Goethes *Faust* gilt vor allem auch für den *Faust*. Und doch, so verschieden die Interpretationsversuche in den vergangenen zwanzig Jahren waren, eines gilt für alle Aufführungen, alle Regisseure. Und zwar seit 1945. Der ungeheuerliche deutsch-faustische Drang, "der Menschheit Krone zu erringen, / Nach der sich alle Sinne dringen" (1804–5), dieser sinnlich-übersinnliche Erkenntnis- (wohl auch Macht-) Hunger, ohne Rücksicht auf Verluste, unter Einsatz der eigenen und aller anderen Existenzen, mit Herzenskraft, Leidenschaft, absoluter Egozentrik und Selbstüberschätzung dem eigenen Genius Genüge tun zu wollen: das sogenannte Faustische ist deutschen Regisseuren und wahrscheinlich auch dem größten Teil der deutschen Zuschauer peinlich geworden. Unerträglich.

Seit 1945 zeichnen sich *Faust*-Aufführungen dadurch aus, daß sie entpathetisiert sind.

Das gilt auch schon für die Inszenierung von Gustaf Gründgens, die, 1957 entstanden, noch immer als die gültige, die richtigste—so man denn richtig steigern kann—Interpretation in Deutschland angesehen wird. Wir Jüngeren kennen zwar nur die Filmversion, doch auch sie beweist, daß es danach keine Aufführung mehr gab, die sich Goethes Text zugleich ehrfurchtsvoll und mutig näherte, den Text unbeschadet ließ und schon jene Skepsis am Faustischen anmeldete, die die meisten Regisseure der siebziger und achtziger Jahre zum eigentlichen Thema ihrer Inszenierungen machten.

Ich möchte Sie jetzt nicht langweilen mit einer chronologischen Aneinanderreihung der wichtigsten deutschsprachigen *Faust*-Aufführungen, sondern Sie nur bekanntmachen mit jenen Arbeiten, die das Verständnis des Dramas veränderten, die eine neue Sicht auf dieses, den deutschen Bildungsbürgern immer noch heilige Werk erlaubten.

Alle diese Theaterarbeiten haben eines gemeinsam: die Kritik an der Gestalt des Faust. Lassen Sie es mich mit einem Wort von Botho Strauß ausdrücken: Die Regisseure der Nachkriegszeit haben den Faust "heruntergedemokratisiert." Er wurde, selbst in mißlungen-ärgerlichen Inszenierungen, immer ein Mensch wie du und ich. Kein Regisseur baute ihm mehr einen deutschen Piedestal. Claus Peymann machte ihn in seiner 1977 entstandenen *Faust I* und *II*-Inszenierung am Württembergischen Staatstheater in Stuttgart ganz einfach lächerlich. Er präsentierte ein genialisch-komisches *Faust*-Kabarett. Es war der lustigste, witzigste *Faust*, den deutsche Zuschauer je zu sehen bekommen haben.

Hans Hollmann wagte sich drei Jahre später an beide *Faust*-Teile, in Hamburg, am Thalia-Theater. Hollmann zeigte ganz deutlich, was er von Goethes Herr und Himmel, von der Faust- und der Mephisto-Gestalt hält: nichts. Wir begegnen Faust und Mephisto, aufs Durchschnittsmaß eher spießiger Bundesbürger verkleinert. Dem Faust nahm Hollmann die das Weltwissen umspannende Intellektualität. Traugott Buhre, der die Titelrolle—neben Boy Gobert als Mephisto—übernommen hatte, spielte einen cholerischen Provinzprofessor, der mehr von seinem Temperament als von seinem Wissenshunger fortgerissen wurde. Von wegen "faustisches Temperament": ein griesgrämig-fahriger Nachfahre des Professor Unrat, ein Heinrich-Mann-Epigone trat uns entgegen.

Nicht viel anders sah Dieter Dorn den Faust. Statt Unrat sah man in den Münchner Kammerspielen, 1987 war's, einen grantelnden, mit dem faden, eher mißlungenen Leben unzufriedenen Dorfschullehrer Heinrich, den die Kumpel am Biertisch gewiß Heinz rufen. Dorn und sein Faust-Darsteller Helmut Griem wollten den Faust, den hehren Deutschen, ganz entschieden und ganz virtuos entzaubern. Diesem miesen Typen, diesem Kraftprotz, der, wenn ihm alles gegen den Strich läuft, immer wieder einen Schluck aus dem Flachmann nimmt, sollten wir nichts abnehmen. Der tönt nur—weiß und will nichts. Dorn inszenierte sehr brillant, aber ebenso fad, ein dämonisches Kleinbürger-Spießer-Panoptikum. Aus dem Renaissance-Menschen Faust war ein überanstrengter Conférencier geworden. Ein grauer, später verjüngter, blonder Mißmut treibt eine schier endlose Märchen- und Ausstattungsrevue voran. Faust, ein Schwätzer, den die Deutschen als Weisen vergöttern—darauf lief Dorns *Faust*-Kritik hinaus.

Ähnlich, doch weit weniger perfekt, schlicht dilettantisch, näherten sich Hansgünther Heyme und Alfred Kirchner dem Text. Der eine inszenierte Goethe

1987 bei den Ruhrfestspielen in Recklinghausen als Musical-Kitsch, als Rockrevue. Er erzählte die alte Geschichte nicht etwa neu, er kostümierte sie nur modisch-schick, verpackte sie, wie Christo es mit Gebäuden und Brücken tut. Nur daß Heyme, anders als Christo, damit nicht größere Aufmerksamkeit für die ver-steckten Objekte schaffte. Sein *Faust* war einem herzlich egal. Und Kirchner ging 1990 am Berliner Schiller-Theater einen ähnlichen Weg, der eine Sackgasse ist: Er inszenierte mit Hilfe der Kostümbildnerin Rosalie eine aufwendige Moden-schau, in deren Zentrum Faust steht. Faust ein Kümmerling. Christian Grashof spielte einen larmoyanten, feigen, stets kraftlosen Mann, der heult und schreit, weint und brüllt und nie recht weiß, wo's langgeht, vor allem mit ihm. Diese Memme steht einem Mann gegenüber, der mit der Philosophiererei, die ohnehin Fausts Sache nicht wirklich ist, kurzen Prozeß macht. Dem timiden Feigling begegnet Mephisto: ein Tatteufel. Der schubst Faust mit Charme und Chuzpe zu neuen Abenteuern. Ein toller Kerl—gespielt von Hilmar Thate—bringt den Langweiler auf Trab. Da gab es hübsche Momente. Doch während in Deutschland und Österreich heftig diskutiert wurde, ob man und wer und unter welchen Umständen seinen Klassiker wiedererkennen muß, zeigte Kirchner einen zur Kenntlichkeit vereinfachten *Faust*. Deutsche Lehrer waren mit dieser Arbeit, ordentlich wie sie war, kritisch nur im Ansatz und ansonsten bemüht, eine theatralische Nacherzählung des Stoffes abzuliefern, gewiß sehr zufrieden. So zufrieden, wie sie gewiß auch mit Giorgio Strehlers Annäherungen an *Faust I und II* (1989/90) gewesen sein werden, falls sie diese opernhafte Aufführung gesehen haben. Strehler—Übersetzer, Regisseur und Titeldarsteller—sprach das Drama, in Ausschnitten. Das heißt, er sprach es nicht—er sang es. Und lieferte wie kein anderer eine *Faust*-Pureté, die sehr schön und sehr hohl war. Ihn interessierte, um Beckett zu zitieren, nicht etwas Besonderes, sondern nur alles. Das kann bei diesem Mammut-Werk nicht gutgehen. Unzufrieden hingegen waren die Goethe-Gralshüter mit jenen *Faust*-Aufführungen, die in dem Text bisher ungeahnte Funde machten; unzufrieden mit Regisseuren, die den Text schamlos benutzten, ihre Weltsicht mit Hilfe des zusammengestrichenen, reduzierten, dekonstruierten Originals auszudrücken.

Zuallererst muß hier Klaus Michael Grüber genannt werden. 1975 arbeitete er zum erstenmal in Frankreich, wo er heute die meisten seiner Inszenierungen herausbringt. Der damalige Direktor des Nationaltheaters im Chaillot, Jack Lang (späterer Kulturminister), verfolgte schon lange den ehrgeizigen Plan, Goethes Werk—und zwar beide Teile—aufzuführen. Grüber erfüllte ihm zwar nicht den Traum vom Mammutspektakel, denn er präsentierte eher *Faust*-Fragmente, aber dieser französische *Faust* von einem deutschen Regisseur war richtungsweisend für die folgenden Inszenierungen. Die Aufführung war eine Sensation. Selten ist dieser Superlativ so angemessen wie hier.

Grüber, der bei all seinen Inszenierungen keine Theorie zugrunde legt, sondern—wie sein Bühnenbildner Gilles Aillaud formulierte—mit einem geradezu "tierischen Instinkt" Texte umsetzt, hatte sich als Raum die dreihundert Jahre alte Chapelle Saint Louis, eine Kirche im ehemaligen Pulvermagazin und

Gefängnis und jetzigen Krankenhaus der Salpêtrière, ausgesucht. Der von Le Vau und Libéral Bruant konzipierte Sakralbau–ein achteckiger Zentralbau mit vier Schiffen und vier Chören–evozierte das Gretchen-Drama. Denn hier in der Kälte litten Manon Lescaut und die Comtesse de la Motte und andere Unglückliche. Hier war im 19. Jahrhundert ein Epileptiker-Spital untergebracht, hier begründete Charcot die Neurologie, hier studierte Sigmund Freud.

Wie immer bei Grüber-Inszenierungen bedeutete der gewählte Raum, ausgestattet von Eduardo Arroyo, dem Maler, bereits Interpretation, er wurde zur Metapher. Hier, in der Chapelle Saint Louis, kamen Erschöpfte, von langer Wanderung Müde zusammen, Reisende, die ihre Seelen in Koffern mit sich schleppten.

"Ja, wir sind erschöpft, wie die Pendler aus den Vorstädten auf dem Gare d'Austerlitz nach einem Arbeitstag," sagte Grüber in einem Gespräch mit *Le Monde*. "Darum dreht es sich: erschöpft zu sein, ohne die Erschöpfung zu interpretieren." Grüber sperrte die Zuschauer in diese Kirche, ließ sie allein mit diesen Wanderern.

Zu Beginn fühlen sich die Zuschauer noch wie in einem Theater, in den Seitenschiffen sitzend und dem Geschehen im Zentrum folgend; später werden sie zu Wanderkumpanen, stehen oder gehen zwischen den Schauspielern herum, setzen sich auf die doppelstöckigen Betten des Asyls oder kauern am Boden, auf feuchten Säcken. Um sie herum Lemuren in schweren Asbestmänteln, einen Hut auf dem Kopf, jeder einen kleinen, grauen Koffer in der Hand. Jedermänner, Clochards, Ausgestoßene–Erschöpfte auf der Suche. Und während aus dem Seesack, der über ihren Köpfen hängt, der Sand rieselt–Zeichen der verrinnenden Zeit, Zeichen für Gretchens nahendes Lebensende–, führt Mephisto, der einzige, der sich durch seine Kleidung von den anderen unterscheidet–rote Handschuhe und ein rotes Glühbirnchen am Mantelrevers, das sein Gesicht dämonisch-dunkel glühen läßt–, seinen Faust durch die Welt, durch die Dunkelheit zu den brennenden Kerzen, in die Blutkapelle, wo zwischen vielen Holzstühlen helle Flämmchen fackeln und sich Faust auf der Kanzel einrichtet.

"Weil das Spiel hier, an diesem Ort, nicht wirklich Spiel im Sinne des Theaters ist; weil die Kirche nicht mehr wirklich Kirche ist, kann sich Goethes Drama in der andauernden Spannung ereignen zwischen einer punktuellen Erscheinung und seinem Verschwinden, also in Klammern. Wir schlagen deshalb einen immer wieder aussetzenden, unterbrochenen, unzusammenhängenden *Faust* vor. Einen Schrumpf-Faust," erklärte Grübers Dramaturg Bernard Pautrant. Und wahrlich war dieser *Faust* eine Verkleinerung. Das bedeutet nicht allein die Streichung des Textes, von dem vielleicht noch ein Zehntel übrig war; Verkleinerung bedeutete auch Reduzierung auf theatralische Mittel, also–wenn man so will–auf armes Theater.

Grüber entdeckte in seiner Inszenierung gerade durch die Reduzierung der Mittel, durch Beschränkung, die Größe der *Faust*-Dichtung. Alles was er benutzte–Raum, Requisit, die Körper der Schauspieler–wurde Metapher der Vergeblichkeit, der Vergänglichkeit. Fausts Koffer enthielt Fausts Seele. Als er, im Vorgefühl von

Glück, die verhängnisvollen Worte spricht, das "Verweile doch, du bist so schön," verliert Faust den Koffer, er rutscht in die Tiefe hinab, wo Gretchen ihn sich nimmt, ihn aufbewahrt zwischen Kerzen. Noch einmal kämpft Mephisto um Fausts Seele, ringt mit Gretchen um den Koffer. Sie siegt und trägt den See-lenkoffer in die Ewigkeit–unter die Kuppel der Kirche.

Ein einziges Wort ist stets Zentrum von Grübers Arbeiten, war auch Zentrum von "Faust Salpêtrière": Ach, Hélas. "Philosophie, hélas! jurisprudence, médicine, et toi aussi, triste théologie. . . ."

Grübers französischer *Faust* war eine extreme Minimalisierung. War ein Sehstück, das die Phantasie des Zuschauers provozierte. Er mußte diese som-nambulischen Dialoge vervollständigen. Natürlich war das "ganz Inkommensura-ble," wie Goethe sein Werk einschätzte, extrem verkleinert. Aber Grüber war der erste deutsche Regisseur, den das "Faustische" am Faust überhaupt nicht inter-essierte. Nicht einmal, um daran Kritik zu üben. Grüber inszenierte einen *Faust*-Traum. Faust war ein von der Suche nach dem möglichen Sinn des Lebens und Leidens Erschöpfter. Am Ende ein "Ach!" Grüber war mit *Faust* auf Becketts Spuren. "Faust Salpêtrière" war ein Endspiel.

Hatte er schon bei dieser Pariser Inszenierung auf die großen Massen- und Volksszenen verzichtet, sein Interesse nur auf die drei Hauptfiguren gelenkt–auf Faust, Mephisto, Gretchen–, so ging er 1982 noch weiter. Ausgerechnet bei der Festaufführung am Abend des 150. Todestages des Dichters verweigerte er den Zuschauern in der Berliner Freien Volksbühne den Text. Aus dem Welt-Stück wurde ein Monodram, aus dem Schau-Spiel mit Dialogen und Massenszenen wurde ein innerer Monolog, ein Drei-Personen-Stück. "Faust Salpêtrière" war ja noch die Reise "vom Himmel durch die Welt zur Hölle" gewesen, der Berliner *Faust* war ein Blick nach innen. Kopf-Theater. Der alte Faust erinnerte sich–und es bleibt nichts als ein müdes verzweifeltes "Ach!" Grüber sah die Figur des Faust mit den Augen des alten Goethe. Dessen Klage aus dem Jahr 1823–"Mir ist das All, ich bin mir selbst verloren"–war der Kristallisationspunkt dieser Inszenierung. Bernhard Minetti, der greise Faust, trägt die ganze Bürde dieser Aufführung. Denn dem Gretchen, einer Laiendarstellerin, hat Grüber fast alle Worte genommen, Mephistos Part arg verkleinert. Natürlich wußte man durch die Lektüre von Fausts Verzweiflung, auch andere Regisseure hatten sie dargestellt, aber Grüber war's, der in Faust Becketts Krapp entdeckte. Und plötzlich–zu einer Zeit, da in Deutschland die jungen Leute demonstrieren gingen mit dem Slogan "no future"–klangen Goethes Sätze, von Minetti voller Grimm gesprochen, er-schreckend: "Nur mit Entsetzen wach' ich morgens auf, / Ich möchte bittre Tränen weinen, / Den Tag zu sehn, der mir in seinem Lauf / Nicht einen Wunsch erfüllen wird, nicht einen." Minetti war da mit Faust ganz nah bei jenen unheldischen Helden, die er in mehreren Texten von Thomas Bernhard gespielt hatte. "Es gibt ja nur Gescheitertes"–diesen Bernhard-Satz hätte auch Grübers Faust sprechen können, oder eben jenes Ach. Hélas.

Es war nur folgerichtig, daß Grüber auch Faustens Verführer, dem Mephisto, alles tatkräftig Starke, glatt Böse nahm. Das Verhältnis Faust-Mephisto ist wundersam zärtlich. Peter Fitz ist eben kein witziger Teufel, sondern ein trauriger Kumpan, besser formuliert, ein Kamerad, ein Freund. Die beiden eint eine Schicksalsgemeinschaft. Denn so wenig wie Faust weiß Mephisto—und er sagt es bei Goethe—der Welt beizukommen. Grüber schuf in Berlin eine Inszenierung der Minimal-Art. Er entdeckte in jenem starken Werk nur die Schwäche: Es ist etwas schiefgegangen mit und in der Schöpfung. Doch Grüber protestiert nicht dagegen, sucht nicht—wie Dorn in Faustens großsprecherischer Schwachheit—den Schuldigen für dieses Malheur. Er stellt die verlorengegangene Harmonie *aus*.

Was Wunder, daß nach dieser Veranstaltung gegen Grüber sich der Zorn erhob, nicht der des Volkes, denn dem ist Goethe so schnuppe wie der *Faust*. Die Bildungsbürger fühlten sich betrogen. Und doch wurde dieser *Faust* eine Kultveranstaltung, genauso wie der "Faust Salpêtrière" zuvor.

Grüber hatte es gewagt, Goethes *Faust* auf ein Drei-Personenstück zu reduzieren.

Jürgen Flimm ging 1983 noch weiter: Ihn interessierte nur noch das Männerpaar, wenngleich er längst nicht so kühn wie Grüber den Text manipulierte. Flimm ist ein genialischer Vereinfacher. Das Leidenspaar stand im Zentrum: Traurig fragt Faust—Hans Christian Rudolph—, während er auf Welt und Leben blickt: "Hier soll ich finden, was mir fehlt?" Und Mephisto findet ohnehin die ganze Schöpfung "herzlich schlecht." Wie Grüber inszenierte Flimm die "Tragödie." Aber seine schöne Aufführung ist die kälteste *Faust*-Inszenierung der letzten dreißig Jahre. Und zum erstenmal, meines Wissens, sind die beiden nicht nur Kumpel, sondern Geliebte. Ihr Verhältnis wird geprägt durch eine durchaus schwule Erotik. Das Gretchen interessiert diesen Kölner Faust weit weniger als der Mephisto.

Mit Grüber und Flimm scheint—für den Moment—die Manier, mit *Faust* den Faust, den deutschen Tat- und Herrenmenschen zu kritisieren, überwunden. Gewiß gab es sie noch, die Regisseure, die sich wie Dieter Dorn des Textes nur bedienten, um zu protestieren, das *Faust*-Drama zu diskreditieren; doch viel eher ging es jetzt darum, skeptisch, ironisch darin die eigene Welt oder den eigenen Untergang zu entdecken. Es war zu einfach, zu geistesschlicht geworden—und war es eigentlich schon zuvor—, nur zu protestieren, mit dem ausgestreckten Finger auf diesen deutschen Fies- und Miesling zu zeigen. Obwohl sich jene Regisseure, die den *Faust* inszenierten, um ihn zu diskreditieren, auf Friedrich Dürrenmatt berufen konnten, der am Beispiel Goethe forderte: "Man kann Klassiker heute nicht einfach hinnehmen. Man muß gegen sie protestieren."

Suchten sich also die einen—um Thomas Mann zu zitieren, der den *Faust* beschrieb als "halb Ausstattungsrevue, halb Weltgedicht"—die Ausstattungsrevue (Kirchner, Heyme, Dorn), suchten die anderen das Endspiel-Weltgedicht wie Grüber und Flimm, suchte eine dritte Gruppe etwas ganz anderes darin: die eigene Vergangenheit. Es waren zwei Regisseure der ehemaligen DDR, Einar Schleef und Wolfgang Engel, der eine als Exilant in Frankfurt, der andere als Noch-DDR-Bürger in Dresden.

Am Vorabend der Währungsunion beider deutscher Staaten, am 30. Juni
1990, zeigte der Regisseur und Autor Schleef (*Gertrud*, 1980/84) etwas Bestür-
zendes. Schleef machte aus dem *Faust* ein Requiem auf sein altes Land, die DDR.
Schleef, den in all seinen Arbeiten für das Theater die Dialoge wenig, chorisches
Sprechen aber überaus interessiert, inszenierte mit Emphase einen höhnischen,
einen großen Abgesang auf die DDR. Er ließ mehrmals das "Lied von den
Moorsoldaten" absingen, ein Gesang, der Westdeutschen eher fremd, von KZ-
Häftlingen gesungen wurde, die bis zum Tod im Moor schuften mußten. In der
DDR kannten selbst Kinder, aufgewachsen mit vielen Parolen des Antifaschismus,
dieses Lied. Damit nicht genug: Gleich in den ersten Momenten der Aufführung,
im Vorspiel, bei dem die beiden Teile der Tragödie bereits verquickt sind, wird
über-deutlich, worauf der Regisseur hinaus will. Auf die Bühne, in einen durch
zwei schwarze seitliche Vorhangwände gebildeten dreieckigen Raum, treten vier
alte Frauen. Es sind der Mangel, die Schuld, die Sorge und die Not. Sie verkünden
den Untergang. Wenig später heben die zwölf Gretchen- und die zwölf Faust-
Darsteller an, einen Choral zu singen. Goethes Lemuren-Chor aus dem zweiten
Faust-Teil singt zur Musik aus der Matthäus-Passion: "Wer hat das Haus so
schlecht gebaut / Mit Schaufeln und mit Spaten? [...] Wer hat den Saal so schlecht
versorgt? / Wo blieben Tisch und Stühle? / Es war auf kurze Zeit geborgt; / Der
Gläubiger sind so viele" (11604–11). So richtig es ist, in diesem Auftritt, der
mehrfach wiederholt wird, Schleefs Abrechnung mit der DDR, diesem Staat, der
ihn verfolgte, zu sehen–die DDR als ein auf Sand und Schlamm und Unrecht
und Pump gebauter Staat der Lemuren–, Schleefs Kritik geht wahrscheinlich
weiter: Er sieht in den Häusern das Grab, im Leben nur ein kurzes Gastmahl.

Und an das freie Volk auf freiem Grund glaubt er weder in der unterge-
gangenen DDR noch in dem neuen großen Einheits-Deutschland. Schleef
inszenierte Scherben des *Faust*-Kosmos: *Urfaust*, *Faust I* und *Faust II*, verquickt,
zerrissen. Dekonstruktion ist sein Mittel, Dekomposition sein Stil. Es entstand
ein musikalisch-szenisches Oratorium, ein gesungenes, getanztes, gesprochenes
Memento mori.

Den Faust- und Gretchen-Darstellern kam wenig Bedeutung zu in diesem
oratorienhaften Theater, dem Mephisto indes die allergrößte. Er ist der Motor
der Aufführung, Theaterdirektor und Regisseur in einer Person. Er bringt die
Faust-Gruppe in Form; er scheucht die alten und die jungen Weiber. Er ist der
Fliegengott Superstar, Rattenfänger und Schnitter Tod. Am Ende betrachtet
Mephisto, der großartige Martin Wuttke, seine Opfer. Er weiß, daß der allgemeine
Untergang das Ende ist. "Es ist vorbei," murmelt er erleichtert, zitiert damit den
Goetheschen Chor des zweiten Teils. Es ist vorbei, das heißt bei Schleef: der
Mensch–und eben nicht allein der DDR-Bürger–hat seine Lektionen beendet.
Allein: er hat nichts gewonnen. Von wegen: ist gerettet?

Man muß gar nicht das Tieck-Wort bemühen, wonach es keinem Sterblichen
gelingen wird, "das vieldeutsame Werk zum Schluß zu singen," um zu erkennen,
daß Einar Schleef–wie Grüber, wie Flimm–nur einen kleinen Teil des Werkes
uns entdeckt hat. Doch besitzen solche höchst fragwürdigen–und die Betonung

liegt auf *würdig*–Versuche, Goethes *Faust* zu okkupieren, zu benutzen und zu nutzen, allemal mehr Kraft und, das auch, Erkenntniswert als die kritisch-oberflächlichen *Faust*-Verunglimpfungen. Faust, der deutsche Schreihals, das deutsche Muttersöhnchen, der deutsche Prahlhans: Das ist hübsch, doch sehr kurz gedacht.

Kurz gedacht ist auch Wolfgang Engels Inszenierung beider *Faust*-Teile in Dresden. Aber dennoch interessant genug, sie Ihnen kurz vorzustellen. In den letzten August-Tagen des Jahres 1990 zeigte er seine Version. Wir sahen den einzigen wirklichen DDR-*Faust*. Aus unerfindlichen Gründen läßt Engel den Faust- und den Mephisto-Darsteller mehrfach die Rollen wechseln. Vielleicht, weil in dieser Inszenierung kein Platz mehr ist für Mephisto. Zwei Seelen in der Brust ist Faust sich selbst Verführter und Verführer. Ihn reizt auch nicht die Wissenschaft, er will nur einmal im Leben alles haben, alles mal gemacht haben. Ein Zu-kurz-Gekommener will nachholen. Was immer passen könnte auf die Situation seiner Landsleute, jeder Halbsatz, der die DDR-Vergangenheit und die damalige DDR-Gegenwart treffen konnte (und es gibt derer erstaunlich viele), wurde bei Engel ausgestellt, mit Lautstärke vorgetragen und mit Lichtspots beleuchtet. Aus der Walpurgisnacht machte Engel eine Hausgemeinschaftsfête im Flur des Betonhochhauses, in dem Marthe Schwerdtlein und Gretchen wohnen. Noch tauglicher für sein Unternehmen war eine andere Szene: Fausts Auftritt bei Hof. Natürlich sind die Mächtigen Narren, die Krisensitzung ist eine Karnevalsveranstaltung, die Ansprachen sind Büttenreden. Weil Engel die größte Lust am erklärenden Vergröbern hat, reichte ihm als Metapher für Währungsunion und falsche Prosperität auch nicht das Papiergeld. Die Schätze sind Spielautomaten, als Faustschen Coup hat er sich Creditcards ausgedacht. Spätestens bei dieser Nummer–denn in der DDR gab es keine Geschäfte, keine Automaten, diese Karten auch zu benutzen–hatte Engel die Lacher auf seiner Seite. Engels *Faust* war eine DDR-Kabarettnummer, stundenlang. Doch es gab eine Szene, die auch für den Zuschauer aus der Bundesrepublik, also aus dem Westen, Kraft hatte. Sie erklärte, was Engel vielleicht mit seinem *Faust* gewollt haben mag. Wenn Faust endlich erkennt, daß er Verführer und Verführter zugleich; wenn er erkennt, daß alles Glück und Unglück mit der Sprache in die Welt kam, wird Engel ernst. "Mit Worten läßt sich trefflich streiten, / Mit Worten ein System bereiten, / An Worte läßt sich trefflich glauben, / Von einem Wort läßt sich kein Jota rauben," druckste Engel, der auch die Faust-Rolle übernommen hatte, heraus; leise, verstört, so als bereite jedes einzelne Wort ihm Qualen. Da wurde klar: Die DDR-Bürger, von ihrem Regime betrogen, standen vor neuem Betrug. Worte, nichts als Worte hatten ihnen die westlichen Politiker und Wirtschaftsmanager zu bieten. Sich selber fremd geworden, fehlte diesen Menschen die Zeit, sich zu suchen. Sich: die eigene Identität.

Der Dresdner *Faust*: ein Drama über das Plaste- und Elaste-Regime und über den Aufbruch, der eine Enttäuschung werden würde. Auch Engel, kein Zweifel, hat die "so hoch aufquellende Masse," wie Schiller das *Faust*-Drama charakterisierte, nicht bewältigt. Aber er hat bewiesen, was sich alles anstellen läßt damit. Auf deutschen Bühnen probiert ein jeder, was er mag. Zum Beispiel auch dies:

Mephisto als *Frau*. Zwar hatte Günter Grass eindringlich in seinem *Butt*-Roman davor gewarnt, doch 1977 sahen wir sie wirklich: die *Mephista*. Maria Becker spielte sie in Michael Degens Inszenierung am Bayerischen Staatsschauspiel in München. Gewonnen war durch diese Besetzung nichts. Außer: der Teufel hat es bei Männern allemal leichter, wenn er sich weiblicher Mittel bedienen kann.

Der *Faust*, so urteilte Hebbel, spiele sich zum Teil von selbst, zum Teil sei er überhaupt nicht zu spielen. Beweise dafür sind in den letzten fünfundzwanzig Jahren genug erbracht worden auf deutschen, auf deutschsprachigen Bühnen. Und–mit Ausnahme der Grüber- und Flimm-Inszenierungen–waren die meisten Aufführungen, wenn überhaupt, nur interessant mißlungen. Das mag an den Regisseuren liegen. Aber vielleicht liegt es auch an dem Stück. Ich werde den Verdacht nicht los, daß in jedem Shakespeare-Stück mehr Leben und Leiden, mehr Welterkenntnis versteckt ist als in Goethes *Faust*. Goethe-Liebhaber, Goethe-Kenner werden mir widersprechen. Ich erwarte Widersprüche und danke Ihnen für Ihre Aufmerksamkeit.

Index of Names